MASTRO-DON GESUALDO

GIOVANNI VERGA

MASTRO-DON GESUALDO

A Novel

Translated, with an Introduction, by

GIOVANNI CECCHETTI

UNIVERSITY OF CALIFORNIA PRESS
Berkeley • Los Angeles • London

University of California Press
Berkeley and Los Angeles, California

University of California Press, Ltd.
London, England

Library of Congress Catalog Card Number: 77-020331
Copyright © 1979 by The Regents of the University of California

First Paperback Printing 1984
ISBN 0-520-05077-0

Printed in the United States of America

CONTENTS

1

In 1874, after acquiring some measure of notoriety as the author of intensely passionate novels, Verga published the story of a peasant girl "crouched on the lowest step of the human ladder" and forced to accept her cruel destiny. It was "Nedda," his first Sicilian tale. Soon after he began to write *Padron 'Ntoni*, "a novelette about fishermen," as he himself defined it in an 1875 letter to his publisher, which he kept rewriting for the next six years, and which turned into one of the great novels of the century. During this period Verga became further acquainted with the works of Balzac and Zola and was fascinated by the vast and sweeping visions that had produced *La Comédie Humaine* and were producing *Les Rougon-Macquart*. He also read the main works of Charles Darwin and accepted the principle of the struggle for survival. Additionally, his own deep-seated conviction that only financial security grants the possibility of expanding and fulfilling all other needs contributed to his meditation on the essence of human progress and to its ultimate identification with the achievement of that financial security. He thus conceived the grand design of a cycle of five novels—with *Padron 'Ntoni*, later retitled *I Malavoglia* ("The House by the Medlar Tree") as the first of the five—intended to present and analyze the successive stages of man's efforts to secure material success and then to assert himself in an ever-widening social context. This design became clear to Verga in early 1878, when he wrote to Salvatore Paola: "I am thinking of a work which I consider great and beautiful, a sort of phantasmagoria of the struggle for existence, extending from the rag-picker to the cabinet minister and to the artist, taking all forms, from ambition to greed, and lending itself to a thousand representations of the great human tragicomedy." Originally the collective title of the five novels was to be *La marea* ("The Tide"), but it was later changed to *I vinti* ("The Doomed"), thereby acquiring a more fatalistic connotation.

In the preface to *I Malavoglia,* published in February 1881, Verga presents his plan to the public, synthesizing both the basic ideas upon which it rests and the artistic principles that should guide its realization. He defines that novel as "the sincere and dispassionate study of how the first anxious desires for material well-being must probably originate and develop in the humblest social conditions; and of the perturbations" brought about "by the vague yearning of the unknown, and by the realization that one . . . could be better off." Then he reviews the next step on the ladder of social progress, and continues with the following statements:

> As this search for economic betterment by which man is tormented grows and widens, it also tends to rise and to follow its ascending movement into the various social classes. In *I Malavoglia* it is still only the struggle for material needs. Once these needs are satisfied, the search will turn into greed for riches, and will be embodied in a middle-class character, *Mastro-don Gesualdo,* who will be placed within the still narrow framework of a provincial town, with its colors somewhat brightened and its design broader and more varied.

Mastro-don Gesualdo, then, was at once conceived as an independent work, as the continuation of the preceding novel, and finally as the indispensable premise of the three novels to follow — which, incidentally, remained little more than titles. It was also viewed as a chapter in mankind's fateful, strenuous, and feverish march toward progress, which (Verga continues in his introduction) appears grandiose in its outcome, if seen as a whole, from a distance. For in its glorious light are lost the anxieties, the ambitions, the greed, the selfish compulsions that on an individual level prompted its movement in the great flood sweeping everybody away. The observer, himself carried by the flood, may become interested in those who fall by the wayside under the brutal steps of those who are hurrying on — the victors of today, who will be the doomed of tomorrow. This is Verga's vision of mankind. There are no winners, only losers. Mastro-don Gesualdo is one of the most conspicuous of them.

2

Between the publication of *I Malavoglia* and the appearance of the first version of *Mastro-don Gesualdo,* Verga wrote a number of short stories in which he often experimented with characters and themes similar to those to be treated in the novel. This was necessary for the purpose of enucleating and mastering the human attitudes and the expressive patterns coinciding with the new social level. As he himself had stated in the introduction to *I Malavoglia,* if in the first novel the "mechanism of passions" was "less complicated" and consequently all that was needed was "to leave the picture its own genuine and simple colors," in the following novel, as the range of human action broadened, also the language would become enriched "with all the nuances and the ambiguities of sentiments, all the artifices of words." Thus these basic principles, which came to him from *verismo* (to create works of art that are true to life), led him to the adoption of a specific language which each time was to suit a specific environment, as if born of that environment itself. The language of *Mastro-don Gesualdo* encompasses three different social levels — the common people, the wasted but still proud aristocracy, and the Sicilian bourgeoisie of the last century — and it must, therefore, be viewed as the amalgamation of three different languages. These extremely complex expressive requirements may explain why, before devoting himself to the composition of the second novel of his series, Verga felt he needed to practice and sharpen his skills on the pages of shorter narratives. It may also explain why he could not proceed with the writing of the other three novels, which had to be in a language full of reticent nuances on one side and of the empty words of the totally self-centered aristocratic parasites on the other.

The most important short stories written soon after *I Malavoglia* were collected in 1883 under the general title of *Novelle rusticane* ("Rustic Tales"). The protagonist of one of them, "Il reverendo" ("The Reverend Father"), is obviously a study for one of the shrewdest, most hypocritical, and least attractive characters in the novel, the Canon-priest Lupi. But the story that offers a preview of Mastro-don Gesualdo himself is "La roba" ("Property"), whose protagonist, Mazzarò, is totally — and successfully — dedicated to building up an immense fortune. He is a self-made man. He is illiterate, but his mind is sharper than the Baron's, whose property he has swallowed up piece by piece. With grim determination and incessant work, he has been able to rise from the level of poor laborer to the sphere of those who own vast lands and huge herds. But in so doing he has alienated himself from life; he has rejected the love of women, as well as the possibility of having children and grandchildren. Thus, when the time comes for him to die, he finally discovers that he has devoted all his energies to a false god. But it is too late. It is true that between Mazzarò and Mastro-don Gesualdo there are great similarities; even the language and the style of "La roba" are more elaborate than those of the preceding "Sicilian" stories. Yet it must be recognized that Mazzarò is far less complex and far less sophisticated than his younger brother of the great novel. In fact, he could be defined as a pre-Don Gesualdo.

In the summer and the fall of 1888 *Mastro-don Gesualdo* was serialized in the prestigious Italian journal, *Nuova Antologia*. Very probably Verga began to publish it well before he had completed it. In fact, the second half seems written in a hurry, just to fulfill a commitment. As soon as the last installment appeared, Verga began to rewrite the novel; and, while he left the first chapters without substantial revisions, he transformed all the others in such a way that the general structure, the style, and even the very personalities of the characters were greatly altered. He made important changes and additions even on the printer's proofs. This ability to turn a fairly approximate narration into what is generally regarded as a masterpiece within such a short period of time (the final version of the novel was published in the fall of 1889) is in itself cause for admiration. It seems obvious that the entire sequence of human events, and the most suitable medium through which they could find their definitive expression, were so ripe in Verga's mind that he could transfer them to paper in only a period of months.

3

Mastro-don Gesualdo is the epic of the economic compulsion that relentlessly drives a man toward the acquisition of great wealth and the power that such wealth generates. Throughout his previous works Verga had consistently stressed the importance of financial well-being and how its presence, or its absence, conditions all other aspects of human existence and of human relations. Now he pulls together all those past remarks to fuse them into a new and powerful unity. Greed for riches obsesses nearly every one of the extremely numerous characters of the novel, from Baroness Rubiera to Nanni l'Orbo, yet only the protagonist, Don Gesualdo, rises above the pettiness and the abjection of most of them. He stands like a giant, so much so that he seems to ennoble even what in others may appear sordid. He wants wealth, but he does not view it as an end in itself. To him it is a means to the achievement of power—the power to fulfill many other aspirations, such as reaching all the way to the top of the social ladder and dominating the whole town. His philosophy, and the philosophy behind the novel, may be found in two undisputed aphorisms: "The world belongs to those who have money," and "Everyone looks after his own interest." But although Don Gesualdo's plans and actions are in harmony with these principles, he never appears narrow-minded or narrowly self-centered. "His own interest" often involves the interest of several other people. The philosophy that brings him success, however, carries within itself the seeds of his destruction. Unlike Mazzarò, Don Gesualdo uses his wealth to achieve respectability and power by marrying into the town's aristocracy, thereby renouncing Diodata, the only person capable of self-sacrifice and of love. It will be precisely his social vanity—a new and different kind of greed—that will cause him to lose all his wealth to his equally greedy aristocratic son-in-law, and to die alone, tolerated by his own daughter and despised by her servants. Yet, throughout the novel, both the town and every one of its inhabitants exist only as a function of Don Gesualdo: their actions, even their thoughts, originate in the shadow of his overwhelming personality. And they are all perfectly conscious of their dependence on him.

In this sense the ironic double epithet—*Mastro-don*—is significant. It evokes the standing of Gesualdo Motta, the name of a plebeian, in the society of Vizzini, a large town in eastern Sicily where the Verga family owned some property and where the action of the novel takes place. *Mastro,* on the one hand, defines a workman, a skilled laborer or, as in our case, a mason; *don,* on the other hand, designates a member of the land-owning gentry. *Mastro-don,* therefore, gives at once the past and the present of the protagonist, his roots in the working class as well as his claims to the social level of the local aristocracy. At the same time it points out the attitude of the town toward him. As Verga himself wrote to his Swiss translator, "*Mastro-don* is the sarcastic nickname pinned by the town's backbiters on the lowly laborer who has become wealthy."

As already implied in this "sarcastic nickname," the novel rests on a set of basic confrontations involving on one side Don Gesualdo himself and on the other his own relatives and especially his wife and her relations, who constitute the proud, and empty, aristocracy that cannot accept a plebeian in their midst. While Don Gesualdo is extremely vital and apparently represents the future, his wife, her brothers, Baroness Rubiera, and even Don Ninì Rubiera represent a past that is rapidly disappearing. They are Don Gesualdo's antagonists. Bianca cannot understand him and cannot overcome her innate repugnance for him; her two old brothers, Don Diego and Don Ferdinando Trao, cannot even imagine being on speaking terms with their lowly brother-in-law. Verga offers them to us like the remnants of another world, lifeless, like mummies. Yet, in his representation of their existence, he writes some extremely moving pages, such as the beginning of Part Two, chapter 3, where the two brothers first are seen by the townspeople as they repeat their daily gestures, day after day, month after month, and then as they in turn look at the townspeople and mechanically count them — as if life were nothing more than distant glimpses that could be constantly enumerated in the same way.

The initial impression of the reader is that Don Gesualdo is victorious in his battle to wrestle wealth from the aristocracy and to dominate all his antagonists. But as the novel proceeds we discover that he is victorious only as long as he keeps his antagonists at a distance. As soon as he tries to become one of them, he starts on the path to defeat and ruin. Through his "daughter" all his wealth returns precisely to the social class from which he has wrestled it. This is a very interesting conclusion, in that it reveals, among other things, how the story of Don Gesualdo develops according to an internal logic of its own, and not according to the writer's intentions. In Verga's plan for the five novels of *I vinti* ("The Doomed"), Don Gesualdo was intended to be the builder of a great fortune and the social climber, whose descendants would rise to a high social and political status because of that wealth. But in fact he loses his fortune to a penniless aristocrat through a daughter who is an aristocrat herself, though illegitimately, with the result that her possible children will not be his descendants.

At the beginning of Part Three, Don Gesualdo surveys his own human condition, thereby attempting to uncover the reasons for his failures. But he cannot go beyond self-serving rationalizations:

After the baby's birth Bianca had never recovered her health; as a matter of fact, she was declining from day to day, gnawed inside by the same worm that had eaten up all the Traos—and it was certain that she wouldn't have any more children . . . a bad bargain; although the man was careful not to complain, not even with the Canon-priest Lupi, who had first proposed it to him. When you have made a blunder you'd better keep quiet and not talk about it, not to let your enemies have the upper hand. —Nothing, nothing had that marriage brought him; neither dowry, nor male child, nor the new relatives' help, not even what Diodata used to give him: a moment of relaxation, an hour of pleasure, like a glass of wine for a poor man who has toiled all day! Not even that! . . . But he wasn't taken in, no! True, he was a peasant, but he had a peasant's sharp nose too! And he had his pride. The pride of a man who, with his own hands and his own work, had managed to earn those fine linen sheets in which they slept turning their backs on each other, and those delicacies he ate with uneasiness under the eyes of that Trao wife of his. . . . Now Bianca, as if she guessed she didn't have long to live, didn't want to be separated from her little daughter. But he was the boss, Don Gesualdo. He was good, loving, in his own way; he didn't let her go without anything: doctors, drugs, just as if she had brought him a fat dowry.

This complex passage, of which I have reported the most salient points, is spoken by the usual Verghian popular narrator who repeats Don Gesualdo's own remarks so faithfully as to let us hear his voice—according to the technique of the "free indirect speech" that Verga had perfected in *Vita dei campi* ("Life in the Fields")* and in *I Malavoglia*. In the context of the novel this passage was prompted by Bianca's implied opposition to Don Gesualdo's decision to send their daughter Isabella to a faraway boarding school. But once it has begun rolling forward, it quickly reaches much farther than

---

*Most of the stories in this book are available in my own translation in Part I of *The She-Wolf and Other Stories* (Berkeley, Los Angeles, London: University of California Press, 1973). In the introduction to the same volume the reader will also find a brief analysis of Verga's style (pp. XV-XX). For a further discussion of the same subject as well as of the originality of Verga's language—and for a more detailed study of *Mastro-don Gesualdo*—I am taking the liberty of referring to my recent book, *Giovanni Verga* (Boston: Twayne Publishers, 1978), passim; see the Index.

even the outer confines of a refutation. In it Don Gesualdo offers his own view of the reasons for his unhappiness and for his failures. But while his remarks may indeed contain such reasons, he is constitutionally unable to grasp them as such. Being unceasingly driven by economic motivations, he can only speak in the jargon of business, even when he discusses the most personally intimate matters. Before his sick wife, he can state that he is "a good, loving" husband only because he does not "let her go without anything...just as if she had brought him a fat dowry." He calls his marriage "a bad bargain," a business transaction that had turned sour—which, in view of his way of thinking, it had indeed been.

Characteristic is Don Gesualdo's attitude toward his daughter Isabella. He wants her to have everything, but the more he gives her, the more alienated she becomes. He cannot understand her profound involvement with Corrado La Gurna, in whom he can see but a greedy destitute who, through her, wants to get rich quickly. Thus, in Don Gesualdo's mind, his daughter and his property become identified; by protecting one, he feels he is protecting the other. His decision to have Isabella marry a nobleman is predicated on the conviction that, with money, she will rise to heights he himself could not attain. But, as a consequence, his lands and his money go to the Duke of Leyra—not just in the form of a dowry, but to indemnify him for a scandalous situation. Had Don Gesualdo allowed Isabella to marry Corrado La Gurna, everything would have proceeded without significant losses. But this was not to happen, for, like the heroes of Greek tragedies, he carried within himself the logic of his own destruction and had to collaborate with his own merciless destiny.

If it is true that Don Gesualdo fails because he relentlessly follows his economic compulsion, it is also true that he causes everyone else to fail. For everyone in the novel is doomed, and everyone stands alone, in life as well as in death. The isolation born of greed, of ambition, and of the consequent impossibility to understand one another, is the tragic theme of the novel. It is a profoundly modern theme; Verga explores it and develops it with extraordinary penetration and coherence.

Giovanni Cecchetti

September 1978
Pacific Palisades, California

A NOTE ON THE TRANSLATION

This translation is as close to the original as possible. A constant effort was made to convey the nuances of the Italian text, to reproduce its expressive patterns, to preserve its language mixture so that the voices of the popular narrator and of the characters could be heard, and to recreate the unmistakable rhythm of its prose. A few liberties were taken: the prefixes *compare* and *comare* which in the speech of southern Italians are a little more than recurring notes, were left out. The other prefixes, which indicate a difference in social status, are given in Italian: *massaro* is a man who owns or rents the land he farms; *mastro* a skilled laborer or an artisan; *Don* a professional man or a landowner, often belonging to the local aristocracy; *Donna* the wife of a *Don,* or a woman who hopes to become one. Names of old currencies and weights are also given in Italian: an *onza* was a Sicilian gold coin worth approximately 13 lire (ca. $50.00 in today's U.S. money), and a *tarì* a silver coin worth forty-two hundreds of a lira; a *tumolo* was the equivalent of about 30 pounds and a *cafiso* a measure of volume equal to four gallons; a *salma,* as a measure of volume, was approximately 275 liters, or 600 pounds, and, as a measure of land, about 4.35 acres. A few recurrent words were translated literally for the purpose of retaining some of the color of the local speech. Thus *cristiani,* which simply indicates "human beings" in general, is consistently rendered with "Christians." In the rare instances when it was necessary to explain an obscure reference, a footnote was added.

The text translated is the text of the 1889 Treves edition of *Mastro-don Gesualdo.* With one exception, I also have adopted the few corrections proposed by Carla Riccardi in her critical edition of the novel, Milano, Mondadori ("Il Saggiatore"), 1979.

At this point I would like to express my gratitude to the colleagues who urged me to undertake the translation of Giovanni Verga's *Mastro-don Gesualdo,* and to Karen Del Antonelli who helped me to make it a reality.

G. C.

CAST OF CHARACTERS

Gesualdo Motta: Mastro-don Gesualdo
Mastro Nunzio Motta: his father
Santo Motta: his brother
Speranza: his sister, married to:
Massaro Fortunato Burgio
Uncle Mescalise: his uncle
Donna Bianca Trao: his wife
Don Diego Trao: Donna Bianca's brother
Don Ferdinando Trao: Donna Bianca's brother
Isabella Trao Motta: Gesualdo and Bianca's "daughter"

Aristocrats / Bianca's relatives

Baron Zacco
Baroness Zacco: his wife
Donna Lavinia: their daughter
Donna Marietta: their daughter

Baroness Rubiera: Donna Bianca's aunt
Don Ninì (Antonino) Rubiera: her son
Donna Giuseppina Alòsi: his wife

Don Filippo Margarone
Donna Bellonia: his wife
Donna Fifì ⎱
Donna Mita ⎰ their daughters
Donna Giovannina ⎰
Nicolino: their son

Donna Sarina (Sara) Cirmena: Donna Bianca's aunt
Corrado La Gurna: her ward

Donna Chiara Macrì: Donna Bianca's aunt
Donna Agrippina: her daughter

Mrs. Marianna Sganci: Donna Bianca's aunt

Duke of Leyra (Alvaro Filippo Maria Ferdinando Gargantas di
    Leyra): Isabella's husband
Marina di Leyra: his sister and one of Isabella's schoolmates
Balì di Leyra: his uncle
Alimena: another of Isabella's schoolmates

Marquis Alfonso Limòli: Donna Bianca's uncle

Baron Mèndola

Others

Canon-priest Lupi
Archpriest Bugno
Father Angiolino: Donna Bianca's father confessor
Don Luca: sacristan
Grazia: his wife

Don Bastiano Stangafame: Captain at Arms and Donna Fifì's
    husband
Don Liccio Papa: head cop
Mr. Captain: Chief of Police
Mrs. Capitana: his wife

Fiscal Attorney
Notary Neri
Mommino Neri: his son
Notary Sghembi: from Militello

Doctor Tavuso: town doctor
Don Margheritino: his son and also a town doctor
Arcangelo Bomma: pharmacist
Doctor Muscio: one of Don Gesualdo's doctors
Don Vincenzo Capra: one of Don Gesualdo's doctors

Cavaliere Peperito

Townspeople

Nanni l'Orbo: works for Don Gesualdo
Diodata: his wife; formerly Don Gesualdo's mistress
Nunzio: her son
Gesualdo: her son
Vito Orlando
Brasi Camauro
Agostino: overseer
Mastro Cola: mason
Massaro Carmine
Mariano: mason
Masi: helper boy
Mastro Nardo: mason

Mastro Lio Pirtuso: middleman and broker

Canali
Don Roberto Ciolla
Giacalone
Pelagatti

Alessio
Rosaria } work for Baroness Rubiera
Gerbido

Mastro Titta: Mrs. Sganci's house barber
Don Giuseppe Barabba: Mrs. Sganci's butler

Fra Girolamo of the Mercenaries: revolutionary cleric

Giacinto: sherbert shop owner
Nanni Ninnarò: inn owner
Mastro Cosimo: carpenter
Don Anselmo: a Caffè dei Nobili waiter

Signora Aglae: actress
Signor Pallante: actor

Don Leopoldo: Don Gesualdo's manservant in Palermo
Donna Carmelina: Isabella's wardrobe maid

PART ONE

I

The dawn mass was ringing at San Giovanni's, but the town was still fast asleep, because it had been raining for three days, and in the wheat fields you'd sink all the way up to your knees. Suddenly, in the silence, a commotion, the shrill bell of Sant'Agata's calling for help, doors and windows slamming, people running out in their nightshirts, yelling:

"Earthquake! Saint Gregory, help us!"

It was still dark. Far off, in the vast black expanse of Alia, only a coalman's lamp was blinking, and to the left the morning star, above a big low-hanging cloud that cut through the dawn in the long plateau of the Paradiso. Throughout the countryside spread the mournful howling of dogs. And all at once, from the lower side of town came the grave sound of San Giovanni's big bell also sounding the alarm; then San Vito's cracked bell, and the other from the mother church, farther away, and Sant'Agata's that seemed to be falling on the very heads of those in the square. One after the other the bells of the monasteries had awakened too; the Collegio's, Santa Maria's, San Sebastiano's, Santa Teresa's: a general clanging that ran in fright over the roofs—in the darkness.

"No! No! It's fire! . . . Fire at the Trao house! . . . Saint John the Baptist!"

The men rushed over shouting, pants in hand. The women put lanterns in the windows; the whole town up on the hill was swarming with lanterns, as if it were Thursday evening, when the second hour of the night rings; something to make your hair stand on end, if you saw it from afar.

"Don Diego! Don Ferdinando!" was the call you could hear at the end of the square; and someone banging at the front door with a rock.

From up the grade toward Piazza Grande, and from the other alleys, people kept coming: a continual trampling of hobnailed boots on the cobblestones; from time to time a name was shouted from afar; and that insistent door banging at the end of the little Sant'Agata Square, and that voice calling:

"Don Diego! Don Ferdinando! Are you all dead?"

From the Trao palace, above the toothless cornice, one could in fact see globes of dense smoke, in waves scattered with sparks, rise in the whitening dawn. And a reddish glare rained down from above and lit up the anxious faces of the neighbors gathered in front of the ramshackle door — their noses in the air. Suddenly you heard a window rattle, and a shrill voice cry out from up there:

"Help!...thieves!...Christians, help!"

"Fire!...your house is on fire! Open up, Don Ferdinando!"

"Diego! Diego!"

Behind Don Ferdinando Trao's wild face then appeared at the window, Don Diego's filthy nightcap and fluttering gray hair. You'd also hear his hoarse, consumptive voice shout:

"Help!... There are thieves in the house! Help!"

"What thieves!... What would they go up there for?" jeered someone in the crowd.

"Bianca! Bianca! Help! Help!"

At that point Nanni l'Orbo arrived out of breath, swearing he himself had seen thieves in the Trao house.

"With these very eyes!... Someone who wanted to jump out of Donna Bianca's window and who ran inside again, when he saw people coming."

"The palace is burning, understand? The whole neighborhood will go up in flames! My house is next door, by God!" Mastro-don Gesualdo Motta began to shout.

The others meanwhile, pushing and levering against the front door, were able to get into the courtyard, one by one, shouting, screeching, armed with buckets and jugs filled with water, the grass up to their knees; Cosimo carrying his hatchet, Don Luça, the sacristan wanting to ring the bells again to call the people to arms, Pelagatti as he was when he ran up at the first alarm, holding the big rusted pistol he had dug up from under a pile of fodder.

From the courtyard the fire could not yet be seen. Only, from time to time, depending on how the wind blew from the northwest, great waves of smoke passed by overhead, and disappeared behind the dry wall of the garden, among the branches of the blooming almond trees. Under the collapsing shed were piled some bundles of firewood, and at the far end, leaning straight up against neighbor Motta's house, there was more wood: scaffolding, rotten joists, beams, a millstone post which had been impossible to sell.

"It's worse than tinder, can't you see!" shouted Mastro-don

Gesualdo, "it will send the whole neighborhood up in flames!...
Goddammit!... And they lean it up against my wall; because they
have nothing to lose, God damn it!..."

At the top of the stairs, Don Ferdinando—bundled up in an old
shabby overcoat, with a filthy kerchief tied around his head, an
eight-day beard, and wild, mad, grayish eyes rolling in his asthmatic
parchment-face—kept repeating like a goose:

"This way! This way!"

But no one dared to climb up the shaky staircase. A real big
hovel that house: broken-down walls, plasterless and battered;
cracks all the way from the cornice to the ground; broken-down
glassless windows; the family crest worn-out, chipped at the corners,
hanging from a rusty hook above the door. Mastro-don Gesualdo
first wanted to throw all that wood piled in the courtyard into the
square.

"It would take a month!" answered Pelagatti who looked on
yawning, big pistol in hand.

"Goddammit! It's piled up against my wall!... Will you listen,
yes or no?"

Giacalone suggested knocking down the shed; Don Luca, the
sacristan assured them that for the time being there was no danger.
A real tower of Babel!

Other neighbors had run up. Santo Motta, his hands in his
pockets, a jovial face and always a joke on his lips; Speranza, his sister, green with anger, wringing her withered breast into her baby's
mouth, spitting poison against the Traos.

"Gentlemen...look at that! Our warehouses are next door!"
—And she got angry even at her husband Burgio, who was there in
his shirtsleeves:

"You don't say anything! You stand there like an idiot! What
did you come here for?"

Mastro-don Gesualdo was the first to dart up the stairs, howling. The others behind, like so many lions, running through the
dark and empty rooms. At each step an army of rats that frightened
the people.

"Careful! Careful! The floor is collapsing!"

Nanni l'Orbo who was still worried about the one at the window, kept shouting:

"There he is! There he is!"

And in the library, which was falling to pieces, he almost killed the sacristan with Pelagatti's big pistol. You could still hear, in the dark, Don Ferdinando's hoarse voice calling:

"Bianca! Bianca!"

While Don Diego, banging and storming behind a door, was stopping those who passed, grabbing them by their clothes, he too screaming:

"Bianca! My sister!..."

"Are you kidding?" answered Mastro-don Gesualdo, red as a tomato, tearing himself free. "My house is next door, understand? The whole neighborhood will go up in flames!"

There was a furious running in the ramshackle palace; women bringing water; children chasing each other, squawking in the midst of all that confusion, as if it was a feast day; onlookers who roamed around open-mouthed, tearing off shreds of fabric that were still hanging from the walls, touching the carvings on the window posts, shouting to hear the echoes in the large empty rooms, raising their noses in the air to examine the gold-plated stuccos, and the family portraits; all those sooty Traos who seemed to be opening their eyes wide in seeing such a mob in their house. A coming and going that kept the floor shaking.

"There! There! The roof is about to collapse!" jeered Santo Motta, scurrying in the water: puddles at every step, among the misplaced or missing bricks. Don Diego and Don Ferdinando, pushed about in a daze, were run over in the midst of the crowd that was rummaging through every corner of their miserable house, kept screeching in a daze:

"Bianca!... My sister!..."

"Your house is on fire, do you understand?" Santo Motta shouted in their ears. "There will be some fireworks with all this old stuff!"

"This way, this way!" a voice was heard from the alley, "the fire is up there, in the kitchen..."

Mastro Nunzio, Gesualdo's father, who had climbed up on a ladder, was waving his arms in the air, from the roof of the house across the street. Giacalone had attached a pulley to the railing of the balcony to draw water from the Motta cistern. *Mastro* Cosimo, the carpenter, had climbed up on the eaves and was furiously axing down the skylight.

"No! No!" they shouted from below. "If you air the fire, in a moment the whole place will go!"

Then Don Diego hit his forehead with his hand, and stammered:

"The family papers! The papers of the lawsuit!"

And Don Ferdinando ran off, also shouting, his hands in his hair.

From the windows, from the balcony, as the wind blew, gusts of dense smoke billowed in, making Don Diego cough, as he continued to call from behind the door:

"Bianca! Bianca! the fire! . . ."

Mastro-don Gesualdo, who had darted furiously up the small kitchen stairway, came back blinded by the smoke, as pale as a dead man, his eyes out of their sockets, half suffocated:

"Goddammit! . . . We can't get in this way! . . . I'm ruined! . . ."

The others shouted all at once, each saying his own piece: a hairraising uproar:

"Throw down the roof tiles!"

"Lean the ladder against the chimney!"

Mastro Nunzio, standing on the roof of his house, jounced as if he were possessed. Don Luca, the sacristan, had really rushed to hang on to the bells. The people in the square were as thick as flies. From the corridor Speranza managed to make herself heard; hoarse from shouting, she was tearing the clothes off people to get through, foaming at the mouth, her nails unsheathed like a cat's:

"From the staircase down there, at the end of the corridor!"

Everyone ran in that direction, leaving Don Diego, who kept calling behind his sister's door:

"Bianca! Bianca! . . ."

A commotion could be heard behind that door; a crazed running as if someone had lost his mind. Then the sound of a chair being overturned. Again Nanni l'Orbo began to yell at the end of the corridor:

"There he is! There he is!"

And the explosion of Pelagatti's big pistol sounded like a cannon shot.

"The law! Here come the cops!" shouted Santo Motta from the courtyard.

Then suddenly the door opened and Donna Bianca appeared,

her clothes in disorder, as pale as a dead woman, groping with shaky hands, without uttering a word, staring at her brother with her eyes crazed with terror and anguish. Suddenly she fell to her knees, grabbing onto the doorpost, stammering:

"Kill me, Don Diego!... Kill me!...but don't let anyone come in here!..."

What happened next, behind that door which Don Diego had again closed after pushing his sister into the bedroom, no one ever knew. You only heard his voice, a voice full of desperate anguish, stammering:

"You?...you here?..."

The Police Captain, the fiscal Attorney, all of the police force rushed up. Don Liccio Papa, the head cop, shouted from afar, brandishing his unsheathed sword:

"Wait! Wait! Stop! Stop!"

And the Police Captain behind him, panting like Don Liccio, throwing his stick before him:

"Make way! Make way! Let the police through!"

The fiscal Attorney ordered that the door be knocked down. "Don Diego! Donna Bianca! Open up! What happened to you?"

Don Diego leaned out of the door. He had aged ten years in one minute—dismayed, wild-eyed, with a frightening vision deep down inside his gray pupils, a cold sweat on his brow, his voice choked with an immense grief:

"Nothing!... My sister!... The fright!... No one must go in!"

Pelagatti was furious with Nanni l'Orbo:

"What a nice thing you almost made me do!... I almost killed Santo!..."

Even the Police Captain gave him a good dressing down:

"Playing with firearms!... Are you joking?... You're a jack-ass!"

"Captain, Sir, I thought it was a thief, down there in the dark. ... I saw him with these very eyes!"

"Shut up! Shut up! You drunk!" chided the fiscal Attorney. "Rather, let's go see the fire."

Now, from the corridor and from the garden staircase, everyone was bringing water. Cosimo had climbed onto the roof and was hacking away at the cross-beams with his ax. Everywhere they were making shingles, stones, pieces of dishes rain on the smoking ceiling. Burgio, on the ladder, took potshots at the fire, and from the other side Pelagatti, lying in wait near the chimney stack, mercilessly loaded and unloaded his big pistol. Don Luca kept ringing the bells as loud as he could; the crowd in the square shouting and gesticulating, and the neighbors at their windows. The Margarones were watching from their balcony above the roofs across the square — the daughters with their hair still in curlers, Don Filippo giving advice from afar, with his bamboo cane directing the operations of those who were working at putting out the fire.

Don Ferdinando, who was returning at that moment loaded down with old papers, bumped into Giacalone who was running along the dark corridor.

"Excuse me, Don Ferdinando. I'm going to call the doctor for your sister."

"Doctor Tavuso!" shouted behind him Aunt Macrì, a relative who was just as poor as they, and who had been the first to rush over. "Just nearby, at Bomma's pharmacy."

Bianca was having convulsions: a terrible attack; four people were not enough to hold her down in her little bed. Don Diego was beside himself too, pale as a dead body, and with his shaky and fleshless hands he was trying to push back all of those people.

"No!...it's nothing!... Leave her alone!..."

The Police Captain finally began letting his stick come down in all directions, wherever it happened to fall, on the curious neighbors, who crowded by the front door.

"What are you looking at? What do you want? Get away from here? Lazy bums! Tramps! You, Don Liccio Papa, stand guard at the door."

A moment later Baron Mendola arrived, for show, and so did Donna Sarina Cirmena who stuck her nose in everyone's business; and the canon-priest Lupi on Baroness Rubiera's behalf. Aunt Sganci and the other relatives sent their servants to inquire about their niece. Don Diego, barely able to stand on his feet, stuck his head out of the door, and answered each one:

"She's a little better.... She's calmer!... She wants to be left alone...."

"Eh! eh!" muttered the canon-priest shaking his head and looking around at the squalid walls of the room: "I remember how this used to be!... What happened to the riches of the house of Trao?..."

The Baron also shook his head, while his hairy hand stroked his chin covered with hard bristles. Aunt Cirmena let out:

"They are crazy! They should both be tied up! Don Ferdinando has always been an idiot...and Don Diego...remember? When our cousin, Donna Sganci, had found him that job at the mills?... No sir!...a Trao could not accept a salary!...but charity, yes, they can accept that!..."

"Oh! oh!" cut in the canon-priest, malice laughing inside his little mouse-eyes, while he tightened his thin lips.

"Yes sir!... What else would you call it? All the relatives getting together about what they must send for Easter and for Christmas.... Wine, oil, cheese...even some wheat.... The girl is already entirely dressed with gifts from Aunt Rubiera."

"Eh! eh!..."

The canon-priest with an incredulous little smile, kept nudging first Donna Sarina and then the Baron, who bowed his head and still scratched his chin discreetly, pretending to look elsewhere, as if to say:

"Eh! eh! I think so too!..."

At that moment Doctor Tavuso showed up in a hurry, his hat on his head, without greeting anyone, and entered the sick girl's room.

A little later he came out, shrugging his shoulders and swelling his cheeks, accompanied by a thin Don Ferdinando looking like an old owl. Aunt Macrì and the canon-priest Lupi ran after the doctor. Aunt Cirmena wanted to know everything and planted her round eyes on your face worse than the fiscal Attorney.

"Eh? What was it?... Do you know? Today they call it nerves ...a fashionable disease.... They send for you for no reason at all ...as if they could afford to pay for the doctor's visits!" answered Tavuso gruffly. Then he too planted his eyes on Donna Sarina's face:

"Do you want me to tell you? At a certain age, a girl should be given a husband!"

And he turned his back breathing heavily, coughing, spitting.

The relatives looked at each other in the face. The canon-priest for reasons of discretion, began to hold off Baron Mendola, handing him idle talk and tobacco, spitting here and there, trying to glimpse at what was happening behind Donna Bianca's half-closed door, tightening his parched lips as if he were constantly swallowing:

"Of course!... The fright!... They'd made her think there were thieves in the house!... Poor Donna Bianca!... She's so young!...so delicate!..."

"Listen, Cousin!" said Donna Sarina taking Mrs. Macrì aside.

Don Ferdinando, the fool, wanted to get closer so that he too could hear:

"Wait a minute! What ways are these!" chided Aunt Cirmena. "I must say something to your aunt!... Why don't you go and get a glass of water for Bianca; it will do her good...."

Santo Motta descended from up there, rubbing his hands, with a happy air:

"The kitchen is in ruins! There is no longer a place to cook an egg!... It must be rebuilt!"

Since no one paid any attention to him, he stared first one and then the other in the face with his stupid smile.

To get rid of him, the canon-priest Lupi finally said to him:

"All right, all right. We'll talk about it later..."

As soon as Santo Motta turned around, Baron Mendola finally spoke his piece:

"We'll think about it?... If there is the money to think about it! I always told him... Sell half of the house, dear Cousin...even one or two rooms...enough to get by! No sir!... Sell the Trao house?... Instead, when a room falls into ruin they close the door and make do with those that are left.... And that's what they will do with the kitchen.... They will cook eggs here in the living room when they have any to cook.... Sell one or two rooms?... No sir, they couldn't even if they wanted to.... The archive room? there are the family papers!... The balcony room? and there will be no place to look from when the "Corpus Domini" procession passes by. ... The cuckoo clock room?... They even have a room for the cuckoo clock, understand!"

After that outburst the Baron left them all there roaring with laughter.

Donna Sarina, before going away again knocked at her niece's door to find out how she was. Don Diego stuck his cardboard face out and repeated:

"Better...she's calmer!... She wants to be left alone...."

"Poor Diego!" sighed Aunt Macrì.

Aunt Cirmena took a few more steps in the entryroom so that Don Ferdinando who came to close the door could not hear, and she added in a whisper:

"I have known it for a while.... Do you remember the evening of the Immaculate Conception, when there was such a big snowfall? I saw the young Baron Rubiera in the alley right near here.... All wrapped up in his cloak like a thief...."

The canon-priest Lupi crossed the courtyard, lifting up his cassock over his large boots, among the weeds; he turned his face back to the dismantled house, to make sure they couldn't hear him, and then, before the front door, looking uneasily here and there, he concluded:

"Did you hear Doctor Tavuso? We can talk because we are all close friends and relatives.... At a certain age a girl should be given a husband!"

II

In the square, as they saw Don Diego Trao pass by with his greasy hat and the greatcoat he wore on special occasions, it was a big event.

"It took the fire to get you out of the house!"

Cousin Zacco even wanted to take him to the Caffè dei Nobili:

"Tell us, tell us how it was..."

The old man tried to ward him off the best he could; besides, he wasn't even a member; poor, yes, but the Traos had never taken their hats off to anyone. He took the long way around in order to avoid the Bomma Pharmacy, where Doctor Tavuso lectured all day long; but while climbing the Condotto, hugging the wall, he ran into that busybody Ciolla, who was always on the lookout for scandals:

"What brings you here, Don Diego! Are you going to see your cousin, Baroness Rubiera?"

He blushed. Everyone seemed to read his secret on his face! He turned around again haltingly, cautiously, before entering the alley, fearing that Ciolla would spy on him. Fortunately, Ciolla had stopped to talk to the canon-priest Lupi, giving out roars of laughter, and the canon-priest himself responded by also composing his mouth into a discrete laugh.

Baroness Rubiera was having some wheat sieved. Don Diego saw her as he passed in front of the storehouse door. She was in the middle of a cloud of chaff, her arms bare, the hem of her cotton skirt tucked into her waistband, her hair dusty, despite the kerchief she had pulled down to her nose, like a little roof. She was arguing with that thief of a grain broker Pirtuso, who wanted to steal her spelt by paying two tari less a salma for it, her face flushed, her hairy arms waving, her belly jumping up and down:

"Don't you have any conscience, Judas! . . ."

Then, as she saw Don Diego, she turned smiling:

"Greetings, Cousin Trao. What brings you around here?"

"I am just coming, in fact, Cousin . . ." and Don Diego, choked by the dust, began to cough.

"Move, move! away from here, Cousin. You're not used to this," cut in the Baroness. "Look what I must do? Jesus! What a face you have! Last night's scare, eh?"

From the trapdoor at the top of the little wooden staircase, appeared two old shoes and thick blue stockings, and then the beautiful voice of a young girl was heard:

"Baroness, here they are."

"Is the Baron back?"

"I hear *Marchese* barking down there."

"All right, I'm coming. Well, what are we going to do about the spelt, *mastro* Lio?"

Pirtuso was still squatting down on the bushel measure, calmly, as if to say that the spelt was no concern of his, carelessly looking here and there at the strange things that were in the storehouse as big as a church. Once, at the time of the height of splendor of the Rubieras, there was even a theater. You could still see the arch painted with nude women, and with columns, as if it were a chapel;

facing it the family box, with shreds of fabric dangling from the parapet; a big broken-down carved wooden bed in a corner; several leather armchairs disemboweled to make shoes out of them; a dusty velvet saddle, straddling the beam of a loom; sieves of all sizes hung all around; heaps of shovels and brooms; a sedan chair was stuck under the stairs leading up to the family box, with the Rubiera coat of arms on its door, and an ancient lantern placed on its roof like a crown. Giacalone, and Vito Orlando, in the middle of heaps of wheat as tall as mountains, restlessly fidgeted about the immense sieves, as if obsessed, all sweaty and white with chaff, singing in rhythm, while Gerbido, the helper boy, kept piling up the grain with a broom.

"In my day, Baroness, I saw comedy played in this storehouse," answered Pirtuso to divert the question.

"I know! I know! That's how the Rubieras lost their wealth! Now you want them to continue!... Do you want that spelt? yes or no?"

"I told you: at five onze and twenty."

"No, in all conscience, I cannot. I am already losing one tarì per bushel."

"God bless...Baroness!"

"Come now, *mastro* Lio, now that the Baroness has spoken!" added Giacalone, still making the sieve dance.

But the broker took up his bushel measure and left without answering. The Baroness ran after him and yelled from the doorway:

"At five and twenty-one. Is that all right?"

"God bless...God bless!"

But out of the corner of her eye she noticed that the broker had stopped to talk to the canon-priest Lupi who, having finally gotten rid of Ciolla, was strolling up the alley. Then, reassured, she turned to her cousin Trao, talking about other things:

"I was just thinking about you, Cousin. I would like to send you some of that spelt...no, no, you're welcome to it...we are relatives. A good harvest must help everybody. Then the Lord will help us!... Your house was on fire, eh? God help us! They tell me that Bianca is still half dead with fright.... I couldn't leave things here. ... You must forgive me."

"Yes ... I came precisely ... I must speak to you...."

"Tell me, please tell me ... but now, while you're down there, look to see if Pirtuso is coming back ... so as not to be seen...."

"He's a jackass!" ansered Vito Orlando, still fidgeting restlessly about the sieve. "I know *mastro* Lio. He's a jackass! He will not come back."

At that moment the canon-priest Lupi came in smiling with the nice amiable face that made people feel at ease, and behind him the broker with the bushel measure in hand.

"*Deo Gratias!* Thanks to God! Baroness, are we going to arrange this wedding?"

When he noticed Don Diego Trao, who was waiting meekly to one side, the canon-priest immediately changed his tone and his manner, his lips tightened. Pretending to keep to one side also, discreetly, only intent upon the wheat deal.

They bargained a little longer; *mastro* Lio now ranted and raved as if they wanted to steal money out of his very pocket. The Baroness, however, with an air of indifference was turning her back and calling toward the trap door:

"Rosaria! Rosaria!"

"Be quiet!" finally exclaimed the canon-priest, hitting *mastro* Lio on the shoulders with his big hand. "I know for whom you're buying. It's for Mastro-don Gesualdo."

Giacalone nodded yes, winking.

"It's not true! Mastro-don Gesualdo has nothing to do with it!" the broker began to shout. "Mastro-don Gesualdo's not in this business!"

But finally, as they agreed on a price, Pirtuso calmed down. The canon-priest added:

"Don't worry, everything is Mastro-don Gesualdo's business if he can make a profit."

Pirtuso, who had noticed Giacalone's winking, went to tell him face to face what he thought about the whole thing:

"What's the matter with you? Don't you want to eat bread? Don't you know that you never talk when people are making deals?"

On the other hand, as the broker turned his back to the Baroness, she too winked at the canon-priest Lupi, as if to say that regarding the price it wasn't too bad at all.

"Yes, yes," he answered in a whisper. "Baron Zacco is about to sell at a lower price. But Mastro-don Gesualdo doesn't know about it yet."

"Ah! Mastro-don Gesualdo has even become a wheat merchant? Is he no longer a mason?"

"That devil does a little of everything! They are saying that he even wants to bid at the auction for the levies on the city lands...."

Then the Baroness opened her eyes wide:

"Cousin Zacco's lands!... The levies that have passed from father to son for fifty years?... It's highway robbery!"

"I can't say no; I can't say no. Today nobody has any respect for anybody. They say that whoever has more money is the one who's right...."

Then he turned toward Don Diego, and with great emphasis, began to complain about modern times:

"Today there is no other God! A gentleman at times...or a young girl born to a good family...yet, they have no luck! Instead one who has come up from nothing...a man like Mastro-don Gesualdo, for example!..."

The canon-priest continued in a mysterious tone, speaking softly to the Baroness and to Don Diego Trao, spitting here and there:

"He has a good head, that Mastro-don Gesualdo! He will become rich I'm telling you that! He would make an excellent husband for a nice girl...like there are many, without much of a dowry."

This time *mastro* Lio was really leaving. "Well, Baroness, may I come to load the wheat?"

The Baroness, again in a good mood, answered:

"Yes, but you know what tavern keepers say? 'Here you eat and here you drink; but without money you don't come in.'"

"Cash in hand, Baroness. Thank God, you'll see that we pay on time."

"I told you so!" exclaimed Giacalone breathing heavily on the sieve. "It's Mastro-don Gesualdo!"

The canon-priest exchanged another sign of understanding with the Baroness, and after Pirtuso had left he said:

"Do you know what I've been thinking? You should bid at the

auction too, ma'am, with someone else.... I would go along, too...."

"No, no, I already have got too many irons in the fire!...besides I wouldn't like to do a bad turn to Cousin Zacco! As you well know...we are in this world...at times we need one another."

"I know,...but let someone else stand in...Mastro-don Gesualdo Motta, for example. He has some capital; I know that for a fact.... You could lend your name...we could set up a partnership, the three of us...."

Then, feeling that Don Diego Trao was listening to their plans, for he was waiting for the right moment to talk to his cousin, Baroness Rubiera—but rigid as he was in his long coat, the poor man had other things on his mind—the canon-priest immediately changed the subject.

"Eh, eh, how many things this storehouse has seen! I remember, as a child, seeing Marquis Limòli perform *Adelaide e Comingio** with Mrs. Margarone, rest in peace, Don Filippo's mother, the one who later ended up at Salonia. 'Adelaide! where are you?' the charterhouse scene...you should have seen it! Everyone with his handkerchief to his eyes! So much so that Don Alessandro Spina cried out with emotion: 'Tell them that's really you!...' and he even cursed at her.... Then there is the story of the potshot someone took at Marquis Limòli, while he was taking a breath of fresh air, after dinner. And the one about Don Nicola Margarone who took his wife to the country and never let her see another living soul. Now they are resting together, husband and wife, in the Church of the Rosario, peace to their souls!"

The Baroness nodded her head, now and then separating the wheat from the dross with her broom.

"That's how families used to go to ruin. If it hadn't been for me, the Rubiera house!... You can imagine what would have remained of so much grandeur! Thank God, I keep my feet on the ground! I have remained just as my father and mother made me...

---

*The names of the two protagonists of a theatrical version of *Mémoires du comte de Comminges* (1735) by Alexandrine Guérin de Tencin (1682-1749), a popular romantic story about a young couple in love, who are not allowed to marry. Adelaide is finally wed to a rich and jealous man and Comingio retreats to a monastery, where Adelaide also secretly goes after the death of her husband.

country folk, people who built their house with their own hands, instead of destroying it! It is because of them that there is still some of God's bounty in the Rubiera storehouse, rather than parties and theaters. . . ."

At that point the driver with his loaded-down mules arrived.

"Rosaria! Rosaria!" the Baroness began shouting again toward the staircase.

Finally, from the trap door appeared the old shoes and the blue stockings, followed by the monkeylike figure of the maid, dirty, unkempt, her hands constantly in her hair.

"Don Ninì was not at the Vignazza," she said calmly. "Alessio came back with the dog, but the Baron wasn't there."

"Oh Holy Mother of God!" the Baroness began to shout, losing some of her old color. "Oh Holy Mother of God! And where can he be? What happened to my boy?"

Hearing this, Don Diego turned red and white from one moment to the next. His face looked as if he wanted to say: "Open up earth, and swallow me up!" He coughed, he looked for his handkerchief in his hat, he opened his mouth to speak; then he turned away, wiping his sweat. The canon-priest gave a hurried answer while he looked at Don Diego Trao stealthily:

"He must have gone somewhere else. . . . When one goes hunting, you know . . ."

"He has all of his father's bad habits, rest in peace! Hunting, gambling, amusements! . . . Without ever thinking about anything else . . . and without even telling me! . . . Imagine, last night, when the bells rang the fire alarm, I went to look for him in his room and he wasn't there! He'll get a piece of my mind! . . . Oh, will he! . . ."

The canon-priest was trying to cut this subject short—his face uneasy, and his smile idiotic:

"Eh, eh, Baroness! your son is no longer a child, he's twenty-six years old!"

"Even if he were a hundred! . . . Until he gets married, understand! . . . And even after!"

"Baroness, where should we unload the mules?" Rosaria asked, scratching her head.

"I'm coming, I'm coming. Let's go this way. The two of you will go through the courtyard when you're finished."

She locked Giacalone and Vito Orlando inside the storehouse, and headed toward the front door.

The Baroness's house was very large; it had been put together by bits and pieces — as her parents had managed to flush out the various owners to the point of ending up in the Rubiera palace with their daughter and bringing everything together: high and low roofs, windows of all sizes, here and there at random; the elegant front door stuck in the middle of facades worthy of shacks. The building took up nearly the entire length of the alley.

The Baroness, who was whispering to the canon-priest Lupi, had almost forgotten about her cousin, who followed them step by step. But as they reached the front door, the canon-priest pulled back cautiously:

"Another time, I'll come back later. Your cousin has to talk to you. Now you can discuss your business, Don Diego."

"Ah, forgive me, Cousin. Please come in."

Immediately, from the huge and dark hall, which was flanked by small, low doors, grated like those of a prison, you could tell that you were in an affluent house; an odor of oil and cheese that choked you and then a smell of mold and cellar. Up from the wide open cellar gate, as if from the depths of a cavern, came the laughter of Alessio and the maid who were filling the barrels, and the weak glimmer of the lantern sitting on a cask.

"Rosaria! Rosaria!" the Baroness again shouted in a threatening voice. Then turning to her cousin Trao:

"Many times you've got to raise your voice with that blessed girl; because when you've got men around it's a serious business! But, on the other hand, you can trust her and you must be patient. What can I do?... A house full of stuff like mine!..."

Farther down, in the courtyard that looked like that of a big farm — crowded with chickens, geese, and turkeys flocking and squawking around the Baroness — the odor changed into a stench of heaps of manure and piles of forage. Two or three of the long line of mules under the shed stretched their necks, braying; pigeons swarmed down from the roof; a ferocious sheep dog began to bark, tearing at his chain; some rabbits lifted their uneasy ears, in the mysterious darkness of the woodshed. The Baroness, surrounded by all that bounty, said to her cousin:

"I want to send you a couple of pigeons, for Bianca...."

The poor man coughed, blew his nose, but not even then could he find an answer. Finally, after a maze of corridors and staircases, through big dark rooms, cluttered with all kinds of stuff—piles of fava beans and of barley covered with trellises, farming tools, trunks full of linens—they reached the Baroness's whitewashed room with her wedding bed unchanged after twenty years of widowhood, with the blessed olive branch at the foot of the crucifix, and her husband's shotgun beside the bolster.

Baroness Rubiera again began to complain about her son:

"Just like his father, rest his soul! Without a care in the world, neither for his mother nor for his own interests!..."

Seeing her cousin Trao nailed to the door, shrunken in his big overcoat, she offered him a seat:

"Come in, come in, Cousin Trao."

The poor man let himself fall into the chair, as if his legs were broken, sweating like Jesus in the Garden. He then removed his greasy old hat, wiping his forehead with his handkerchief.

"Do you have something to tell me, Cousin? Speak, please tell me."

He clasped his hands tightly, one inside the other, inside his hat, and stammered with a hoarse voice, his lips pale and shaky, his eyes damp and sad avoiding his cousin's eyes:

"Yes, ma'am...I have to talk to you...."

At first, when she saw that face of his, she thought that he had come to ask her for money. True, it would have been the first time: the Trao cousins were too proud; a little gift, the kind that helped them get by, wine, oil, wheat, they would accept from their rich relatives—herself, Cousin Sganci, Baron Mendola—but they had never held out their hand. But there are times when need makes even prouder people bow their heads!... The instinctive prudence that was in her blood froze her benevolent smile. For a moment. Then she thought of the fire they had had in their house, of Bianca's sickness—the Baroness was a good woman after all. Don Diego had such a pitiful face.... She moved her chair next to his to give him courage, and added:

"Tell me, tell me, Cousin... Whatever I can do...as you know...we are relatives.... The times are not very good...but what can be done...not much...but what little I can...among relatives...please tell me...."

But he couldn't, no! With his jaws tightened, his mouth bitter, at every moment raising his eyes toward her, and opening his lips without uttering a sound. Finally, he took out his handkerchief to wipe off the sweat, he passed it over his parched lips, stammering:

"Something terrible happened!... Something terrible!..."

The Baroness feared she had let herself go too far. In her eyes, which avoided her cousin's tearful ones, began to flash the uneasiness of the peasant who fears for his property:

"What!...what!..."

"Your son is so rich!... My sister, on the other hand, isn't..."

At these words Baroness Rubiera stretched out her ears, her face tightened into her forefather's mask, stamped with the gruff mistrust of those peasants who had put their blood in her veins and had built her house piece by piece with their own hands. She got up and went to hang the key on the doorpost, rummaging throughout the drawers of the dresser. Finally, seeing that Don Diego didn't say anything else:

"But, speak clearly, Cousin. You know that I have got a lot to do..."

Instead of speaking clearly, Don Diego burst into tears like a child, hiding his parchment-face in his cotton handkerchief, his back bent and shaken with sobs, while he kept repeating:

"Bianca! my sister!... A terrible thing happened to my poor sister... Ah, Cousin Rubiera!...you, you who are a mother!..."

Now Cousin Rubiera had a totally different expression: her lips tightened so as not to lose her temper, and a wrinkle in the center of her forehead—the wrinkle of those who have been in the rain and in the sun to accumulate property—and who must defend it. In a flash she remembered many of the things she had neglected in the rush of her constant business: some half words of her Cousin Macrì; the rumors that Don Luca, the sacristan had spread: certain of her son's subterfuges. All of a sudden she felt a taste as bitter as gall in her mouth.

"I don't know, Cousin," she answered him dryly. "I don't know what this has to do with me..."

Don Diego took a moment to find the words, staring at her with eyes that said so much—in between those tears of shame and grief, and he then again hid his face in his hands, nodding his head in time with his voice that barely came out:

"Yes!... Yes!...your son, Nini..."

This time it was the Baroness who could not find words—her eyes darting out of her large apoplectic face and fixed on her cousin Trao, as if she wanted to devour him. Then she sprang to her feet as if she were twenty years old, and throwing open the window in anger, shouted:

"Rosaria! Alessi! Come here!"

"For God's sake! Please," begged Don Diego with clasped hands, running after her. "Don't make scandals, please!"

And he shut up, suffocated by his cough, pressing his breast.

But the Baroness, who was beside herself, did not listen to him. It felt like an earthquake throughout the house: the chickens's squawking; the dog's yelping; Alessi's and Rosaria's big old shoes running up at breakneck speed—both of them disheveled and panting, their eyes downcast.

"Where did my son go? What did they tell you at Vignazza? Speak, you idiot!"

Alessi, shifting his weight from one leg to the other, stammering, looking here and there uneasily, kept repeating the same thing: the Baron was not at Vignazza. He had left his dog, *Marchese*, there the night before, and had gone away:

"On foot, yes Ma'am. That's what the factor told me."

The maid tidying herself up on the sly, her head bent, added that when he was going hunting early in the morning, the Baron used to go out through the stable door, so as not to wake anyone:

"The key?...I don't know.... He threatened to break every bone in my body.... It's not my fault, Baroness."

The Baroness looked like she was having a stroke. They both slunk away with long faces. On the stairs you could again hear the noise of their big old shoes running after each other rapidly.

Don Diego, looking like a dead body, his handkerchief over his mouth to stop his cough, suffocated, kept stammering senseless words:

"He was there...behind that door!... It would have been better if he had killed me.... Then he pointed his pistols at my chest ...at me!...the pistols at my chest, Cousin Rubiera!..."

The Baroness wiped her lips as bitter as gall with a cotton handkerchief:

"No, I never expected that!...tell me the truth, Don Diego. I didn't deserve this!... I have always treated you like relatives.... And that cold fish of a Bianca, whom I would take into my house for entire days at a time...just like a daughter..."

"Forget it, Cousin Rubiera!" cut in Don Diego, with a remainder of the old Trao blood in his cheeks.

"Yes, yes, let's forget it! I'll take care of my son, don't worry! He'll do as I say, that young Baron. Crook! murderer! He'll be the death of me!..."

And tears welled up in her eyes. Don Diego, dejected, did not dare look up. He could see before him the merciless Ciolla, Bomma's Pharmacy, the ironic laughter of the neighbors, the women's gossip, and even, insistent and painful, the clear sight of his own house which a man had entered at night — the old house that seemed to start at the echo of those thieving steps — and Bianca, his own sister, his own child, his own blood, who had lied to him, who in the darkness had silently clung to the man who was coming to inflict such a mortal outrage on the Traos — her poor delicate and fragile body in the arms of a stranger!... His tears fell bitter and hot, down the fleshless cheeks he was hiding behind his hands.

Finally, the Baroness, wiped her eyes, and sighed turning to the crucifix:

"May God's will be done! Cousin Trao, you must have a bitter taste in your mouth, too! What do you want! It's up to us who carry the burden of the house on our shoulders!... God knows if I have worn myself out from morning to night. If I have kept bread out of my mouth for the love of property!... Then all of a sudden something like this comes down on you!... But it's the last time the noble Baron pulls a stunt like this!... I'll take care of him, you can be sure. After all, he is not a child...I'll find him the kind of wife I see fit.... The chain around his neck, that's what he needs!... But you, let me tell you, you should have kept your eyes open, Cousin Trao!... I'm not speaking of your brother Ferdinando, who's an idiot, the poor man, even if he's the first born...but of you, you who have more sense...and aren't a child either! You should have been on guard!... When there is a girl in the house!... Man is a hunter, we all know!... You should have guarded your sister yourself...or rather she should have guarded herself.... We could almost say that it was...her fault!...who knows what she'd gotten into her head?...maybe even to become Baroness Rubiera...."

Cousin Trao flushed and paled in a moment.

"Baroness...we're poor...it's true... But as far as birth goes..."

"Eh, my dear cousin! birth...ancestors... They're all nice things...I don't deny it.... But the ancestors who made my son a Baron...do you want to know who they were? Those who hoed the soil!...with the sweat of their brow, understand?... They didn't work themselves to death to let their property fall into just anybody's hands.... Understand?..."

Just then someone knocked at the front door with the heavy iron knocker, and the bang echoed throughout the house, again stirring up the squawking of the chickens and the howling of the dog. As the Baroness went to the window to see who it was, Rosaria yelled from the courtyard:

"There is the broker about the wheat..."

"I'm coming, coming!" The Baroness kept grumbling, again taking the storehouse key from its nail. "See what it takes to earn a tarì per salma, with Pirtuso and all the rest. If I have worked all my life, and have taken the very bread out of my mouth, for love of the house, I intend my daughter-in-law to bring along a good dowry as well...."

Don Diego scurried as fast as he could after Cousin Rubiera through the corridors and the big dark rooms full of all kinds of stuff, and kept saying:

"My sister isn't rich...Cousin Rubiera.... She doesn't have the dowry she should have.... We'll give her the house and everything.... We'll strip ourselves for her...Ferdinando and I..."

"In fact, as I was telling you!... Watch out! There's a broken step...I want my son to marry a good dowry. I'm the boss; I'm the one who made him a Baron. He isn't the one who made the property! Come in, come in, *mastro* Lio. There, through the wooden gate. It's open..."

"But your son knew that my sister wasn't rich!..." argued poor

Don Diego, who could not make up his mind to leave — as Cousin Rubiera had so much to do.

Then she turned around like a fighting cock, her fists on her hips, at the top of the stairs:

"I'll take care of my son myself, as I tell you again! You take care of your sister.... Man is a hunter...I'll send him away from here! I'll put him under lock and key! At the bottom of the sea! I'll not let him back in town unless he's married! With the chain around his neck! I tell you! He is my cross! my downfall!..."

Then, moved to compassion by the mute despair of the poor man, who could hardly stand up, she added, as she very slowly came down the stairs:

"By the way...listen, Don Diego...I'll do all I can for Bianca too...I too am a mother!...I too am a Christian!...I can imagine the thorn you must have inside you!..."

"Baroness, he says that the spelt is not full weight," shouted Alessi from the storehouse door.

"What? What is he saying?...Now the weight too?... Is he backing down? Not again!... To force me to lower the price still more!"

And the Baroness left like a fury. For a while you could hear a great uproar coming from the depth of the storehouse; as if they had come to blows, Pirtuso screamed worse than a lamb in the hands of the butcher; Giacalone and Vito Orlando were also shouting to make peace; and the Baroness, beside herself, was saying the wildest things. Then, as she saw Cousin Trao, who was leaving with his tail between his legs, his head sunk in his shoulders, staggering, she stopped him at the door and suddenly changed her face and her manner:

"Listen, listen... We'll settle this business between us.... After all, what could it have been?... Nothing bad, I'm sure. A God-fearing girl... The thing will remain between you and me.... We'll settle it between us...I'll help you too, Don Diego...I'm a mother after all...I'm a Christian... We'll marry her to an honest man...."

Don Diego shook his head bitterly, dejected, staggering like a drunk as he was leaving.

"Yes, yes, we'll find her an honest man...I'll help you too, all I can... What else?... I'll make a sacrifice!..."

At those words he stopped, shaking all over, his eyes wide open: "You? Cousin Rubiera?... No!... No!... That cannot be..."

At that moment the broker was coming out of the storehouse, covered with chaff, looking tough all the way to the beard that darkened his face even if freshly shaven: his small eyes as gray as two silver tarì, under the two brows knitted by his being always in the sun and in the wind of the countryside.

"Kiss your hand, Baroness!"

"What? Are you leaving like that? What now? Don't you like the spelt?"

The other signaled "no" with his head, just like Don Diego Trao, who was going off hugging the wall, still shaking his head, as if he had had a stroke, and stumbling on the stones every moment.

"What?" the Baroness kept bawling. "After agreeing on the deal!..."

"Is there a deposit, by any chance, dear Baroness?"

"There is no deposit, but there is your word!..."

"In that case, Baroness, I kiss your hand!"

And he walked away, as stubborn as a mule. The Baroness, in a rage, yelled after him:

"These are dirty tricks, worthy of you! A pretext for breaking off the deal...worthy of that Mastro-don Gesualdo who has sent you—now that he has changed his mind..."

Giacalone and Vito Orlando were running after him too, frantically trying to make him listen to reason. But Pirtuso kept walking, without even answering, saying to Don Diego Trao, who was not paying attention to him:

"The Baroness can talk as much as she likes.... In my shoes she would have done the same thing herself!... Now that Baron Zacco is selling under the market... Whether a peasant or a Baroness, the deposit is what counts. Am I right or not, sir?"

III

Mrs. Sganci's house was full of people who had come to see the procession of the patron saint; even the staircase was lit up; the five balconies showered fire and flames on the square, which was black with people; and Don Giuseppe Barabba, in dress uniform and with cotton gloves, announced the arrivals.

"Mastro-don Gesualdo!" he shouted suddenly, sticking his mussed-up head between the gilded leaves of the door. "Should I let him in, Ma'am?"

The cream of the town aristocracy was there: Archpriest Bugno, dressed in shiny black satin; Donna Giuseppina Alòsi, loaded with jewels; Marquis Limòli, with a face and a wig from the last century. Mrs. Sganci, taken by surprise in front of so many people, could not control herself:

"Jackass! You're a jackass! You should say Don Gesualdo Motta! You jackass!"

In this fashion, Mastro-don Gesualdo made his entrance among the big shots of the town! He was clean shaven, dressed in fine cloth, with a brand new hat in his lime-eaten hands.

"Come in, come in, Don Gesualdo!" screamed Marquis Limòli, with his sour piercing little voice, "Make yourself at home!"

But Mastro-don Gesualdo still hesitated somewhat—intimidated, in the middle of that large room papered with yellow damask, under the eyes of all those Sgancis who looked at him haughtily from their portraits, hanging on the walls.

The lady of the house gave him courage:

"Here, here, there's room for you too, Don Gesualdo."

There was in fact the alley balcony, which faced the square at an angle. It was used for second-class guests and for poor relatives: Donna Chiara Macrì, who was so humble and so modest that you'd have thought she was a servant; her daughter Donna Agrippina, "a house nun," a girl with quite a moustache, a large, brown, warty face like a begging friar's, and two large eyes as black as sin, which searched men. In the front row sat Cousin Don Ferdinando, more curious than a child, who had elbowed himself forward, and stretched his neck out of his big black tie toward Piazza Grande, like a turtle—his little eyes gray and wild, his pointed chin the color of soot, his large quivering Trao nose, his curved ponytail looking like a dog's and resting on the greasy collar that reached up to his hairy ears; and his sister Donna Bianca, huddled behind him, with her shoulders slightly bent, her chest thin and flat, her hair smooth, her face wan, washed out, and wearing a thin woolen dress among all her relatives in their evening clothes.

Aunt Sganci repeated:

"Come here, Don Gesualdo, I have saved a seat for you. Here, next to my nephew and my niece."

Bianca moved over timidly. Don Ferdinando, fearing that he would be disturbed, turned his head for a moment, frowning, and Mastro-don Gesualdo walked toward the balcony, tripping, stammering, drowning himself in apologies. He stayed there, behind the backs of those who were in front of him, raising his head at each firework that came up from the square to give himself a less embarrassed bearing.

"Excuse me, excuse me," puffed Donna Agrippina Macrì, wrinkling up her nose, making way with her powerful hips, disdainfully straightening her white kerchief on her enormous breasts. She ended up in the group where Aunt Cirmena was with the other ladies, on the great balcony, in the midst of a great murmuring, all of them turning to look at the alley balcony at the far end of the room.

"They put him there...at my side, understand!... An outrage!"

"Ah, is that the groom?" asked Donna Giuseppina Alòsi, in a whisper, her eyes smiling in the middle of her placid moon-shaped face.

"Quiet! Quiet! I'll go see..." said Donna Cirmena, and crossed the room—like a sea of light in her yellow satin dress—to go and smell what was cooking on the alley balcony.

There everyone seemed to be on pins and needles: Aunt Macrì pretending to look down at the square, Bianca quiet in a corner and Don Ferdinando, the only one who was enjoying the festivities, turning his head here and there, without saying a word.

"Are you all having a good time here? Are you, Bianca?"

Don Ferdinando turned his head, annoyed; then, seeing Cousin Cirmena, he grumbled:

"Ah...Donna Sarina...good evening! good evening!"

And again he turned away, Bianca raised her sweet and humble eyes toward her aunt without answering. Donna Macrì sketched a discreet smile.

Aunt Cirmena went on immediately, looking at Don Gesualdo:

"Hot, isn't it? Stifling! There are too many people this time... Cousin Sganci invited the whole town...."

Mastro-don Gesualdo tried to move aside:

"No, no, stay, stay, my friend. By the way, listen to this, Cousin Macrì..."

"Ma'am, Ma'am!" shouted Don Giuseppe Barabba, at that moment, signaling the lady of the house.

"No," she answered, "the procession must go by first."

Marquis Limòli caught her on the run while she was going away, grabbing her by the dress:

"Cousin, Cousin, satisfy my curiosity: what are you scheming with Mastro-don Gesualdo?"

"I should have known...you gossip!" grumbled Mrs. Sganci; and she left him there, without paying any more attention to him, while he was sinking into a large armchair and grinning between his naked gums like a malicious mummy.

Just then entered Notary Neri—short, bald, a veritable spinning top, with a petulant belly, a loud laugh, and a speech that ran out squeaking like a pulley.

"Donna Mariannina!... Ladies and Gentlemen!... How many people!... How many beauties!..."

Then, discovering also Mastro-don Gesualdo, all dressed up, he pretended to lean forward in order to see better, as if he were seeing double, arching his eyebrows, shading his eyes with his hand, he made the sign of the cross and sped toward the great balcony, throwing himself elbowing into the crowd, grumbling:

"This is the last straw, I swear to God!"

Instinctively, Donna Giuseppina Alòsi rushed a hand over her jewels; and Mrs. Capitana, who didn't have any to show off but displayed other riches, feeling someone searching her shoulders, turned around like a viper.

"Excuse me, excuse me," stammered the Notary. "I am looking for Baron Zacco."

From Via San Sebastiano, above the roofs, you could see a glow of fire swelling toward the square, out of which, from time to time, fireworks sped off, in front of the statue of the saint and accompanied by the crowd's uproar growing like a storm.

"The procession! the procession!" screamed the children pressed up against the railing. The others pushed forward; but the procession still didn't appear. Cavaliere Peperito, who was devouring Donna Giuseppina Alòsi's jewels with his eyes — such eyes as those of a hungry wolf, in his thin face that was completely covered with a bluish beard — took advantage of the confusion to whisper once more in her ear:

"You look like a young girl, Donna Giuseppina! I give you my word!"

"Quiet, you rascal!" the widow answered. "Rather ask for help of the Patron Saint who is just coming."

"Yes, yes, if he grants me my wish..."

From the armchair, where Marquis Limòli was huddled, rose his cracked voice:

"Talk, talk as much as you like! I am deaf, as you know."

Baron Zacco, red as a tomato, came in from the balcony, without paying attention to the saint, letting off steam with Notary Neri:

"It's all the canon-priest Lupi's doing.... Now they are also going to stick Mastro-don Gesualdo into my affairs, to bid at the auction of the City lands!... But they will not take 'em away from me, even if I were to sell Fontanarossa, see!... Lands that have been in my family for forty years!..."

All of a sudden, under the balconies, the band burst into a wild double-pace rhythm and spilled over into the square with a wave of people that looked like a threat. Mrs. Capitana pulled back, curling up her nose.

"What an odor of people is coming up from down there!"

"Understand?" Baron Zacco kept bawling. "Lands for which I already pay three onze per salma! As if it weren't enough!"

Notary Neri, who didn't like to let people know his business, turned to Mrs. Capitana who was flirting with a group of young men, her dress so low cut that it was truly indecent — she used the excuse that she had her clothes sent from Palermo.

"Mrs. Capitana! Mrs. Capitana! So this is how you steal the feast away from the saint! Everybody is turning his back on him!"

"How stupid you all are!" answered Mrs. Capitana, jubilant, "I'm going to stand next to the Marquis, who has more sense than you."

"Alas! alas! my dear lady!..."

The Marquis, whose eyes were now awake, kept sniffing her bergamot perfume, to such an extent that she had to shield herself with her fan, while the little old man persisted:

"No! let me recite my prayers my way!..."

The Archpriest took some snuff, expectorated, coughed, finally stood up, and made a move to leave, puffing out his cheeks—his shining cheeks, his shining dress, his shining large ring, so big that the gossips said it was fake—while the Marquis shouted after him:

"Don Calogero! Don Calogero! I said it in jest, what the hell! At my age..."

As soon as the laughter had ceased after the Marquis's remark, Donna Giuseppina Alòsi was heard confiding to the Cavaliere:

"...as if I were free, understand! My two oldest daughters at the Collegio di Maria; my son in the Seminary; only the youngest son, Sarino is left at home, and he's shorter than this fan. Then my children were taken care of by their father, rest his soul...."

Donna Sarina came back toward the great balcony, whispering to Cousin Macrì, shaking her head and smiling as if to say:

"But I just don't understand the mystery Cousin Sganci wants to make out of the whole thing!... We are Bianca's relatives too, after all!"

"Is it that one? That one there?" Donna Giuseppina asked again, with the same malicious smile as before.

Aunt Cirmena nodded yes, tightening her thin lips, her eyes looking elsewhere, she too with an air of mystery. Finally she couldn't hold it in any more:

"They are doing things in secret...as if it were something dirty. They too feel that they are handling dirty things.... But people are not so foolish not to notice.... It's a month that the canon-priest Lupi has been scheming about this deal...always back and forth between Mrs. Sganci and Baroness Rubiera...."

"Don't tell me!" exclaimed Peperito. "A Trao marrying Mastrodon Gesualdo!... Don't tell me!... When I see an illustrious family like that stoop so low my stomach hurts, I swear to you!"

And he turned his back blowing his nose into his filthy handkerchief and sounding like a trumpet, trembling with indignation all over his wretched little person, after having shot an eloquent stare at Donna Giuseppina.

"Who's going to marry her?...without a dowry!..." Aunt

Cirmena retorted to the Cavaliere who was already some distance away. "And then, after what happened?"

"At least she'll put herself in the grace of God!" Aunt Macri observed quietly.

Her daughter who was listening without saying a word, staring those who spoke in the face with her large fiery eyes, shook her frock, almost as if she feared to dirty it in the midst of so much filth, and murmured in her masculine voice with her large indignant lips on which the black hairs seemed to tremble, turned toward the glow of the procession, which was approaching above the street roofs, like a fire:

"Patron Saint! Protect me!"

"These are the results!... The girl had gotten I don't know what into her head... A disgrace for all her relatives!... Cousin Sganci did well to mend the situation.... I don't say no!... But she should have talked to us too, who are as much Bianca's relatives as she is.... Instead of doing things on the sly...I bet that not even Don Ferdinando knows anything...."

"But the other brother...Don Diego, what does he say about it?..."

"Ah, Don Diego?...he's probably rummaging through his dirty old papers. The papers of the law suit!... He thinks of nothing else.... He believes the law suit will make him rich.... You see that he hasn't gotten out of the house even for the feast.... Then maybe he is ashamed to let himself be seen!... They are all like that, those Traos. Idiots!... People who will starve to death in their own home, rather than open their mouths for..."

"The canon-priest, no!" the Notary was saying while he approached the balcony and whispered to Baron Zacco. "Rather the Baroness...if one offers her a profit.... She isn't stubborn!... She's not afraid of the canon-priest...."

And then all smiles to the women:

"Ah!...Donna Chiara!... The beautiful nun you have at home!... A real gift of God!..."

"Eh, Marquis? eh? Would you ever have believed it, in your day?...that you would have seen the procession of the patron saint while standing shoulder to shoulder with Mastro-don Gesualdo, in the Sganci house!" added Baron Zacco, who was always thinking of the same thing, and could not swallow it, as he looked here and there with his ugly ghostlike eyes, winking at the women to make them laugh.

The Marquis, inscrutable, only answered:

"Eh, eh, dear Baron! Eh, eh!"

"Do you know how much Mastro-don Gesualdo made building the mills?" the Notary cut in with a quiet voice and an air of mystery. "Quite a sum! I'm telling you!... He pulled himself up from nothing.... I can remember when he was a mason's helper, carrying rocks on his shoulders...yes sir!... *Mastro* Nunzio, his father, couldn't pay for the stubble to burn the gypsum in his kiln....
—Now he's got the contract for the bridge at Fiumegrande!... His son has shelled out the warranty money, all twelve-tari pieces, one on top of the other.... He's got his fingers in all of the town's affairs.... They say that he's planning to speculate on land too.... The more you eat the hungrier you get.... He's quite hungry... and he's got good teeth too, I'm telling you!... If they let him keep on doing what he wants, in a while they'll say he owns the town!"

At that point, the Marquis raised his little monkey head for an instant; but then he shrugged his shoulders and answered with his cutting little smile:

"As for me...I don't care. I don't own anything."

"Own...own the town? After all those who were born before him are dead!... And born better than he! I'll sell Fontanarossa; but Mastro-don Gesualdo isn't going to take the city lands away from me! Neither by himself nor with Baroness Rubiera's help!"

"What's going on? What's going on?" cut in the Notary as he ran to the balcony, to change the subject, because the Baron could not restrain himself and shouted too loudly.

Down below in the square, in front of the door of the Sganci house, you could see a flurry of light-colored dresses in the middle of the crowd, caps flying in the air, and somebody who was meting out cudgel blows right and left to make his way. Immediately afterward Don Giuseppe Barabba appeared in the doorway of the entry-room —strangled by reverence, his hands in the air.

"Ma'am!... Ma'am!..."

This time it was the whole Margarone family: Donna Fifì, Donna Giovannina, Donna Mita, the Margarone mother, Donna

Bellonia of the Bracalanti di Pietraperzia, no less! suffocating inside her green satin corset, purple in the face and smiling, and behind them the Margarone father, dignified, swelling out his cheeks, leaning on the gold knob of his bamboo cane, without even turning his head, holding by the hand the youngest Margarone, Nicolino, who was screaming and kicking because they wouldn't let him see the Saint from the square. The father brandishing his bamboo cane, wanted to teach him good manners.

"And what now?" jeered the Marquis to calm him down. "Today, during the feast? Leave that poor child alone, Don Filippo!"

Don Filippo let go of him, being content with darting some looks of authority now and then at the boy who was paying no attention. Meanwhile, the others were making a lot of noise welcoming the Margarone women:

"Donna Bellonia!... Donna Fifì!... What a pleasure, tonight!..."

Even Don Giuseppe Barabba, in his own way, busied himself carrying in more chairs and snuffing the candles. Then from the balcony he began to play telegraph with someone down in the square, shouting to make himself heard above the loud buzzing of the crowd.

"Baron, Sir! Baron, Sir!" and finally he ran to his boss, Mrs. Sganci, triumphantly:

"Ma'am! Ma'am! There he is, he's coming! There is Don Nini..."

Donna Giuseppina Alòsi sketched a faint and discreet smile as Baron Zacco planted an elbow in her ribs. Mrs. Capitana, on the other hand, straightened up in her corset as if her beautiful shoulders were just then blooming out of her puffed sleeves.

"Idiot! You can't do anything right! What's all this commotion? That's not the way to do things!"

Don Giuseppe went away grumbling.

But just then Don Nini Rubiera walked in—a tall, stout young man who could hardly go through the door, his face red and white, his hair curly, and his eyes somewhat sleepy, such that they turned the heads of the girls. Donna Giovannina Margarone, who was quite a dish herself, strapped inside her corset just like her mother, blushed as red as a poppy, as she saw the young Baron walk in. But her mother kept telling her that first it was the turn of her older sister, Donna Fifì—dried up and yellow from the long celibacy, all hairy, with such front teeth that looked as if they were meant to snatch a husband from the air—loaded up with ribbons, frills, and trinkets, just like a rare bird.

"Fifì was the first to spot you in the crowd!... What a crowd, eh! My husband had to use his stick to get through. Quite a beautiful feast! Fifì said: 'There's Baron Rubiera, next to the band platform!...'"

Don Nini was looking around uneasily. Suddenly, as he spotted his cousin Bianca huddled in a corner of the alley balcony, her face deadly pale, he was startled, lost for a moment his fine vivid color, and answered stammering:

"Yes, Ma'am... In fact...I'm on the Committee...."

"Great! Great! Quite a beautiful feast indeed! You know how to do things well!... And where's your mother, Don Nini?...."

"Hurry! Hurry up!" called Aunt Sganci from the balcony. "The Saint is here!"

Marquis Limòli, who was afraid of the evening dampness, had grabbed the Margarone mother by her green satin dress, playing Casanova:

"There is no hurry, there is no hurry! The Saint comes back every year. Come here, Donna Bellonia. Let's make room for the young, we who have seen so many feasts!"

And kept mumbling spicy jokes into her ear which seemed to be blushing with embarrassment. He was amused by the serious face Don Filippo was making above his big satin necktie; while Mrs. Capitana, to show that she could hold her own in a social chat, laughed like a madwoman, leaning forward every moment, screening herself with her fan so as to hide her white teeth, her white breasts, all those beautiful things the effects of which she studied out of the corner of her eye, as she pretended to get angry when the Marquis took some excessive liberty—now that they were alone, as he said with his satyr's toothless grin.

"Mita! Mita!" finally called the Margarone mother.

"No, No! Don't run away, Donna Bellonia!... Don't leave me alone with Mrs. Capitana...at my age!... Donna Mita knows what to do. She is as big and tall as her sisters put together; she knows that she must behave like a child, not to wrong the other two."

Notary Neri, who due to his profession knew the affairs of the entire town and talked about them freely, asked Mrs. Margarone:

"Well then, when shall we eat Donna Fifì's wedding cake?"

Don Filippo coughed loudly. Donna Bellonia answered that so far it was all gossip; people talked because they knew that Don Ninì Rubiera was rather regular with his attentions to her daughter.

"Nothing serious. Nothing definite . . ."

But you could see that she wanted very much not to be believed. Marquis Limòli found the right word, as usual:

"You should not talk about it in public before the relatives have agreed on the dowry."

Don Filippo nodded his head, and Donna Bellonia, seeing her husband's approval, ventured to say:

"It's true."

"They'll make a beautiful couple!" added Mrs. Capitana graciously.

Cavaliere Peperito, not to keep his mouth closed like an idiot, in the middle of the group where Donna Giuseppina had planted him so that he would not attract attention, burst out saying:

"But Baroness Rubiera didn't come! . . . Why didn't Baroness Rubiera come to Cousin Sganci's?"

There was a moment of silence. Only Baron Zacco, like the clodhopper that he was, to give vent to the anger he kept in his belly, took the trouble to answer aloud, as if they were all deaf:

"She's ill! . . . She's got a headache! . . ."

And meanwhile he was signaling "no" with his head. Then, driving himself into the midst of the people, his voice lower and his face afire:

"She sent Mastro-don Gesualdo in her place! . . . Her future partner! Yessir! . . . Don't you know? They'll lease the city lands. . . . Those that we've held for forty years. . . . All the Zaccos, from father to son! . . . Highway robbery! They have ganged up together, the three of them: Father, son, and holy ghost! The Baroness doesn't dare to look me in the face after that trick they are planning to play on me. . . . I don't mean that she stayed home not to meet me. . . . What the hell! Everyone works in his own interest. . . . Nowadays one's own interest comes before one's relatives. . . . Besides, I don't

much care about ours.... We all know Baroness Rubiera's family
background!... And she works in her own interest... Yessir!... I
know about it from people who are in the know!... The canon-
priest acts as a prompter; Mastro-don Gesualdo lays out the capital,
and the Baroness...nothing at all...just the support of her
name!... We'll see which one is worth more, hers or mine!... We'll
most certainly see... For the moment, just a trial balloon, they
push Mastro-don Gesualdo forward.... See him there, on the balcony, where the Traos are?..."

"Bianca, Bianca!" called Marquis Limòli.

"Me, Uncle?"

"Yes, come here."

"Doesn't she look lovely?" remarked Mrs. Capitana to flatter
the Marquis, as the girl walked across the hall in her thin woolen
dress, timid, and with the humble and uncomfortable air of poor
girls.

"Yes," replied the Marquis. "She is of a good family."

"Here he is! Here he is!" someone shouted at that moment
among those who were looking out. "Here is the Saint!"

Peperito seized the opportunity to plunge head-on into the
crowd behind Donna Alòsi. Mrs. Capitana rose on tiptoe; the
Notary gallantly offered to lift her up in his arms. Donna Bellonia
ran to act as a mother next to her offspring; and her husband was
satisfied with stepping on a chair in order to see.

"What are you doing there with Mastro-don Gesualdo?" grumbled the Marquis now that he was alone with his niece.

For a moment Bianca stared at her uncle with her big and
sweet dark-blue eyes — the only real beauty on her thin and washed-
out Trao face — and answered:

"Well...my Aunt brought him there...."

"Come here, come here. I'll find you a place myself."

All of a sudden the square seemed to flare up in a vast fire,
upon which were stamped the windows of the houses, the cornices of
the roofs, and the long balcony of the City Hall, swarming with
people. In the openings behind the balconies the guests' heads clus-
tered together, black against that fiery background; and in the cen-
tral opening the angular figure of Donna Fifì Margarone, caught by
surprise in that light, greener than usual, her surly face intent upon

appearing moved with emotion, her flat corset panting like bellows, her eyes dismayed behind the clouds of smoke, and only her teeth still ferocious; almost abandoning herself, shoulder to shoulder, against the young Baron Rubiera, who looked purple in that light, embedded between her and Donna Giovannina; while Mita opened her childish eyes wide, so as not to see, and Nicolino kept pinching people's legs, so that he could stick his head through and push himself forward.

"What's the matter? Don't you feel well?" said the Marquis, seeing his niece so pale.

"It's nothing . . . The smoke's bothering me. . . . Don't say anything, Uncle Limòli! Don't trouble anybody! . . ."

Every once in a while she pressed to her lips the imitation-batiste handkerchief she herself had embroidered, and coughed very quietly, bending her head; her thin woolen dress made folds on her slim shoulders. She did not say a word, she was busy watching the fireworks, her face sharp and pale, as if stretched toward the corners of her mouth, where you could see two painful folds, her eyes open wide and shiny, almost wet. Only the hand leaning on the back of her chair trembled a little, while the other, hanging at her side, opened and closed mechanically—emaciated and quivering white hands.

"*Viva* the Patron Saint! *Viva* Saint Gregory the Great!"

In the crowd in the square below, the canon-priest Lupi was howling as if possessed, in the midst of the peasants and was gesticulating toward the balconies of the Sganci palace, his face upturned, calling his acquaintances in a loud voice:

"Donna Marianna! . . . Eh! . . . Eh! . . . Baron Rubiera must be happy about it! . . . Baron, Don Nini, are you happy? . . . How d'you do, Mastro-don Gesualdo! Great! Great! Are you up there? . . ."

Then he ran upstairs headlong, frantic, red in the face, out of breath, his cassock tucked up, his cloak and his three-cornered hat under his arm, his hands filthy with dust, drowning in sweat.

"What a feast, eh! Donna Sganci!"

And he called Don Giuseppe Barabba to bring him a glass of water:

"I'm dying of thirst, Donna Marianna! Beautiful fireworks, eh? . . . About two thousand rockets! I've lighted more than two hundred with my own hands. Look at these hands, Marquis!... Ah, you are here, Don Gesualdo? Good! Good! Don Giuseppe? Who knows where that old fool of a Don Giuseppe has holed up."

Don Giuseppe had gone up to the attic, to see the fireworks from the dormer at the risk of falling into the square. Finally he appeared—all dusty and covered with spider webs—the glass of water in hand, after Mrs. Sganci and the canon-priest Lupi had shouted themselves hoarse calling him through all the rooms.

The canon-priest Lupi, who was familiar with the place, gave him a tongue-lashing too. Then, turning toward Mastro-don Gesualdo with a beaming face:

"Great, great, Don Gesualdo! I'm ecstatic to see you here. Mrs. Sganci had been telling me for a long time: 'Next year I want Don Gesualdo to come to my house to see the procession!'"

Marquis Limòli, who had gentlemanly greeted the Patron Saint as he passed, by bowing over the chair, straightened up his back with a grimace.

"Ah! Dear me! Thank God this too is done!... Whoever lives the year through sees all the feasts."

"But you'll never expect to see again what you have seen this time!" jeered Baron Zacco, nodding toward Mastro-don Gesualdo. —"No! No! I can remember him with rocks on his shoulders...and his shoulders scratched and in rags.... On the scaffoldings, this great friend of mine with whom we are here today, face to face!"

But the lady of the house was all kindness to Mastro-don Gesualdo. Now that the Saint had started out on the street where his house was, it seemed as if the entire feast were for him: Donna Marianna talking to him about this and that; the canon-priest Lupi clapping him on the shoulder; Donna Macrì who had even given up her place for him; even Don Filippo Margarone who let drop from the height of his big necktie such compliments as:

"High birth is an accident, not a virtue!... To rise up from nothing, that's the real merit! The first mill you built under contract, eh? With the money you borrowed at twenty per cent!..."

"Yessir," Don Gesualdo answered calmly. "I couldn't sleep a wink all night."

Archpriest Bugno, jealous of all the ceremonies directed at someone else, after all those firecrackers, those shouts, that uproar which he thought somewhat dedicated to himself too, as head of the church, had managed to assemble a little group around himself, and was talking about the merits of the Patron Saint:

"A great Saint!...and a really fine statue.... Foreigners used to come just to see it.... It had become known that some Englishmen were ready to pay its weight in gold, to take it down there to their lands, among their idols...."

The Marquis, who was about to burst, finally cut in:

"That's utter nonsense!... Who tells you things like that, Don Calogero? The statue is paper maché...hideous!... The mice have nested inside it... The jewels?... Eh! Eh! They couldn't even make me rich, think of that!... Colored glass...just like so many others you see!... A carnival puppet! Eh? What are you saying? Yes, sacrilege! The one who made that saint must be in hell.... I'm not speaking of the Saint in Paradise...I know, that's something else... Faith is enough...I am a Christian too, what the hell!... And am proud of it!..."

Mrs. Capitana pretended she was insistently staring at Donna Giuseppina Alòsi's necklace, just as she was rebuking the Marquis:

"You heretic, heretic!"

Peperito had covered his ears. Archpriest Bugno started all over again:

"The work of a master, that statue!... The King, God forbid, wanted to sell it at the time of the war against the Jacobins!... A Saint that works miracles!..."

"What's new, Don Gesualdo?" the Marquis, fed up, finally shouted with his little cracked voice, turning his back on the archpriest. "Some new deal in the wind?"

Baron Zacco began to laugh loudly, his eyes popping out of their sockets, but Mastro-don Gesualdo somewhat stunned by their crowding around him, did not answer.

"You can tell it to me, my friend," continued the malicious old man. "You cannot fear my competition!"

The squabble amused even those who had no interest in it. As for Baron Zacco, you can imagine!

"Eh! Eh! Marquis!... You're not in competition?... Eh! eh!..."

Mastro-don Gesualdo glanced around, at all those laughing people, and answered calmly:

"What can I tell you, Marquis!... Everyone does what he can...."

"Go on, go on, my dear friend. As for me, I have nothing to complain about...."

Don Giuseppe Barabba drew near Mrs. Sganci on tiptoe, and said in her ear with great mystery:

"Should I serve the sherbet, now that the procession has gone?"

"Wait a minute! Wait a minute!" cut in the canon-priest Lupi. "Let me wash my hands."

"If I don't bring it right away," added the servant, "it will get to be slosh. Don Giacinto sent it quite a while ago, and it was half melted even then."

"All right, all right...Bianca?"

"Yes, Aunt Sganci."

"Do me a favor, help me."

A little later, from the wide open double doors, Don Giuseppe and *mastro* Titta, the house barber, came in weighed down with two large, dripping silver trays. The two of them began to make the rounds of the guests, step by step—just like another procession. First the archpriest, Donna Giuseppina Alòsi, Mrs. Capitana—the most important guests. The canon-priest Lupi elbowed the barber who was passing before Mastro-don Gesualdo without stopping.

"What do I know... You see strange things nowadays," grumbled *mastro* Titta.

The Margarone boy stuck his fingers everywhere.

"Uncle Limòli!"

"Thanks, my dear Bianca...I have the cough...I'm an invalid...just like your brother...."

"Donna Bellonia, there, on the balcony!" suggested Aunt Sganci, who also frantically busied herself to serve her guests.

After the initial general stirring, with a maneuvering of chairs to avoid the rain of syrup, there followed some moments of silence, a circumspect clicking of plates, and a cautious and quiet working of spoons, as if it were a solemn ritual. Donna Mita Margarone, greedy, without lifting her nose from her plate, Barabba and *mastro* Titta, standing aside after they put down the trays, wiping their sweat with their cotton handkerchiefs.

Young Baron Rubiera, who was talking in a corner of the great balcony nose to nose with Donna Fifì, looking into her eyes—two eyes that were melting like the sherbet—abruptly moved away as he saw his cousin Bianca appear, and became somewhat pale. Donna Bellonia took the plate from Bianca's hands, with an awkward bow:

"How kind of you!... It's too much...too much!..."

Her daughter pretended to notice her friend just at that moment:

"Oh, Bianca...are you here?... What a surprise!... They had told me you were ill...."

"Yes...a little... Now I'm all right...."

"Yes, I can see.... You're looking well... And you're wearing a nice dress too...simple, but becoming!..."

Donna Fifi bowed, pretending she was inspecting the material, but for the purpose of having the topazes around her neck glitter. Bianca answered, as she blushed:

"It's light wool...my Aunt's present...."

"Ah!...ah..."

The young Baron, who was on pins and needles, suggested that they go back into the hall:

"It's beginning to be damp.... We'll catch a cold...."

"Yes!... Fifi! Fifi..." said Donna Bellonia Margarone.

Donna Fifi had to follow her mother, with her droopy walk which she thought extremely romantic, her little head somewhat bent on her shoulder, her eyelids fluttering—as if hit by a strong light—on her languid sleepy eyes.

As he was just about to sneak away from the balcony, Bianca rested her hand on her cousin's arm tenderly, like a caress, like a prayer. She was trembling all over, her voice stifled in her throat:

"Nini!... Listen, Nini! Please!... Only one word!... I've come only for this.... If I don't talk to you now, it's all over for me!... It's all over!..."

"Careful!... There are so many people!..." her cousin retorted in a whisper, looking here and there with fleeting eyes. She kept hers fixed on him—her beautiful, pleading eyes—with great wistfulness, great painful abandonment in all her person, in her pale and spent face, in her humble attitude, in her inert arms that opened in desolation.

"What do you answer me, Nini?... What do you tell me to do?... Look...I am in your hands... Like Mother Dolorosa!..."

He then began to beat his head with his fists. He too moved, his heart heavy, careful not to make noise and making sure that nobody was coming to the balcony. Bianca caught his hand.

"You're right, we're both doomed!... My mother doesn't even leave me free to blow my nose!... Understand? understand?... Do you think I don't think about you?... Do you think?... At night ...I can't sleep a wink!... I am a poor, doomed fellow!... People think I am happy and content..."

He was looking down into the square, now deserted, so as to avoid the desperate eyes of his cousin, which went through his heart. He was grieved too, his eyes almost wet.

"See?" he added. "I wish I were a poor devil...like Santo Motta, down there!...in Pecu-Pecu's tavern... Poor and happy..."

"Aunt Rubiera is opposed?"

"Yes, yes, she is opposed!... What can I do?... She's the boss!"

From the hall came the voice of Baron Zacco, who was arguing heatedly; and, during his moments of silence, the chattering of the ladies, just like a bunch of sparrows, with the shrill laughter of Mrs. Capitana that sounded like a piccolo.

"We must confess everything to Aunt Rubiera!"

Don Nini stretched his neck toward the balcony opening cautiously. Then he answered, lowering his voice still more:

"Your brother told her.... There was a tremendous uproar!... Didn't you know?"

Don Giuseppe Barabba came onto the balcony, carrying a plate in each hand.

"Donna Bianca, your aunt says...before it's all gone...."

"Thank you; put it there, on that flower pot...."

"Better hurry, Donna Bianca. There is hardly any left."

Then Don Nini put his nose in his plate, pretending not to pay attention to anything else:

"Don't you want some?"

She didn't answer. After a while, when the servant was no longer around, you could again hear her muted voice:

"Is it true that you're getting married?"

"Me?..."

"You...to Fifi Margarone..."

"It's not true!... Who told you so?"

"They all say so."

"I wouldn't like to.... It's my mother that has gotten it into her head ... About you too ...they say that they want you to marry Don Gesualdo Motta ..."

"Me?..."

"Yes, they all say so ...Aunt Sganci ...even my mother..."

Donna Giuseppina Alòsi stuck her face in for a moment, as if looking for someone; and, as she saw the two of them at the far end of the balcony, pulled back into the hall at once.

"See? See?" he said. "They all keep their eyes on us!... Eat your sherbet ...for my sake ...for the sake of the people who are watching us.... They all keep their eyes on us!..."

She tenderly took from his hands the plate that she had put on the pot of carnations; but she was trembling so that two or three times you could hear her little spoon clinking against her glass.

Immediately Barabba came running:

"Here I am! Here I am!"

"Just a moment! Just a moment, Don Giuseppe!"

Baron Rubiera would have liked to pay something out of his own pocket to keep Barabba on the balcony.

"How are you enjoying the feast, Don Giuseppe?"

"What can I say, Baron?... Everything's on my shoulders!... the house to put in order, the slipcovers to take off, the lights to prepare.... Donna Bianca here, who gave me a hand, can tell you. *Mastro* Titta was called for the reception only. And tomorrow I must again sweep and put the slipcovers back on...."

Still grumbling, Don Giuseppe left with the empty glasses. From the hall came the sound of a general guffawing—immediately following a remark by Notary Neri, which one couldn't hear well simply because when the Notary told a really dirty joke, he lowered his voice.

"Let's go back inside too," said the Baron. "Not to give them reason for suspicion ..."

But Bianca didn't move. She was crying silently in the shadow, and now and then you could see her white handkerchief being lifted to her eyes.

"There! It's you who make people talk!" blurted out her cousin, who was on pins and needles.

"What do you care?" she answered. "What do you care? Now!..."

"Sure, sure! Do you think I don't love you anymore..."

An excruciating longing, an infinite bitterness rose from the vast expanse of Alia, straight ahead, beyond the Barresi houses — from the Giolio vineyards and olive groves, which you could vaguely make out, beyond Via del Rosario still swarming with lights — from the long Casalgilardo plateau, broken up by the corner wall of the Collegio — from the deep sky, embroidered with stars — while one of them brighter than the others, up there, seemed to be watching, cold, sad, and solitary. The noise of the feast day was fading and dying up there, toward San Vito. A desolate silence fell now and then — a silence that wrung your heart. Bianca was standing against the wall, motionless; her wan hands and face seemed to waver in the uncertain glimmer rising from the nougat peddler's stand. Her cousin was leaning on the railing, pretending to be intently watching the man who was putting out the lights in the deserted square, and the decorator's assistant, who was running up and down the band platform, like a big black cat, taking nails out, hammering, throwing down the festoons and the paper garlands. From time to time the rockets still burst up in the distance, behind the black mass of City Hall, the decorator's hammer blows, the intermittent cries, tired and drunken, seemed to be dying out far off, in the vast, solitary countryside. Together with the pungent odor of gunpowder that was now dissipating, you could feel a sweet scent of carnations coming up. Some people passed by singing. You could hear a loud confusion of chatter and laughter in the hall, just next to them, during the laceration of that last good-bye without words.

A lean shadow passed by the lighted opening of the balcony, and you could hear Marquis Limòli's little cough:

"Eh, eh, children!... For heaven's sake!... I came to see the feast...now that it's over...Bianca, my dear niece... Beware of the evening air; it's not good for you...."

"No, Uncle Limòli," she answered in her muted voice. "It's stifling inside there."

"Patience!... You've got to be always patient in this world.... Better sweat than cough.... You there Nini, the Margarone ladies are leaving...."

"I'm going, Uncle Limòli."

"Go then, go, or you'll see some teeth. . . . I wouldn't like to have them on myself either!. . . Even if I cannot afford to be finnicky!. . . What the hell has your mother gotten into her, to have you marry those teeth?. . ."

"Ah. . . Uncle Limòli!. . ."

"You're an idiot! You should let her kick up a big fuss—as big as she likes—your mother!. . . You are an only child!. . . Whom do you think she is going to leave her property to, when she dies?"

"Eh. . . in thirty years!. . . There is plenty of time to starve to death!. . . My mother is in better health than you and me, and can easily live another thirty years!. . ."

"You're right!" answered the Marquis. "Your mother wouldn't especially like being begrudged the years she still has to live. . . . But it is her fault."

"Ah! my dear Uncle!. . . Believe me: this is an awful mess!. . ."

"Calm down! Calm down! Find some consolation in thinking about those who are worse off than you are."

Mrs. Capitana put her head inside—quick, restless, looking with a smile on this and on that side of the street.

"My husband?. . . Isn't he coming yet?. . ."

"The Saint isn't back yet," answered Don Nini. "As he gets into the church and the other rites begin, you can hear the big bell of San Giovanni."

But people began to leave the Sganci house. The first who was seen to go out the door was Cavaliere Peperito, who disappeared behind the corner wall of Bomma's pharmacy. A moment later appeared the big lantern leading the way for Donna Giuseppina Alòsi, who crossed the square—dirty with burnt paper, fava bean and nut shells—on tiptoe, holding up her skirt with her hand, walking up the Rosario; and immediately after, from the pharmacy, Peperito's shadow again showed up around the corner and began to follow her, stealthily, hugging the wall. Mrs. Capitana gave out a shrill little laugh, and young Baron Rubiera confirmed:

"It's him!. . . Peperito!. . . I swear to God!"

The Marquis took his niece's arm and walked back into the hall with her. At that moment Mastro-don Gesualdo, standing near the balcony, was talking with the canon-priest Lupi—the latter fervently pleading, in a low voice and with an air of mystery, pressing closer and closer, as if he wanted to get into his pocket, with his ferretlike face. Don Gesualdo was serious, his chin in his hand, without saying a word, only nodding from time to time.

"Just like a Minister!" jeered Baron Zacco.

The canon-priest concluded with an emphatic handshake, glancing toward the Baron, who, red as a rooster, pretended not to notice. The hostess was bringing the mantillas and the hats to the ladies, while all the Margarones had risen to their feet and were turning the house upside down to say good-bye.

"Hi!... Bianca!... I thought you have already left!" remarked Donna Fifì with a biting smile.

Bianca answered only with a stunned glance—so dismayed and suffering she was; while her cousin was busying himself in the midst of the mantillas and the hats, his head low.

"Just a moment! Just a moment!" exclaimed Don Filippo, raising his free arm, while with the other he was holding the sleeping Nicolino.

You could hear a scuffle in the square; screams in the distance; the people were running toward San Giovanni, and the big bell was ringing full blast, down there.

Mrs. Capitana came in from the balcony covering her ears with her beautiful white hands, screaming in falsetto:

"My husband!... They're fighting!..."

And she slumped on the sofa, her eyes closed. The ladies began to shout all at once; the hostess yelled at Barabba to go down and bolt the front door; while Donna Bellonia herded her girls into Donna Mariannina's bedroom, and Marquis Limòli tapped Mrs. Capitana's hands with little sharp blows. Notary Neri suggested that her corset be untied.

"What?..." she said jumping to her feet in a fury. "Who do you think I am, you Don Jackass?"

Just then the Police Captain arrived, followed by Don Liccio Papa, who was clamoring in the entryroom, reporting what had happened—a hundred people wouldn't have been able to hold him back.

"The same story as every year!" said the Police Captain finally, after he had gotten back his spirits by emptying a glass of water in one breath. "The faithful of San Giovanni ringing out the big bell fifteen minutes ahead of time!... An outrage!... And those of San Vito who can't take it!... Mad cudgel blows...that's what it was!..."

"The same story as every year!" repeated the canon-priest Lupi. "A disgrace! The law doesn't do anything to prevent..."

The Police Captain, standing in the middle of the hall, stretching his forefinger toward him, finally blurted out:

"Listen to him!... Why don't you go there yourself? Another minute and they would have polished me off too!... Donna Carolina, your husband's life was in danger too!..."

Mrs. Capitana, tightening her little mouth, clasped her hands:

"Holy heavens!... Our Most Holy Lady of Peril..."

"You're in trouble!" grumbled Notary Neri turning toward her. "You're in trouble indeed!...if you wait for your husband to risk his hide to make you a widow!..."

Don Nini Rubiera, as he was looking for his hat, ran into his cousin, who was following him like a ghost, stunned, stumbling at every step.

"Careful!..." he said. "Careful!... They're watching us!... There's Mastro-don Gesualdo over there!..."

"Bianca! Bianca! The mantillas for these ladies!" shouted Aunt Sganci from the bedroom, where the entire Margarone flock had stuck themselves.

Bianca was searching in the heap, her hands trembling. Her cousin was also so upset that he kept looking for his hat.

"Look! I have it on! I don't even know what I'm doing."

As they were all looking for their things in the entryroom, he glanced around like a thief, and then he drew her aside toward the door.

"Listen...for God's sake!...be careful!... Nobody knows anything about it.... Certainly your brother didn't tell...I didn't either.... Know that I have loved you more than my own soul!..."

She didn't answer a word; only her eyes were speaking, and saying many things.

"Don't look at me with that face, Bianca!... No!... Don't look at me like that...I would betray myself too!..."

Donna Fifi walked out with her hat and her mantilla, dried up stiff, her lips so tight as if they had been sewn together; and since her sister, always cheerful, turned to say good-bye to Bianca, she called at her with a sour voice:

"Giovannina! Let's go! Let's go!"

"This one is not so bad!" grumbled young Baron Rubiera. "But her sister is a punishment of God."

As she saw the Margarones to the door, Aunt Sganci said to Mastro-don Gesualdo who was busying himself with a profusion of bows on the landing, risking a tumble down the stairs:

"Don Gesualdo, be so kind as to accompany the Traos, my nephew and niece.... You're neighbors...Don Ferdinando can't see very well at night...."

"Listen! Listen!" said the canon-priest to him.

Baron Zacco couldn't stand still; he pretended he was looking for the lamp in the entryroom chests, to give it to Mastro-don Gesualdo.

"Since he has to accompany Donna Bianca...a Trao... It couldn't even have entered Mastro-don Gesualdo's head that he would be so highly honored!"

But Mastro-don Gesualdo could not hear, for he was waiting in the square, chatting with the canon-priest. Only Don Liccio Papa, who was the last one to come in, holding the saber on his shoulder, began to laugh.

"Ah! Ah!"

"What's the matter?" asked the Police Captain, who was giving his arm to his bundled-up wife. "What's the matter, you insubordinate idiot?"

"Nothing," answered the Marquis. "It's Baron Zacco barking at the moon."

Then as he was going down the stairs with Bianca, leaning on his little cane step by step, he said in her ear:

"Listen... Nowadays the world belongs to those who have money.... They are all clamoring out of envy. If the Baron had a daughter of marriageable age, he would most certainly give her to Mastro-don Gesualdo!... I can tell you; I am an old man and know what poverty is...."

"Eh? What is it?" inquired Don Ferdinando, who was slowly

walking behind them, counting the stones.

"Nothing... We were saying what a beautiful evening, Cousin Trao!"

The other looked up, and repeated like a parrot:

"Beautiful evening! Beautiful evening!"

Don Gesualdo was waiting before the front door, together with the canon-priest Lupi, who was whispering in his face:

"Eh? eh: Don Gesualdo?... What do you think of it?"

And the other one nodded, while with his big hand he stroked his beard-hardened chin.

"A jewel! A girl who doesn't know anything but home and church!... Frugal... She won't cost you anything.... At home she is not used to spending for sure!... But of good family!... She'll bring prestige into your house!... You'll become a relative of the entire aristocracy.... Did you see tonight?... What kind of welcome they gave you?... Your affairs would go full blast. Even for that business of the city lands.... It's better to have the support of all the big shots!"

Don Gesualdo didn't answer right away, his head low, deep in thought, following Donna Bianca step by step, as she was starting home by the way of the stairs of Sant'Agata, together with her uncle, the Marquis and her brother, Don Ferdinando.

"Yes...yes...I can't say 'No'.... But it's a question one must think about...a serious question.... I am afraid it's too big a deal for me, my dear canon-priest.... After all she's a lady.... Besides, I have so many things to settle before I can decide.... Everyone has his own problems.... I must sleep on it. Night brings good counsel, my dear Canon Lupi."

Bianca, who was walking with a heavy heart, listening to her uncle's indifferent chatter, next to her silent, lanky, and emaciated brother, heard those last words.

Night brings good counsel. The dark and desolate night in her poor little bedroom. The night that was carrying away the last sounds of the feast day, the last light, the last hope.... Like her vision of him who was walking away with another woman, without turning around, without telling her anything, without answering her call to him from the depths of her heart, with a deep moaning, with a sick lament—as she buried her face into her pillow, wet with hot and silent tears.

IV

While the masons were still taking shelter from the downpour, playing quoits, inside the Giolio olive mill that was as big as a church, the boy who guarded the door walked in biting a piece of bread and shouting with his mouth full:

"The boss!... Here comes the boss!..."

Behind him appeared Mastro-don Gesualdo, soaking wet, pulling the mule that was shaking its ears.

"Great!... Very good!... Have a good time! You get paid just the same!... Dammit!... Goddammit!..."

Agostino, the overseer, groping, mumbling, looking out the door at the still cloudy sky with his blind eye, finally found the answer:

"What were we supposed to do? Get all wet?... The storm's just over.... Are we Christians or pigs?... If I get a bad fever my mother will not make another Agostino any more, no sir!"

"Yes, yes, you're right!... I'm the jackass!... I'm the one with the tough hide!... I did the right thing to send my brother here to look after my interests!... It's obvious!... He too spends his time playing, thank God!..."

Santo, open-mouthed, who was squatting in front of the wooden plate with the money, rose to his feet in confusion, scratching his head.

While the others, long-faced, busied themselves, Gesualdo measured the new wall with a rod; he climbed the ladder; weighed the gypsum sacks, lifting them off the ground:

"Goddammit!... As if I were stealing my money!... All of them ganging up to do me in!... Two days to put up three rods of wall? I'll make a lot of money on this contract for sure!... The sacks of plaster are half empty! Neli? Neli? Where is that s.o.b. who brought the gypsum?... And that lime that's turning into dust, eh? ...that lime?... Don't you have any conscience? Aren't you Christians? God in heaven!... Even the rain is against me!... I still have the sheaves in the yard!... Couldn't you put up the millstone while it was raining?... Come on, let's get to it, the millstone! I'll give you a hand while I'm here...."

But Santo wanted to light a fire to dry off Gesualdo's clothes.

"Never mind," he answered. "I have let a lot of water dry on my shoulders!... If I'd been like you, I'd still be carrying gypsum on my shoulders!... Do you remember?... And you wouldn't be here playing quoits!..."

Grumbling, busying himself to ready the lever, the wedges, the props, Santo turned around to throw dirty looks at him.

"Dammit!" he exclaimed. "Always the same old story!..."

And he went to stand in the doorway, frowning, his arms crossed, looking here and there. The workmen dawdled, walking around the enormous stone; the oldest, *mastro* Cola, holding his chin in his hand, shaking his head, knitting his brow, looking at the millstone like at an enemy. Finally, he declared that they were too few to push it onto the platform:

"If the lever gives way, God save us!... Who will put himself underneath to change the wedges? Not me, I swear to God!... If the lever gives way!... My mother will not make another *mastro* Cola Ventura any more!... Eh, eh!... We need more hands...a jack... Then tie a pulley to the ceiling beams...then some wedges underneath...see, sir, if you have the wedges, you stay on the side and there is no danger."

"Good! now you think you are a master mason! Give me the bar! ...I'm not afraid!... While we are here talking, time is passing!... The day goes by, just the same, eh?... As if I'd stolen my money!... Let's go! Over there!... Don't worry about me, my hide is tough!... Come on!... Let's go!... *Viva Gesù!*... *Viva Maria!*...more!... Watch out! Watch out!... Mariano! dammit, you're killing me!... Up!... *Viva Maria!*... Oh, my back! My back! up!... What are you doing, jackass, over there?... Up!...we made it! It's ours!... more...over there!... Don't be afraid, the pope won't die... Up! ...up!...if the lever gives way!...more!...if I'd treasured my hide ...more!...as my brother Santo does...dammit! dammit! watch out... Now I would be carrying gypsum on my shoulders!... Need ...go on!...go on!...need brings the wolf out of the woods... more!...up!...the wolf out of the woods!... See my brother Santo who's standing there, watching us?... If it weren't for me, he would be under...under the millstone...in my place...instead of scratching himself...to push the millstone...and the house... All on my shoulders!... Ah! thank God!"

Finally, after securing the millstone on the platform, he sat down on a rock, out of breath, still shaking and with his heart beating fast, wiping off his sweat with a cotton handkerchief.

"See how you dry yourself off from the rain? Water inside and water outside!"

Santo proposed to pass around the bottle of wine.

"Ah?...for all the work you did?...to wipe off your sweat too?... Stick your head in the watering trough...right outside the door...."

The rainy weather had let up. A ray of sun came in through the door open wide to the countryside, that now seemed to spread out, smiling, with the town down there on the hill and its windows sparkling.

"Quick, quick, boys! on the bridge, let's go! Let's earn a full day's pay.... Put yourselves in the shoes of the boss who's paying you!... I'll almost break my neck with this contract!... I'm already losing, I swear to God!... Agostino! be careful! keep your eyes sharp!... Speak softly and keep your eyes sharp!... *Mastro* Cola, you who are the master mason!...who taught you how to hold the ruler?... Damn you! Mariano, give me the ruler, up here, on the bridge.... Don't you have eyes, dammit!... The plaster cracking and coming loose!... Then the architect will give me a piece of his mind, damn all of you!... When that gypsum man comes back, put that s.o.b. in his place!...tell Neli that I know the job too!... We'll talk about it again on Saturday, when we settle the accounts!..."

He took care of everything, going about here and there, rummaging through the heaps of tiles and bricks, testing the materials, raising his head to examine the work done, his hand over his eyes, against the glaring sunlight that had just come.

"Santo! Santo! Bring my mule here... At least do this job for your brother!"

Agostino wanted to detain him to have a bite, since it was almost noon and the sun was burning so hot as to bring on a stroke to whoever went around the countryside at that time.

"No, no, I have to stop by Camemi...it takes two hours...I have so much else to do! If the sun is hot all the better! I'll be dry when I get to Camemi.... Let's hurry up, boys! Remember that I am always on your backs, like God's presence! You'll see me appear when you least expect it! I know the job too, and later I'll find out if you have worked!..."

As he was leaving, Santo ran after him, stroking the mule's neck and holding the stirrup. Finally, when he saw that Gesualdo mounted without paying any attention, he planted himself in the middle of the road scratching his ear:

"You leave me like this? Without even asking me if I need anything?"

"Yes, I understand, the money I gave you Monday, you gambled it away. I understand! I understand! Here is the rest. And have a good time playing quoits, since I am the one who pays...everyone's debtor!..."

Still grumbling, as he went off at the mule's pace under the boiling sun—a sun that split rocks now, and made the stubble pop as if it were on fire. In the ravine, between the two mountains, it felt like a furnace; and the town on top of the hill, climbing above the precipices, scattered among enormous cliffs, undermined by caverns that left it as if suspended in air—blackish, rusty, looking abandoned, without a shadow, with all the windows opened wide in the torrid heat, like so many black holes, and the crosses of the bell towers swaying in the misty sky. Even the mule, covered with sweat, panted up the steep road. On the way Don Gesualdo met a poor old man, loaded with sheaves, exhausted, who began to grumble:

"Oh, where are you going, sir, at this time?... You have so much money, and you give your soul to the devil!"

Gesualdo reached the town as the noon hour struck, while everyone rushed home as if there were a thunderstorm. From Rosario came the canon-priest Lupi, sweating, his three-cornered hat on the back of his head, breathing hard:

"Ah, ah, Don Gesualdo!... Are you going to get a bite to eat?... Not I, unfortunately! I haven't had anything all day.... I'm going to say holy mass...the noon mass!...one of Monsignore's whims!"

"I came up to the town just for you!... I made this asinine trip!... It's hot, eh!" Meanwhile, he wiped off the sweat with his handkerchief. "I'm afraid they are going to play a bad trick on me, regarding the contract of the city streets, Canon Lupi. You who have a voice in town...have you thought about it? Then I'll meet my obligations!..."

"Oh don't mention it!...between us!...I'm working on it... By the way, what are we going to do about that other deal? Have you thought about it? What's your answer?"

Don Gesualdo, who had brought his mule to a walk, was going alongside him, hunched over the saddle, and a little stunned by the great sun, answered:

"What deal? I have so many of them!... Which deal are you talking about, sir?"

"Ah! ah! so that's how you take it?... Excuse me... Please excuse me!..."

The canon-priest immediately changed the subject, as if it didn't matter to him either; he spoke about the other deal of the city lands, that they had to come to an agreement with Baroness Rubiera:

"Something else's new... Notary Neri has ganged up with Baron Zacco...I'm afraid that..."

Don Gesualdo then got off his mule, thoughtful, pulling it behind him by the reins, as he was walking in step with the priest, all ears, his head bowed and his chin in his hand.

"I'm afraid they will change the Baroness's mind!... I saw the Baron scheming with that idiot of a Don Nini...last night, behind the Collegio.... I pretended to go into the pharmacy so as not to be seen. Understand? a big deal!... It's nearly 500 salme of land... There's a lot of money to be made from that auction."

Don Gesualdo was getting excited too; his eyes, lit up by the torrid heat, gleamed at those words. However, he feared the schemes of his adversaries — all big shots, the kind that have a say in matters. The canon-priest, on the other hand, was getting cooler and cooler, knitting his brow, tightening up his shoulders, staring at him from time to time, and shaking his head up and down, as if calling him an ass.

"That's why I was saying... But you take it your own way!... Excuse me, please, excuse me!... With that deal, I meant to get you the support of family relations that really count in this town... the highest aristocracy... But you seem unconcerned.... All right then, excuse me!... Also to give an answer to Mrs. Sganci, who has worked so hard at it!... Excuse me, but it's a dirty deal!..."

"Ah, are you talking about that marriage deal?..."

This time the canon-priest pretended not to be listening:

"Ah! Here is your brother-in-law! How do you do, *massaro* Fortunato!"

Burgio's face was a foot long, scowling and sulking with its big hanging jowls.

"I saw you coming from down there, brother-in-law. I have been waiting for you there, at the observation point. Did you hear the news? The fava beans barely came to fifteen salme!... Not even enough to cover the costs, I swear to God!... I came here just to tell you..."

"I thank you! Thanks a lot! Now what do you want from me? I told you when you decided to farm that field!... Good only for thorns! You always want to do everything your way, and you never make the right decisions, my dear fellow!" Gesualdo answered in anger.

"Good, you're right. I'll leave that field. I don't want it any more! What else do you want from me?"

"You don't want it?... Your lease is for two more years! Who's going to take it?... Not everyone is such a jerk!..."

The canon-priest, as he saw that the argument was going to last some time, turned away:

"Good-bye...Don Luca, the sacristan, is waiting for me...he too has been without food till now!"

And he took the stairway to the upper neighborhood.

Then Don Gesualdo, furious, took it out on his brother-in-law:

"And you came here just to give me this piece of news?... While I was discussing my own business...at the high point? Spoiling a deal I was working out!... You really know how to make deals! Who do you think is going to take it...that field?"

Massaro Fortunato, standing behind his brother-in-law, kept saying:

"If we look hard enough...we'll find someone to take it!... The land is already fallow for next year.... It costs me a fortune. ... Your sister is making a hell of a racket...she won't give me a moment's peace!... You know what a punishment of God your sister is!"

"It costs you, it costs you!... I know who it costs!" grumbled Gesualdo, without turning around. "All your great deals end up on my shoulders!..."

Burgio became offended at those words:

"What do you mean? Explain yourself, brother-in-law!... I'm my own boss! I don't sponge off anyone, no sir!"

"All right, all right, now I must even plead with you? As if I weren't already carrying your field on my shoulders... as if I hadn't guaranteed the land for you...."

Thus grumbling, they both went off to find Pirtuso, who was at Fosso, down there toward San Giovanni. *Mastro* Lio was eating a few fava beans, his door ajar.

"Come in, come in, Don Gesualdo. God bless, sir! What can I do for you? At your service!"

Then, when he heard them talk about the field that Burgio wanted to unload on someone else, his happy face became dark, as he scratched his head.

"Eh! eh!... Purgatory field? It's tough! No one wants it, not even for grazing land."

Burgio ran out of breath trying to praise it — flat land, deep land, which had given him thirty salme of fava beans that year alone, already fallow for the new year!... His brother-in-law cut him short as one who has many irons in the fire, and doesn't have time to waste.

"Well, *mastro* Lio, I want to get rid of it. You do what you think is right...but with discretion!..."

"This is what I call talking!" Pirtuso answered. "You sir, know what to do and how to talk...."

And now he winked with his sleepy eye, and a cunning smile traveled among the wrinkles of his chin covered with filthy hairs.

On the sunbathed road, deserted at that time, a peasant was waiting, yellow and trembling with fever, his kerchief tied under his chin, and his hands in his pockets. Respectful, sketching a sad smile, moving his hand as if to push back the cap he held under his kerchief:

"God bless, Mastro-don Gesualdo...I recognized your mule. ... I've been looking for you for a long time! What shall we do about those few of Giolio's olives? I haven't got the money to have them picked.... D'you see the condition I'm in? Five months of tertian fever, yes sir, may God save you! I'm only skin and bones...no bread by day, no light by night...never mind! But I can't afford to

have the olives picked, I really can't.... If you want them, sir...
You'd be doing a work of charity, sir...."

"Eh! eh! money is scarce for everybody, old man!... Why did
you put the cart before the horse?... When you can't... You're all
alike... You would take on a whole estate, if you were allowed to.
... We'll see...I don't say no... It all depends on the deal...."

And he let fall the smallest possible offer, as he was walking
away on the road, without turning around. The other kept complaining for some time, while he ran after him, calling God and the
saints as witnesses, whimpering, cursing, and finally accepting —
suddenly cheering up, changing his tone and his manner.

"Lio, did you hear? The deal is closed! A good deal for Don
Gesualdo...never mind!... But it's done! As for me, it's the same
as if we'd gone to the Notary!"

And he headed back, his hands in his pockets.

"Listen here, *mastro* Lio," said Gesualdo pulling Pirtuso aside.

Burgio walked away discreetly, with the mule — for he knew
that secrecy is the soul of business — while his brother-in-law told the
broker to get him all the sumac he could find, at the market price.
He heard only *mastro* Lio guffawing, his mouth open from ear to
ear:

"Ah!...ah!...you're a devil.... You must have talked with
the devil! You know a week ahead of time what we should buy and
sell.... All right, it's a deal.... Now I'll go back home. I've got
those few fava beans waiting for me."

Burgio couldn't stand on his feet, he was so hungry. He started
grumbling when he found out that his brother-in-law wanted to stop
by the post office.

"Always mysteries... Always schemes!"

Don Gesualdo came back happy, reading a letter full of scrawl-
ings and sealed with bread crumbs.

"You see, the devil whispering in my ear, eh? He has given me
good news too. I must go and see *mastro* Lio again."

"I don't know anything.... My father didn't teach me how to
do these things!..." answered Burgio grumbling. "I do as my father
did.... Rather, would you like to come home and have a bite? I
can't stand on my feet, I swear to God!"

"No, I can't; I don't have time. I must stop at Camemi, before going on to Canziria. I have twenty men working on the road...the sheaves in the yard...I can't..."

And he went off under the scorching sun, pulling the tired mule behind him.

It was suffocating in that Petraio gorge. The barren cliffs seemed red-hot. Not a patch of shade, not a blade of grass, hill after hill, piled upon one another, bare, parched, rocky, scattered with sparse and scrawny olive trees, with dusty prickly pear trees — the plain under Budarturo like a waste burned by the sun, the mountains dark with mist, in the distance. Some crows flew away croaking from a carcass that stank in the ditch. Sirocco flurries burnt his face and cut his breath short; a maddening thirst, the sun beating on his head just like the hammering of his men who were working on the Camemi road. But when he got there, he found them all lying on their stomachs in the ditch, here and there, their faces covered with flies, and their arms stretched out. Only an old man was breaking stones, seated on the ground under a dilapidated umbrella, his bare chest copper-colored and sprinkled with white hairs, his arms fleshless, his shins white with dust, just like his face, which seemed a mask — only his eyes burning in the midst of so much dust.

"Great! Great!... I like that.... Fortune comes while you're asleep.... I've come to bring it to you!... And so the day goes by! ... How many rods of pavement did you do today? Let's see... Not even three rods!... Is that why you're resting now? You must be really tired, Goddammit!... I'll really make a lot of money here!... I'll go to rack and ruin to keep you all resting and sleeping...dammit!...dammit!..."

As they saw him with that burning and parched face, white with dust only on his hair and in the sockets of his eyes — such eyes as those of the fever-stricken — his lips thin and pale, no one dared answer him. The hammering started again like a chorus in the vast silent valley, with the dust rising upon the sunburnt flesh of the men, upon their fluttering rags, together with a dry panting that accompanied every blow. The crows again flew overhead, croaking, in the ruthless sky. The old man then raised his dusty face to look at them, his eyes flaming, as if he knew what they wanted and he were waiting for them.

When Gesualdo finally got to Canziria, it was almost two hours after nightfall. The door of the farmhouse was still open. Diodata was there waiting on the threshold, dozing. *Massaro* Carmine, the field-watchman, was lying on his stomach in the yard, the shotgun between his legs; Brasi Camauro and Nanni l'Orbo had gone off here and there, just like dogs at night when they smell a bitch in the vicinity. And there were only the dogs to welcome the boss, barking around the farmhouse.

"Eh! Nobody here? No one to watch over anything when I'm not around!"

Diodata, suddenly awakened, was looking for a lamp, gropingly, still half asleep. Uncle Carmine, rubbing his eyes, his mouth contracted by yawns, was looking for an excuse.

"Ah!... Thank God! You're asleep in one corner and Diodata in another, in the dark!... What were you doing in the dark?... Waiting for somebody?... Brasi Camauro, or Nanni l'Orbo?"

The girl took the outburst with her head bent, as she was quickly lighting the fire, while her boss kept complaining, outside, in the dark, and reviewing the oxen tied to the poles around the yard. The field-watchman, crestfallen, walked behind him to answer questions:

"Yes, sir! Red is a little better: I fed him crabgrass to clear his stomach. Whitey is becoming listless too.... We should have them graze in a different place...all the animals... The evil eye, yes sir! I'm sure someone's been here with the evil eye!... I've even strewn the pastures with St. John's bread.... The sheep are all right, thank God...and the harvest too...Nanni l'Orbo? Down there at Passanitello, carrying on with that witch.... Someday he's going to come back home with broken legs...I swear to God!...and Brasi Camauro too, for the sake of a handful of wheat ears."

Diodata yelled from the door that it was ready.

"If there isn't anything else I should do, sir, I'm going to lie down a while...."

Thank God, after a twenty-four hour fast, finally Don Gesualdo could get to the table; he sat facing the door, his shirtsleeves rolled back above his elbows, his aching feet in his old slippers that were quite a blessing too. The girl had prepared a fresh fava bean soup with an onion, four fresh eggs and two tomatoes she herself had picked gropingly behind the house. The eggs were frying in the pan, and the full bottle of wine was standing before him. Through the door a cool breeze that was indeed a pleasure came in, together with the chirping of the crickets and the scent of the sheaves in the yard —his harvest, right there, under his eyes, and the mule that was biting greedily at the barley stack, poor animal; each bite a bundle. Down the slope, from time to time, you could hear the herd's bell in the enclosure. And the oxen crouched around the yard, tied to the big baskets full of hay, lifted their sluggish heads, breathing heavily; and you could see the glittering of their drowsy eyes scurrying in the dark, like a procession of disappearing fireflies.

Putting down his wine bottle, Don Gesualdo sighed deeply, then he leaned his elbows on the little table:

"You're not eating?... What's the matter?"

Diodata was in a corner, quiet, sitting on a wine barrel; at those words there passed through her eyes the smile of a caressed dog.

"You must be hungry too. Eat! Eat!"

She put the soup plate on her knees, made the sign of the cross before beginning, and then she said:

"God bless...you, sir!"

She was eating very slowly, her back bent and her head bowed. She had a mass of soft fine hair, in spite of the frost and the harsh mountain wind; rich people's hair, and brown eyes, the same color as her hair, timid and sweet: beautiful dog's eyes, caressing and patient, that stubbornly wanted you to like them—like all her entreating face. A face over which had passed hardships, hunger, blows, brutal caresses; filing it, furrowing it, eroding it; leaving on it the scorching of the dog days, the premature wrinkles of the days without bread, the bruises of the tired nights—only her eyes still young, inside those bruised sockets. Curled up like that, she really looked like a little girl—her bust slender and svelte, the nape of her neck showing her white skin where the sun had not burnt. Her hands, blackened, were small and thin—two poor hands for her hard work!...

"Eat, eat. You must be tired too!..."

She smiled, happy, without raising her eyes. The boss handed her the bottle too:

"Here, drink! Don't be shy!"

Diodata, still somewhat hesitant, wiped her mouth with the back of her hand, put the bottle to her lips, throwing back her head. You could almost see the wine, generous and warm, go down her amber-colored throat at every gulp; her breasts, still young and firm, seemed to swell. At that the boss began to laugh.

"Great! great! You sure know how to play the trumpet!..."

She smiled too, wiping her mouth again with the back of her hand, blushing deeply.

"God bless you, sir!"

He went outside to get some fresh air. He sat down on a sheaf by the door, his back against the wall, his hands hanging between his legs. The moon must have been already high behind the mountain, toward Francofonte. The whole Passanitello plain, at the mouth of the valley, was lit up by a dawnlike glimmer. Slowly, as that glimmer kept spreading, on the slope too there began to appear the heaps of sheaves, like so many boulders in rows. Other black dots were moving down the slope and, on the wind, there came the grave distant sound of the bells worn by the bigger animals, as they went down, step by step, toward the creek. Every once in a while, there blew also a few breaths of a cooler wind from the west, and for the whole length of the valley you could hear the rustling of the still standing wheat. In the yard, the high and still dark stack seemed crowned with silver, and in the shade there were dim hints of more heaps of sheaves; more cattle were ruminating; another long silver stripe softly came to rest on the rooftop of the storehouse, which was growing immense in the dark.

"Eh, Diodata! Are you asleep, you lazy-bones?..."

"No, sir, no!..."

She appeared, all disheveled and forcing her sleepy eyes wide open. She began to sweep in front of the door with her hands, on all fours, throwing away the twigs, rubbing her eyes every once in a while so that she wouldn't be overcome by sleep—her chin relaxed, her legs weary.

"Were you asleep!...I told you, you were asleep!..."

And he dealt her a smack on the back, just like a caress.

As for him, he wasn't sleepy. He felt his heart swell. So many pleasant memories came to him. How many stones had he carried on his shoulders before he built that storehouse! How many days had he gone without bread, before becoming the owner of all that property! As a young boy... It was like going back to the time when he carried gypsum from his father's kiln to Donferrante! How many times had he traveled that Licodia road, behind the donkeys that fell along the way and sometimes died under the load! How had he cried and called on saints and Christians for help! *Mastro* Nunzio then recited the prayers for the dead by whipping his son on the back with the very rope of the pack.... Each time a donkey died, it was ten or twelve tari that fell out of his pocket, the poor man! —saddled with a big family! Santo, who already made him gnaw his hands in despair; Speranza, who was beginning to want a husband; mother, with the fever thirteen months a year!... More rope whippings than bread! Then when his uncle, Mescalise, took him along as an assistant mason in search of good fortune...his father didn't want to let him go, for he had his pride too, having always been his own boss, at the kiln; it burnt him up to think that his own flesh and blood was taking orders from someone else. It took him seven years to forgive him, and it was when finally Gesualdo managed to get the first contract on his own...the Molinazzo job.... About two hundred salme of gypsum left the kiln at *mastro* Nunzio's price...plus Speranza's dowry, for the girl couldn't stay in the family home any longer.... And all the arguments when he started speculating on land!... *Mastro* Nunzio wouldn't have anything to do with it.... He said that it wasn't the business they were born to. "Stick to the trade you know!" —But then, when his son took him to see the land he had bought, right there, at Canziria, he couldn't stop measuring it, in all directions—the poor old man—with long paces, as if he had the surveyor's rod in his legs.... And he gave orders—"this must be done, and that,"—just to put forth his own authority, and not have to admit that his son might have a sharper head than he did. —Mother did not live long enough to see this, poor woman. She died telling everybody to take care of Santo, who had always been her favorite, and of Speranza who was saddled with a big family, just as she herself had been...a child every year.... All on Gesualdo's back, for he made enough for everybody. And he, how much money had he made! How much property had he gotten together! How many rough days and sleepless nights! For twenty years he had never once gone to bed without first looking at the sky to see what

kind of weather to expect. —How many Hail Mary's, of the kind
that must really reach all the way up there, for rain or for good
weather! —So many irons in the fire! So many worries, so much
anxiety, so much work!... Tilling and cultivating the land, selling
the produce and the harvest; the risk of the leased lands, the speculations of brother-in-law Burgio, who couldn't guess anything right,
and then left all the losses on his shoulders!... —*Mastro* Nunzio,
who stubbornly insisted on risking his son's money on contracts of
his own, just to prove that he was the boss in his own house!...
Always on the go, always tired, always on his feet, here and there, in
the wind, in the sun, in the rain; his head heavy with worries, his
heart swollen with anxieties, his bones broken with weariness; getting a couple of hours of sleep when it came in handy, as it came
handy—in a corner of the stable, behind a hedge, in the yard, with
rocks under his back; eating a piece of hard black bread wherever he
was—on his mule's packsaddle, in the shadow of an olive tree, along
the edge of a ditch, in the malaria, in the midst of a cloud of mos-
quitoes. —No holidays, no Sundays, never a moment of cheerful
laughter, everybody wanting something from him: his time, his
work, or his money; never an hour such as those his brother Santo
gave himself at the tavern at his expense! —And at home each time
being met by Speranza's surly face, by his brother-in-law's complaints, or by the children's whimpering—and the fights among all
of them, when things didn't go well! —Forced to defend his own
property against everybody, so that he could look after his own interest. —In town, not one man who wasn't either his enemy or his dangerous and feared ally. —Always to have to hide the fever of profit,
the blow of a piece of bad news, the elation of success; always to have
to keep your face straight, your eyes peeled, your lips unsmiling! The
everyday schemes; the devious language even to say "hello"; the uneasy handshakes with your ear stretched out; the struggles fought
with false smiles, or with faces red with rage, foaming and threatening—the night always restless, the day after always loaded with hope
and fear...

"You've worked too, on your boss's property!... You have big
shoulders too...poor Diodata!"

As she saw that he was speaking to her, she moved close to him
happily, sat at his feet, on a rock, her face whitened by the moon,

her chin on her knees, all curled up like a ball. And there passed by the tinkling of the cattle bells, the heavy and slow trampling of the animals across the expanse, as they went down toward the creek, their heavy and sluggish bellows, the voices of the herdsmen driving them — voices that carried far away in the sonorous air. The moon, which now had come down as far as the yard, stamped black shadows into a cold pale glow; it sketched the wandering shadows of the watchdogs that had smelled the cattle, the inert mass of the field watchman, lying face down.

"Nanni l'Orbo, eh?...or Brasi Camauro? Which one are you carrying on with?" resumed Don Gesualdo, who was in a joking mood.

Diodata smiled:

"No sir!... Nobody!..."

But the boss was having fun:

"Sure, sure!... Either one...or both together!... I'm going to find out!... I'm going to catch you with them! Sooner or later! Down there in the valley!..."

She kept smiling in the same way, with that sweet and happy smile, at her boss's jokes, which seemed to light up her face, thinned by the soft pale glow; her eyes like two stars; her beautiful braids loosened on her neck; her mouth a little large with thick lips, but young and fresh.

The boss looked at her for a moment, smiling too, and gave her another affectionate smack on the back.

"This is not stuff for that rascal of a Brasi or for Nanni l'Orbo! No!"

"Oh, my God!..." she exclaimed, crossing herself.

"I know, I know. I'm joking, jackass!..."

He was silent for a short time, then he said:

"You are a good girl!... Good and faithful! Keeping an eye on your boss's interests; you've always been..."

"The boss has given me bread," she answered simply. "I would be a wicked..."

"I know! I know!... My poor girl...that's why I'm fond of you!"

Little by little, seated in the cool air, after supper, with that beautiful moonlight, he let himself drift into tender memories:

"My poor Diodata! You have worked too!... We've had quite a few bad days!... Always on the lookout, just like your boss! Always bustling about...doing something! Always looking after my property!... As faithful as a dog!... It's taken some doing, I can tell you, to put together all this property!..."

He was silent for a moment, moved. Then, after a while, he resumed, changing his tone:

"D'you know? They want me to get married."

The girl did not answer. He didn't notice and went on:

"To gain support... To join up with the big shots in town.... Without them one can't do anything!... They want me to become one of the family...with the support of all the relatives, understand?... Not to have 'em all against me, in time of need.... Eh? What d'you think?"

She kept silent a little longer, her face in her hands. Then she answered, with a tone of voice that made his blood boil:

"You're the boss, sir..."

"I know, I know...I'm talking about it now for the sake of talking...because you're fond of me...I'm not considering it yet... But sooner or later I'll have to give in.... Whom have I been working for after all?... I don't have any children...."

Then he saw her face, turned toward the ground, very pale and all wet.

"What are you crying for, jackass?"

"Nothing, sir!... Just!... Don't pay attention..."

"What did you get into your head, tell me?"

"Nothing, nothing, Don Gesualdo..."

"Goddammit! Goddammit!" he began to scream, fuming, up and down the yard.

At that noise the field-watchman lifted his drowsy head, and asked:

"What's the matter?... Did the mule get loose? Should I get up?..."

"No, no, sleep, Uncle Carmine."

Diodata was walking behind him step by step, her voice humble and subdued:

"Why did you get angry, sir?... What did I say?..."

"I'm getting angry with my destiny.... Troubles and head-

aches everywhere . . . everywhere I turn! . . . You too, now! . . . With
your tears! . . . Jackass! . . . D'you think that in case I would leave you
in the middle of the street . . . without help? . . ."

"No, sir . . . It isn't for me . . . I was thinking about those poor
innocent children . . ."

"Now that too? . . . What can be done about them? That's the
way the world goes! . . . Then the City takes care of them! . . . The
City must support them at its own expense . . . with everybody's
money! . . . I pay taxes too! . . . I know how much, each time I go to
the tax collector! . . ."

He scratched his head for a moment, then went on:

"See, everyone comes into this world under his own star. . . .
You yourself . . . Was there by any chance a father or a mother to
help you? You came into this world alone, the same way as God
sends the grass and the plants no one has sown. You came into this
world just like your name says . . . Diodata . . . God-given! Which
means that you belong to no one! . . . And you may even be a
Baron's daughter, and your brothers are now eating chicken and
squab! The Lord is there for everybody! You have found a way to
make a living too! . . . And my property? . . . Did I get it from my
parents by any chance? Didn't I make myself what I am? Everyone
carries his own destiny with him! . . . I have made my own property,
thank God, and my brother doesn't have anything. . . ."

So he kept grumbling as he walked up and down the yard, in
front of the door. Then, seeing that the girl was still crying — very
quietly, not to annoy him — he sat by her again, calm:

"That's the way it goes. A man can't always do what he likes.
I'm no longer as free as when I was a poor devil with nothing. . . .
Now I have so much property to leave behind . . . I cannot go look
for heirs here and there, in the street . . . or in foundling hospitals. It
means that the other children I'll have, if God helps me, will be
born under a lucky star! . . ."

"You're the boss, sir . . ."

He thought about it a little bit longer, because that kind of talk
stung him worse than a wasp, and then he added:

"You too . . . You haven't had either father or mother . . . And
yet what did you have to go without? Tell me? . . ."

"Nothing, thank God!"

"The Lord is there for everybody...I wouldn't leave you in the middle of the street, I'm telling you... My conscience won't let me. ... I'd find you a husband..."

"Oh...as for me, Don Gesualdo!..."

"Sure, sure, you'll have to be married!... You're young, you cannot stay alone.... I wouldn't leave you without support...I'd find you a good young man, honest...Nanni l'Orbo, that's it! I'd give you a dowry...."

"May the Lord repay you..."

"I'm a Christian! I'm an honest man! Besides, you deserve it. Where would you end up, otherwise? I'll take care of everything. I've so many things to take care of!... And now this one too! You know I'm fond of you. It won't take much to find you a husband. You're young...a beautiful girl... Yes, yes, beautiful!... Let me be the one to judge; I know. You're first-class stuff.... You're a Baron's daughter for sure!..."

Now he was addressing her in another manner, with a cunning smile and itching hands. He took her cheeks with two fingers and he forced her to lift her head, which she stubbornly insisted in keeping low to hide her tears.

"Anyway, for the moment this is nothing but talk.... I'm fond of you as I am of no one else, that's sure!... Now, up with that head of yours, you silly!... You silly girl!..."

As he saw that she went on crying, stubbornly, he burst out cursing again, like an enraged steer.

"Goddammit! What a hell of a destiny!... Always troubles and tears!..."

V

Masi, the helper-boy, ran to wake up Don Gesualdo before dawn, with a voice that would freeze the blood in your veins:

"Sir, get up, sir; the assistant mason from Fiumegrande is here and wants to talk to you right away."

"From Fiumegrande?... At this time?..."

Mastro-don Gesualdo was groping in the dark, picking up his

clothes, still half asleep, with a mess inside his head. All of a sudden he yelled:

"The bridge!... Something must have gone wrong!..."

Down below in the stable he found the assistant mason seated on the bench, soaked to the bone from the rain, drying his few rags by a straw fire. As soon as he saw the boss, he began whimpering again:

"The bridge!... *Mastro* Nunzio, your father, said that it was time to take the frame down! Nardo was caught under it."

The whole house was in an uproar. Speranza, his sister, plunging down the stairs, while her husband was putting his pants on; Santo, still half drunk, rolling down the trapdoor ladder, howling as if he were being murdered. The assistant mason kept repeating to whoever got there:

"The bridge!... The frame!... *Mastro* Nunzio says that it was the bad weather!..."

Don Gesualdo was walking up and down the stable, pale, without speaking a word, without looking anybody in the face, waiting for them to saddle his mule that, also frightened, was shooting kicks right and left, while Masi, all confused, couldn't manage to saddle it. At a certain point Don Gesualdo, his eyes ready to jump out of their sockets, put his fists before the boy's face.

"When? Goddammit!... How long does it take, plague on you!"

"It's all your fault! I told you! Those aren't jobs for the like of us!" bawled his sister in her nightgown, her hair disheveled — a real fury. *Massaro* Fortunato, calmer, nodded agreement with his wife, as he sat silently on the bench that looked like a millstone.

"You're not saying anything! You just sit there like an idiot!"

Now Speranza was attacking her husband:

"When it comes to helping you, who are his brother-in-law after all!... Saddled with lots of children too...then all kinds of difficulties turn up!... There is no money!... The money that was lost with that damned bridge!"

At first Gesualdo turned toward her furiously, foaming at the mouth. Then he swallowed his rage, and began to hum a tune while he buckled the mule's head-harness: the kind of cheerfulness that ate up his insides. He made the sign of the cross, put his foot in the stirrup; finally from up there, almost touching the roof with his head, he spat out his piece before leaving:

"You're right! Your husband has really made some great deals for me! The seed we threw away at Donninga! The vineyard he made me plant where not even pasture grass grows!... He's got a jewel of a head—your husband! I had to pay for your great speculations out of my own pocket! But I'm tired, tired, of carrying the load. When the donkey is tired, he lies in the middle of the road and doesn't go on any more..."

And he spurred the mule as he was still grumbling; his sister shouting after him from the stable doorway, until the animal's shoes could be heard on the cobblestones of the little road, in the dark. The assistant mason began to run, panting, limping; but the boss, whose head was going a mile a minute, didn't notice him. Only when they arrived at the Carmine fields, Don Gesualdo turned his head at the noise of footsteps in the mud, and had him climb up behind. The boy, his voice broken by the pace of the mule, kept repeating the same thing:

"*Mastro* Nunzio said it was time to take the frame down.... It had stopped raining in the early afternoon... 'No, sir,' said *mastro* Nardo; 'let's leave it on until tomorrow...' *Mastro* Nunzio said: 'You talk like that because you want to pocket another day's pay....' Meanwhile, I was cooking the soup for the men.... From the mountain came the shout: 'The flood! Christians!' And while Nardo was untying the last rope..."

Gesualdo, his face to the wind, whipped by the tempest, kept spurring the mule with his heels, without opening his mouth.

"Eh!... What d'you say, Don Gesualdo?... Don't you answer?..."

"Doesn't your tongue ever fall out?" answered the boss finally.

Dawn was beginning to break before reaching the Torretta. They met a peasant who was pushing his donkey forward, getting the downpour through his cotton jacket, his kerchief around his head and his hands in his pockets. He wanted to say something; he was pointing down there, toward the river, while the wind carried his voice far off. Farther on, a little old woman huddled under a carob tree began to scream:

"You can't get through, you can't!... The river!... Watch out!"

In the distance, inside the fog of the river and of the rain, you could hardly make out an enormous pile of ruins, like a mountain that had caved into the river, and on the pillar—still standing, lost in the mist of the low clouds—something black that was moving, arms that were signaling from far away. On both sides of the debris, the river overflowed in large muddy pools. Farther down, some men in a row, up to their knees in the water, bent forward all at once and then pulled together with an *Oooh* that sounded like a lament.

"No! no!" howled the masons, as they held Don Gesualdo by the arm. "Do you really want to drown yourself, sir?"

He didn't answer, in the mud up to his knees, going up and down the eroded bank, his hair flying in the wind. *Mastro* Nunzio, from the top of the pillar, cried out something at him—a cry that the gusts tore from his mouth and then shredded in the distance.

"What are you doing up there now?... Are you crying over the dead body? Leave it...leave it alone!" answered Gesualdo from the bank.

The roar of the water devoured his enraged words as well. The old man, high up, in the fog, kept signaling "No," stubbornly. Other people were crying out also from the opposite bank, under their big umbrellas of oilcloth, without being able to make themselves heard, pointing to where men were salvaging beams. Depending on the wind, even from that upstream area, came voices that seemed to be falling from the sky, desperate cries, and the hoarse sound of a horn.

Gesualdo, bent under the downpour, wobbling in the mud on the bank, was helping to salvage the timbers of the frame that the furious current kept shaking and smashing.

"Here!... Good God!... Don't you see that it's carrying those off too?..."

At a certain point he staggered and was about to sink into the foamy slime that was rising all around.

"Goddammit! D'you want to leave your hide there too?" howled the foreman, grabbing him by the collar. "You nearly dragged me to hell too!"

Pale as a dead man, his eyes wide open, his hair standing on end, almost foaming at the mouth, he answered:

"Let me go to hell! What do you care about all this!... You talk like that because your own blood is not there in the middle of the water!... Let me go to hell!..."

As he saw his son raving that way, *mastro* Nunzio wanted to throw himself headlong into the river, no less:

"Not to have to hear him anymore!... Now he'll say that it was all my fault!... You'll see!... I'm not free to lift a finger in my own house...I'm only to be made fun of.... Then it's better to end it once and for all!..." And he kept trying the water with his foot.

"Listen!" cut in his son in a muted voice. "Leave me alone, you too! I let you do as you liked, I did! You wanted me to take the bridge contract not to stay idle.... See how it turned out?... And we have to start all over again if I'm not to lose the bond.... You could have stayed home in peace and quiet.... Did I let you go without anything?... Leave me alone at least. After all, you haven't lost anything yourself...."

"Ah! I haven't lost anything?... I knew very well that you would have thrown it back into your own father's face...your father's. In fact, I don't count for anything! I don't know how to do anything any more!... I've made you what you are!... As if I weren't the head of the family!... As if I didn't know my job!..."

"Ah!...your job?...because you had the gympsum kiln?... And I even had to buy it back twice for you!... You think you are a structural engineer!... That's the kind of job you know!..."

Mastro Nunzio gave his son a furious look, groping, stirring up his lips without being able to speak a word, rolling his eyes around to look again for the best place to drown himself, and finally grumbled:

"Why do you hold me back then?... Why don't you want me to throw myself into the river? Why?"

Gesualdo began to tear his hair, to bite his arms, to spit toward the sky. Then he planted himself desperately before his father, shaking his clasped hands in his face:

"For God's sake!... For the sake of my mother's soul!... With this kind of disaster on my back...you understand that now I don't feel like fooling around!..."

The foreman intervened to calm them down.

"After all, what's done is done. The dead man will never come back again. Words can't change anything. Rather, come and dry yourselves off, both of you, who are risking to catch pneumonia too, soaked as you are."

They had started a big fire in the shed with rushes and broken-up timber. Pieces of beams on which there still were stuck the images of the saints who had to protect the bridge — rest its soul! *Mastro* Nunzio, who in that plight was even losing his faith, spat on them a couple of times, with a surly face. As they were drying their wet clothes, they were all crying and rubbing their eyes from the smoke. In a corner, under those few broken-down roof tiles, was lying Nardo — the assistant mason who had broken his leg — sweating and agonizing. He too wanted to put a good word in to ease the bad feelings between father and son:

"I've got the worst of it," he complained. "Now I'll be a cripple and unable to earn my bread."

One of his fellow workers, seeing that he couldn't move, piled up some straw under his head. *Mastro* Nunzio, standing in the doorway, his fists raised to the sky, spat fire and flames.

"Hell, damn it! Goddammit! That's what we needed!... Just now!... All this wealth from heaven!..."

Everyone had something to say. There were neighbors who had come to see; and passersby, who wanted to cross the river, waited under cover, their backs to the fire.

"Great job! You did a great job indeed! All that money gone! City money!... Who knows how long it will take now, before we see another bridge.... How did you built it?... With mush?..."

"They too, now!... You're coming just at the right time!.... D'you want me to make God and the saints come down, from up there?..." bawled *mastro* Nunzio.

Gesualdo didn't say a word, seated on a rock, his face the color of the earth, his hands hanging between his legs. Then he began to give vent to his anger by turning to the assistant mason.

"Look at that bastard there! He left the mule outside! With this weather! You lazy-good-for-nothing! Your boss' enemy!"

"Don't take it so hard, sir!" whimpered Nardo from his corner. "As long as there's health, the rest is nothing!..."

Gesualdo looked at him furiously.

"He can talk this way...he doesn't have anything to lose!"

"No, no, sir!... Don't talk that way; God may punish you!..."

Mastro Nunzio, leaning against the doorpost, had been chewing an idea between his toothless gums for some time. Finally he spat it out, suddenly turning to his son:

"And d'you know what I'd tell you? That I don't want to have anything more to do with this cursed bridge! We should rather build a mill with the materials we manage to salvage...that's a safe bet!..."

"That's a new one!" sprang up Don Gesualdo. "You've really gone mad? And the bond? You want me to lose that one too? If I were to leave things to you!... When I began to build mills, I had to hear that it was a disaster.... Now that you know better, you wouldn't build anything else.... As if the entire town were just to grind their bones night and day, beginning with my own!... Goddammit!..."

The fight flared up all over again. *Mastro* Nunzio was screaming and complaining that he was not respected.

"Don't you see that I'm just a puppet?... Just a joker?... The head of the family...gentlemen!... Look at this!..."

To stop it, Don Gesualdo, green with anger, jumped onto the back of his mule once more, and went off while it was still raining cats and dogs, his head in his shoulders, soaked to the bone, his heart blacker than the cloudy sky before his eyes; the town gray and sad too in the rain, up on top of the mountain, the ringing of the noon hour passing by in waves, carried by the wind, and losing itself in the distance.

All those who met him, knowing of the disaster that had befallen him, forgot to greet him and kept going. He gave furious glances and from time to time he grumbled to himself:

"I'm still on my feet! My name is Mastro-don Gesualdo! As long as I'm on my feet, I know how to help myself!"

Only one man, a poor devil, who was going the same way, offered to take him under his umbrella. He answered:

"I need far more than an umbrella, my friend! Don't worry, I'm not afraid of the rain, or of the hail, not me!"

He reached the town after midday. The canon-priest Lupi had just gone to lie down for his nap, right after lunch.

"I'm coming, I'm coming, Don Gesualdo!" he shouted from the window as he was called.

Someone going about his own business at that time, seeing him soaked through and raining down like an umbrella, said:

"Eh, Don Gesualdo?... What a disaster!..."

He stood there, like a rock, a bitter smile on his pale and thin lips, and answered:

"Eh, those are things that happen. If you walk in the rain you'll get wet, and if you ride a horse you'll fall. But as long as there is nobody dead, all the rest can be managed."

Most people kept going, only turning around in curiosity after they had passed. Finally the canon-priest appeared in the little door, buttoning his cassock.

"Eh! eh! Don Gesualdo! Here you are...here you are!..."

Don Gesualdo tried to look as cheerful as he could, in spite of the malignant fever he carried inside his stomach.

"Yes sir, here I am!" he answered with the broad smile he tried to spread all across his dark face. "Here I am, at your disposal...at your orders.... But, tell me the truth, you talk with the devil, don't you?"

The canon-priest pretended not to understand:

"Why? About the bridge? No, I assure you! As a matter of fact, I'm very sorry!..."

"No, no, I'm not talking about the bridge!... But we'd better go upstairs, sir. This is not the kind of talk to be done here, in the street..."

In the canon-priest's room the bed was still unmade; all around the walls a good number of little cages, in which the canon-priest — a great bird hunter with nets — kept his decoy birds; an enormous black crucifix in front of the door, and under it the confraternity chest, just like a coffin, in which he kept the collaterals for the money he lent; some images of saints, here and there, stuck on the walls with hosts and dirtied by the birds; and a smell that would kill you, in the midst of all those animals.

Immediately, Don Gesualdo began to give vent to his troubles: his father who stubbornly insisted on doing things his own way to prove that he was still the boss, after having squandered the family fortune.... He had had to buy it back twice for him, that gypsum kiln! And his father kept getting him into all kinds of trouble!...

And if he uttered a word of complaint when he had to let his veins be opened to bleed more payments, then his father yelled that he was not respected enough. His sister and his brother-in-law were fleecing him on the other side. A jackass, that brother-in-law Burgio, a jackass and also arrogant! And the one who had to pay each time, it was he, Gesualdo!... His brother Santo, eating and drinking at his expense, without doing anything from morning to night:

"With my money, d'you understand, sir? With my blood! I know what it costs me! When I left my father with the gypsum kiln in bankruptcy, and we didn't know how to feed those four pack-donkeys, I left with only my shirt on my back...and a pair of pants that almost didn't hold together any longer...without shoes on my feet, yes sir. My uncle Mescalise had to lend me the first trowel so that I could start working as a mason.... And my father raving because I was leaving the job in which I was born.... And then, when I took the first contract job...he screamed as if it were the end of the world! I've had some courage, my dear Canon Lupi. I know what it costs me, whatever I have! It all comes from my own sweat.... And when I see them throwing it away, one from one side and one from another...well, sir...my blood boils!... So far I haven't said anything not to have fights in the family...to be able to eat a mouthful of bread in peace, when I come back home tired ... But now it's enough. Even the donkey, when he's tired, lies in the middle of the road and doesn't go on any more.... You know what kind of punishment of God my sister Speranza is!... I want to put an end to it. Everyone in his own home. Am I right, my dear Canon Lupi?"

Meanwhile, the canon-priest was feeding his birds.

"If you're not listening, sir, why am I talking?"

"Yes, yes, I'm listening. What the hell! It doesn't take a Saint Augustine to understand what you mean!... The point is that you want to salvage the bond, isn't it so? —You want some help from City Hall."

"Yes, sir...the bond..."

Then Gesualdo planted his piercing gray eyes on him, and went on:

"There is something more...I was telling you that I want my own home...on my own...if I find the wife that suits me.... But if you're not listening, sir...then why am I... Or if you pretend not to understand . . . D'you remember . . . what you told me the evening of the Patron Saint's feast? . . . But if you pretend you don't understand . . . why I've come here to see you . . . when I told you first of all . . . I told you: 'Here I am, at your disposal . . .' "

"Ah! . . . Ah! . . ." answered the canon-priest lifting his head like a donkey that's pulling at the halter.

Then he stopped the careful dusting of his three-cornered hat and planted on Don Gesualdo his own eyes — the eyes of a man who doesn't let anybody fool him.

"Listen, Don Gesualdo . . . This is not the kind of talk that belongs here, in this manner! Or you don't know your friends from your enemies, good God! I'm glad to see that you yourself have realized that the advice I gave you then was pure gold! A girl who's a jewel, used to all kinds of trouble, who would do whatever you wish, and from a top aristocratic family too! . . . Who would make you a relative of all the big shots in town! . . . You see now what kind of help she would be to you? You'd have the judges and all the others on your side. And also for the other business of the City lands, if you want to come in along with us . . ."

"Yes sir," answered Don Gesualdo vaguely. "We could do many things . . . . We could talk about it . . ."

"We should talk about it in plain words, my friend. Do you think I'm a child? One hand washes the other. If you help yourself, I'll help you, says the Holy Spirit. My dear Don Gesualdo, you have the fault of thinking that everyone is a much bigger fool than you are. First you pretend not to know anything, that you are deaf in that ear, and then, in case of need, if the house caves in on you, you come to me with a face like that."

"It must be the heat . . . it must be all those birds . . ." stammered Don Gesualdo, his mind in disarray. "I'd like you to be in my shoes, my dear Canon Lupi!" he finally exclaimed.

"In your shoes? Certainly. I'm ready to put myself in them! I want you to see and to realize if I really care for you or not! Here I am with you. Let's think about that business of the bridge first . . . about salvaging the bond with a subsidy from City Hall. Let's go now to see the Captain . . . and the judges who won't be against us. . . . Too bad Baron Zacco is already suspicious about that business of the City lands! . . . Let me think . . ."

As he was tying his cloak around his neck, he was collecting his ideas, knitting his brow, looking here and there on the floor.

"That's it! First I'll go to Mrs. Sganci.... No! No! I won't tell her anything for the moment! Just a few casual words ... somewhat academically.... All we need is that Donna Marianna writes a couple of lines to the Captain. As for Baroness Rubiera, there's nothing to worry about ... she is as safe as you yourself.... But no monkey business, eh! ..."

The canon-priest opened his eyes wide. Don Gesualdo stretched his arm toward the crucifix.

"No, I'm talking about the other deal, the City lands. I wouldn't like to be passing the buck between us, my dear Don Gesualdo."

The latter wanted to stretch out his arm again; but the canon-priest had already gone through the door.

"You'll wait for me downstairs inside the front door. I'll be back in a moment."

He came back rubbing his hands:

"Didn't I tell you. For Donna Marianna that niece is the apple of her eye. It will be a fantastic deal for you!"

As they started out in the street, they ran into Notary Neri, who was going to open his office, and who nodded in sympathy to Don Gesualdo:

"Bad business, eh! I am sorry!"

But you could see that underneath it all he was jubilant. The canon-priest cut it short and answered:

"Nothing serious ... The devil is not so black ... We'll manage.... We've salvaged the materials...."

Afterward, when they were some distance away and the Notary, his key in the lock was still looking at them, laughing, the canon-priest whispered into Mastro-don Gesualdo's ear:

"The fact is that your face is such, my dear friend ..."

"Me?"

"Yes. You don't know, but it is! With a face like that, people will walk all over you! ... With a face like that, a man doesn't go to ask for a favor.... Wait for me here, I'll go up a moment to see Cavaliere Peperito. He's a jackass, but they have made him a judge."

As soon as the canon-priest had gone up the dilapidated and unplastered staircase, the Cavaliere arrived from his little farm, riding an emaciated donkey that also carried a packsaddle full of fava beans. To get into his favor, Don Gesualdo helped him to unload the fava beans, and to tie the donkey to the manger, under the arch of the stairway; but the Cavaliere seemed annoyed at being caught in that gear, all muddy and in his ragged country clothes.

"Nothing to do," said the canon-priest when he came back a while later. "He's a jackass! He thinks he's a real cavaliere, a real knight. He must have it in for you.... We must find the right man. ... Ciolla? Eh! Ciolla? I'm talking to you, Ciolla! D'you know if Don Filippo is home? Did you see him go out?

Ciolla winked with one eye, twisting his paralyzed mouth some more.

"No, Canali's still there, at Bomma's; he's waiting for him to take him to his sister-in-law's, the candle maker, you know? Their usual walk, after lunch ... to fool around with her, behind the bookcase.... What's new, Don Gesualdo? Are you going to have the bridge blessed, together with the canon-priest?"

Finally Don Gesualdo gave vent to his anger, making cursing gestures with both hands.

"That bridge was sitting on your chest!... As if you had to pay for it out of your own pocket!..."

The canon-priest pulled him by the arm:

"Let's go! Let's go! D'you think you can shut up all the lazy bums?"

As they were going up the Margarones' lane, they met Marquis Limòli, who was taking his usual evening walk, from Rosario to Santa Maria di Gesù, always alone, the red umbrella under his arm. While answering the ceremonious hat-raising of the Marquis, the canon-priest had an inspiration:

"Wait, wait a moment!"

A little later he rejoined Don Gesualdo with quite a different face.

"A real devil, that Marquis! As poor as Job, but his words count! They help one another, all together!... a good word, at the right time!... They cannot say no to one another ... They'd let him starve to death, but they couldn't deny him a favor...."

Don Filippo was still at home, busy drawing lines for Nicolino's pothooks:

"How lucky! How lucky!"

Then, seeing that Don Gesualdo was coming in too behind the canon-priest, he lowered his glasses on his nose again.

"I'm so very busy!... Ah, yes...the bond?... D'you want City Hall to help to fish it out? You want some help to start the work again?... We'll see... We'll find out.... You went wrong on this damned bridge the first time.... It's a serious business.... I don't know what, actually...I don't know the details.... I haven't had anything to do with these things for some time! I'm so very busy!... I don't even have time to blow my nose.... We'll see... We'll find out...."

Just then Canali came in. He was looking for Margarone, for he was surprised not to have seen him at the usual time. He knew about the bridge too, and he seemed to have great fun stretching out his expressions of sympathy—the venom running behind his large yellow face:

"Ah! Ah! Don Gesualdo!... It was a big job!... A blow to knock you down!... You had too many irons in the fire, in your family!..."

Don Filippo, now that he felt this support, turned on Don Gesualdo too:

"You must cut the coat according to the cloth, my dear man! ... Did you want to knock down the sky with your own fists?... Everyone in his place, my friend!... You can't get it into your head that you can bring an entire town to its knees!..."

At that point Don Gesualdo lost his patience. He suddenly stood up, as red as a fighting-rooster, and opened his mouth to vent his anger. But the canon-priest covered it with his hand.

"Keep quiet! Let me do the talking! Listen here, Don Filippo!"

He pulled him by the coattail into the entryroom. After a while they came back, arm in arm—Don Filippo again as sweet as sugar with Don Gesualdo, planting his big ox eyes on him, as if he were seeing him then for the first time:

"We'll see!... As for me...whatever I can do...I was speaking in your own interest, my dear Don Gesualdo...."

As he was going down the staircase, Don Gesualdo was still grumbling:

"Why should they all be against me?... I'm not hurting anyone!... I just look after my business...."

"Eh, my dear Don Gesualdo!" blurted out the canon-priest, finally. "Your business clashes with everybody else's business, what the hell!... That's why we must draw them to your side.... Among themselves they're hand in glove with one another.... They're all relatives.... You're the stranger...you're the enemy, what the hell!"

The canon-priest stopped cold in the middle of the square, before the Trao palace — high, black, and dilapidated — and looking straight at Don Gesualdo with his sharp little rat's eyes that seemed to pierce him like two pins, his blade-shaped face sliding away on all sides:

"D'you see?... When you've come into their camp... That's the dowry Donna Bianca would bring you!... It's good money for a man like you, who has so many business deals on his hands."

Again Mastro-don Gesualdo stroked his chin, as when he was making a deal with someone shrewder than himself; he looked at the palace; then he looked at the canon-priest, and answered:

"But with deposit in hand, eh! Dear Canon Lupi! First I want to see how her relatives will take it."

"They'll take it with open arms, they will!... I'm telling you! It's as if the river rebuilt your bridge better than before; and you go and sleep on it."

In the nearby alley, next to his house, he met Diodata who was there waiting with her mantilla on her head, huddled under the arch of the landing, for they didn't want her in the house — especially Speranza — and tolerated her only in the country, for the heavy work. As soon as the girl saw her boss, she began to cry and lament, as if the bridge had fallen on top of her:

"Don Gesualdo, what a disaster! I'd have been happier to drown myself...I've come to see you, sir... with this thorn that you must have in your heart!..."

"This too now! Why did you come? You're all wet!... Look at you!... Like an animal!... All the way from Canziria, on foot!... Just to cry and moan.... As if I didn't have enough trouble of my own!.... Now where are you going at this time?"

He had her go into the stable. As she moved away from the wall, she left a pool of water in front of the door where she had been waiting. He felt his bones broken too. Besides, his sister welcomed him like a dog:

"Are you back from the feast? You really made a big profit, didn't you?"

Then she turned to her husband like a viper—black, thin as a nail, her eyes the color of coal, her mouth wide open, as if she wanted to eat people up:

"You don't say anything?... Your blood isn't boiling?"

Burgio, more peaceful, was trying to stay out of it, shrugging his shoulders, lowering his big ox-head.

"That's it!... Nobody gives a damn about all our trouble!... I'm the only one to eat my heart out!..."

Her brother, Gesualdo, his mouth bitter, repeated:

"Cut it out, Speranza! Leave me alone; I've got enough trouble, even without your sermon!"

"You don't even want to hear my sermon?... You don't want me to complain?... With all that money lost?... What? Don't you earn your money, you?..."

To get away from that wasp, he kept looking in the kitchen for something to put between his teeth, after that kind of a day. He rummaged in the breadbin. Speranza followed him, like a real punishment of God.

"Soon, if things keep going this way, there won't be any bread in the bin, there won't...the bin won't be there either!... The whole house will go to hell!..."

Santo, who was coming home hungry from lounging all day in the square, went into a rage as he found the fire still out—like a real animal. The children were screaming; all the neighbors at their windows to enjoy the scene; so that finally Gesualdo lost his patience:

"D'you want me to tell you? You'll make me do something you'll be really sorry for! I've promised it to you so many times!... Now I really mean it, I swear to God! When the donkey can't stand it any more, he lies down and good-bye everybody!"

And he went into the stable, while Speranza kept screaming after him:

"You run away too? To go to Diodata? D'you think I didn't see her? Half the day she's been waiting for you, that bitch!..."

He slammed the door. At first he didn't even want to eat—and he had gone twenty-four hours without food—his stomach full of all kinds of aches. Diodata—soaked to the bone like him and with her throat dry—went to buy him some bread and salami. There, on the stable bench, before a straw fire, he could at least swallow a little bit of food in peace.

"You like it, eh...isn't it a great life? Don't you think?" he asked as he was chewing full mouthed, and still sulking.

She watched him eat, her face reddened by the flame, and said yes, as he wished—with a happy smile, now. The day was ending clear. A glimmer of sunlight spread like gold on the cornice of the Trao palace, across the way, and Donna Bianca, who was hanging some worn-out laundry on the terrace, which couldn't be seen from the square—her hands fine and delicate, her figure looking taller and more slender in her poor dress, as she rose on tiptoe to reach the ropes strung from wall to wall.

"See whom they want me to marry?" he said. "A Trao!... And a good housegirl too!... They've told me the truth!..."

And he sat there watching, deep in thought, as he was slowly chewing. Diodata watched too, without saying anything, with a heavy heart. Some goats passed down the alley, bleating. Donna Bianca, as if she finally felt those eyes fixed on her, turned her pale and tired face, and brusquely drew back.

"Now she is lighting the lamp," continued Don Gesualdo. "She does everything herself in that house!... Eh, eh...there isn't much to waste in that house!... I like her because she is used to all kinds of trouble, and she'd do whatever I wished.... Say, what d'you think?"

Diodata turned her back, and went toward the far corner of the stable to give the mule a handful of fresh grass, and after a while she answered, in a hoarse voice:

"You're the boss, sir..."

"True... But...what a jackass! You must be hungry too.... Eat, eat, you poor thing. Don't just mind the mule."

VI

Don Luca the sacristan was putting out the candles on the high altar one by one, with a little tuft of grass tied to the top of a reed, while keeping an eye on a band of urchins who now and then burst into the church — almost deserted at that hot hour — and who were pursued by his angry words. Donna Bianca Trao, kneeling before the confessional, bent her humble head; abandoned to desolate depression, she mumbled muted words that sounded like sighs. From the confessional there answered a calm voice that crept into her like a caress — soothing her anguish, appeasing her scruples, forgiving her mistakes, vaguely opening something like a new life, a new blue sky, in the future, in the unknown. The noon sun darted in through the curtains up above, and made the wounds of Sant'Agata bloom again on the high altar — like two big roses in the middle of her breast. At that point Donna Bianca anxiously lifted her spirit, glowing with consolation, avidly clinging to the side of the confessional, her voice more fervent, her forehead leaning onto her crossed hands to let herself be penetrated by that sweetness. From the place and from the hour of the day came a buzzing of sleepy flies, a smell of incense and melted wax, and a heavy torpor resembling a profound weariness. An old woman was waiting, crouched on the steps of the altar, like a filthy mantilla lying on top of a bundle of laundry; and when she woke up grumbling, Don Luca rebuked her:

"Some manners indeed! Don't you see there is a Lady ahead of you at the confessional?... Hers is not the kind of nonsense you bring to the Tribunal of Penance!... Family matters, my dear!... Important business!..."

In the shadow of the confessional appeared a white hand making the sign of the cross, and Donna Bianca finally got up, staggering, wrapped in her cloak reaching down to her feet, her face radiant with sweet serenity. Don Luca, seeing that the old woman would not bring herself to leave, touched her mantilla with his reed:

"Hey! hey! Aunt Filomena?... Today it's too late, too late. Noon will soon strike, and the father-confessor must go for lunch."

The old woman raised her dazed head, and had him repeat the same thing two or three times, stubborn and benumbed as she was.

"Sure, I'm about to close the church. You can go now, mother. This afternoon?... Not either!... Father Angelino is threshing at Passo di Cava. Busy days, my dear!..."

Slowly he managed to send her away, grumbling and dragging her slippers. Then, as the priest slipped through the door to the sacristy, Don Luca had to chase away those urchins, overturning benches and chairs, pretending to throw the incense burner at them.

"Out! out! Go and play in the square!"

Meanwhile he kept passing by Donna Bianca, who was kneeling and praying in the chapel of the Sacrament — which was ablaze with gold and with colors so brilliant as to blind you — coughing, spitting, blowing his nose, grumbling:

"Not even in church!... One cannot collect one's thoughts and pray!..."

Donna Bianca rose to her feet, crossing herself, her lips still full of Hail Marys. The sacristan spoke to her directly, as she was starting out toward the door:

"Are you satisfied, Donna Bianca? A Saint, that Father Angelino! He's a really good confessor, isn't he? Are you satisfied with him?"

She nodded yes, with a brief smile, slackening her pace out of courtesy.

"A good man! A sensible man! He can really give you good advice...better than your brother Don Ferdinando...and even than Don Diego, for sure..."

He looked around with those cat eyes of his used to seeing in the dark of the church and of the bell tower ladder, and added in a whisper, changing his tone, with an air of great mystery:

"D'you know what they answered Don Gesualdo Motta? Yesterday, after lunch, he had the formal marriage proposal delivered by the canon-priest Lupi..."

Bianca blushed without raising her head. The sacristan, who was looking into her lowered eyes, as he followed her step by step, continued aloud:

"They said no!... Just as I'm saying it now!... The canon-priest was flabbergasted!... Nobody would have expected such an answer, don't you think?... The canon-priest, Donna Marianna, even your aunt the Baroness, they had all made every effort!... Even that Christ made of wood would have been moved, see! Nobody would have thought him so hardheaded, that Don Diego, your brother! Such a good and humble gentleman that we almost felt we could go to him for confession!.... I'm not speaking of Don Ferdinando, who's worse than a child, the poor man!..."

He had managed to stop Donna Bianca, planting himself

before her, his eyes shiny and his face ablaze; again he lowered his voice as if confiding a decisive piece of news:

"Don Gesualdo seems gone mad!... He says he can't swallow it! That it will cause him to get ill, I swear to God!... I went to see him at Canziria.... He was threshing the wheat.... 'Don Gesualdo, is this the way to take it?... You'll leave your hide there, yes sir!...' 'Leave me alone, my dear Don Luca, don't I know!... Ever since the canon-priest brought me that great answer!...' He really looks like he has been sick for a hundred years!... His beard unshaven... He doesn't sleep nor eat anymore..."

Just then came the noise of church people's footsteps. Don Luca suddenly raised his voice, as if he were speaking to a deaf person:

"Today Father Angelino is threshing at Passo di Cava. If you have some other sin to confess, there's Archpriest Bugno, who's idle ...very good too! a true servant of God...."

But as he saw the canon-priest Lupi, who was coming toward them, bowing at every altar, his right hand dripping holy water, his three-cornered hat hanging in his left:

"Bless, Canon Lupi! How come you are here?"

Instead of replying, the canon-priest turned to Donna Bianca with an idiotic little smile on his sharp ferrety face the color of soot.

"Let's do good, Donna Bianca! Let's pray to the Lord! I saw you walk into the church as I was going to Don Gesualdo Motta's close by, and said to myself: 'There is Donna Bianca going to the Forty Hours, and giving a good example to me, unworthy priest that I am...'"

"Yes...here is our canon-priest!... If you need to go to confession again, Donna Bianca..."

"Sorry, I can't! Monsignore has not allowed me to hear confession, because he knows that I don't have the time...."

Then he added with that little smile of his, stroking his bristled chin:

"Besides, your brothers wouldn't want..."

Donna Bianca, as red as if she had had on her face the reflection of the curtain veiling the altar of the Crucifix, pretended not to understand. The canon-priest went on, changing his tune:

"I have a lot of serious business on my shoulders...of my own and of others.... I was just going to see Don Gesualdo on your aunt's behalf. D'you know about that big deal they are planning together, he and the Baroness?"

Donna Bianca signaled no with her head.

"A big deal indeed. . . . It's about leasing the municipal lands of the whole County!. . . Don Gesualdo's heart is bigger than this church!. . . and the money too!. . . Lots of it! Lots of it, Donna Bianca! Much more than people think. . . . A man who'll get as rich as Croesus, with that fine head he's got!"

Don Luca, as he was taking off his vestments, his face still inside the surplice, his arms in the air, his voice muted, could not help saying:

"You should see his Canziria harvest, you should see that!"

"Ah, ah! are you coming from there?"

"Yes sir," answered the sacristan, pulling out his red and embarrassed face. "Just going for a walk. . . I go there every year for the church alms. . . . Don Gesualdo is a devotee of Sant'Agata's!"

"A heart of gold!" cut in the canon-priest. "Generous, charitable!. . . Too bad that. . ."

And he put his hand over his mouth.

"Just what I was telling Donna Bianca!. . ." confirmed Don Luca, as he recovered his spirit—his little eyes again impertinent.

"Enough! enough! Everyone is king in his own house! I'm now leaving you to your own business. Regards to Don Diego and Don Ferdinando!"

Donna Bianca, embarrassed, wanted to leave too; but the sacristan detained her:

"Just a moment! What should I tell Father Angelino, if you want to regain God's Grace before Saint John's Day?"

The canon-priest insisted too:

"No, no, stay, Donna Bianca; tend to your business."

Then, as soon as the canon-priest went out letting the door-curtain fall, Don Luca winked:

"So? What should I tell Don Gesualdo, if I happen to run into him?. . ."

She seemed to hesitate. She kept walking toward the main door of the church, step by step, keeping her eyes lowered, as if annoyed by the sacristan's insistence.

"Since my brothers have said no . . ."

"That was a stupid thing to say! I would have liked to take them to Canziria by the hand, and show them if it isn't worth all your sooty portraits!... Excuse me, Donna Bianca!... I'm talking in your own interest, Ma'am.... Your brothers hang onto that soot because they're old...they've got their feet in the grave, they have! ... But what's going to happen to you who are young? Nobody can ruin a sister this way!... Not even Saint Joseph, the father of Providence, can send you a husband like that!... They're crazy to say no, those brothers of yours!...fit to be put in an asylum!... He will pick up all those County lands, he, Don Gesualdo!.... And then, he has his fingers in every pie. Not a stone is put into a wall without him making a profit.... Like God himself on earth! Bridges, mills, factories, paved roads!... He turns the world upside down, that demon! Soon we'll go all the way to Militello by coach—thanks to God and to Don Gesualdo Motta!... His wife will wallow in luxury! ... She'll walk on fine gold, I swear to God! Father Angelino too must have given you the same advice.... I didn't hear anything, not to violate the seal of confession, but Father Angelino is a sensible man...he must have certainly advised you to marry a good man... to regain the Grace of God."

Donna Bianca looked at him in dismay while her pointed Trao chin seemed convulsed. Then she raised her eyes wet with tears toward the crucifix—her pale lips tightened in a painful fold. With those bloodless lips she finally answered in a whisper:

"My brothers are the bosses.... It's up to them to decide...."

Don Luca, being short of supporting arguments, was for a moment almost stunned, as he planted himself before her, not to let her run away—stifled as he was by so many good reasons in his throat, stammering, groping, furiously scratching his head, his little shiny eyes searching her from head to foot to find a weak spot. He shook his clasped hands before her threatening and pleading. Finally he blurted out:

"But is it right, good God? is it right to cause so much suffering to a good man who's so fond of you?... To kick fortune in the shins? ... Sorry, Donna Bianca! I'm talking in your own interest.... You must make up your mind yourself! You're no longer under age, after all!... I'm getting excited about you because I'm a good servant of your family...a great house!... Too bad it isn't what it used to be anymore!... Now that you have the chance to lift up the Trao name again!... This means to kick fortune in the shins!... This means being ungrateful to Divine Providence."

She kept walking toward the door, hesitating, her head low. Don Luca at her heels, getting excited, harping on all the strings, changing his tune at every chord:

"And those days, Donna Bianca!... Those days that dawn in your house!... I won't say more; sorry; I'm talking about this simply because I'm always hanging around there to help you, together with my wife.... And when your relatives forget that you exist...those winter days that God sends! No more!... You could be the town's queen, instead! Think about it. Don Gesualdo would pick the sun and the moon out of the sky to please you!... He can't reason anymore!... He looks like a madman, no less."

Donna Bianca had stopped abruptly, her head high, while a sudden flame seemed to be thrown on her face by the door-curtain that somebody entering the church was lifting at that moment. There appeared an emaciated woman, her ragged skirt lifted by pregnancy over her thin shins; she was filthy and disheveled as if all her life she had done nothing else but carry that belly; she had the look of a mother hen stupefied by hatching, two small round eyes on a pointed face, yellow and parchmentlike, and the shredded kerchief of a sick person tied under her chin; nothing more on her shoulders, just like one who feels quite at home in the good Lord's house. She began to moan from the threshold as if she were in labor:

"Don Luca...aren't you going to strike noon?...the pot is about to boil...."

"Why did you put it on the fire so soon? The sun is still here, on the threshold.... The archpriest raises hell because of this business of striking noon before the time.... But now, since you have already made a mess, here is the key to the bell tower...."

Don Luca, still holding his surplice under his arm and looking as skinny in his filthy cassock as his wife's belly was enormous, went on arguing with her:

"You've got a clock right there, in your belly!... You can only think of eating!... It takes some food!... Our neighbors are still all out in the fields.... Burgio's children are right there..."

"They're waiting too!..." whimpered his wife, in the same tone of voice. "They're waiting for you to strike noon . . ." And she went off, her belly ahead of her.

"Don Gesualdo's nephews!" continued the sacristan, winking meaningfully at Donna Bianca while he was coming back. "They're there to spy on us! . . . Their mother, Speranza, sends them for that purpose, to know everything we are doing! She has her eyes on the property, that one! . . . As if it were her own! . . . She has made plans! . . . When we meet, she looks as if she wanted to bite me to pieces! . . ."

He pretended he was leading the way for Donna Bianca in order to lift the door-curtain, so that he would keep her another moment:

"He really makes me feel sorry for him! . . . A sick man's face! . . . He kept talking about you the entire time, Ma'am. . . . He says that maybe the canon-priest Lupi didn't convey the message the right way . . . that he would like to talk to you . . . to see . . . to find out . . ."

Donna Bianca became as red as fire.

"He's in love, and that's it! In love like a madman. You should talk to your brothers again. Send him a good word . . . a more Christian answer . . . I'll come and get it myself, after noon, when Don Diego and Don Ferdinando are resting . . . with the excuse of the flowers for the Virgin Mary . . . All right? What d'you say? . . ."

She quickly lowered her head, as she walked under the curtain, and went out. Don Luca thought she was searching in her pocket, and as he ran after her:

"What are you doing? No! You offend me! Some other time . . . later . . . when you can. . . . I just thought it might be better if I send my wife, to get your answer. I wouldn't like your brothers to see me hanging around the house and suspect that it was the canon-priest who sent me. . . ."

After vespers he quickly got through with church work and ran to Canziria; five miles uphill — never mind, for love of Don Gesualdo, who surely deserved it, after all!

"She's about to fall, Don Gesualdo! As yet she hasn't said a clear 'yes' with her mouth; but you can tell she's wavering, just like a pear when it's ripe. I've experience with these things, because every day in church I see women who have recourse to the Tribunal of Pen-

ance . . . before and after. . . . She made me sweat it out, though! . . .
But now I tell you that the pear is ripe! Another shake and it will fall
into your arms; I assure you! You should go back to town and strike
the iron while it's hot."

But Don Gesualdo did not welcome the love message he happened to receive at that moment.

"See, Don Luca, the entire harvest is in the yard. . . . I've been
up since last night. . . . I don't keep the wind in my pockets so that I
can do the threshing whenever I like! . . ."

The yard was as vast as a town square. Ten mules trotted
around continuously; and behind the mules ran Nanni l'Orbo and
Brasi Camauro, sinking into the chaff up to their knees, panting,
shouting, singing, howling. On one side, in a white cloud, a band of
peasants armed with pitchforks seemed to be digging in the wheat —
their shirts flying open; while uncle Carmine, blackened by the sun,
on top of the stack, kept making more sheaves rain down. Sledges
loaded with more wheat kept arriving from the nearby fields; workers put the wheat into sacks and carried it to the storehouse, where
you'd constantly hear Pirtuso's lamenting voice, as he sang "Viva
Maria" every twenty bushels. All around there fluttered flocks of
hens, and in the air a cloud of pigeons; emaciated little donkeys
were hungrily biting at the straw — their eyes dead; other beasts of
burden were scattered here and there; and little barrels of wine
passed from one hand to the next, as if to put out a fire. Don Gesualdo always on the go, a bundle of tally sheets in his hand, marking
the sacks of wheat, putting down a cross for every little barrel of
wine, counting the arriving sledges, scolding Diodata, arguing with
the broker, shouting to his workers from the distance, sweating,
having almost lost his voice, his face burning, his shirt open, a cotton kerchief tied around his neck, an old dirty straw hat on his head.

"You see, Don Luca, if I can waste time now! . . . Wine, here!
Give Don Luca something to drink! . . . Yes, yes, I'll come; but when
I can. . . . For the moment I can't leave, not even if the world caved
in! . . . Diodata . . . be sure the wind doesn't push the flame toward
the yard, Goddammit! . . . No, Don Luca! . . . I'm not angry because
of her brothers' refusal. . . . Come here, come closer, for it's better
not to let anybody know our business! . . . Everyone has his own
ideas. . . . Besides, she's the one who must decide. . . . If she says yes,

I won't back out. . . . But today I can't come . . . nor can I tomorrow
. . . Well! the day after tomorrow! . . . The day after tomorrow I
must come for the business of the City lands; we'll talk about it
then."

Don Luca also suggested to send a few words in writing:

"There is my wife who's just the kind of person to deliver them
secretly to Donna Bianca, without arousing any suspicion. A nice
little letter, with a couple of those words that turn a girl's head!
D'you understand, sir? Ciolla knows how to do that. . . . I can talk to
Ciolla myself, in confidence, without having to rack your brains
yourself; and he'll make you look good. Then with a big bottle of
wine you'll keep Ciolla's mouth shut."

Don Gesualdo didn't want to hear of a letter.

"Not to save the wine; but what kind of stories are you telling
me? If it's true that she likes the deal, why all these schemes?"

"All right! All right!" concluded Don Luca. "I only meant to
keep hitting the nail on the head. But you're the boss."

Don Luca went home happy, with a lamb and a cheese. Out of
prudence he sent his wife to deliver the message, with an excuse:

"As to that matter you discussed with my husband, Donna
Bianca, he says that the father confessor will come the day after
tomorrow to get your answer! . . . The father confessor expects the
answer on Sunday! . . ."

Don Ferdinando, who had heard the front door being opened,
appeared at that very moment like a ghost.

"The father confessor! . . ." repeated Grazia without anyone
having asked anything. "Donna Bianca wanted to go to confession!
. . . Today the father confessor can't . . . tomorrow he can't either . . .
But Sunday's all right, if you let him know that you're ready. . . ."

The poor woman, under Don Ferdinando's suspicious, restless,
and wild eyes that seemed to look through her, became confused,
stammered, groped for words. Then, seeing that he kept silent and
didn't move, scraggy as he was, she stopped talking too, her eyes
empty, her mouth open, her hands on her belly. Bianca, to cut the
matter short, led her to the storage pantry to give her an apronful
of fava beans. Don Ferdinando, following, sewn to their heels,
speechless, looking into every corner, suspicious. He too bent over
the little pile of fava beans, shielding it with his body, measuring it

by sight, feeling it with his hands. And after the sacristan's wife had gone, like a duck, holding her full apron on her enormous belly, he began to grumble:

"Too many!... You gave her too many!... They're nearly finished!... Aunt Rubiera won't send us any more before Christmas!"

His sister wanted to leave; but he kept searching, rummaging, examining whatever was in the storage pantry: two little sausages hanging from a big ring; a cheese nibbled by mice; some rotten pears on a plank; a little oil jar hanging inside a container that would have held twenty *cafisi;* a sack of flour at the bottom of a chest as large as a granary; the big wicker basket that was still waiting for Baroness Rubiera's wheat.

Finally he started again:

"We need God's help!... We're three mouths to feed, in the house!... D'you think it's nothing? We should also have some broth for Diego...I haven't liked his looks for some time now!... Did you see his face? The same as our dear father's, rest in peace, d'you remember?... When he went to bed not to get up again! And the doctor won't even come, because he's afraid that he won't be paid ...after all that money that he swallowed up during our dear father's last illness!... Aunt Rubiera has forgotten we are alive... and Aunt Sganci too..."

Grumbling these words, he followed his sister step by step, bending down to pick up from the floor the fava beans that had fallen from Grazia's apron. Then, as if waking up from a dream, he asked:

"Why don't you go to Aunt Rubiera's any more? She would have sent a pair of squabs, if she knew that Diego is not well...to make him some broth...."

Bianca became as red as cinders and lowered her eyes. For a while Don Ferdinando, blinking his eyelids and with his mouth open, waited for her answer. Then he went back to the storage pantry to put away the fava beans he had picked up from the floor. Soon after she saw him appear before her again, with that stunned look of his:

"If the sacristan's wife comes back, don't give her anything... next time! Leeches, that's what they are! The fava beans are nearly finished, didn't you see?... Something else... You should go to

Aunt Sganci's for a little oil . . . borrowing it . . . Be sure you tell her that you want to borrow it, because we weren't born to go begging for our food . . . since your aunt hasn't thought about it. . . . Soon we'll be in the dark . . . for Diego too who's sick . . . all night long! . . ."

And he opened his eyes wide, still motioning with both his hands and his head, a vague fright on his stunned face. In the distance you could hear from time to time the cough that was eating up Don Diego — across the doors, along the corridor, all over the house — implacable and painful as it was. . . . Bianca started each time, her heart bursting; she would bend to listen, or she would run away as if terrified, covering her ears.

"I can't stand it! No, I can't stand it! . . ."

Finally God gave her the strength to appear before him again — that day when Don Ferdinando had told her that their brother had taken a turn for the worse — in his filthy little room, as he lay on that miserable bed that looked like a dog's pallet. Don Diego was neither better nor worse. He lay there, waiting for what God would send him, just like all the Traos, without complaining, without trying to escape his destiny, careful only not to inconvenience others, and to keep his troubles and his miseries to himself. As he saw his sister come in, he turned his head, as if a shadow had fallen on his parchmentlike face. Then he motioned to her with his hand to come closer to his bed.

"I'm better . . . I'm better . . . my poor Bianca! . . . And you, how are you? . . . Why d'you show up only now? . . . why? . . ."

He stroked her head with the dirty and fleshless hand of a destitute sick man. A flaming-red color lingered on his hollow cheeks sprinkled with gray hairs.

"My poor Bianca! . . . I'm still your brother, you know? . . . Your brother who loves you . . . my poor Bianca! . . ."

"Don Ferdinando told me . . ." she stammered timidly. "Would you like some broth? . . ."

At first the sick man signaled no with his head, looking into the air as he was lying on his back. Then he turned his head, staring at her with his greedy eyes from the depths of his sockets, which seemed empty, sooty.

"Broth, you said? You have meat? . . ."

"I'll send to my aunt . . . to Aunt Sganci! . . ." Bianca quickly added, her cheeks suddenly ablaze.

A similar flame had passed over her brother's face.

"No! no!...I don't want it."

He didn't want the doctor either.

"No! no! What good will the doctor do?... Nothing but a fraud!...to wring money out of us.... The true doctor is up there! ...Whatever God wills... Besides, I feel better."

He really seemed to improve, after a few days; good broth and some old wine sent by Aunt Sganci helped him get out of bed, though he was still battered and short of breath. Even Donna Marianna came in person to see him; considerate in every way, she had a benevolent reproach on her genial face.

"Why? You are in this condition and I don't know anything about it? Are we among Turks? Are we relatives or aren't we? All these secrets! Always touchy and distant, all of you Traos!... Burrowed up like bears in this den! One of these mornings they'll suddenly find you stone-dead, and it will be a disgrace for all the relatives!... You haven't even said anything to me about that deal of the marriage!..."

Then she began to harp on this other string. Were they crazy, or what, to turn down a proposal like that?... A man on his way to becoming so wealthy, like Don Gesualdo Motta!...

"Don Gesualdo! Yes sir! Don't pay attention to the crazy ones! ...You can see very well the state they have brought you to!... A brother-in-law who could help you in all kinds of ways...who would lift you out of so many problems!... Ah!...ah!..."

Donna Marianna was looking around the squalid, dilapidated room, shaking her head. The others didn't breathe a word; Bianca with her head lowered; Don Ferdinando waiting for his brother to speak, his old owl's eyes staring at him.

At first Don Diego was stunned, and grumbled:

"Mastro-don Gesualdo!... Have we gotten to this point?... Mastro-don Gesualdo who wants to marry a Trao!..."

"Sure! Who d'you think is going to marry her?... Without a dowry? She is no longer a child either!... It's nothing but a treacherous blow!... What will she do when you close your eyes, you and your brother?... She'll become a servant, eh! Aunt Rubiera's servant, or somebody else's?..."

Don Diego got up from his bed as he was, in a flannel undershirt and with a kerchief on his head, his skinny legs shaking like leaves inside his worn-out underpants—an Ecce Homo! He began to roam about the room, wild-eyed, gesticulating and making incoherent speeches, coughing, breathing with difficulty, blowing his nose as if he were sounding a trumpet.

"Mastro-don Gesualdo!... She thinks we have gotten to this point, that a Trao would marry Mastro-don Gesualdo! You, would you agree, Bianca?... Tell us, would you say yes?..."

Bianca, extremely pale, without raising her eyes from the ground, nodded yes, slowly.

He threw his trembling arms in the air, and was not able to utter one more word. Don Ferdinando was not breathing a word either, frightened that Don Diego could not manage to convince Bianca.

"What can I tell you?" exclaimed their aunt. "D'you think it's a great future, to grow old like you...with so many problems?.. Sorry, I'm talking about this because we're relatives.... I do all I can myself to help you . . . but, after all, it's not very pleasant for you either.... And now that fortune offers itself to you, you answer by kicking it in the shins.... Sorry, but I'd call it a disgrace!"

All of a sudden Don Diego began to laugh, as if struck by an inspiration, winking his eye, rubbing his hands, and auspiciously nodding his head.

"All right! all right!... Is that all?... Because at the moment we have some problems?... It troubles you, doesn't it?... You're troubled by this life full of problems, my poor Bianca?... Are you afraid of the future?..."

He rubbed his hairy chin with his skeletal hand, as he kept winking and tried to make his pale smile look cunning.

"Come here...I won't tell you any more!... You too, Aunt! ... Come and see!..."

He climbed tremblingly on a chair to open a little cabinet inside the wall, just above the window, and pulled out piles of old dirty papers and parchments—the papers of the lawsuit—which was to be the great resource for the family, as soon as they would have enough money to prove their rights against the king of Spain; yellow, worn out, and dusty volumes that made him cough each time he turned a page. On the bed there lay spread out like a sheet an enormous genealogical tree: the family tree that sank its roots in the blood of a libertine king, as its coat of arms declared—red with three golden lilies on a golden bar, and the motto glorifying the fall of the foundress: *Virtutem a sanguine traho*—I draw strength from my bloodline.

He had put his glasses on, leaning his elbows on the side of his little old bed, face down, his eyes flaring up in the depths of his livid sockets.

"Six hundred years of interest, they owe us!... Quite a sum of money!... You'll solve your problems once and for all!..."

Bianca had grown up in the midst of such talk, which helped them pass the sad days. She had always seen those dirty old books spread out on the rickety tables and over the lamé chairs. Thus she didn't answer. Finally, her brother turned his head toward her, with an affable and melancholy smile.

"I'm talking for you two...for you and for Ferdinando.... At least you two will enjoy it.... As for me...I'm almost there... Here!... Here's the key!... You keep it!..."

At that kind of talk, Aunt Sganci first jumped up like a spring:

"My dear nephew, you're like a child!"

But she quickly calmed down, with the indulgent smile of one who is precisely intent upon making a child understand reason:

"All right!... It's quite all right!... Meanwhile, marry her to the man who's available now, and then, if you become so many Croesuses, so much the better."

Don Diego was disconcerted, seeing that his sister did not take the key, and started again:

"You too, Bianca?... You say 'yes' too?..."

She, slumped on a chair, lowered her head in silence.

"All right!... Since you want it...since you're not courageous enough to wait..."

Donna Marianna kept pleading Don Gesualdo's case, saying that that marriage was a golden deal, a lucky strike for all of them; congratulating herself with her niece, who was staring out of the window, her eyes shiny with tears; turning even to Don Ferdinando, who was looking at all of them one by one, stunned; patting on the shoulders Don Diego, who seemed not to hear anything—his eyes nailed on his sister, and shaking all over. At a certain point he stopped his aunt, stammering:

"Leave me alone with Bianca . . . I must say a few words to her . . . Leave us alone . . ."

Bianca raised her eyes in dismay — face to face with her corpse-like brother — after her aunt and Don Ferdinando had gone out.

The poor man still hesitated before adding what he had left to say, and stared at his sister with a more piercing and profound grief. Then he grasped her hands, as he shook his head and moved his lips without being able to utter a word.

"Tell me the truth, Bianca! . . . Why d'you want to leave your house? . . . Why d'you want to leave your brothers? . . . I know! I know! . . . Because of the other one! . . . You're ashamed to stay with us after the disaster that befell you! . . ."

He kept nodding his head, with an immense excruciating longing in his voice and on his face, bitter tears running down the bristly gray hairs of his beard.

"God forgives . . . Ferdinando doesn't know! . . . I . . . I . . . Bianca! . . . I love you like a daughter! . . . You're my child . . . Bianca! . . ."

He stopped, overwhelmed by a burst of tears.

More dead than alive, she shook her head slowly and mumbled: "No . . . no . . . It's not because of that . . ."

Very slowly Don Diego let his sister's hands fall, as if an abyss were opening between them.

"Then! . . . Do whatever you like . . . Do whatever you like . . . ."

And he turned his back, bent, without adding anything, dragging his feet.

VII

In the old La Gurna house that had been rented by Gesualdo Motta, they were expecting the bride and the groom. Before the door there was a band of urchins that Burgio's son, in his function as relative, struggled to keep back, threatening them with a stick. The stairway sprinkled with orange leaves; a four-burner lamp sitting on the railing of the landing; and Brasi Camauro — wearing a worsted blue hunting jacket, a laundry-clean shirt, and new boots — giving the last sweep inside the freshly painted doorway. Every moment there was a false alarm. The children shouted:

"Here they come! Here they come!"

Camauro dropped the broom, and people came looking from the lit-up balconies.

About an hour after dark there arrived Marquis Limòli, making room for himself with his bamboo cane. He saw the lamp, he saw the orange leaves, and said:

"Great!" But as he went upstairs, he almost broke his neck, and then he also could not restrain himself from swearing:

"Jackasses!... They've made a garbage dump here!..."

Brasi ran over with his broom.

"Should I sweep everything away, Marquis, sir? Should I throw everything out?"

"No! no... Now I've made it through. Rather, don't scratch too much with that broom.... We can smell the stable."

As he heard voices, Santo Motto who was waiting upstairs — dressed in new clothes, the bottom of his pants well strapped and his vest made of flowered satin — looked down the landing while he was putting his tailcoat on.

"Here I am! Here I am!... I'm here!... Ah, Marquis, sir!... Kiss your hand!..."

And he became somewhat confused when he did not see anyone but Limòli.

"Your servant, your servant, my dear Don Santo!... Don't kiss anything any more...now we're relatives."

At the top of the stairs appeared also Donna Sara Cirmena — the only one of all the bride's relatives who had been gracious enough to come — with a bunch of flowers on her head, her silk dress that had wrinkled like paper in her linen chest, and the family earrings that tore her ears — herself annoyed for having waited such a long time in a bath of perspiration. She began to scream from up there:

"But what are they doing? Something else happened?"

"Nothing, nothing," answered the Marquis going up very slowly. "I left first not to let them see that I was the only one of all the relatives in church...I came just to look around."

Don Gesualdo had done some shopping: new furniture,

brought especially from Catania, mirrors with gilded frames, stuffed chairs, lamps with crystal bell-glasses; a suite of lit-up rooms; when you saw them that way, with all the doors wide open, it was like looking into the lens of a *cosmorama*.

Don Santo walked ahead giving explanations, while he kept pulling up his sleeves that reached all the way to his finger tips.

"What? Nobody's here yet?" exclaimed the Marquis, as they got to the wedding chamber, all decked out like an altar. Santo pulled his head into his velvet collar, just like a turtle.

"Nothing's missing...I've been here since the Angelus bell. Everything's ready..."

"I thought I'd find at least your other relatives...*Mastro* Nunzio...your sister..."

"No, sir...they wouldn't feel at home.... There was a hell of a commotion! I came to keep an eye on the refreshments...."

And he opened the door to show them to him: a big table loaded with sweets and with bottles of liqueurs, still wrapped up in special paper as they had come from the city, and scattered carnations and Arabian jasmine—all that could be found in town, because Mrs. Capitana had sent word that flowers were needed; as many candlesticks as could be borrowed, from Sant'Agata's as well as from the other churches. Diodata had even beautifully arranged all the napkins, by standing them rolled up like so many skittle pins, each one with a flower at the top.

"Good! good!" approved the Marquis. "I've never seen anything like that!... And these two here...what are they doing?"

On either side of the table, like the Jews at the Holy Sepulcher, stood Pelagatti and Giacalone, who seemed made of papier-mâché, well washed and combed as they were.

"To serve the refreshments, yes sir!... *Mastro* Titta and the other barber, his friend, refused with an excuse!... They work only in aristocratic houses, those bums!... They were afraid to dirty their hands here, those two who play so many dirty tricks!..."

Giacalone, considerate, ran over with a bottle in each hand. The Marquis warded him off:

"Thank you, son!... You'll ruin my suit, look out!"

"Over there are the tubs with the sherbets," added Santo.

But as soon as he opened the kitchen door, they saw some

women, who had been looking through the keyhoke, running away.

"I see, I see, my friend. Leave'm alone; don't frighten them."

At that moment an uproar rose from the street and they ran to the balcony just in time to see the carriage arrive with the bride and groom. Nanni l'Orbo, seated on the box, his hat pulled down to his ears, cracked the whip like a real cart driver, and shouted:

"Make room!... You!... Watch out!..."

The mules, just taken from the herd, were kicking and snorting, so much so that the canon-priest Lupi suggested that they get out where they were, and Burgio had already gotten up to jump over the coach window. But suddenly the mules lowered their heads together and darted through the doorway at top speed.

"Oh, Hell!" exclaimed the canon-priest, falling with his nose to the bride's knees.

They were going upstairs arm in arm. Don Gesualdo with a glittering pin right in the center of his big satin necktie, his shoes shiny, gilded buttons on his suit, a wedding smile on his freshly shaven face; only the velvet collar, too high, bothered him. She looked younger and prettier in that white and fluffy dress, with bare arms, a little of her breast also bare, and the Trao angular profile softened by the hairdo then in fashion—her hair curled at the temples and fastened on top of her head with a high tortoise comb— which made the canon-priest smack his tongue, while the bride kept greeting the guests by nodding her head right and left—somewhat pale, timid, almost dismayed, with all that nakedness of hers, which blushed to display itself for the first time before so many eyes and so many lights.

"Long live the bride! Long live the groom!" The canon-priest began to shout cheerfully, waving his handkerchief.

Bianca received Aunt Cirmena's kiss, Uncle the Marquis' kiss, and walked along into the beautiful rooms, where there was no living soul.

"Hey! Hey! Careful! Don't lose your husband!" her uncle the Marquis shouted after her, in a general laughter.

"Are we all here?" grumbled Donna Sarina in a whisper.

The canon-priest was quick to answer:

"Yes, Ma'am. Small company, happy company."

Behind them Alessi was coming up, hat in hand, disconcerted

by all those lights and by all that pomp. He was hardly on the threshold when he began to stammer:

"Baroness Rubiera sends me... She says she can't come because she has a headache.... She sends regards to her niece, and to Don Gesualdo too...."

"Go in the kitchen, this way," answered the Marquis. "Tell them to give you something to drink."

Don Gesualdo caught that moment to whisper some advice to his brother.

"Watch out before all these people!... Sit down and don't move. And do what you see me do."

"All right. Leave it to me!"

Aunt Cirmena had taken charge of the bride, and had put on a matronly air that made her look angry. After everyone had found a place in the beautiful hall with mirrors, there was silence—everyone looking here and there to do something, and nodding his head in admiration. Finally the canon-priest thought he should break the ice:

"Don Santo, sit here. Come on here; don't be afraid."

"Me?" answered Santo, who heard himself addressed with a "Don."

"This is your brother-in-law," said the Marquis to Bianca.

The canon-priest went on a moment later:

"Look! Look! It's like Christopher Columbus' landing!"

At the entryroom doorway you could see a bunch of heads crowding against one another, some curious, some bashful, as if a mine were about to explode. The canon-priest spotted Don Gesualdo's nephew, Nunzio, among the urchins and winked at him to come inside. But the boy ran away like a savage. Still smiling, the canon-priest said:

"What a little devil!...just like his mother...."

The Marquis, stretched out in the armchair near his niece, looked like a president, and kept chattering as if to himself:

"Great! great!... Your husband has done things well!... Nothing's missing in this house!... You'll be like a princess here!... You just have to say a word...show a wish..."

"Then tell him to buy you different mules," put in the canon-priest laughing.

"It's true; you are a little pale.... Did you get scared in the carriage?"

"Those mules are too young...just taken from the herd... They're not used to it.... Nowadays they normally use horses for carriages," said the canon-priest.

"Of course! of course!" Don Gesualdo quickly answered. "As soon as I can. Money is there to be spent...when it's there."

The Marquis and the canon-priest kept the conversation going, Don Gesualdo approving by nodding. The others listened: Aunt Cirmena with her hands on her belly and with an affable smile that made words fall off your lips—a smile that said: "You just must!... Since I've come!... It was really worth dressing up like this!..."

Bianca looked like a stranger, in the midst of all that luxury. And her husband was embarrassed too, among so many people—his bride, his friends, the servants—before those mirrors in which he saw himself from head to toe, in his new clothes, reduced to watching how the others acted, even if he wanted to blow his nose.

"The harvest has turned out well!" said the Marquis aloud, so that the others would follow what he was leading up to. "I'm just repeating what I heard. Eh? Is it so, *massaro* Fortunato?..."

"Yes sir, thank God!... It's the prices that are not as they should be!..."

"There must be a lot of work in the fields! Nobody's in town any more."

At that Aunt Cirmena couldn't restrain herself:

"I saw Cousin Sganci on her balcony...I thought she was coming, as a matter of fact!..."

"Who knows? Who knows? The rain has turned the road into a mud puddle!... I almost broke my neck. But they say that it's good for the vines. Eh? eh? Isn't it so, *massaro* Fortunato?..."

"Yes sir, let's hope to God!..."

"They must all be busy getting ready for the grape-picking. Except us, Donna Sarina! We drink the wine without praying to God for the rain!... You must take your bride to Giolio for the grape-picking, Don Gesualdo!... Those are some vines; you'll see Bianca!"

"Of course!... She's the mistress!...of course!..."

"Just a moment!..." exclaimed the canon-priest, jumping to his feet. "I think I hear somebody!..."

Santo, who kept on his toes, his eyes on his brother, motioned him to ask if it was time to start with the refreshments. But the canon-priest came back in from the balcony almost immediately, shaking his head.

"No!... They're peasants walking back to town. Today's Saturday, and people are coming in until late."

"I thought so!" said Cirmena. "I've a sharp ear!... Whom are you waiting for?"

"Donna Giuseppina Alòsi, by God!... At least she always shows up!"

"The cavaliere must have detained her..." blurted out the Marquis, losing his patience.

Santo, who had already gotten up, sat down again, crestfallen.

"Excuse me! excuse me!" said the canon-priest. "Just a moment! I'll be right back!"

Donna Sarina ran after him into the entryhall, and you could hear the canon-priest answer aloud:

"No! close by...to the Captain's!..."

The Marquis, who was all ears, still pretended to admire the furniture and the rooms, and again said:

"Good! good!... An elegant house! You've been lucky to get into the La Gurna's nest!... Eh! eh!... There have been quite a few parties...in this very place!... I remember...the baptism of the youngest La Gurna...little Corrado.... Now they have moved to Siracusa...the entire family...after squandering whatever was left!... *Mors tua vita mea!*... Your death is my life!... Here you'll live like princes!... Eh! eh!... I'm old and have learned a lot!... We would do well here too, eh, Donna Sarina?...eh!..."

Donna Sarina fidgeted on her chair, as she was trying to hold her tongue:

"As for me!..." she said after a while, "thank God!... The proof is that the La Gurna boy, little Corrado, spends his summer vacations at my place. It isn't his fault, poor innocent boy!"

"No, no, it's better to sit in a soft chair like this, than having to go here and there to earn your bread and butter, like the La Gurnas! ...and if they can earn it!... And to have a good table ready, and a carriage to go for a little ride after your meals, and a vineyard for your vacation, and everything else!... Especially a table loaded

with good food!... I'm old and sorry that the title of Marquis cannot itself be served at the table...smoke is good only in the kitchen.
... I've learned a lot.... In many houses there is more smoke in the kitchen than steak on the table...those are the houses with the biggest coats-of-arms above the front door. And the most finnicky!... If I'm born again, I want to be *mastro* Alfonso Limòli, and be as rich as you are, my dear nephew.... To enjoy my money by myself ...without inviting anybody...no!"

"Quiet!... The bell's ringing!" cut in Donna Sarina. "It has been ringing for quite some time while you've been lecturing...."

However, it was the subdued tinkling typical of the poor. Santo ran to open and found himself face to face with the sacristan, followed by his wife, who was carrying under her arm a napkin that looked like a sack, as if she had come to pack for house moving. At first, Don Luca was embarrassed, as he saw the brother of Speranza, who together with her husband Burgio, had sent him lots of insults; but he didn't lose heart because of this, and soon found an excuse:

"Is the canon-priest Lupi here?... My wife told me that he was riding in the carriage with the bride and the groom...."

Grazia then entered unfolding her napkin very slowly, drawing out a little flask of perfumed water, plugged up with a tuft of rags.

"The holy water!... It's for Donna Bianca!"

And both husband and wife stood in the middle of the hall waiting calmly.

Just then the canon-priest Lupi came back, his face red, puffing, and wiping his sweat. And to avert any question, he immediately turned to the master of the house, with an indifferent air, smiling:

"Don Gesualdo...if you have plans for us to taste some sweet stuff!...I think it's about time!...I have to say mass at dawn, before going to the fields."

"Should I go?" blurted out Santo. "Should we start?"

The bride rose to her feet; all the others rose after her, and stood still in their places, waiting for whose job it was to lead the march. The canon-priest was busy making signs to Santo, and, seeing that he did not understand, he breathed his deep voice toward him just as he did in church, when he made a mistake during the service:

"You!... Give your arm to your sister-in-law!..."

But the brother-in-law did not feel up to that. Finally, they forced him by pushing him forward. Uncle Limòli, meanwhile, had gone ahead with the bride, and the canon-priest grumbled into Don Gesualdo's ear:

"Would you believe it?... Even Mrs. Capitana is being haughty! That one, who never fails to turn up when there are plates to lick! She's being haughty too! As if we didn't know where she came from, that grand dame!... No! No! What are you doing!..." he suddenly exclaimed, as he darted toward Santo.

Having lost his patience, Santo was quietly rolling up the sleeves of his jacket. Fortunately, his sister-in-law was talking with Uncle Limòli and didn't notice it. The Marquis, on the other hand, had something else on his mind, as he was trying to avoid Giacalone and Pelagatti, who wanted to give him a helping at all costs.

"They'll cause trouble, those two fellows!" he finally grumbled.

At that even Bianca managed a smile; then both of them moved away from the table, to avoid the danger.

"She doesn't want anything!..." said brother-in-law Don Santo coming back, as if a great load had been lifted from his stomach. "As for me, I did offer it to her!..."

"Not even a small glass of *Perfect Love?*" put in the canon-priest gallantly.

Aunt Cirmena began to laugh, and Santo looked at his brother to see what he was supposed to do.

"Eh! eh!..." added the Marquis with his dry little cough. "Eh! eh!..."

"Would you like something, Uncle?"

"Thank you, thank you, my dear Bianca...I've no more teeth or stomach...I'm an invalid...I'm just looking on...I can't do anything else...."

The canon-priest let them plead with him for a while, and then drew from his pocket a handkerchief that looked like a sheet. Meanwhile, Aunt Cirmena was filling the big purse she carried on her arm—a purse on which there was embroidered a whole dog, and which could hold an awful lot of stuff. The canon-priest, on the other hand, had pockets that reached all the way to his knees, under his cassock—two veritable sacks—and he could pack them with whatever he wanted, without being noticed. Bianca even presented her brother-in-law Santo a box of wedding candies with her own hands.

"For your sister and her children..."

"Say that she sent 'em herself...her sister-in-law..." added Mastro-don Gesualdo, gratefully smiling at her.

They were standing off to one side, while all the others crowded around the table. Then he whispered to her, with a certain tenderness:

"Great! I like you because you are wise and try to put peace in the family.... You don't know the commotion!... Especially my sister!... They have turned everything to poison for me, even my wedding day!..."

As she inspired trust in him, with her sweet face, he was about to unload himself of all the rest, when Aunt Cirmena came to interrupt him, by saying:

"Take care of the sacristan; he's there waiting with his wife."

As he saw so many good things come his way, Don Luca pretended to be surprised.

"No, no, sir! We didn't come for the sweets!... Don't bother, sir."

Meanwhile, his wife was spreading out her tablecloth, that looked like the one on the altar. But he, to show his gratitude, pretended to look into the air, arching his eyebrows with surprise.

"Look, Grazia!... All that stuff!... It costs a heck of a lot!"

Then, as soon as Don Gesualdo turned his back, he helped to load up.

"As if we had the plague!" grumbled Donna Sarina, her big purse full, as she came back in together with the canon-priest Lupi. "Not even her brothers came!...did you see?..."

"Poor old men!... Poor old men!..." he answered, waving his hand before his forehead, as if to say that those two no longer had any sense in their heads. Then he looked around, and lowering his voice:

"It was as if somebody had died, when we went to pick up the bride! Two old owls, that's what they are!... They kept creeping away from room to room, in the dark... Two old owls, that's what they are!... Donna Bianca, instead, wanted to do things properly ...at least for other people's sake!... After all, if she has brought herself to take this step!..."

He made another sign, with his thumb and his forefinger on his mouth. And seeing out of the corner of his eye that Bianca and her husband were coming back into the hall too, he said aloud, as if he were following up on another topic, and showing his full handkerchief:

"My fringe benefits!... The fruits of the ministry...."

The sacristan's wife, who had not noticed the bride, added:

"They're still there, both of them, behind the windowpanes, in the dark, looking into the square where there is nobody!...just like two mummies!...."

Donna Bianca heard those words as she went by.

"Best of health to you!" cut in the sacristan as he saw the mistress of the house. "It will be a feast for those children, when we get home!... Five children, Donna Bianca!..."

Then, turning to his wife who was staggering away with that other load on her belly:

"Best of health and male children!... As for property, you have plenty. We'll pray to the Lord to give you children.... We want you to look like Grazia in nine months..."

The Marquis stopped him by saying good-bye:

"Very good! Good evening, dear Don Luca!"

The guests had hardly left, when there was in the next room a hell of an uproar. The neighbors, the house servants, Brasi Camauro, Giacalone, and Nanni l'Orbo—a starving throng hurled themselves upon the leftovers, fighting over the sweets, tearing them out of each other's hands, coming to blows. And Santo, with the excuse of protecting those things, grabbed all he could, and stuffed it everywhere—in his mouth, in his pockets, inside his shirt. Nunzio, Burgio's son, had slipped in like a cat and had climbed onto the table, where he did his best too with kicks and punches, screaming as if possessed—the other urchins crawling on all fours underneath. Don Gesualdo, furious, wanted to run in and stop that racket with his stick; but his uncle, the Marquis, held him back by the arm:

"Leave them alone...by now!..."

Aunt Cirmena, who had at least enjoyed it a little, planted herself right in the center of the room, staring people in the face, as if to say that it was time to leave. Just at that moment the sacristan ran back in, panting, with an air of great mystery:

"There is the whole town!... Down in the street...they're watching!...Baron Zacco, the Margarones, Mendola's wife too... all the cream of the town!... Your wedding is making a sensation, Don Gesualdo!..."

And he left the same way he had come, in a hurry, elated.

Aunt Cirmena grumbled:

"What a nuisance!... At least if there were another way out!"

But the canon-priest, curious, decided to go and see.

Across the street, at the San Sebastiano corner, there was a gang of people; you could see white clothes showing against the dark of the street. Others were passing by slowly, on tiptoe, hugging the wall, their faces turned upward. You could hear people speaking in whispers, with stifled laughter too, and the noise of stealthy footsteps. Two men, who were coming back from the area of Santa Maria di Gesù, stopped when they saw the balcony being opened. And all of them slunk away here and there. There remained only Ciolla, who pretended to be going about his own business, singing:

"Love, oh love, what have you made me do?"

Donna Sarina and Marquis Limòli had also come close to the balcony. Then the Marquis said:

"Now you can leave, Donna Sarina. There isn't anybody left down there!..."

Aunt Cirmena jumped up like a spring:

"I'm not afraid, Don Alfonso!... I do what I like!... I'm here in Bianca's mother's place...since there is no other close female relative. We can't turn our backs on the bride as if she were an orphan...for the sake of family pride, if for nothing else!..."

"Ah? ah?..." meanwhile jeered the Marquis.

Donna Sarina hammered it again in his face, hardly restraining her voice:

"Don't pretend you don't know, Don Alfonso!... You know better than I!... It must matter to you too, who are one of the family... We must do it for the sake of others...if not for hers!..." And she rushed through the door to the wedding chamber, while she kept on shouting.

"All right, all right! Don't get angry... So we'll have to go!...

Eh, eh, Canon Lupi . . . I think it's time to go! . . . A little consideration! . . ."

"Ah! ah! . . . Ah! ah!" cackled the canon-priest.

"Good night, dear niece and nephew! I give you my blessing,
which costs nothing. . . ."

Bianca had become as pale as a washed-out rag. She rose to her
feet too, with a slight trembling in the muscles of her chin, her beautiful deep blue eyes bewildered, while she stumbled in her new dress,
and stammered:

"Uncle Limòli! Listen, Uncle Limòli! . . ." And she drew him
aside to speak to him in whispers, vehemently.

"They're all mad," cut in the Marquis aloud, he too becoming
vehement. "Fit to be put in an asylum! If I'm born again—I'll tell
'em too—I want to be *mastro* Alfonso Limòli! . . ."

"Great!" jeered the canon-priest. "I like what you say!"

"Good night! good night! Don't think about it! I'll go and see
them tomorrow morning . . . and in nine months, don't forget, I
want to be invited again for the baptism . . . the canon-priest Lupi
and myself . . . only the two of us. . . . There won't be any need for
Cousin Cirmena! . . ."

"Small company, happy company!" concluded the canon-
priest.

Don Gesualdo saw them to the door, tickled inside by the compliments of the canon-priest, who couldn't stop telling him how well
he had done things:

"Too bad that not all those invited came! They would have seen
that you spend like Caesar, I'm surprised about Mrs. Sganci! . . .
Baroness Rubiera too would have been happy to see how you respect
her niece . . . that you're not tight-fisted . . . since you have to be partners soon."

"Eh, eh!" answered Don Gesualdo, who at that moment felt the
ill-spent money surge inside him. "There's time! There's time! First a
lot of water will have to pass under the bridge that isn't there any
more. . . . Please, tell the Baroness!"

"What? What? Hadn't it already been decided? That you were
to be partners?"

"My partners are right here!" said Don Gesualdo slapping his vest pocket. "I wouldn't like Baroness Rubiera to be ashamed of having me as an associate.... Please, tell her!"

"He's right!" added the Marquis, stopping halfway down the stairs. "He's got the pride of his money, what the hell!... Cousin Rubiera could have been gracious enough.... She wouldn't have to suffer too much for so little, not she!"

"Who knows? Who knows why she didn't come?... There must be some other reason.... And her business...it's something else. ... Think it over!... You'll be without her support!... Then everybody will be against you!..."

"Everybody against me... How nice! Why?"

"Because of your money, by God!... Because you can put your finger in the pie too!... Besides, you have become one of them with this marriage!... That's a slap in the face, my friend! A slap in the face for all of them."

"D'you know what I can tell you?" the Marquis began to scream at that moment, lifting his head upward, "that if I didn't have my fixed income as a Knight of Malta, which saves me from starvation, I too would be forced to slap my aristocratic family past in the face ...I would be forced to become a street cleaner!"

And he left grumbling.

"Don Gesualdo," said Nanni l'Orbo, sticking his head in from the kitchen. "Here are the house servants who would like to kiss the mistress' hand...if everybody else is gone...."

"Hurry up! hurry up!" he answered, annoyed.

First they crowded in the doorway like a flock of sheep; then, they all filed by behind Nanni l'Orbo, smiling awkwardly, caps in hand, and the women huddled in their mantillas, genuflecting all the way to the floor like in church.

"This is Diodata," said Nani l'Orbo. "A poor orphan the boss has supported out of charity."

"Yes, Ma'am!... Best of health to you!..." And Diodata could not say more.

"He has a really big heart, Don Gesualdo!" continued Nanni l'Orbo vehemently. "He has given her a dowry! The good God rewards him for this."

Don Gesualdo was putting out the lights. Then he turned

around, all dressed up in new clothes, so much so that Diodata wouldn't dare raise her eyes on him, and concluded:

"All right. Are you happy?"

"Yes sir," answered Nanni l'Orbo, tenderly looking at Diodata. "Very happy!...she can say so too!..."

"Nanni had his eyes on that money for some time, not to let it get away!" added Brasi Camauro. "He was born with a silver spoon in his mouth!"

"He's marrying Diodata," Don Gesualdo then told his wife. "I'm marrying her to him."

The field-watchman added some other information, laughing:

"They were running after each other! We had to keep a watch on them too!... The boss still owes me an additional gift for this extra guard duty that wasn't in the bargain."

Then they all burst out laughing, for Carmine was very funny, as usual. The girl, her face ablaze, darted a wild animal's glance at him.

"It's not true! No, sir, Don Gesualdo!..."

"Yes! yes! And Brasi Camauro too! And Giacalone, when he came over for the cart!... All in perfect agreement, together!..."

There was no end to the laughter; beginning with Nanni l'Orbo, who was holding his sides. Only Diodata, as red as fire, with tears in her eyes, couldn't stop repeating:

"No, sir!... It isn't true! How could you say that, Carmine?... Don't you have a conscience?"

Donna Sarina appeared in the doorway again, her arms crossed, not saying a word; only the flowers being tossed about on her head were speaking for her.

"Enough now!" concluded the boss. "It's late, you can go now."

They offered their regards once more, bowing awkwardly, stammering confusedly all together, bumping into one another on their way out, and left with a heavy stamping of feet—like cattle. As soon as they were outside they began to laugh and joke together; Brasi Camauro and Pelagatti charging into each other; Nanni l'Orbo and Carmine exchanging dirty words and atrocious insults, their arms around each other's necks, like two brothers made cheerful by wine. The kind of boisterous frolicking that caused even Don Gesualdo to laugh.

"They're like animals!" he said, coming back. "Don't pay attention, my dear Bianca!"

"Just a moment!" screamed Aunt Cirmena pushing him back with her hands, as if he were forcing himself on her. "You can't come in now! Out! Out!"

And she shut the door in his face.

Diodata ran back upstairs at that moment, all excited and out of breath, with tears in her eyes.

"Don Gesualdo!... They won't let me go! Can you hear them down there?... Nanni and all the others!..."

"All right! What's the matter? Isn't he going to be your husband?..."

"Yes, sir... He says that's why!...that he's the boss.... They won't let me go in peace!... All of them!"

"Wait! Wait! I'm going to get a stick!"

"No! no!" screamed Nanni from the street. "We're going home. Nobody's going to touch her."

"D'you hear? Nobody's going to touch you. Go home... What are you doing now?"

She, standing two steps below him on the stairs, had secretly taken his hand, and kept kissing it, just like a really affectionate and faithful dog:

"Bless!...bless!..."

"Now the whimpering's beginning again!" he snorted. "I won't have a moment's peace tonight!..."

"No, sir...no whimpering.... Best of health to you, sir!... and to your bride too!... I only wanted to kiss your hand for the last time!... My legs are a little shaky... For you've been so good to me, you sir!"

"Good! Good!... Have fun too!... This must be a day to have fun! You've found a good husband too.... He'll be a good provider. ... And if there is a bad harvest, remember that my storehouse is open.... Aren't you happy too? Aren't you?"

She answered that she was happy, bowing repeatedly, for she had a knot in her throat and couldn't speak.

"All right! Now go home happy...and without thinking of anything, all right?...without thinking of anything!..."

As she was looking at him in a certain way, with her grieving eyes which seemed to read also the hidden pain in his heart, he began to shout so as not to think about it, as if he were angry:

"And without splitting hairs!... Without thinking of this, that, and the other.... The Lord is there for everybody.... Even if you are a poor foundling, and the Lord has helped you!... Besides, in case of need, I'm here...I'll do all I can...I don't have a heart of stone, no I don't!... You know! Go, go; go home happy!..."

But Diodata, who was turning her back on him, her breast pressed against the railing, as if she felt she was dying of a broken heart, could not suppress her sobs, which shook her from head to foot. Then her boss burst out swearing:

"Damn it!... Goddammit!"

At that moment Aunt Cirmena appeared at the top of the stairs, her shawl over her head, her big purse on her arm, and her eyes wet with tears, as was becoming the mother-role that had then fallen on her.

"Here I am, Don Gesualdo! here I am!" and she stretched out her arms like a crucifix to throw them around his neck. "There is no need for a lecture. You're a sensible man.... My poor Bianca!... I'm so moved; see!"

She looked for her batiste handkerchief among all the things stuffed in her big purse, and wiped her eyes. Then she again kissed the groom, and called the servant who was downstairs waiting with a lantern:

"Don Camillo! Light up; it's time to go. Don Camillo? Hey? What are you doing? Are you asleep?"

From the street Ciolla answered passing by again with his guitar:

"Love, oh love, what have you made me do?"

And some other loafers were following him, accompanying him with grunts.

"No!" exclaimed Aunt Cirmena, planting herself before her nephew, as if she wanted to prevent him from doing something foolish. "Don't listen.... They're drunk! They're rabble, full of envy! Go to your wife, instead. Take good care of her.... She cannot be handled like anybody else.... We come from another mold...the

whole family . . . I feel I'm leaving my own blood in your hands, now!
. . . I never had a daughter. . . . I never went through anything like
this! . . . I feel all upset! . . . No! No! Don't listen to me! . . . I'll calm
down . . . You, Don Camillo, walk ahead with the lantern. . . ."

He turned his back:

"Why so much talk? After all, are we husband and wife, yes or
no?"

As he entered the wedding chamber, he drew a big sigh.

"Ah! thank God, it's over! It's taken some doing . . . but it's over,
thank God! . . . I wouldn't do it again, I swear to God, if we were to
start all over again! . . ."

He wanted to make his bride laugh too, to put her in a good
mood, so that they would be more at ease together, the way it should
be between husband and wife. But she, who was sitting before the
mirror, turning her back to the door, started as she heard him come
in, her face ablaze. Then she became paler than before, and her
delicate features suddenly looked even sharper.

Just what Aunt Cirmena had said! A girl who fainted for no
reason at all, and tied up your tongue and your hands. He was
annoyed—that's it—by that wedding day that hadn't given him a
single good moment.

"Hey? . . . Why don't you say anything? . . . What's the
matter? . . ."

He remained embarrassed for a moment, without knowing
what to say either, humiliated in his new clothes, in the middle of
his furniture, which had cost him a fortune.

"Listen . . . if that's the way it is . . . if you take it that way too.
. . . Then I'll say good-bye and sleep on a chair, I swear to God! . . ."

She stammered some unintelligible words, a gurgle of timid
and confused sounds, and bowed her head obediently to begin to
take off her tortoise comb, with her frail hands, a little wasted at the
tips—the hands of a poor girl accustomed to doing everything in the
house.

"Great! great! That's how I like you! . . . If we get along the way
I mean, our home will prosper . . . prosper a lot! I assure you! we'll
make those who envy us bite the dust. . . . Did you see tonight? How
they wouldn't come to the wedding! . . . So much money thrown
away! . . . Did you see how I was eating my heart out, and yet I was

laughing?... He who laughs last laughs longest!... Come on, come
on, why are your hands trembling?... Am I not your husband now?
... In spite of those who envy us!... What are you afraid of?...
Listen...that Ciolla...will make me do something foolish!..."

She once more stammered a few unclear words, which again
died out on her pale lips, and for the first time she raised her eyes to
him—those sweet, deep blue eyes that promised him she would be
the loving and obedient wife people had said she would. Then,
happy and with the broad laughter that smoothened his face and his
heart, he answered:

"Let him sing. Now I don't care about Ciolla...about him and
all the others!... They're dying with envy because my business is
going great guns, thank God! No, you won't regret what you did!...
You're good!... You're not as stuck up as all your people...."

His heart was swollen with an unusual tenderness, as he was
helping her to undo her hair. His big hands helping a Trao, and
feeling themselves become very light in the midst of all that fine
hair! His eyes lit up at the lace veiling her white, delicate shoulders,
at her short, puffed sleeves that almost put wings on those shoulders.
He liked the golden down blooming in the last joints of her spine,
the scars left by the awkward vaccinator on her slender and white
arms, those small hands that had worked as much as his own, and
were trembling under his eyes, that nape which paled and flushed,
all those humble signs of hardship that brought her closer to him.

"I want you to be better than a queen, if we can get along the
way I hope!... I want to put the whole town at your feet!... All
those jackasses that are now laughing and gloating over us!...
You'll see! You'll see!... He's got a good stomach, Mastro-don Gesualdo...to store up for years and years all that he wants to...and
good legs too...to get wherever he wants to.... You're good and
you're beautiful! First class stuff you are!... First class!..."

She pulled her head into her shoulders, like a trembling dove
that's about to be seized.

"Now I really love you, you know?... I'm afraid to touch you
with my hands.... My hands are big and rough because I've worked
so much...I'm not ashamed to say so...I've worked to get this far.
... Who could have known?... No, I'm not ashamed, no! You're
beautiful and you're good...I want to make you like a queen...."

Everybody at your feet!... These nice little feet! You decided yourself to come...with these nice little feet...into my house... The
mistress!... My own beautiful lady!... Look, you make me talk
nonsense!..."

But she was listening to something else. She seemed to look into
the mirror, far, far away.

"What are you thinking about? Still about Ciolla!... I'm going
to end up in jail, on my wedding night!..."

"No!" she cut in stammering, in a whisper. "No...listen...I
must tell you something..."

She looked as if she didn't have a drop of blood left in her veins,
so pale and beaten she was. She moved her trembling lips two or
three times.

"Speak up," he answered. "Whatever you wish. I want you to
be happy too!..."

As it was July and very hot, he also took off his suit, waiting.
She brusquely drew back, as if she had received a blow in the chest;
and became stiff, very pale, her eyes circled by black rings.

"Speak up, speak up!... Tell me in this ear...here, where
nobody else can hear us!"

He was laughing happily, with his broad peasant laugh, in the
warm impulse that was beginning to make his head turn, stammering incoherent words, in shirtsleeves, pressing on his heart—which
was beating all the way up to his throat—that delicate body which
he felt shudder and almost rebel; and as he lifted her head gently,
he immediately became dispirited. She wiped her feverish eyes, her
face still painfully contracted.

"Ah!...what a pleasure!... Aunt Cirmena was right!... Great
fun indeed!... After so much hard work, so many bitter pills!... So
much money spent!... We could be really happy here...two people who love each other!... No sir! Not even this do I get! Not even
on my wedding day.... Goddammit!... At least tell me what's the
matter!"

"Don't pay attention to me...I'm much too upset..."

"Ah! that Ciolla!... Again!... I swear to God, I'm going to
throw a flowerpot at him!... I'm going to put an end to him too, on
my wedding night!"

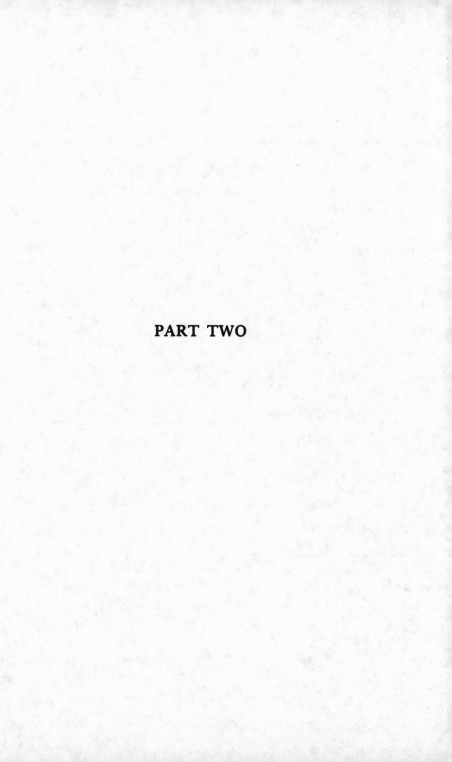

PART TWO

I

"Three onze and fifteen!... One!...two!..."

"Four onze!" replied Don Gesualdo matter-of-factly.

Baron Zacco got up, as red as if he was having a stroke. He groped about looking for his hat, and started on his way out. But as he reached the threshold, he ran back headlong, foaming at the mouth, almost beside himself, screaming:

"Four and fifteen!..."

And he stopped panting before the desk of the judges, burning up his opponent with lightning looks. Don Filippo Margarone, Peperito, and the others of City Hall, who were presiding at the auction of the City lands, whispered into each other's ears. Don Gesualdo took a pinch of snuff, as he quietly kept on figuring in the little notebook on his knees. Then he raised his head, and countered in a calm voice:

"Five onze."

Suddenly the Baron became as white as a sheet. He blew his nose, pressed his hat down on his head, and then he walked through the door shouting:

"Ah!... If that's the way it is... If it's a stupid whim!... If it's a personal attack!... Good-bye to those who stay!"

The judges were figeting about on their chairs as if they had the colic. Canon-priest Lupi suddenly got up and ran to whisper a word in Don Gesualdo's ear, with his arm around his neck.

"No, sir," answered Don Gesualdo aloud. "No such nonsense ...I'm looking after my own interest and nothing more."

A murmur ran through the people attending the auction. All the other bidders had stepped back, stunned, sticking out their tongues. Then young Baron Rubiera stood up, haughtily pushing his chest out, stroking his scanty beard, without paying attention to the signs Don Filippo was making from a distance, and let his own bid fall, with the sleepy air of one who does not care about money:

"Five onze and six!... I say...!"

"For God's sake," Notary Neri whispered into his ear pulling one of his coattails. "Baron, sir, let's not be foolish!..."

"Five onze and six!" The young Baron repeated without paying attention and looking around triumphantly.

"Five fifteen."

Don Nini became red in the face, and opened his mouth to bid; but the Notary covered it with his hand. Margarone thought that the moment had come for him to take on a presidential air.

"Don Gesualdo!... This is not a game!... You certainly have money...I don't deny it...but that is a big figure...for a man who until yesterday carried rocks on his shoulders...if I may say so without offense.... Honestly... "Look at what I am, not at what I was," says the proverb.... But City Hall wants a warranty.... Think about it!... They are about five hundred salme... They add up to...they add up to..."

And he put his glasses on and began to write figures atop figures.

"I know what they add up to," answered Don Gesualdo laughing. "I thought about it while carrying rocks on my shoulders.... Ah! Don Filippo, you don't know what a great satisfaction it is to have gotten as far as this, face to face with you, sir, and with all those that were my bosses, and each one of us stating his own reasons, and looking after his own interest!"

Don Filippo lay his glasses on the old sheet of paper; he gave a stunned look at his colleagues, right and left, and kept silent, dazed. In the crowd pressing against the doorway there was a commotion. *Mastro* Nunzio Motta wanted to get inside at any cost, to give a beating to that son of his, who was throwing money away like that. Burgio had a hard time keeping him back. Margarone rang the bell to call for silence.

"All right!... Yes, all right!... However, the law states..."

As he kept stammering, yellow-faced Canali suggested the answer, pretending to blow his nose:

"Sure!... Who guarantees for you?... The law states..."

"I'm my own guarantee," answered Don Gesualdo laying on the desk a sack of gold coins which he had pulled out of his hunting jacket.

At that they all opened their eyes wide. Don Filippo was dumbfounded.

"Gentlemen!" yelled Baron Zacco in a fury, as he was coming back in. "Gentlemen!...look at that...look to what point we've come!..."

"Five fifteen!" repeated Don Gesualdo taking another pinch of snuff. "I bid five onze and fifteen tarì a salma for the lease of the City lands. Let's go on with the auction, Don Filippo."

Young Baron Rubiera jumped up like a spring, all his blood rushing to his face. Not even chains could have held him back.

"Six onze," he stammered beside himself. "I bid six onze a salma."

"Take him outside! Take him away!" screamed Don Filippo getting halfway up.

Some people were applauding. But Don Nini was persisting, as pale as his shirt, now.

"Yes, sir! Six onze a salma! Secretary, write down my bid!"

"Stop!" shouted the Notary raising both his hands in the air. "As to the legality of the bid!... I've my reservations!..."

And he rushed at the young Baron, as if they were coming to blows. There, in the opening to the balcony, face to face, his eyes jumping out of his head, blowing his fiery breath into Nini's face:

"Baron, sir!... If you want to throw your money out of the window!...go and play cards!...gamble only the money out of your pocket!..."

Don Nini was snorting worse than a furious bull. Peperito had nodded to the canon-priest Lupi to come to him, and they had begun to whisper together, bending over the desk, and shaking their heads like two hens pecking in the same pot. Such was the excitement that the canon-priest's hands were shaking on top of the old papers. The Cavaliere took him by the arm and together they joined the Notary and the young Baron, who were loudly arguing in a corner of the hall. Don Nini was beginning to give in, his face limp and his legs weak. Then the canon-priest motioned to Don Gesualdo to come close too.

"No," signaled the latter without moving.

"Listen!... There is that business of the bond!... The bridge is gone, never mind!... We can fix that business of the bond now...."

"No," continued Don Gesualdo. He was like a stone wall. "The business of the bridge...a trifle, in comparison."

"Peasant! Mule! Bullhead!" the Baron began to inveigh once more under his breath.

Don Filippo, after the first moment of excitement, had again sat down, and was gravely wiping his sweat. While the canon-priest was talking in whispers to Mastro-don Gesualdo, the Notary began to make signs from the distance. Don Filippo bowed toward Canali's ear. Stealthily, in a falsetto voice, the auctioneer repeated:

"The last bid for the City lands! Six onze a salma!... One!... two!..."

"Just a moment, gentlemen!" cut in Don Gesualdo. "Who guarantees this last bid?"

At that remark they were all left open-mouthed. Don Filippo opened and closed his own mouth without finding a word. Finally, he answered:

"Baron Rubiera's bid!... Eh? eh?"

"Yes, sir. Who'll guarantee for Baron Rubiera?"

The Notary threw himself against Don Nini who seemed intent upon making a slaughter. Peperito was twisting about as if he had been slapped in the face. Even the canon-priest was dismayed. Margarone stammered wild-eyed:

"Who'll guarantee for Baron Rubiera?... Who'll guarantee?..." All of a sudden he changed his tone, turning it into a joke:

"Who'll guarantee for Baron Rubiera?... Ah! ah! Great! that's a good one!"

And many people, like him, held their sides from laughter.

"Yes, sir," replied Don Gesualdo matter-of-factly. "Who'll guarantee for him? The property belongs to his mother."

At those words the laughter stopped, and Don Filippo began stammering again. People crowded in the doorway as at a theater. The canon-priest, who looked still paler under a four-day beard, pulled his companion by the jacket. The Notary had managed to push the young Baron against the wall, while the latter, in the midst of the commotion, blurted out:

"Cuckold!... Happy cuckold!... Woman savior!"

"The Baron's word!" finally said Don Filippo. "Baron Rubiera's word is worth more than your gold coins!...Don...Don..."

"Don Filippo!" cut in Don Gesualdo without losing his great calm. "I've witnesses here to enter everything in the official record."

"All right! We'll enter everything in the official record!... Write that Baron Rubiera has made the bid on behalf of his mother!..."

"Very well!" added Don Gesualdo. "If that's the way it is, you may write that I bid six onze and fifteen a salma."

"Madman! murderer! enemy of God!" You could hear *mastro* Nunzio shout from the middle of the crowd in the next room.

There was an uproar. The Notary and Peperito pushed out of the door the young Baron who was ranting and raving, shaking his hands in the air. Meanwhile, the canon-priest, convulsed, threw himself at Don Gesualdo, pressing close against him, almost sitting on his knees, his arms around his neck, beseeching him in whispers, with a desperate air, with fiery words, pouring himself down his ears, shaking him by the lapels of his jacket, as if he wanted to work him over, to make him listen to reason.

"It's crazy!... What do you intend to do, my dear Don Gesualdo?..."

"Don't worry, my dear Canon Lupi. I have figured everything out. I don't lose my head, I don't."

Don Filippo Margarone had been ringing the bell for five minutes, to ask for a glass of water. His colleagues were also wiping their sweat, out of breath. Only Don Gesualdo remained seated in his place like a rock, next to his sack of gold coins. At a certain point, out of the racket in the next room, burst into the hall *mastro* Nunzio Motta, wild-eyed, shaking with anger, his white hair standing on end, towing behind him his son-in-law, Burgio, who was trying to hold him back by a sleeve of his jacket, like a madman.

"Don Filippo, sir!... Am I the father, yes or no?... Am I the boss, yes or no?... If my son Gesualdo is crazy!...if he wants to send us all to rack and ruin!...there's the Law, Don Filippo, sir!... Send for Don Liccio Papa!..."

Speranza, in the doorway, her baby at her breast, was tearing her hair and howling, as if she were being slaughtered.

"For God's sake! For God's sake!" pleaded the canon-priest, running from one to the other.

"The bridge money!... He wants to ruin me!... He's his own father's enemy!" howled *mastro* Nunzio.

"Was it any of your money, by any chance?" the canon-priest finally blurted out. "Wasn't it your son's own blood? Didn't he make that money himself, with his own hard work?"

They were all standing up, shouting. You could hear Canali scream louder than the others, trying to quiet Don Nini Rubiera.

Baron Zacco, dispirited, was standing with his shoulders against the wall, his hat on the back of his head. The Notary had rushed downstairs, taking the steps four at a time, so as to run to Baroness Rubiera's. On the stairs there was a coming and going of curious people, arriving at every moment, attracted by the racket coming from City Hall. From the square Santo Motta pointed at the balcony, shouting at anybody who wasn't interested, about his brother's exploits. Even Donna Marianna Sganci had put her head out, under her little umbrella, shading her eyes with her hand.

"I swear to God!... I made him and I'm going to unmake him!" howled old Motta, as ferocious as ever.

"Make room! Make room!" you could hear from the midst of the crowd.

It was Giuseppe Barabba, waving a note in the air.

"Canon! Canon Lupi!..."

The canon-priest elbowed himself forward.

"All right," he said after reading it. "Tell Mrs. Sganci that it's all right, and I'll be with her in a second."

Barabba ran to deliver the same message in the next room. He was almost suffocated by the rush. The canon-priest even tore his cassock, while the Baron stretched his arms to read the note. Canali, Barabba, and Don Nini were quarreling. Then Canali began to shout:

"Make room! Make room!" and he walked forward smiling, toward Don Gesualdo:

"Young Baron Rubiera is right here and would like to shake hands with you!"

"Why not? He's welcome! I'm not angry at anybody!"

"That's what I mean! What the hell! Now you're relatives, after all!..."

And pulling the young Baron by his jacket, he hugged them both, almost forcing them to kiss each other. Baron Zacco ran to throw himself into their arms too, big tears shining in his eyes.

"Damned be the devil!... I'm not made of bronze!... What nonsense!..."

The Notary arrived at that very minute. First he went to take a quick look at the secretary's old papers, and then he began to clap his hands.

"Long live peace! Long live harmony!... Haven't I always told you?"

"Look what your aunt Donna Marianna Sganci is writing to me!..." said the canon-priest, moved, showing the open letter to Don Gesualdo.

And he went to the balcony and waved the sheet of paper in the air, like a white flag; while Mrs. Sganci from her balcony answered by nodding her head.

"Peace! Peace!... You're all one family!..."

Canali ran to grab *mastro* Nunzio, Burgio, even Santo Motta—in shirtsleeves—and pushed them into the arms of their new relatives. The canon-priest embraced even Speranza and her baby. The very stones would have wept.

"His wife makes you cousins..."

"True enough," added Don Nini, still somewhat red in the face. "Bianca and I grew up together...just like brother and sister.

"Dear Don Nunzio...d'you remember the gypsum kiln...near Fontanarossa?..."

The grumpy old man shrugged his shoulders, to shake off Baron Zacco's heavy hand, and answered rudely:

"My name's *mastro* Nunzio, Baron, sir. I don't have a swelled head like my son."

"And why then? For whose benefit are you fighting?... Who can enjoy all that money thrown away?..." concluded Canali heatedly.

"It's crazy! Childish!... A rash decision!... The hot day!... A silly whim...a misunderstanding.... Now it's all over! Let's go! Let's not make the whole town laugh at us!..."

And the Notary was trying to lead them all out of there.

"Just a moment," cut in Don Gesualdo. "The candle is still burning. Let's first see if they have written down my last bid."

"What, what?... What are you talking about?... What d'you mean!... Are we starting all over again?..." Again there was an uproar. "Aren't we friends any more? Aren't we relatives?"

But Don Gesualdo persisted, worse than a mule:

"Yes, sir, we're relatives. But we came here for the lease of the City lands. I've bid six onze and fifteen tarì a salma."

"Peasant! Bullhead!"

In the midst of all that commotion, Don Filippo was forced to sit down again in his arm chair, puffing. He gulped a full glass of water, and rang the bell.

"Gentlemen," shouted the secretary, "the last bid . . . at six onze and fifteen."

They had all gone into the next room to argue, at the top of their lungs, leaving Don Gesualdo alone before the desk. In vain the canon-priest, uneasy, breathed into his ear:

"You won't make it, no! . . . They've all banded together on this! . . ."

"Six onze and fifteen a salma! . . . Last bid!"

"Don Gesualdo! Don Gesualdo!" yelled the Notary, as if the roof were about to cave in.

They all came back in again, like a procession: Baron Zacco, fanning himself with his hat; the canon-priest and Canali, arguing together in whispers; Don Ninì, more restive, behind the others. The Notary made a circular gesture with his arms, to group them all around himself:

"Don Gesualdo! . . . Listen here! . . ."

He glanced around, like a conspirator, and lowered his voice:

"A serious proposal!" and made another meaningful pause. "First of all the bond money, a large sum! . . . It was bad luck . . . an accident . . . but it wasn't your fault, Don Gesualdo . . . nor was it yours, *mastro* Nunzio. . . . It's only fair that you don't lose it! . . . We'll fix everything! . . . You, Baron Zacco, sir, you hate leaving the lands that have been in your family for forty years? . . . All right! . . . Baroness Rubiera now wants her share too? . . . She has more than three thousand head of cattle on her hands. . . . This is all right too. Don Gesualdo, here, has money to spend too; he wants to speculate on the leases . . . . Very well! Divide the lands among the three of you . . . without quarrels, without stupid whims, without fighting for other people's benefit. . . . For whose benefit, after all? . . . City Hall's! Which means nobody's! Let's throw over the auction! . . . I'll find an excuse! . . . In a week we start the bidding again at the original price; with one bid only . . . I won't . . . nor will they! . . . Canon Lupi! . . . In your name, Don Gesualdo. . . . We trust one another. . . . We're gentlemen! One bid at the original price; and the lands will be awarded to you without a cent's increase. Only a small commission for me and the canon-priest.... And you divide the rest among the three of you, casually and informally...all in perfect agreement. How d'you like it? Is it clear?"

"No, sir," answered Don Gesualdo. "I'll take all the lands myself."

As the others were happily nodding their approval at the triumphant glances the Notary was again casting around, that answer fell on top of them like a bucket of cold water. The Notary at first was dumbfounded; then he turned around on his heels and walked away humming a tune. Don Nini ran away without saying anything. The Baron this time pretended he was really pressing his hat down on his head. The canon-priest himself jumped up like a fury:

"Then I don't want to have anything to do with you!... If you want to break your neck, the balcony is right there!... They offer you a good deal!... They hold out their hands to you!... I'll leave you to yourself, I swear to God!"

But Don Gesualdo persisted, his silly little smile on his lips—he being the only one who would not lose his head in that racket.

"You're a jackass!" he told him still smiling.

The canon-priest opened his eyes wide and became docile again, as he wanted to see what that devil of a Mastro-don Gesualdo was scheming now.

The Notary, careful, managed to control himself before the others, and came back with a smile on his lips and his snuffbox in his hand.

"So...you want them all?"

"Eh...eh... What are we here for then!" answered Don Gesualdo.

Notary Neri offered him his open snuffbox, and continued in a low voice, with a tone of cordial confidence:

"What the hell will you do with them?... About five hundred salme of land!..."

Don Gesualdo shrugged his shoulders.

"My dear Notary, did I ever stick my nose into those dirty old books of yours? Did I?"

"If you take it that way, Don Gesualdo, listen to me...let's talk about it between us...and let's forget about whims...even about friendship...let's stick to business...."

At each phrase he bent his head to the right and to the left with a rhythm that he thought convincing.

"If you want them all, we'll make you pay twice as much, and half your profit will vanish right away...without considering the risks...the bad harvests!... Leave us the bone, my dear Don Gesualdo! Stop our mouths... We have teeth, and know how to bite! We'll go to rack and ruin, and so will you!"

Don Gesualdo kept shaking his head, jeering as if to say: "No, sir! Only you will go to rack and ruin!" And he kept repeating:

"Did I ever stick my nose into those old papers of yours?"

Then, seeing that the Notary was becoming green with anger, he decided to offer him a pinch of snuff himself.

"Since I see that you're speaking to me straight from the heart, I'll explain this mystery to you in a few words. I'll lease the City lands...the County lands too...all of them, understand, Notary, sir? Then I can fix the prices of the harvests, understand?... I'm telling you this because you're a friend, and because to be able to do this one must have a great deal of capital in hand, and a heart as big as the plain of Santa Margherita, my dear Notary. That's why I'm going to push the auction where you and the others can't reach. But watch out! At a certain point, if it isn't in my interest, I'll pull out, and will leave you with a burden that will break your backs...."

"This is it?"

"Eh? eh? How d'you like it?"

The Notary looked here and there, as if he were searching for something on the floor, pressed his hat definitely on his head, and turned his back:

"All the best to those who stay!...I'm leaving.... There is nothing more to do."

The canon-priest, who had been there listening open-mouthed, moved close to his partner with enthusiasm — as soon as they were alone.

"What a coup, eh? Don Gesualdo! You're quite something!... My commission will still be there?"

Don Gesualdo reassured the canon-priest by nodding, then he said to Margarone:

"Don Filippo, sir, let's go on...."

"I'm not going any further," Margarone finally answered in

anger. "The law states . . . There is no competition any more! . . . I don't see any guarantee! . . . I must consult with my colleagues."

And he began to gather his old papers together as fast as he could.

"Ah! that's how you treat people? . . . That's the way? . . . All right! We'll talk about it later, Don Filippo, sir . . . A petition to His Majesty! . . ."

The canon-priest, with his cloak on his arm like a Roman orator, pleaded his friend's cause, threatening. Instead Don Gesualdo, calmer, picked up his money and his notebook crammed with figures.

"I'll still be here, Don Filippo, sir, when you reopen the auction."

"Gentlemen! . . . Just look at that. . . . We've gotten to this point!" grumbled Margarone.

On the steps of City Hall, and in the whole town, there was a turmoil — when they heard about the battle that had been fought to take away from Baron Zacco the City lands that had been in his family for forty years, and about the price they had commanded. People put their heads out of the doors to see Mastro-don Gesualdo pass by.

"Just look, my dear gentlemen, what it has come to! . . ."

Mastro-don Gesualdo was going home as cool as a glass of water, his hands in his pockets. . . . He had more money in his pockets than hair on his head! . . . and was causing trouble for the big shots in town! In the entry room Don Giuseppe Barabba was waiting, in uniform:

"Don Gesualdo, sir, my mistress came to see you . . . she's inside . . . yes sir!"

Donna Marianna, all dressed up, was sitting on the silk sofa, under the big mirror, in the beautiful yellow room.

"My dear nephew, now you've done it! You've stirred up hell in the whole family! . . . Sure! . . . Cousin Zacco's wife came to show me her bruises! . . . The Baron seems to have gone mad! . . . He vents his anger on anyone within reach . . . And Cousin Rubiera too . . . she says that's a treacherous blow! that the canon-priest Lupi had put you all in perfect agreement, and then all of a sudden . . . Is it true, my dear nephew? . . . I came just to talk about it with Bianca. . . .

Come, Bianca, help me. Let's try to straighten things out. You, Don
Gesualdo, will give her this present . . . to your wife. Eh? Won't you?"

Bianca was glancing timidly first at her and then at her husband, huddled as she was in a corner of the sofa, her hands on her
belly, and on her head the silk kerchief she had hastily put on to
receive her aunt. She opened her mouth to answer something, while
she was made to feel uneasy by Donna Marianna, who kept on urg-
ing her.

"Eh? what d'you say? Now it's your business too."

Bianca again looked at her husband, and remained silent, in
embarrassment. But he helped her solve the problem.

"I say no," he answered simply.

"Ah? ah? Is that what you say?"

Donna Marianna was open-mouthed too for a moment. Then
she became as red as a rooster:

"Ah! you say no? . . . Excuse me . . . It isn't any of my business. I
just came here to talk about it with my niece, because I wouldn't like
quarrels and fights among relatives. . . . Even with your brothers,
Bianca . . . what didn't I do to convince them too . . . especially Don
Diego, who's so stubborn! . . . A disaster . . . A punishment of God!"

"What can you do?" answered Don Gesualdo. "Not all deals
come out right. I too, if I had known . . . I'm not talking about the
woman I married, no! I've no regrets! . . . Good, concerned, obedient . . . I'm telling you here, in front of her. . . . But as for the rest
. . . let's forget it!"

"You're right, let's forget it. That's why I came to have a talk
with Bianca, because I know that you love her. Now you're husband
and wife, as God wills. She's the boss too . . ."

"Yes, Ma'am, she's the boss. But I am her husband . . ."

"Obviously I was wrong," said Mrs. Sganci, stung to the quick.

"No, you weren't wrong, Ma'am. The point is that Bianca
doesn't know about these things, poor girl! Isn't it true, Bianca, that
you don't know, tell us!"

Bianca, obediently, said "yes" lowering her head.

"Let it be as if we hadn't said anything. Let's not talk about it
any longer. I've done my duty as a good aunt, trying to bring you
together. . . . Today too, down there, at City Hall, did you see? . . .
What I had Canon Lupi tell you? . . ."

"*Lupus in fabula*, speak of the devil . . . ," he exclaimed walking in as if in his own house, hat on, his cloak swaying behind him, rubbing his hands. "You were maligning me, eh? My ears were burning . . . ."

"You rather, you old scoundrel. You look like somebody who's just won the lottery!"

"The lottery? You rub it in too? A poor devil who works hard from morning to night! . . ."

"We were talking about the City lands lease . . ." said Don Gesualdo calmly, taking a pinch of snuff, "just to chat a little . . . ."

"Ah! ah!" answered the canon-priest; and he began to stare into the air.

Aunt Sganci observed the new furniture, turning her head here and there.

"Beautiful! Beautiful! Cousin Cirmena had told me. Too bad I wasn't feeling well on the evening of your wedding . . . ."

"And the others weren't either, Donna Marianna!" answered the canon-priest with a little laugh. "It was an epidemic! . . ."

"No! no! I can assure you! On my word! . . . Baroness Rubiera, the poor woman! . . . And her son too . . . I can still hear him complaining . . . 'Aunt, how could I?' "

Donna Marianna stopped.

"But we said that we wouldn't talk about it any more. Yet he's sorry not to be able to come to pay his respects . . . . There are always conflicts, I'd say, between brothers and sisters . . . . But they'll pass, with God's help . . . . You know, Bianca? Your cousin is getting married. Now there is no need for secrecy, because everything is arranged. Don Filippo gives his Salonia property—thirty salme of land! Quite a dowry."

Bianca's face was suddenly flushed, then she became as pale as a rag; but she didn't move, nor did she speak a word.

The canon-priest himself, answered instead, with bitterness still in his mouth.

"We know! we know! We understood that much today, at City Hall! . . ."

Finally, he could not contain himself any more, as if he were the one with a burning wound.

"Baroness Rubiera tried to trip me too! . . . Me, who had suggested the deal to her in the first place!... She ganged up with the other side! All against us!... The wife's relatives siding against the husband!... The kind of scandal nobody has ever seen.... They've announced another competition for the bridge...so that he'll lose his bond, this poor unlucky man! Nothing but abuses!... For the construction of new roads, they're bringing in bidders all the way from Caltagirone and from Lentini... 'At least from there we won't be saddled with another relative!...' Baron Mendola said these very words, in the pharmacy."

Donna Marianna turned a hundred colors, and bit her lips, to keep from spitting out her piece. Don Gesualdo, on the other hand, was laughing quietly, stretched out on his beautiful soft sofa, and at a certain moment he even put his hand over the canon-priest's mouth.

"Don't bother!... This is all talk that doesn't bring anything to the mill. Everyone looks after his own interest."

"I was trying to answer Donna Marianna. D'you want to hear something else? It's the best one yet! They have even ganged up together to sell the wheat way under the market, to make the price tumble. A swindle! Young Baron Rubiera said that he doesn't mind losing one hundred onze, as long as he can make Don Gesualdo lose a thousand—with his storehouses full.... His cousin's husband! Shame! I've twenty salme of wheat fields too, understand, sir? A dirty trick!"

The canon-priest was getting more excited by the minute. He turned to Mastro-don Gesualdo:

"You really made quite a profit, by becoming a relative of people like that. Who would have expected this...eh? It was a mistake! ... Sorry, Donna Bianca, I'm not talking about you, who are a jewel!... Then, dear Donna Marianna, then, if it's that way, let Samson die with all the Philistines."

"And let 'em die," said Mrs. Sganci getting up. "After all, the world is not going to come to an end because of this."

Since her niece had also gotten up from the sofa, mortified by that kind of talk, her hands crossed on her belly, Donna Marianna went on, laughing and staring at her:

"It's true, Bianca, that you yourself will see to it that the world doesn't come to an end, won't you?"

Bianca blushed again.

"*Evviva!* Congratulations. Now that you have this beautiful house, you must have a great baptism . . . with all the relatives . . . in total harmony. Otherwise, what did you spend so much money for?"

Don Gesualdo didn't want his enemies to have it their own way, but he was gnawed inside, because it was true that all that money spent was not doing him much good.

"Eh, eh," he answered in whatever good mood he could show under the circumstances. "Never mind! It will do good to those who come after us, if God wills!"

And he affectionately patted his wife's shoulder, smiling with love, while he was thinking that if his children were to have the same destiny as himself, it would really be money thrown away — all that work, and even the very profit, always with that great result! Then, when Aunt Sganci was gone, he began to grumble at Bianca because she hadn't put on a better dress to receive her aunt:

"Then what d'you have all those things for? They'll say that I treat you like a servant. What good is it to spend so much money if nobody enjoys it, neither ourselves nor the others!"

"Let's forget about all this nonsense, and let's talk about serious things!" cut in the canon-priest, whose face had become gloomy. "There's a hell of a racket. They're trying to set the whole town against you; saying that you've got long arms, and that you want to grab as much land as you can see with your eyes, to starve everybody. . . . That jackass, Ciolla, is going around lecturing for them. . . . They want to unleash even the peasants against us . . . against you and me, my friend! They say that I'm holding the bag . . . I can't set foot outside of my house . . ."

Don Gesualdo was shrugging his shoulders.

"Ah, the peasants? We'll talk about it later, when winter comes. And you, what are you afraid of?"

"What am I afraid of, by gosh! . . . Don't you know that in Palermo there was a revolution?"

He tiptoed over to close the door, and came back with a dark and sour face.

"The *Carbonari,** understand? . . . They have brought that

---

*Members of a secret political society especially active in southern Italy and committed to the overthrow of the foreign autocratic governments that had been chosen by the Congress of Vienna in 1816.

great novelty here too! I can talk, for I wasn't told under the seal of confession. We have that sect here too!"

And he explained what it was all about: to make new laws and overthrow all those who had been in charge until then.

"A sect, understand? Like putting Tavuso in Margarone's place; and all of them with their fingers in the pie! Every peasant wanting a piece of land for himself! Big fish and small fry, all together. They say that even the king's son is involved, no less, the duke of Calabria!"

Don Gesualdo, who had been listening with his eyes wide open, blurted out:

"If that's the way it is...I'm for it! It's just what I'm looking for!... And you tell me about it with a face like that? You almost scared me to death, for God's sake!"

The canon-priest was open-mouthed:

"Are you joking? Or you don't know what revolution means? What they did in France, understand? But you don't read history books..."

"No, no," said Don Gesualdo. "I don't care."

"But I care. Revolution means to turn the basket upside down, and those who were on the bottom move to the top: the starving, the indigent!..."

"Well? What was I twenty years ago?"

"But not now! Now you have a lot to lose, you, my dear Christian! D'you know how it is? Today they want the City lands, and tomorrow they'll want yours too, and mine as well! No, thanks! Thanks a lot! I haven't sold my soul to the devil, for so many years, to..."

"That's it! We've got to help one another not to end up at the bottom of the basket, dear Canon Lupi! We must keep afloat, if we don't want the peasants to help themselves with their own hands. I know them...I know what to do, don't worry."

And he explained his own idea better: take the chestnuts out of the fire with cat's paws; bring the grist to your own mill, and if you happen to get hold of the shovel for even only fifteen minutes, and can trip all those big shots you hadn't been able to win over even by marrying one of theirs, with no dowry and with nothing—so much the better....

At that moment his eyes wandered to Bianca who was huddled in a corner of the sofa, deadly pale from fear, looking now at one and now at the other, without daring to open her mouth.

"I'm not talking about you, you know. I'm not sorry about what I've done. It wasn't your fault. Not all deals come out the same way. Then if you happen to do some good, at the same time . . . ."

The canon-priest, his mouth and his eyes twisted, deep in thought, was beginning to get the gist of it and also was supporting his partner's ideas:

"They didn't want to touch a hair on anybody's head . . . if they could get hold of the shovel early enough. . . . They could really do a lot of things. . . . "

"You should do one of them now! . . ." cut in Don Gesualdo. "Talk to those who are involved in this business, and tell them that we want to be in it too."

"Eh? What d'you mean? . . . A priest!"

"Forget it, Canon Lupi . . . If the king's son is in it, you can be too!"

"Sure! They are not going to cut the king's son's head off, for sure!"

"Don't be afraid; they're not going to cut your head off! As a matter of fact, if things are the way you say, they should cut the head off a whole town. Do you think I haven't been figuring things out, during this time? . . . When we're there, to see what's brewing . . . We must stand close to the shovel . . . with a bit of discretion . . . with money . . . I know what I'm talking about."

Then Bianca began to stammer:

"Oh, Good Lord! . . . What are you planning to do? . . . A family man!"

The canon-priest, hesitant, looked at her with uneasiness, almost as if he felt the noose around his neck. To reassure him, Don Gesualdo added:

"No, no. My wife doesn't know what she's talking about. . . . She speaks out of too much love, the poor girl."

Then, as he accompanied his partner to the entryroom, he said:

"D'you see? She's beginning to love me. After all, children are a great bond. Let's hope at least they grow up happy; because as for me . . . Shall I tell you, eh, Canon Lupi, as if I were at the point of death? I've killed myself with work . . . I've killed myself putting property together. . . . Now I'm even risking my hide according to what you're saying! . . . And what have I gotten out of all this, eh? you tell me! . . ."

II

There was a great excitement in town. They were all waiting for the news from Palermo. Bomma was lecturing in the pharmacy, and Ciolla was shouting here and there. There were agitators arousing even the peasants with speeches that made them open their eyes wide: the city lands going out of the Zacco household after forty years . . . a price that had never been seen before! . . . Mastro-don Gesualdo's arms were much too long. . . . If they had made the lands rise to that price, it meant that there was still some profit to be made! . . . Just poor people's blood! City property . . . Which meant that everybody had a right to it! . . . Then why shouldn't everybody grab his own piece?

It was a Sunday, the feast of the Assumption. The night before a letter had come from Palermo setting the powder afire, as if everybody had read it. At daybreak Piazza Grande was already crammed full of peasants: a swarming of white caps; a threatening murmur. Brother Girolamo of the Mercenaries was sitting in the shade together with the other evil planners, on the steps before Notary Neri's office, and as he saw Baron Zacco pass by with his tail between his legs, he showed him the pistol he carried inside his big sleeve.

"See, Baron, sir? . . . The times of arrogance are now over! . . . From now on we're all equal! . . ."

There were also rumors about Brother Girolamo's plans: to leave his cassock in his cell, and grab an estate at Passaneto for himself, and Margarone's youngest daughter too, for a wife.

The Notary who had come to remove some important papers from his study had to take his hat off to Brother Girolamo to get inside.

"May I? . . . Gentlemen? . . ."

Then he went to join Don Filippo Margarone in the little square of Santa Teresa:

"Listen here; I have to tell you something!"

And he took him by the arm, walking toward his house while talking in whispers. Don Filippo was dismayed at every gesture the Notary cut through the air with his hand; but stubbornly kept saying no, yellow with fear. The other pressed his arm tightly, as they crossed the alley from Masera to climb toward Sant'Antonio.

"D'you see them? d'you hear them? You want them to seize us and do us in, those peasants?"

At the end of the alley the square looked like a nest of angry hornets. Nanni l'Orbo, Pelagatti, and other agitators, all excited, moved from one group of people to another, shouting, gesticulating, spitting gall. *Mastro* Titta's customers stuck their heads out every minute. In Bomma's pharmacy they were arguing, shaking their hands in one another's faces. Across the square, on the Caffè dei Nobili sidewalk, Don Anselmo, the waiter, had lined up the chairs in the shade as usual; but there was only Marquis Limòli, who was calmly watching the threatening crowd with his cane between his legs.

"What do they want, Don Anselmo? What the hell's gotten into them today? D'you know?"

"They want the City lands, Marquis, sir. They say that up to now you rich people have exploited them and that now it's our turn, because we're all equal."

"They're the bosses! They're the bosses! As for me, I won't say no! All equal!... Bring me a glass of water, Don Anselmo."

Every once in a while, from Rosario and from Via di San Giovanni there started out a wave of people, and a more threatening grumbling that spread out in a flash. Then Santo Motta came out of Pecu-Pecu's tavern, and began to shout, his hand on his cheek:

"The City lands! Who wants the City lands?... One!...two! ...three!..." And ended with a jeering laugh.

"Make room!...make room!..."

People ran toward Masera. Above the crowd you could see young Baron Rubiera, with his whip raised in the air high above the head of his horse that was snorting in fright. The field watchman who stayed at his side, armed to the teeth, screamed as if possessed:

"Baron, sir!... This is not the right day!... Today we must be cautious!..."

From the Sant'Agata district the Police Captain showed up for a moment too, so that he could intimidate the mutinous crowd with his presence. He planted himself on top of the steps, leaning against his bamboo cane — Don Liccio Papa behind him, squinting in the sun, his white baldric reaching all the way across his belly. But in front of that sea of heads, they both quickly sneaked away. At the windows you could see uneasy faces show up now and then, behind the panes, as if it were raining. The Sganci palace was hermetically sealed and Don Giuseppe Barabba was perched up by the dormer window. Even Bomma had sent his friends home earlier than usual, for fear of broken glass. Once in a while, on the Margarones' balcony, above the roofs piling up toward the Castello, appeared Don Filippo's skullcap and yellow face. At noon, when the high mass rang everyone went about his own business, and only Santo Motta remained in the deserted square, shouting:

"Did you see the way it ended?"

Ciolla rushed to have lunch too. Don Liccio Papa, now that nobody was around, showed up again in the streets, his hand on his saber, fiercely staring at the closed doors. Finally he went into Pecu-Pecu's tavern and sat down at the table together with Santo.

"Did you see the way it ended?"

Ciolla used to have lunch as fast as he could, his hat on his head and his stick between his legs, in order to run back into the square to finish his last mouthful there, carrying in his pocket a handful of lupins or of roasted garbanzos — during the winter he even carried his portable brazier under his cloak — loafing about, hâving something to say to everybody, spitting here and there, scattering the ground with shells.

"Did you see the way it ended?"

First he stopped at the shoemaker's, then at the cafè, as soon as it opened, without ever ordering anything; in the summer he followed the shade, and in the winter he went after the sun. And things again kept going their usual course, just like Ciolla. Giacinto brought his tables outside for the sherbet, Don Anselmo lined up his chairs on the sidewalk of the Caffè dei Nobili. Only the last clouds of the storm remained: a few groups of people here and there, before

Pecu-Pecu's tavern and before City Hall; people who were casting uneasy looks around, and those who out of curiosity ran over and got together at the slightest noise. But otherwise everything had resumed its usual Sunday look. Archpriest Bugno spending an hour licking his sherbet with a teaspoon; the Marquis and the other aristocrats sitting in a row before the Caffè; Bomma lecturing in the midst of the usual group in the doorway of his pharmacy; a swarm of peasants a little farther away at the proper distance; and every ten minutes the old coach of Baron Mendola taking his mother who was as deaf as a gopher for a ride from Rosario to Santa Maria di Gesù — his mules' hairy and weary ears dangling in the crowd, the coachman perched up on the box with the whip between his legs, next to the uniformed hunter, whose freshly washed stockings looked as if stuffed with walnuts — and the yellow plumes of the Baroness' large hat passing back and forth in the midst of the rippling sea of white caps.

All of a sudden there was a turmoil; a kind of brawl before the tavern. Don Liccio Papa was trying to arrest Santo Motta because he had been shouting that morning; and the Police Captain was inciting him from afar, brandishing his bamboo cane:

"Stop! stop!... The Law!"

But Santo freed himself with a shove and began to run toward Sant'Agata. The crowd whistled and howled behind the cop who was trying to pursue him.

"Ah! Ah!" said Bomma who had climbed on a chair to see. "If they have no more respect for the authorities!..."

Tavuso signaled him to keep quiet, by putting his forefinger across his lips.

"Listen, Don Bastiano!"

And they began talking in whispers, drawing aside.

From the Maddalena area, the Notary was coming down very slowly, holding his stick behind his back. Bomma began to signal to him from the distance; but the Notary pretended not to notice; he nodded to the Police Captain who had started out toward the Collegio, and walked into the church through the small side door. As he passed by the pharmacy, the Police Captain burned up the libertines with a lightning look, and grumbled, as he turned to the leader:

"Watch out, you have wives and children!..."

"Dammit!... Goddammit!..." the pharmacist felt like shouting.

At that moment the bell rang from the church for benediction, and all those in the square knelt. Soon after Ciolla, who was killing time by crunching fava beans, sitting before the sherbet shop, saw something that made him perk up his ears: Notary Neri and the canon-priest Lupi coming out of the church together and walking up toward Maddalena, step by step, talking in whispers. The Notary shrugged his shoulders, looking stealthily here and there. Ciolla tried to join them, but they walked away from him. Bomma, from a distance, did not lose sight of them, shaking his head.

"Watch out!... Watch out for your hide!..." the Police Captain told him passing by him again.

"Cuckold!" the pharmacist wanted to yell at him. "You'd better watch out for yourself!..."

But the doctor forced him inside. Ciolla had run after the canon-priest and Notary Neri up Via di San Sebastiano, when he saw them still standing under the great arch of the Condotto, almost in the dark and in spite of the stench, talking in whispers and gesticulating. As soon as they noticed Ciolla, they quickly sneaked away, one to this side and the other to that. The Notary kept climbing the rocky little road, and the canon-priest determinedly went down at breakneck speed toward San Sebastiano, stopping Ciolla as if by accident.

"That Notary...he really tricked me!... He had an agreement with *massaro* Sbrendola...a regular contract...and now he says he can't remember!"

"Come on now, come on, I'm not going to swallow that one!" Ciolla murmured to himself, as soon as the canon-priest had turned his back.

And he immediately ran to the pharmacy.

"There are big things in the air! Cats and dogs are sleeping together! There are big things in the making!"

Tavuso swelled his cheeks and didn't answer. Instead the pharmacist blurted out:

"I know! I know!"

And he hit his lips with his open hand, as the doctor burned him with a lightninglike glance.

Almost two hours after dark, Don Gesualdo was about to have dinner, when in a great mystery the canon-priest came to see him, dressed as a shepherd. Bianca was on the point of having a miscarriage out of fright.

"Don Gesualdo, we're ready; if you want to come; our friends are waiting for you."

But the poor man's voice was shaking. Don Gesualdo himself, at the point of jumping into the deal, had some frightening thoughts; he grew pale and his fork fell from his hand. And Bianca got up convulsed, stumbling here and there, quarreling with the canon-priest, who was putting a family man into such a predicament.

"If that's the way you feel . . ." stammered the canon-priest. "If you now can even wish me to go to hell . . . then, good night!"

Don Gesualdo was trying to laugh it off, with his lips pale.

"You're great, Canon Lupi! Now we'll see if you're a man! . . . I'm glad, you see, Bianca! I'm even glad to head toward rack and ruin, just to find out that you're beginning to be fond of me and of the house . . . ."

All sweaty, his hands a little shaky, he covered himself with a hood — just out of caution — and the two of them went down into the street. There wasn't a living soul. On the Collegio balcony an unknown hand had even put out the lamp before the statue of the Immaculate Conception — something to give you goose pimples, on a night like that! He then felt his heart wrung by an unusual tenderness, as he thought about his house and his relatives.

"Poor Bianca! Did you see? She's good, yes, deep down . . . I really didn't believe it! . . ."

"Quiet!" cut in the canon-priest. "If you let them know you by your voice, it's useless to hide and to sweat it out like animals!"

Every moment they turned around afraid that they were being spied on. When they got to Via di San Giovanni they saw a shadow moving up toward the square, and the canon-priest said in a low voice:

"See? . . . That's one of us! He's going where we are going."

It was in one of the Grancore storehouses, down in the middle of the crooked alleys that seemed made for that purpose, toward San Francesco. A little low house with a window lighted as a signal. You had to knock three times in a certain way at the little door that could be reached by walking down three steps; you had to cross a big dark and steep courtyard, at the end of which there was a large unlighted room where, from the buzzing you could hear from behind the door, you realized that there were a lot of people talking together. The canon-priest said:

"It's here!" and he gave the secret signal.

The two of them had their hearts in their throats. Fortunately, another conspirator arrived at that very moment, all wrapped up too, walking on tiptoe on the stones of the courtyard, and repeating the same signal.

"Don Gesualdo," said Notary Neri, drawing his nose out of a big scarf. "Is it you? I could recognize you because of the canon-priest, who looks like an old owl, the poor man!"

The Notary was taking it cheerfully. He was saying that in Palermo they had made a mess; they had killed the Prince of Aci and had occupied Castellammare:

"The one in charge now is a priest, a certain Ascenso!"

"Ah!" answered the canon-priest, who felt involved... "Ah!"

"Let's keep quiet for the moment!... Let's go slowly! You know how it is?... Who must be the first to tie a bell to the cat? And no honest man would like to step into a trap. But if there are many of us... Even Baron Zacco is here tonight."

"Why aren't we going inside, gentlemen?" cut in Don Gesualdo at that news, becoming as brave as a lion.

When they came out, after quite a while, they were all more dead than alive. Bomma was doing his best to play the braggart; Tavuso did not speak a word; and the Notary himself was deep in thought. Zacco ran to take Don Gesualdo's arm, as if they had really become brothers.

"Listen, Cousin, I want to talk to you." And they kept on walking arm in arm, in silence.

"Ssst! somebody's whistling!... Toward the Capuchins!"

The Baron pulled out his pistol; their hearts were beating wildly. They heard dogs barking.

"Stop!..." exclaimed the canon-priest in a whisper, grabbing the Baron's arm that was holding the pistol aiming in the dark. "It's Brother Girolamo, who doesn't want to be seen around here!"

When they heard the door being closed again, after a white cassock had flashed in the opening, the pharmacist grumbled breathing heavily:

"We had a really close call, I assure you!"

Instead the Baron pressed Don Gesualdo's arm tightly without saying anything. Then he let everyone go his own way—Bomma up, toward Piazza Grande, the canon-priest at the foot of the steps leading toward San Sebastiano.

"This way, Don Gesualdo...you come with me."

And he had him go all around by the Capuchins, then climbing up toward Santa Maria di Gesù through such dark alleys that you would not have known where to put your feet. All of a sudden he stopped, staring at his newfound friend's face with his eyes glistening in the dark.

"Don Gesualdo, did you hear all that nice talk? Now we're all brothers. We're going to swim in milk and honey, from now on.... You believe it, don't you?"

Don Gesualdo said neither yes nor no, cautious, as he waited for what was coming.

"I don't...I don't trust all these brothers whom my mother didn't give birth to."

"Then why did you come, sir?"

"So that you yourself wouldn't have to come, dammit! I'm not mysterious. We're playing at undercutting each other, we who have something to lose—and here is the great result! Cooking for cats and risking our property and our heads!... I watch out for my interests, just like you.... I don't have a swelled head, like so many other people.... Relatives! Sure! As for me, I'm happy about it.... Then let's rather get together, ourselves...."

"All right! What d'you want to do?"

"Ah? what do I want to do?... Is that how you take it? You pretend not to know?... Then forget I said anything.... Each one after his own interest! Brothers! *Carbonari!* We'll have the revolution! we'll even turn the world upside down!...I'm not afraid!..."

In the heat of the argument the Baron leaned against the gate to a courtyard. A dog began to bark furiously. Frightened, Zacco took to his heels with the pistol in his hand, and Don Gesualdo followed him, panting. Before they reached the Santa Maria di Gesù square, a man who ran toward them stopped him, putting his hand on his chest.

"Don Gesualdo, sir!... Where are you going?... The police are in your house!"

Just what the canon-priest was afraid of! What Bianca was afraid of! He kept running in the dark, without knowing where, a great confusion in his head, and his heart bursting out of his chest. Then, hearing that man plodding along behind him, with a peculiar noise, as if he were hitting the ground with a stick, he asked:

"Who are you?"

"Nardo, the assistant mason, the one who left his leg under the bridge. You don't recognize me any more, sir? Donna Bianca had me awakened during the night."

And he told him that the Armed Forces had arrived suddenly, four hours after dark. The Captain at Arms and other soldiers were in Don Gesualdo's house. Up there, toward the Castello, there were lights gleaming; there was also a lantern hanging at the door of the stable, at Poggio, with soldiers currying their horses. Farther ahead, near Piazza Grande, from time to time you could hear voices: a confused murmuring, footsteps echoing in the night, dogs barking all over town.

Don Gesualdo stopped to think.

"Where are we going, sir?" Nardo asked.

"I've thought about it. Don't make noise. Ah! Holy Virgin of Peril! Go and call Nanni l'Orbo. D'you know him? Diodata's husband?"

It was beginning to dawn. But on the out-of-the-way paths they had taken you would not yet meet a living soul. Diodata's little house was hidden inside a pile of small blackish huts and cactus thickets, where there was mud even in the summer. A vine trellis leaned above the landing, and a light shone through the worn-out shutters.

"You knock, in case..." said Don Gesualdo.

As she saw her former boss appear before her all out of breath, Diodata began to shake like a leaf.

"What d'you want at this hour?... For God's sake! Leave me in peace, Don Gesualdo!... If my husband comes back!... He just went out to pick a few prickly pears!... Close by."

"Jackass!" said he. "I've something else on my mind. The police are after me!..."

"What's the matter?" asked Diodata frightened.

With his hand he motioned to her not to speak. At that moment Nardo came back running; his wooden leg could be heard from a distance on the cobblestones.

"There he is!... There he comes!..."

Nanni l'Orbo walked in, grim, the reed to pick prickly pears on his shoulder, his surly eyes darting lightning glances here and there. In vain Diodata kept swearing over and over again, her arms crossed.

"Boss!" exclaimed Nanni. "What kind of game is this? This is not the way!..."

"Jackass!" shouted Don Gesualdo, losing his patience. "I've the gallows before my eyes, and you speak of jealousy."

At the clamor the neighbors rushed up.

"D'you see?" repeated Nanni in a fury. "What do I look like before them, boss? In all conscience, what you gave her to marry her off is a trifle, in comparison to what you make me look like!"

"Keep quiet! You'll make the cops run over with that racket! What d'you want? I'll give you what you want!..."

"I want my honor, Don Gesualdo! My honor, which money can't buy!"

The neighborhood dogs began to bark.

"D'you want the Carmine field?...a piece of land you've been coveting?"

Finally, Nardo managed to make them agree about the Carmine field.

"Goddammit! Property helps in emergencies like this...jail, illness, and persecution... You've put it together, Don Gesualdo, and now it helps to save your hide...."

With a funereal face, Don Gesualdo grumbled:

"Talk! Shout! You're right! Now you're the one who's right!"

"But then take the other people into account, sir! A wife to support...the children who'll be born...and if the others come back

home too?... Those who arrived first? I must support them as if
they were my own...because I'm Diodata's husband.... People
will probably say that it was me who brought them into the
world!..."

"Enough! Enough! Haven't I said 'yes' about the field?"

"An honest man's word? In front of these witnesses? If that's the
way it is...since you tell me you came here only to save your hide,
you can stay as long as you like. I'm a good-natured, helpful man, as
you know!..."

It had gotten late. Nanni, now fully calmed down, even suggested to go and see what was happening out there:

"Make yourself completely at home, Don Gesualdo.... Nardo
will come with me. When we get back, I'll give the signal by knocking three times. But don't open to anybody else, not even to the
devil."

The whole town was terrorized: doors and windows still shut,
soldiers in the streets, noise of sabers and of spurs. The Margarone
girls, wearing their frills and with round pads like fireworks on their
heads, kept running to the balcony every minute. Don Filippo, his
head swelled with pride and his chest pushed forward, was seated at
the Caffè dei Nobili, together with the Police Captain and the Fiscal
Attorney, making all those who passed tremble with his stares. In
Don Gesualdo's stable the orderlies were feeding the horses, and the
Commander was smoking on the balcony, in his slippers, as if he
were in his own house.

Nanni l'Orbo came back roaring with laughter. But before
going inside he knocked the way he had said, coughed, blew his
nose, even stopped for a while to talk aloud with a neighbor who was
combing her hair on her landing. Don Gesualdo was eating an onion
salad to ward off any illness brought about by fright.

"Enjoy your food! Enjoy your food, Don Gesualdo! I found
strangers in your house, just exactly as you are here in mine. Baron
Zacco is still running!... They saw him before dawn on the other
side of Passaneto, believe it or not! All the way out there!... Behind
a hedge, more dead than alive!... His wife seems to have lost her
mind.... I also went to look for Notary Neri—just in case we should
have a few words written about the Carmine field that you're giving
my wife for services rendered.... Not that I don't trust you... As

you well know...I'm at your service in life and in death. But nobody has seen the Notary! They say that he's hidden in the monastery of San Sebastiano...dressed like a woman...yes sir!... The
cops are searching everywhere! But here there is nothing to fear, sir!
... D'you hear? D'you hear?"

He seemed to enjoy making the blood freeze in the veins of
others, that ruffian. You could, in fact, hear the confused voices of
women, the running of hobnailed boots, the screeching of children.
Diodata climbed to the granary dormer to see. Then Nanni came in
to say:

"It's the viaticum, God save us!... It's going up toward
Sant'Agata. I saw the canon-priest Lupi carrying the Host...with
his eyes to the ground!... A saint's face, I swear to God!"

"Tonight, as soon as it's dark, please let me find a horse or a
mule down at Masera, and give me some clothes to disguise myself,"
said Don Gesualdo, who looked even paler in the light of the small
skylight.

"Why? Don't you like to stay in my house any longer? Has Diodata been rude to you?"

"No, no...I'm really anxious to be far away..."

"But here there is nothing to fear.... The cops are not coming
to look for you here! But certainly they will in your own house!
Watch out!..."

In fact the night before, three hours after dark, Bianca had
seen the Captain at Arms, a handsome man with a round-shaped
beard and a military moustache, come by with a lodging order in his
hands. Bianca, who was already restless about her husband, did not
know what to do, and sent for Uncle Limòli, who arrived yawning
and in a bad mood. In vain the Captain at Arms kept saying in a
deep voice, as he stroked that moustache he had recently grown:

"Don't be afraid!... Please calm down, you beautiful lady!...
We soldiers are gallant with the fair sex!..."

"Then," added the Marquis, "these people are military just so-
to-speak; just the same way as I have taken the vow of chastity only
because I'm a Knight of Malta."

The Captain at Arms frowned, but the Marquis continued
without noticing it, informally patting him on the shoulder:

"I know you, Don Bastiano!... You were this small, your little

pants open, when your father and I were having escapades together.
. . . At that time my vow bothered me as much as that little spring
scale at your side bothers you. . . . Happy days!. . . A fine man your
father! His heart and his purse always open!. . . Don Marcantonio
Stangafame!. . . Of the Ragusa Stangafames!. . . One of the most
illustrious families in the county! Too bad that there are so many of
you! You did the right thing to have yourself made Captain at Arms!
. . . Four hundred onze a year, just to investigate the thefts in the
fields. . . . It's a good sum of money. . . . And it all remains in your
pocket . . . because the area is peaceful!. . . Except for those twelve
soldiers you have to support . . . two tarì a day each, eh!. . . "

"Enough, Goddammit!" shouted the Captain at Arms hitting
the ground with his sabre. "You seem to want to make a mockery of
me, Goddammit!"

"Hey, hey! calm down, Captain, sir! I'm Marquis Limòli, and I
still have friends in Naples, to have you uncaptained and to have
that fresh moustache of yours shaven off, you know?"

At that very moment, the sacristan's son happened to come to
deliver an urgent message, stammering, getting confused, always
repeating the same thing, red with embarrassment. The Marquis,
who was beginning to get a little deaf, stretched his ears, grimaced,
and intimidated him more and more, yelling:

"Eh! What the hell d'you want?"

But Bianca uttered a lacerating cry—a cry that left her Uncle
open-mouthed—and she rushed about the house, looking for her
cloak, looking for something to throw over her head, to get out of
the house, to run.

III

Everyday at the same time for many years, Donna Giuseppina
Alosi who sat knitting on her balcony waiting for Peperito to pass
by; Don Filippo Margarone who turned the tomato paste drying on
his terrace; Archpriest Bugno who hung the canary cage; even those
who sat yawning in Bomma's pharmacy—if they raised their eyes
toward the Castello, above the roofs, would see Don Diego and Don

Ferdinando Trao, who cautiously stuck their heads out of the window, one after the other, glancing to the right and to the left, looking up into the air, and then withdrawing their heads like snails. Finally, after a few minutes, the door to the great balcony opened, screeching, trembling, pushed apart a little at a time, and Don Diego appeared, bent, emaciated, his cotton cap pressed down to his ears, coughing, spitting, holding on to the railing with one hand; and behind him Don Ferdinando, carrying the watering can — yellow, lanky, and fleshless, a veritable ghost. Don Diego watered, weeded, trimmed Bianca's flowers; he bent down to pick up the dry branches and the withered leaves, stirred up the soil with a piece of broken pot, inspected the new buds, and cherished them with his eyes. Don Ferdinando followed him step by step, most attentively; he too put his wan face to each plant, sharpening his jaw, knitting his brows. Then they leaned their elbows against the railing, and remained there like two hens perched on the same stick, turning their heads here or there, whether *massaro* Fortunato Burgio's mule came by loaded with wheat, or the girl who sold eggs came up from Rosario, or the sacristan's wife crossed the little square to go and ring the *Angelus*. Don Ferdinando was intent on counting how many people could be seen pass through that piece of street that was visible down there, among the roofs sloping in throngs downhill; Don Diego, for his part, followed with his eyes the last rays of the sun, which slowly climbed toward the heights of Paradiso and Monte Lauro, and rejoiced as he saw it suddenly sparkle on the windowpanes of the poor houses that already lost themselves among the fields, like whitish botches. Then he smiled and pointed his fleshless, trembling finger, nudging his brother, who nodded yes, he too smiling like a child. And he told what he himself had seen:

"Today twenty-seven!...twenty-seven went by...Archpriest Bugno was together with Cousin Limòli..."

For a few days, at the beginning of August, only Don Ferdinando had come to water the flowers, barely dragging himself along, his gray hair flying loose, spilling water all over himself at every step. When also Don Diego reappeared, it was like seeing Lazarus risen from the dead: all nose, his ears black, buried alive inside an old overcoat, coughing out his soul at every step — a muted cough, which almost could no longer be heard and that shook from head to foot both him and his brother who had him on his arm, as if he were bowing before every flowerpot.

And it was the last time. From then on you could rarely see the white heads of the two brothers together, behind the windowpanes that had been patched up with paper—both of them looking for the sun, and Don Diego spitting and looking at the floor every moment. The day when there was that uproar in City Hall, with the shouts being heard all the way to the little Sant'Agata square, for an instant the quivering tip of a white cap appeared at the window. But when the San Giuseppe procession stopped before the Trao front door, for the traditional homage to the family, the windows remained closed, in spite of the shouting crowd. Don Ferdinando came downstairs to buy the image of the Saint—swollen as he was with asthma, his eyes burned with lack of sleep, doubled up, his dark hands shaking so badly that they could not find in his pocket the two pennies for the image. The procurator of San Giuseppe, who was in charge of the procession, said to him:

"You'll see how miraculous that image is! So much health and abundance to everyone in your house!"

And he entrusted him also with the saint's silver staff, to be put by the sick man's bolster; a cure-all. And yet it didn't help either.

Cosimo and Pelagatti kept seeing the light in Don Diego's window, whether they left for the fields two hours before dawn, or they came back well after dark. And the Mottas' black dog's whining in the square was like a lament. Then, in the afternoon, Don Luca's boy knocked at the front door, bringing a glass of milk. Occasionally came Don Giuseppe Barabba, carrying a plate covered with a napkin, or the Fiscal Attorney's servant with a fiasco of wine. Slowly even those visits became less and less frequent. The last time, Doctor Tavuso had left shrugging his shoulders. The neighborhood boys played all day long by that front door that did not open any more. Late one evening, the neighbors who were having dinner heard Don Ferdinando's hoarse voice call the sacristan, across the little square—a voice that would make the bread fall out of your mouth. And immediately after, a loud bang of the dilapidated door, and steps rushing off into the dark.

It was just that night when the Company at Arms arrived. A hell of a racket all over town. At the unusual noise even Don Diego opened his eyes for a moment. Burgio was on his landing, with his ear stretched toward Piazza Grande, where you could hear all that commotion, and as he saw people on the Trao balcony he asked anxiously:

"What's the matter?... What's going on?"

"Don Diego!..." answered the sacristan; and he made the sign of the cross, almost as if *massaro* Fortunato could see him in the dark. "Alone like a dog!... They leave him in my hands!... I sent Grazia for the doctor...at this time of night!..."

"D'you hear, down there, toward the square?...d'you hear? ... What a day tomorrow is going to be, God save us!..."

"All it takes is to have a clear conscience, *massaro* Fortunato. I've always been a poor devil!... I kiss the hand that gives me bread...."

"The Doctor!... Him for sure!... He must be shaking all over at this time!... And the canon-priest Lupi too—they say!... Good night!... Walls have ears in the dark!"

In fact Doctor Tavuso, who was the head of all the Jacobins in town and was hiding in the woodshed shaking like a leaf, thought his last hour had come, when he heard that furious banging at the door.

"The cops!... The Company at Arms!..."

Instead when they told him that it was the sacristan's wife calling him for Don Diego, who was dying, he became as furious as an animal.

"Is he still alive?... Send him to hell!... They're coming to frighten me!... At this time of night!... In times like these!... A family man!... You'd better call his relatives...or the viaticum, that's better!..."

Aunt Sganci did not even want to open. Barabba answered from behind the door, which was tightly bolted:

"My good woman, these are not times to go running about the streets at night. Tomorrow morning, if God wills it, those who are alive will see one another."

Fortunately, Grazia did not have anything to fear. Her husband would have sent her in the middle of a regiment of soldiers without worrying. To go around at this late hour, on such a night, was really frightening. Even your Baron Rubiera, who had left the Margarones' house early, had himself accompanied by a man with a lantern.

"Nini! Nini!" Donna Fifi screamed from the balcony in her thin voice, as if her fiancé were running to throw himself into a ravine.

"Don't be afraid . . . don't!" he answered in a deep voice.

As he heard people in the little square, Don Luca came running from the Trao front door, which resounded like a cannon shot.

"Baron, sir! . . . Your cousin, Don Diego is dying! . . . Alone as a dog! . . . There is nobody in the house! . . ."

Across from the black and sad Trao palace shone the lit-up balcony of the Margarones, and Donna Fifi's shadow was outlined in that light to remind him of another shadow that used to wait for him in the past at the window of the dilapidated palace. Don Nini walked off in a hurry, his head lowered, carrying inside him the memory of that window, closed and without light.

"What a dirty trick! . . . They leave him in my hands! . . . With me alone!" grumbled Don Luca going back into the dying man's room.

Don Ferdinando was sitting at the foot of the bed, without saying anything, like a mummy. Every now and then he went to look into his brother's face; then, wild-eyed, he looked at Don Luca, and again he lowered his head on his chest. But at the sacristan's outburst, he suddenly got up as if somebody had given him a jolt, and asked in a whisper, with the voice of one who speaks in a dream:

"Is he asleep?"

"Yes, he's asleep! . . . Go to sleep too, if you like! . . ."

But Don Ferdinando did not move. At first the sick man wanted to know at every moment what time it was; then, toward midnight, he did not ask for anything any more. He was quiet, his nose against the wall, and his blanket all the way to his ears. When Grazia had come back, she had set the door ajar, had put the light nearby, on the night table, and had gone to look around her own house. Her husband made himself as comfortable as he could on two chairs. From time to time Don Ferdinando got up again, on tiptoe, bent over the bed, like a bird of ill omen, and asked in a whisper, in Don Luca's ear:

"What is he doing? Is he asleep?"

"Yes! yes!... Go to sleep too!... Go!"

And he himself accompanied him to his room, at least to get rid of that nuisance. Don Ferdinando dreamed that his neighbor Motta's black dog had crouched on his chest and wouldn't go away, no matter how much he would try to free himself or to shout. The dog's tail, so long that there was no end to it, had twisted all around his neck and his arms, like a snake and was squeezing him, stifling him, strangling his voice in his throat, when he heard another voice that made him jump out of bed, with his heart beating wildly.

"Get up, Don Ferdinando! This is no time to sleep!..."

Don Diego seemed to be snoring loudly; you could hear him from the next room. Lying on his back, his eyes open and lifeless, his nostrils sooty—a face that you could not recognize any more. Don Ferdinando first called him in whispers; then called him again and shook him to no avail, and that little bit of hair on his head stood on end. Stunned, he turned to the sacristan, and pleaded:

"What is he doing now?... What is he doing?..."

"What is he doing?... You can see what he's doing!... Grazia! Grazia!"

"No!... Stop!... Don't open now!..."

It was daylight. Donna Bellonia, in her underskirt, was on her terrace keeping an eye out toward Piazza Grande at her husband's request—frightened as she was by all the commotion that had been going on in town during the night; and Burgio was currying his mule tied to the Trao's front door. When he heard Don Luca's shouts, he raised his head toward the balcony, and asked what was the matter with a nod of his head. The sacristan answered with a gesture of his hand, indicating someone's departure.

"Who? asked Donna Margarone, who noticed it. "Who? Don Diego or Don Ferdinando?"

"Yes, Ma'am, Don Diego! They leave him in my hands alone! ...I'm running to the doctor, at least for the prescription of the viaticum, what the hell!... Gentlemen, is this the way for a Christian to go, without doctor and without pharmacist?..."

Speranza started with scolding her husband who had tied his mule to a dying man's house:

"It brings bad luck! That's all we need!..."

They they began to figure out the lottery numbers together with Donna Bellonia, who had run inside to get Rutilio Benincasa's book.* Donna Giovannina put her head out while drying her face; but the only one to be seen was the sacristan, who was running to call Tavuso, close by—at a little green door, with the bell rope tied up high, so that they wouldn't come to bother him at night. After knocking over and over again, finally Tavuso's maid blurted through the keyhole:

"Stop it! The Doctor won't come out of the house, even if the world caves in! He's more ill than anybody else!"

Bomma, as yellow as saffron, was pounding cream of tartar in the back of the pharmacy, as alone as if he had the plague. Don Luca ran in, breathing heavily:

"Don Arcangelo!... Don Diego Trao's dying. The Doctor doesn't want to come... What should I do?"

"What should you do?... Make him a coffin, that's what you should do, damn you! You've frightened me! This is not the way... now when every honest man carries his soul on his breath!... Go and call a priest instead...right there at the Collegio there is Canon Lupi, who's been busying himself saying masses and matins since dawn, just to make sure they see him in church!... He always falls on his feet, that one! He doesn't give a damn about the cops!... I'm a pharmacist! I pound cream of tartar, since I cannot pound anything else...I can't!"

But as he saw Ciolla pass by, handcuffed like a thief, he bit his tongue, and lowered his head over the mortar.

"Gentlemen," shouted Ciolla, "look here!...an honest man who's in the square minding his own business!..."

The soldiers at arms pushed him forward without paying attention; Don Liccio Papa escorted him with his saber drawn, shouting:

"Make room! Make room for the Law!..."

The Police Captain, from the height of the Caffè dei Nobili sidewalk, pronounced:

"We must make an example of somebody! They'd kick us you

*Rutilio Benincasa (ca. 1555-1626) is the author of the *Almanacco perpetuo* (1593), a handbook for, to quote the author, "astrologers, physiognomists, doctors, physicists, surgeons, barbers, distillers, alchemists, farmers, painters, sailors, wayfarers, camp masters, sergeants, orderlies, and any other curious person."

know where, if you'd let them!... A gang of scoundrels!... A town like this, that used to be like a monastery!... To the Castello! To the Castello! Don Liccio, here are the keys."

Thank God they could breathe again. The right-minded ones began to show up once more in the streets late in the afternoon: the archpriest before the Caffè; Peperito up and down Rosario; Canali arm in arm with Don Filippo toward the wax-seller's house; Don Giuseppe Barabba taking Donna Marianna Sganci's puppy for a walk; and Mrs. Capitana all dressed up, as if it were her birthday—now that there were so many soldiers—her embroidered purse on her arm, her hat loaded with plumes, wagging her behind, laughing, chirping, towing behind her Don Bastiano Stangafame, the lieutenant, and any of the colleagues of her husband, who was there looking like a real blockhead—holding his bamboo cane behind his back—while the others were walking with his wife, splitting like compasses, laughing at the top of their voices, fiercely looking at the women who dared to show themselves at the windows, filling the town with the noise of their sabers and the clinking of their spurs, as if they had bells at their heels. The Margarone girls, crammed on the terrace, were gnawed by envy. Especially for the lieutenant, who had a moustache as big as horse tails, and along his stomach two rows of buttons that glittered from the distance.

So that, in that holiday atmosphere, the viaticum bell sounded still more melancholy. Sinister rumors were also spreading:

"There was a battle!... Some were condemned to death!"

One of those who carried the big lantern behind the canopy said that the viaticum was going to the Traos.

"Another great family dying out!" gravely observed the Fiscal Attorney taking off his hat.

Mrs. Capitana, skipping on her toes so that she could show off her silk stockings, was rebuking Don Bastiano with a kind of smile that would make you damn your soul:

"I know! I know! Sailor's vows!..."

The Captain at Arms winked at Donna Bianca who was passing by at that very moment, as if to say: "This one too!... What fault is it of mine?" And he took off his hat with excessive obsequiousness. But the poor woman did not answer. She was almost running, out of breath, her cloak slipping down her shoulders, her face anxious and pale. Donna Fifì Margarone withdrew from the balcony with a grimace, as soon as she saw her break into the little square by the Sant'Agata steps.

"Ah!...finally...the good sister!... How condescending of her!..."

"Bianca! Bianca!" shouted Uncle Limòli, who could not keep up with her.

Before the wide-open front door, Burgio's and Don Luca's children were crowding. The sacristan's wife walked out at that very moment, disheveled, yellow, without a stomach, and began to deal smacks right and left:

"Go away! Go away from here!... What are you waiting for? A feast?"

Then she rushed into the church. There were curious women at the windows. At the top of the stairs, Don Giuseppe Barabba was dusting some black banners, with holes gnawed into them by mice, carrying the Trao's coat-of-arms: a red spot all moth-eaten. Aunt Macrì had immediately run over with her daughter, and also Baron Mendola, who lived nearby; a coming and going in the house, a smell of incense and of melting wax; a great confusion. In the background, across a half-open door, you could see the foot of a modest low bed, and a swarming of lighted candles, funereal, in the daylight. Bianca did not see anything else, in the midst of all those relatives who were crowding around her, blocking her way:

"No!... Let me in!..."

For a moment Don Ferdinando's stunned face appeared, like a ghost; then the door closed. Some friendly arms supported Bianca, affectionately, while Aunt Macrì kept repeating:

"Wait!... Wait!..."

The sacristan's wife came back, panting, carrying some candlesticks under her apron. Her husband, who again leaned out of the door, said:

"There is the viaticum...the Extreme Unction.... But he is unconscious..."

"I want to see him!... Let him go!"

"Bianca!...at a moment like this!... Bianca!... D'you want to kill him?... If he's startled!... If he recognizes you!... Don't do that, don't, Bianca!... A glass of water!... Quick!..."

Donna Agrippina ran into the kitchen. The door opened again

on the glittering of a procession. The priest, the canopy, the viaticum, big lanterns passed by like an apparition. The Marquis, bowing to the floor, grumbled:

"*Domine, salva me*... Lord, save my soul ..."

"*Amen*," answered the sacristan. "I've done what I could... alone like a dog!... Twice to call the Doctor!... In the middle of the night!... And to call the pharmacist too!... He says the bill is long...and he doesn't have the miracle-herb of Lazarus Risen, after all!..."

"Why?... Why don't you let me in?... What have I done?..."

Bianca was shaking so that her teeth made the glass tinkle, and was almost beside herself, staring at the people with frightened eyes.

"Let me go! Let me in!"

Her uncle, the Marquis, quickly got out his handkerchief, to wipe away all the water that she had spilled on herself. Baron Mendola and Aunt Macrì were talking before the big window.

"A long illness!... All that way, those Traos!... There is nothing that can be done!"

"Look!" exclaimed the Baron, who had been watching intently for some time. "They opened a little window onto my roof...down there!...that thief of a Canali!... Fortunately, I saw it! I'm going to sue him!... It'll be a lawsuit as black as pitch!"

"Don Luca! Don Luca!" someone shouted.

Suddenly the door opened wide, and Don Ferdinando appeared, waving his arms in the air. Don Luca ran over in a flash. There was a moment of confusion: screams, excited voices, a mad running here and there, Donna Agrippina looking for the *Vinegar of the Seven Thieves*, the others who could hardly hold Bianca back —who was like a madwoman, foaming at the mouth, and with her no longer recognizable eyes darting flashes of lightning.

"Why?... Why don't you want me to? Let me go! let me go!... Let me in!..."

"Yes! yes!" said her uncle, the Marquis. "It's only right that she sees him!... Let her in."

She saw a long, stiff body in the low little bed, a sharp chin, bristling with grayish beard turned upward, and two blue eyes, wide-open.

"Diego!... Diego!... Brother!..."

"Don't do that, Donna Bianca!" whispered Don Luca. "If he can still hear you, can you imagine the scare!..."

She stopped, shaking all over, frightened, her hands in her hair, looking around, stunned. Suddenly she fixed her dry and burning eyes on Don Ferdinando, who was groping around in a daze, as if he wanted to push her away from the bed.

"Nothing!... You let me know nothing!... I don't mean anything...a stranger!... I'm shut out of your house and of your heart!... Out!...of everywhere!"

"Quiet!..." stammered Don Ferdinando placing his trembling finger on his lips. "Later!...later!... Now quiet!... All these people, see!..."

"Bianca! Bianca!..." pleaded the others, hugging her, pushing her, pulling her by her dress.

"Take her away!..." shouted Aunt Macrì from the doorway. "In her condition, the poor girl...there will be a tragedy!..."

Meanwhile, Donna Sarina Cirmena arrived, all out of breath, streaming with sweat.

"I just found out!" she stammered letting herself down into the leather armchair in the midst of all the relatives gathered in the hall. "What can you expect? With all that commotion in town! If it weren't because of the viaticum I saw coming this way!..."

The Marquis nodded toward the door leading to the other room. Aunt Cirmena, slumped on the armchair, her handkerchief to her eyes, whimpered:

"I can't stand these scenes!... I'm all upset!..."

And since she kept asking this person or that with her eyes, Donna Agrippina answered in a whisper, with an anguished look, making the sign of the cross:

"Just now!... Five minutes ago!"

Don Giuseppe came in carrying a bundle of banners:

"Here!... I've told the carpenter."

Baron Mendola got up to go and find out what he wanted.

"All right, all right," said Baron Mendola. "In a while we'll take care of everything. Don Luca? Hey? Don Luca?"

As the sacristan stuck his head through the doorway, they heard such screams that would tear your heart to shreds.

"Poor Bianca!... D'you hear?"

"She's like a madwoman!" confirmed Don Luca. "She's tearing her hair out . . ."

Baron Mendola asked him in front of everybody:

"You've taken care of everything, eh, Don Luca?"

"Yes sir. The catafalque, the banners, as many masses as there are priests. But who's going to pay?"

"Go! go!" cut in Aunt Cirmena sharply, pushing the sacristan by the shoulders toward the dead man's room, where the commotion was increasing.

"Too bad!" observed Aunt Macrì getting up to see how far the sun had reached. "Too bad it's getting late, and at home there's nobody to prepare a bite to eat."

Out of the dead man's room came Don Luca, his face upset.

"It's a serious business. . . . We'll have to take her away, whether she likes it or not! . . . I tell you that it's a serious business!"

"May we come in? May we?"

It was the deep voice of the hunter, accompanying Baroness Mendola, who was wearing her plumed hat and her stockings full of walnuts. The old woman, without needing to hear more, as straight and stiff as a pole, went to take her place among the relatives who had all grown quiet when she had made her appearance, while they sat around in the ancient armchairs, their faces long and their hands on their bellies. The Baroness looked all around, shouting:

"And Baroness Rubiera? And Cousin Sganci? What shall we do now? We must tell all the relatives about the funeral. . . ."

"There she is!" Donna Sarina whispered into Donna Macrì's ear. "If the world caved in . . . she would still be there! . . . Did you see the kind of commotion there was in the streets?"

The Cousin answered with a pale smile, indicating that the old woman did not fear anything, because she was deaf.

"The fact is . . ." the Baron began.

But just then Donna Agrippina and the sacristan — both red in the face, panting, and out of breath — were carrying Bianca who had fainted, her arms hanging loose.

"As if she were dead!" snorted the sacristan. "Her bones are weighing her down! . . ."

Aunt Macrì advised:

"There, there, in her own bedroom! . . ."

"The fact is . . ." Baron Mendola continued in a whisper, pulling aside Cousin Limòli and Donna Sarina Cirmena, "the fact is that we must plan together for the funeral. Now you'll see that the brother-in-law Motta's relatives will come forward. . . . We're going to make quite a show! . . . Side by side with Burgio and *mastro* Nunzio Motta! . . . But we can't leave her husband out. . . . It's a disaster, I don't deny it . . . but we must swallow Mastro-don Gesualdo, eh? . . ."

"Of course! of course!" answered Aunt Cirmena.

She wanted to raise some other objections. But Marquis Limòli said frankly what he thought:

"Forget it, my dear cousin! . . . As a matter of fact . . . the dead man is dead, and is not going to say anything."

"In that case! . . ." retorted Aunt Cirmena, red in the face. "It's really a disgrace that Mastro-don Gesualdo hasn't even put in an appearance."

Baron Mendola went out to the landing to tell Barabba to run to the Sgancis's.

"We'll need money," he said in a low voice as he came back in. "Did you hear the sacristan? Who's going to cover the cost?"

Aunt Macrì pretended not to hear, as she was talking with Donna Cirmena in whispers:

"Poor Bianca! . . . In that condition! How many months is she? D'you know? . . ."

"Seven . . . They must be seven . . . It's really a serious business! . . ."

Marquis Limòli, who was discussing the funeral plans with Baron Mendola and with Barabba, concluded:

"I would invite the First Confraternity of the Whites, since it's a question of a man of distinction. . . ."

"Of course . . . We must do things properly . . . without pinching pennies! . . ."

But everybody took to the open sea when it came to the point of advancing a cent. Meanwhile, in the dead man's room the dispute was going on between the sacristan's wife, who wanted Don Ferdinando to leave, and him, who persisted in staying; on one side, like the whimpering of a puppy, and on the other the hoarse voice of Aunt Grazia, who kept screaming:

"Holy Virgin! You really don't understand anything?... You're just like a little boy! My own boy would have more sense than you, you see?"

And all of a sudden, in the middle of the group of the relatives who were talking in whispers, appeared Don Ferdinando, dragging his feet, his hair disheveled, his shirt unbuttoned, his face like the face of a dead body, carrying an old sheet of paper which he showed around to everybody:

"Here's the privilege!... King Martin's diploma.... We must put it in the death notice.... We must let people know that we are entitled to be buried in the royal tombs... *una cum regibus!* together with kings! Did you take care of the banners with the coat-of-arms? Did you take care of the funeral plans?"

"Yes, yes, don't worry..."

Since everyone avoided taking a direct commitment, turning their backs on him, Don Ferdinando walked from one to the other, mumbling, with tears in his eyes:

"*Una cum regibus!*...together with kings!... My poor brother! ... *Una cum regibus!*..."

"All right, all right," answered Marquis Limòli. "Don't worry."

Baron Mendola, who had been having conversations with various people outside on the landing, came back in, gesticulating:

"My dear friends!... If you only knew!... I'm thunderstruck!..."

"Quiet!" the Marquis motioned to him. "Quiet! What's the matter now?..."

You could hear a great commotion in Bianca's room; gasping and pleading voices; the sound of blunted movements as if of people wrestling; delirious screams of pain and of anger; then a howl that made everybody start. The door was banged open and suddenly the Marquis walked out, agitated and upset. A moment later Aunt Macrì stuck her head out screaming:

"A doctor! Quick! quick!"

More relatives were then arriving like a procession, with anguished looks, wearing black gloves. In the middle of the noise of the chairs being shifted, Aunt Macrì screamed again:

"Quick! A doctor! Quick!"

IV

"If a conglomeration of formalities shapes not the theme of my utterings, obsequiousness is not unobserved. Thus less fallacious and more stable fonts of messages I esteem the direct pleadings. The favor of a glance from you is what I gasp for, and covet it by the grace of these my long-faced lines.

The 7th hour of the 17th."

BARON ANTONINO RUBIERA

"Of course!" added *mastro* Titta standing in the middle of the doorway to the box, while Donna Fifi was slowly reading the little letter. "He gave it to me himself, the young Baron, to be delivered secretly to the leading lady. But for God's sake, I'm a family man. . . . Don't make me lose my bread and butter."

Donna Fifi, yellow with anger, didn't even answer. Secretly, behind the parapet, she was crumpling up the letter in her feverish hand. Then she passed it to her mother, who was stammering:

"But let's hear it. . . . What does it say? . . ."

"I'm going," said the barber humbly. "I'm going back to the stage because at this time she kills the leading man, and I must comb her hair down over her shoulders. . . . Please, Donna Fifi, I plead with you . . . Don't betray me! . . ."

"But what does it say?" repeated the mother.

Little Nicola stuck his head between them, and got a kick for it. At his screams Don Filippo ran over. He had been walking back and forth in the corridor because the box was crammed full.

"What's the matter? . . . As usual! We'll have the entire theater against us . . . just us! . . ."

Canali stuck his head into the box too.

"Watch carefully! Now comes the scene when they kill each other! . . ."

"Don't I wish it!" muttered Fifi between her teeth.

"Eh? what?"

"Nothing, Fifi has a headache," answered Don Filippo.

Then he whispered to his wife:

"Can you tell me what's the matter?"

"It's stifling!" put in Canali. "Would you please make a little room for me? . . . Look up there! . . . How many people! I'm thinking about taking off my jacket."

There was a wall of heads. Peasants, standing on the gallery benches, held onto the beams of the ceiling to look down into the orchestra; boys almost hanging from the railing, as if they were pruning olive trees; such a crowd that Mrs. Capitana, in the box across, threatened to faint at every moment, her bottle of smelling salts under her nose.

"Why doesn't she let the Captain at Arms untie her corset?" said Canali, who was in the habit of making such remarks.

Baron Mendola, who was paying a visit to Donna Giuseppina Alòsi in the neighboring box, turned around with that silly laugh of his that could be heard throughout the whole theater. Donna Giovannina blushed. Mita opened her eyes wide, and her mother pushed Canali out of the door. Then she said to Fifì:

"Watch out! Mrs. Capitana is looking at you with her binoculars."

"No! She's not looking at me!" she answered shrugging her shoulders.

"D'you want to hear a good one?" continued the Baron insisting on sticking his head through the doorway. "There's a hell of a racket, at Mrs. Capitana's! . . . She's having somebody watch the inn where the first lady is staying. . . . Her husband too, poor man! . . . Apparently, she's uncovered some pretty good goings on! . . ."

The Captain at Arms, annoyed, felt compelled to retort:

"Why don't you worry about what happens in your home, my dear colleague?"

"Hm! Hm!" coughed Don Filippo gravely.

From the orchestra they called for silence too, for the curtain was rising. At that moment Donna Bellonia pulled out her eyeglasses to read the note, hiding it behind Fifì's back.

"But what does it say? I don't understand a thing! . . ."

"Ah, you don't understand? . . . He never wrote me such a beautiful letter! . . . The villain! The traitor! . . ."

The fact is that Ciolla, who prided himself on being a literary man, had squeezed into it the quintessence of his brain, as he was locked up face to face with the young Baron in the back of Giacinto's shop. Don Filippo asked again:

"But what's the matter? Can you tell me?"

"Ssst!!!" they hissed from the orchestra.

You could have heard a fly buzz. The leading lady, all white except her hair that was hanging loose down over her shoulders, just like *mastro* Titta had combed it, gave goose pimples to all those who were listening to her. Out of anxious expectation, some had risen to their feet, in spite of the objections of those who were sitting behind and could not see anything.

Even Canali, moved, blew his nose like a trumpet.

"Look! Look!... Now!..."

"'I, I myself, with this hand that you wedded, swearing eternal faith!...'"

The leading man, a puny little fellow that she could put in her pocket, backed away with well-calculated steps, one hand on his velvet jerkin and the other in his curly hair, expressing horror.

"I can't stand it, I can't," grumbled Canali. And he ran away at the very moment the applause resounded.

"What an actress, eh? what a talent!" exclaimed Don Filippo, waving his arms too. "The plague!... You, peasant!..."

Little Nicola, scared, kicked and pushed himself head on toward the door, screaming that he wanted to go. Down in the orchestra it was like an earthquake, all standing up, shouting and raving. The leading lady bowed her thanks to this side and to that, wagging her hips, darting her neck to the right and to the left like a turtle, throwing kisses and smiles with her fingertips to the whole crowd, her lips sewn up with lipstick, her breasts jumping out, quivering at every bow.

"Dammit!... Goddammit!..." exclaimed Canali who had started applauding again. "I'm married!... I'm a family man!... But I would go to the dogs!..."

"Oh Daddy, Daddy!" then broke out Donna Fifi, as she burst into tears leaning against her father. "If you love me, Daddy, have somebody give that bitch a good beating!..."

"Eh?..." stammered Don Filippo, open-mouthed and with his hands in the air. "What's gotten into you now?"

Donna Bellonia, Mita, Giovannina, all got up together to calm down Fifì, surrounding her, pushing her into the background, toward the door, so as to hide her. In the boxes across, down in the orchestra, there was a waving of heads, bursts of laughter, curious people who aimed their binoculars toward the Margarone box. Don Filippo, to put an end to that scandal, came to the front row with little Nicola, leaning against the railing and greeting the ladies with a light smile on his lips, while he was grumbling in a whisper:

"Stupid fool!... Your brother, so small, has more sense than you, look!..."

You could hear a commotion in the neighboring box too. Donna Giuseppina Alòsi was terribly busy, her bottle of smelling salts in her hand, and Baron Mendola, turning his back to the theater, was shaking with his hands a boy as white as a shirt, almost lifeless on a chair.

"The La Gurna boy got sick,..." said Baron Mendola from Donna Giuseppina's box. "He understands everything, just like the grownups!... A nuisance!"

"Just like my Fifì...just now!... These blessed children! They take everything seriously!..."

The boy, pale, with big, intelligent, and timid eyes, was still staring at the stage, with the curtain down. Out of courtesy, after her little nephew had somewhat recovered his senses, Donna Giuseppina offered her bottle of smelling salts to the Margarones. Don Filippo kept grumbling in whispers:

"Just like the La Gurna boy, who's seven!... It's a disgrace!... but you're not going to catch me here any more, that's sure!"

But he stopped as he saw Baron Mendola coming to pay a visit, all dressed up, his tailcoat bottle-green, his pants apple-blossom, and only his big necktie black, in mourning for his cousin Trao. He went around paying visits from one box to the other, so that he wouldn't have to pay for a seat.

"Don't disturb yourselves...just a couple of inches...in a corner.... You, Canali, can go to Donna Giuseppina's box, next door; there's nobody there!... No, no, really, nobody!... Sarino, her little boy, as tall as her fan—you know the song—and little Corrado La Gurna, her aunt Trao's boy...Donna Giuseppina takes him wherever she goes to use him as a screen...when she's expecting certain people to come visiting . . . understand? They sent him on purpose from Siracusa, just to pester us! . . ."

Then, as soon as Canali was gone:

"Now Peperito's coming too! . . . I don't like this kind of game! . . ."

And he winked. Nobody answered. Then, as he saw those long faces, he continued, changing his tune:

"What a performance, eh! Especially the woman! . . . She made me cry like a child! . . ."

"Same here! Same here!" answered Don Filippo, pretending to turn it into a joke.

"Ah, Donna Fifì . . . cheer up; no, in the third act they make peace. He's only wounded. He's saved by a girl who loves him secretly, and then vice versa they discover that she's his foster sister. . . . A play that was performed two evenings in a row at Caltagirone. . . . Oy! Oy! . . . What's going on now?"

The Captain at Arms, in the box across, thinking he was not being seen, was motioning to them from behind Mrs. Capitana's back with his white handkerchief, pretending to blow his nose. Baron Mendola, as he turned around, caught Donna Giovannina with her handkerchief at her face too. She immediately lowered her eyes and became as red as a tomato.

"Ah! . . . ah! . . . Of course! Quite a company! Lucky that they happened to come to this area. Especially the leading lady! . . . She's staying right there, across from my house, in Nanni Ninnarò's inn. You should see every night, after the performance! . . ."

And he finished his sentence in the ear of Don Filippo, who answered:

"Hm! . . . Hm! . . ."

"I'm going to smack you in the face," meanwhile her mother threatened Giovannina in a whisper, staring at her ferociously, "I'll make you catch my kind of cold! . . ."

"Of course!" continued the Baron aloud, so that the girls would not understand. "Actually the boss is the aristocratic father, the one you saw wearing the big white beard. They pretend to fight every evening on the stage. . . . But then, at home, you should see! . . . I don't have to tell you more! I've made a hole on purpose in the granary window-covering that looks straight into her room. But there are the casual ones, the cheap worshipers, understand? those who bring their offerings. . . . Notary Neri's son sacked the pantry, when his father was a fugitive . . . sausages, strings of dried figs, whole cheeses . . . He kept bringing something in his pocket every day. . . . Oy! Oy!"

Mrs. Capitana was getting ready to leave before the end. Standing in the front of the box, she had rudely pulled the shoulder scarf from the Captain at Arms, and had handed it to the lieutenant, who was arranging it on her naked shoulders, right under his superior's nose, slowly, taking his own time, without giving a damn about all those eyes staring at him. But Don Bastiano Stangafame, fan in hand, and her peaceful husband, were looking on in silence. Baron Mendola nudged Margarone, and they both began to look into the air, scratching their chins. Canali remarked from the nearby box:

"If each gets his share, it's only fair!"

"Mind your own business, rather! Mind yourself! . . ."

"Yes, yes, I saw him come. . . . Now I'm running away before the Cavaliere gets here. . . ."

He ran into Peperito just in the corridor doorway.

"Oh, Cavaliere! . . . Lucky to see you! We were worried around here . . . that's sure! . . ."

"Why?" stammered Peperito becoming red in the face.

"Well . . . A performance such as this . . . the whole town has rushed to see it. . . . We were saying . . . how come that the Cavaliere? . . ."

Peperito hesitated for a while, looking for an answer, not knowing whether or not he should show anger, and then he shut the door in his face.

"Now they want to look like the picture of the Innocents!" added Canali laughing. "I'm going into the orchestra to see it from down there."

"Cheer up, Donna Fifi!" said Baron Mendola later. "There are no dead and no wounded! . . . if we cannot make you laugh no matter what, it will mean . . ."

Just then you could hear the rustle of silk in the corridor, with a noise of sabers and spurs. Donna Giovannina became red as fire, feeling her mother's eyes on her. Mrs. Capitana pushed the door of the box, and put her curly and smiling little head inside.

"No, no, don't disturb yourselves. I came for just a moment to say hello. This performance is really indecent... I'm leaving not to hear any more... And the woman's dress?... Did you see, while she bowed?..."

"Eh! eh!..." answered Don Filippo nodding toward his girls.

"Right! A mother can't even take her daughters to the theater."

"True!" remarked Don Filippo. "The law ought to do something about it..."

The lieutenant, who had been put in high spirits by Mrs. Capitana's attentions, added:

"I'm the law. Now I'm going to run to the stage to see if what I think... I want to put my finger there, just like Saint Thomas!"

But nobody laughed. Only Mrs. Capitana, patting him on the arm, bent smiling toward Donna Bellonia's ear to tell her in confidence about what the lieutenant was saying:

"But I say no. Look at Donna Giovannina... She's almost as heavy as the leading lady, and yet it doesn't show.... A little... maybe...up close...maybe because of the corset that's too tight...."

"How so very beautiful!..." grumbled the Captain at Arms from the corridor. "How so very elegant!..."

Baron Zacco, who was just arriving, was ready to go back as soon as he saw the uniforms—so great was the fear still in him after that *Carboneria* business. But then he got courage, not to arouse suspicion, and went to shake hands with everybody—smiling, and as yellow as a dead man.

"I'm coming from Cousin Bianca Trao's. She's still at her brother's place, poor thing! She can't move!... She wanted to have her baby right in her old home!... I didn't know anything about it; I was in the country looking after my interest."

"But why haven't they baptized that baby girl yet?" asked Margarone. "Archpriest Bugno is making a hell of a racket for that innocent soul who's running the risk of going to limbo."

Then the Police Captain spoke up.

"They're waiting for His Majesty's mandate, God save us.... It was Marquis Limòli's idea to pass the Trao name on to the side descendants, now that the male line is dying out.... I had the papers in my own hands...."

"Yes, a great family...a great name," added Mrs. Capitana.

"I went to pay a visit to Donna Bianca. I saw the baby girl too...a beautiful little face."

"Very well!" concluded Baron Zacco. "So Mastro-don Gesualdo's gain is that not even his daughter is his own."

The crack made them laugh. Canali, who was coming back with his pockets full of roasted chestnuts, wanted to hear it again.

"Good night! Good night! I don't want to hear anything else!" exclaimed Mrs. Capitana smiling and covering her ears with her little gloved hands. "No...I'm going...really!..."

They were all in the corridor—Donna Fifì chewing a smile between her yellow teeth; little Nicola behind Canali, who was handing out roasted chestnuts; even Donna Giuseppina Alòsi had opened her box door not to give people a chance to gossip. Only Donna Giovannina had remained in her seat, nailed down by her mother's gruff face. Don Ninì, who was coming in stealthily not to arouse his fiancee's suspicion, dressed in black and with a small bunch of roses in his hand, was a little surprised when he saw so many people in the corridor. Donna Fifì gave him a dirty look and rudely pulled away by the arm her brother who was climbing all over Don Ninì to search his pockets. The Captain at Arms, looking into the Margarones' box with daring, wide-open eyes, flattered the boy saying:

"What a good looking boy!... So cute!... A great family!..."

Donna Fifì answered with a coy smile, from right under her fiancé's eyes. Mrs. Capitana herself had a sour smile; she looked at Donna Giovannina, whose eyes were shining, and since Peperito was flattering little Corrado La Gurna, so as to court Donna Giuseppina —by saying that he looked distinguished, the very look of the Traos —Mrs. Capitana added, with her sweet little voice:

"It's really surprising the family look they all have. Did you notice how Donna Bianca's little girl looks like Don Ninì?"

"What the hell!" grumbled Canali in her ear. "What kind of stories are you concocting!..."

There followed a few moments of embarrassing silence. Baron Zacco left, humming a tune. Canali announced that the last act was about to begin. There was an exchange of kisses and of stinging smiles among the ladies. Donna Fifì even went so far as to languidly shake the hand the Captain at Arms held out to her in an out-of-town fashion.

"Come, come in for a moment," said Donna Bellonia to the

young Baron. "You can sit in the back of the box, with Fifi—since you are in mourning. Nobody will see you. Get away from there, Giovannina."

"Always the same story!" grumbled Giovannina, furious against her sister. "I must always step back for her!..."

"Mother...let him go...if he's in mourning!... He can see the play from the stage!..." jeered Fifi.

"Me?..."

But she turned her back on him. Baron Mendola had stuck himself into the box in front of all the others—to see the scene he had talked about—and was giving explanations at every word.

"Listen now...we'll find out that the foster sister is somebody else's daughter..."

"These are things that happen!" remarked Canali from the doorway.

"Quiet! Quiet! You backbiter!"

All eyes, including those of the girls, turned to the young Baron, who pretended not to understand.

"If you're annoyed...," grumbled Donna Fifi, "and since you stand there like an idiot...why don't you go?..."

"Me?..."

"There you are!..." Baron Mendola cut in triumphantly. "There you are!...understand?"

"I'm a married man!..." said Canali again. "I'm a family man... But I would be ready to go to the dogs for the leading lady!... Even her name is beautiful!... Aglae..."

"It sounds like Agli... Garlic... What a name!..." jeered Baron Mendola. "I wouldn't know what to do with her...face to face!..."

Don Filippo went right to the point.

"She's a great artist...a first-class leading lady.... So you understand..."

"Of course," Don Nini blurted out rashly, just to say something.

"Ah!... You like her too?..."

"Certainly...but...I mean..."

"Tell us, tell us!... We know all about it!..."

Baron Mendola, smelling a storm, got up to sneak away:

"I know the rest of the play. Good night. Excuse me, Don Filippo. Listen, Canali..."

Unfortunately, the leading lady who was supposed to keep her eyes turned up to the sky while declaiming "If it's written up above ...by Fate..." found herself looking at the Margarones' box. At that point Donna Fifì could not restrain herself any more:

"Yes, we know all about it! The conglomeration of formalities!... The long-faced lines!..."

"Me?... The long-faced lines?"

But she sprang up ferociously, as if she wanted to plant her teeth into his face.

"It takes some gall!... Yes sir! the letter with the long-faced lines!...here it is!..." And she brushed it under his nose, bursting into tears of rage.

At first Don Nini was dumbfounded. Then he too sprang up like a fury, looking for his hat. In the doorway he ran into Don Filippo, who was rushing over at the noise.

"You're an idiot!... A fool!... You surely brought up your daughter beautifully!... Thank God, I won't set foot in your house again!"

And he went off furiously, slamming the door. As soon as the young Baron had left, Don Filippo, open-mouthed, rushed into the box, and in turn shouted at his wife:

"You're an idiot!... You weren't able to bring up our daughters decently!... D'you see what I must hear!... You shouldn't have brought that ruffian into my house!..."

The break was a sensation. Five minutes later people talked about nothing else in the whole theater. The performance almost ended up by being booed. The leading actor got angry at the leading lady, who caused him to be on the wrong side of the most important families in town. But she kept repeating and swearing that she didn't even know what he looked like, that Baron, and she didn't give a damn about him. She was heard by Cosimo, the carpenter, and by all those on the stage. The day after, Don Nini, furious, ran up to see Ciolla, who was going about his business, after those twenty-four hours he had spent at the Castello under lock and key.

"You certainly made me look like an idiot with your 'long-faced lines'!... The whole town knows your letter by heart!..."

"Fine! What does that mean? It means that they liked it, if they know it by heart!..."

"The hell, they liked it! She says that she doesn't give a damn about me!"

"Oh! Oh!... That's impossible!... That letter would have brought down a wall! Obviously, it's your fault, Don Nini... I'm not talking about your looks.... You should have sent a present or two, along with it, my dear Baron! Powder makes the bullet fly!... Did you think you'd make a hit just with that cute face of yours?... With two cents worth of satin-paper?... For you didn't even give me a cent, did you?..."

In vain friends and relatives tried to intervene and bring the young Baron and Donna Fifi back together. Her mother kept repeating:

"What can you do?... Men!... Your father too!..."

Don Filippo tried a different tune.

"Trifles... Youthful pranks!... It was no more than circumstances... The novelty... Leading ladies don't come by every year... You're a Margarone, after all! He can't give up a Margarone for an actress!... Besides, if I am the one to forgive, and yet I've been most offended!..."

But Donna Fifi wouldn't be pacified. She kept saying that she didn't want to have anything more to do with that one—an idiot, a miser, the Baron Long-faced Lines!... In any case, she would most certainly find a suitor a hundred times better than he.... She vilified him with everybody, friends and relatives. Out of rage, Don Nini would have liked to do all kinds of things. He swore that he intended to come out on top, no matter what, and to get the leading lady, out of spite, if for nothing else.

"Ah! I'm going to show that witch!... Powder makes the bullet fly!..."

And he sent presents of sausages, provolone cheese, a big bottle of wine—they covered the table at the inn. People talked about nothing else in the whole town. Baron Mendola told how every night you could see the Cana Wedding feast from his hole. Presents atop presents, so much so that the Baroness had to hide the key to the pantry. Finally *mastro* Titta said to Don Nini:

"She can't hold it any longer, sir! She's lost her head, that leading lady. Every night, while I comb her hair, she doesn't talk about anything else."

"If you can help me get the satisfaction I want!... Under Donna Fifi's own eyes I want to get that satisfaction! I want to make her die of consumption!"

The first meeting was a disappointment. Signora Aglae pretended to play the role of a poor blind woman, and her face was painted like a mask. Nevertheless, she received him like a queen, in her cubicle that was filled with the stench of burned wax, and introduced him to a great big man who was rummaging inside a chest, in shirtsleeves, and who didn't even turn around:

"Baron Rubiera, a distinguished amateur... Signor Pallante, a famous artist."

Then she glanced at the back of the famous artist, who kept on searching and grumbling, she glanced lengthily at Don Nini, and added in a lower voice:

"I already know you!... I see you every night...in the orchestra!..."

He was about to excuse himself by saying that he hadn't gone to the theater because he was in mourning; but just then Signor Pallante turned around, his hands dirty with dust, his face also plastered up, and on his head a bladder-skin, from under which filthy hair was hanging.

"It's not here," he said with a voice so deep that it seemed to come from underground. "I told you!...Dammit!" and he walked out grumbling.

She looked around with an air of mystery, her eyes wild in their black sockets; she went to close the door on tiptoe, and then she turned toward the young man, one hand on her breast, a pale smile at the corner of her mouth.

"Strange how my heart is beating!... No... It's nothing... Please sit down."

Don Nini looked for a chair, his head on fire, his heart beating wildly. Finally he perched on the trunk, looking for some appropriate phrases to make an impression, while she was burning a piece of cork at the flame of the smoking oil lamp.

Another visitor arrived. Mommino Neri, who, finding Baron

Rubiera there, got immediately into a bad mood, and didn't open his mouth, while he was leaning against the doorpost and sucking the knob of his cane. Signora Aglae kept the conversation going all by herself: a great town...an intelligent and cultivated public... handsome your people too...

"Good night," said Mommino.

"Are you going already?..."

"Yes... You can't move in here... We're too many...."

Don Nini accompanied him with a jeer, keeping on drumming the trunk with his heels. She noticed it and shrugged her shoulders, with a fascinating smile, sighing as if a load had been lifted from her chest.

The young Baron, jubilant, began:

"If I'm in your way, too..." and he looked for his hat, which was in his hand.

"Oh no!...not you!" she answered solicitously, lowering her head.

"May I come in?" said the shrill little voice of the curtain raiser behind the door.

"No! no!" repeated Signora Aglae as vividly as if she had been caught doing something wrong.

"We're on!" added Signor Pallante's deep voice. "Hurry up!"

Then she, raising her resigned face toward Don Nini, with a sad smile:

"D'you see!... I'm never free for a moment!... I'm Art's slave!..."

Don Nini seized the opportunity: Art...what a beautiful thing!...it was her realm...her altar!... Everybody admired her! ...she made so many hearts beat!...

"Ah! yes, I've given all of myself to Art... I've given all of myself to it!..."

And she opened her arms, turning toward him, with such abandon—like offering herself to Art, right then and there—that Don Nini sprang from the trunk to his feet.

"Watch out!" she exclaimed in a low voice, quickly. "Watch out!..."

She instinctively stretched her trembling hands toward him,

almost to keep him away. Then she rubbed her eyes, repressing a sigh, and stammered as if waking up:

"Forgive me... One moment... I must dress..."

And in her eyes flashed a malicious smile.

That nuisance of a Mommino Neri was still there, leaning against a wing, talking with Signor Pallante, who was already dressed as a king, wearing a fur cloak and a paper crown. This time it was Don Ninì's turn to become dark in the face. As if she knew, she opened the door ajar again, leaning out her naked arm and shoulder:

"Baron, if you wait until the end of the act...those lines you'd like to read are there, at the bottom of my trunk."

No! No woman had ever given him such joy, such a blazing heat in his heart and in his head; neither the first time Bianca had abandoned herself in his arms, quivering; nor when a Margarone girl had lowered her proud head, showing herself with him in the midst of the whispers they were stirring in the crowd. It was a real seizure of madness. People even said that to bring her presents he had borrowed money from any and everybody. Baroness Rubiera, desperate, had her tenants warned not to advance a cent to her son, or they'd have to deal with her.

"Ah!...ah!...they'll find out! My son doesn't own anything. I'm not going to pay his debts, for sure!..."

There had been violent scenes between mother and son. He was stubborn, worse than a mule, so much more so because Signora Aglae hadn't even let him go up the stairs of her inn. Finally she had told him why, one night, in the dark, right there on the threshold, while Pallante had gone up ahead to light the lamp:

"He's jealous!...I'm his!...I've been his!..."

And she had confessed everything, her head low, her beautiful melodious voice stifled with emotion. He, a great nobleman disinherited by his father because of that unlucky passion, had been in love with her for a long time—madly, desperately; one of those love stories you read about in novels; he had devoted himself to Art only to follow her; he had suffered in silence; he had pleaded, had cried ...finally one night...just like then...still quivering all over and throbbing with the emotions aroused by Art...her compassion...

his sacrifice...she herself didn't know how...while her heart was flying off, far away...dreaming of different horizons...of different ideals.... But afterward, never again!...never again!... She had recovered herself...in shame...repenting...implacable... He still loved her, as much as before...more than before...madly ...he was jealous: jealous of everything and of everybody, of the air, of her dreams, of her thoughts, of him too, Don Nini!...

"Hey!" said a deep voice from upstairs. "D'you want'em fried or with tomato sauce?"

Over her face sweetly veiled by the half darkness, journeyed an angelic smile. "D'you see?... It's always this way!... Always the same devotion!..."

Ciolla, who was Don Nini's confidant, told him later:

"You're really an idiot!... That one is a...Stinkpot!* Together they gorge themselves with whatever you and Neri's son send her."

As a matter of fact, he had often met Mommino on the stage, and also before the inn door, walking up and down like a sentry. Now Mommino was all kindness and smiles, as far as he was concerned. When he thought he was really looking like a fool, he flew into a rage:

"Ah!... You want that?..." she finally told him in a feverish voice.... "All right!... All right... If there is no other way to prove how much I love you... Since I must lose myself no matter what...tonight...after midnight!..."

There was a smell of stables, on that little dark stairway, with the greasy steps broken by all the hobnailed boots of the peasants. Up there on top, a thread of light and a white figure that completely offered herself, brusquely, her hair loose.

"You want me?... Your bayadere... Your odalisque?..."

There were dirty plates on the table, a damask mantle worked with arabesques on the bed, carnations and a lighted lamp on the chest of drawers, in front of a little picture of the Virgin, and a scent

*A popular synonym for happy cuckold—one who lives off of his wife's or his mistress' lovers.

of incense coming out of a small cream vase smoking on the floor. A very beautiful turkish shawl, spotted with oil, was nailed to the door to the next room; and behind that turkish shawl you could hear Signor Pallante snoring his jealousy away.

She threw wide open those eyes of hers that lit up the room, placed her forefinger on her lips, and motioned Baron Rubiera to come close.

"The fact is that she's bewitched him!" The canon-priest Lupi was writing Mastro-don Gesualdo, suggesting that he lend a large sum of money to young Baron Rubiera.

"Don Ninì is in debt up to his neck, and doesn't know where to turn any more. . . . The Baroness swears that as long as she lives she won't pay a cent. But she has no other heirs, and sooner or later she'll have to leave everything to him. As you can see, it's a good deal, if you've got guts. . . ."

"How much?" answered Mastro-don Gesualdo. "How much does the young Baron Rubiera need? If it can be done, I'm here."

Later, when in town they found out about the large sum of money Don Gesualdo had advanced to Baron Rubiera, they all said he was crazy and that he was going to lose his money. He answered with that peculiar smile of his:

"Don't worry. I'm not going to lose my money. The Baron is an honest man . . . and time is still more honest."

So the proverb is really right in saying that woman is the root of all evil. Especially if she's an actress!

V

Don Ninì had hoped to keep the deal secret. But for some time his mother had been quite restless, seeing him so changed, irritable, worried—his face flushed and his beard shaven every morning. At night she would not close her eyes trying to figure out where her son could find the money for those silk handkerchiefs and those bottles of perfume. She had put Rosaria and Alessi at his heels. She kept asking her factor and her field workers. She kept the keys to the storehouse and to the pantry under her pillow. As if her heart was telling her, the poor woman! Cousin Limòli had gotten so far as to point at Signora Aglae, who was full of frills and was wagging her behind.

"D'you see her? It's that one. What d'you think, eh, of your daughter-in-law? Are you happy?"

Just as if Don Diego Trao had cast the evil eye on her when he lay dying.

In small towns there are people who would walk miles to bring you bad news. One morning the Baroness was sitting on her balcony in the shade of the wicker screen, basting some canvas sacks which later Rosaria would sew as best she could—squatted as she was on the step, sharpening her eyes and her lips so that the needle wouldn't fall from her big rough hands, and turning now and then to look down toward the deserted little road.

"That's three!" Rosaria blurted out, seeing Ciolla pass by again with a bailiff look on that face of his, scanning the Baroness' house with his eyes from top to bottom, stopping every two steps, turning back again as if he were waiting for somebody to call him. Baroness Rubiera who had been following that coming and going for some time, from under her eyeglasses, finally bent down to stare at Ciolla in such a way that said clearly enough: What are you doing and what do you want?

"God bless!"

He himself began the conversation. And he stopped right then and there, leaning against the wall across the road, his hat over one eye and in his hand a walking cane that looked like the land-survey-or's measuring rod—waiting. In answer to his greetings, Baroness Rubiera asked, with a bittersweet smile:

"What are you doing there? Are you getting an estimate on my house? D'you want to buy it?"

"Not I! . . . Not I," he repeated in a louder voice, as he saw that she had gone back to her sewing. Then the Baroness, her eyeglasses shining, again bent toward the little road, and the two of them looked at each other for a moment, like two basilisks.

"If you have something to tell me, you may come up."

"Nothing, nothing," Ciolla answered, while he was walking toward the front door.

Rosaria pulled the bolt cord and began to grumble:

"Now what does he want, that Christian? It will soon be time to start the fire."

But you could hear the cackling of the animals in the yard and Ciolla's steps slowly coming upstairs. He came in with his hat on, obsequious, repeating: *Deo gratias! Deo gratias!* Thanks be to God! and praising how orderly everything was in the house.

"House mistresses like you are not born any more, Baroness! That's it! That's it! You're always there, working yourself blind. They've really put property together those hands!... They haven't squandered it, oh no!"

The Baroness, who was waiting with her ears stretched out, began to feel uneasy. Meanwhile, Rosaria had cleared a chair of the canvas piled on it, and was listening, scratching her head.

"Go and see if the hen has laid an egg," said the Baroness.

She then turned to Ciolla again, more amiable than usual, so as to pull out of his mouth whatever he had to say. But Ciolla would still keep it inside. He was talking about the weather, about the crops, about the commotion the Company at Arms had left in the town, about the trouble he had gone through.

"The poor are those who always get clobbered, dear Baroness, and those who've made the mess go scot-free. Blessed you who stay home, looking after your interest. It's good! You're right. Whatever we can see here was made by you! I'm not trying to flatter you! Bless your hands! Your husband, rest his soul!... Well, let's not bring the dead into it...everything slipped through his fingers...just like all the Rubieras.... The estates mortgaged to the hilt...and the house... Finally, what was the Rubiera palace after all?... Those five rooms right there?..."

The Baroness pretended to swallow the flattery, by giving him all the information he wanted, as she accompanied him from room to room, explaining to him where doorways had been cut through the walls so that the new would be connected with the old.

Ciolla kept looking around with those bailiff eyes of his, nodding his head, and drawing outlines with his bamboo cane:

"That's it! Those five rooms there! Everything else is yours. Nobody can stick his claws into your property as long as you live.... May God let you enjoy it for a hundred years! A house like this...a real palace! As vast as a monastery! It would be a mortal sin if your enemies managed to break it up . . . for we all have enemies! . . ."

While she felt herself grow pale, she pretended to laugh, the kind of laughter that was enough to get Ciolla's dander up.

"What? Did I say something foolish? We all have enemies. Mastro-don Gesualdo, for instance! . . . I wouldn't like to find him mixed up in my business . . ."

He too pretended to be looking around, suspicious, as if everywhere he saw Mastro-don Gesualdo's long hands.

"He has gotten it into his head to drive himself into your house . . . little by little . . . if it takes him a hundred years . . . just like a porcupine . . . ."

The Baroness had gone back to the balcony for some fresh air, without paying attention to him, so as to pull the rest out of his mouth. He teeter-tottered a little longer, getting ready to go, taking off his hat to stroke it, looking for the bamboo cane that was in his hand, excusing himself for all that nonsense with which he had filled her ears until then.

"Why all that hurry? D'you have to dress up to go to the baptism of Don Gesualdo's baby girl? It will be quite a baptism . . . in the Trao house! . . . The kind of tricks the devil plays . . . that Mastro-don Gesualdo's baby girl should be born in the Trao house! . . . All the relatives will be there . . . all in peace . . . you're a relative too . . ."

The Baroness kept laughing, and Ciolla followed her, both of them staring each other in the face—their eyes alone having remained serious.

"No? You're not going? You're right! Watch out for that man! I won't tell you more! Your son is a jackass! . . . I won't tell you more! . . ."

"My son has his property and I have mine. . . . If he's made a fool of himself, my son will pay, if he can pay. . . . You can be sure I won't! He'll have to pay, with his own stuff, with those five rooms you've seen. . . . He doesn't have anything else, unfortunately. . . . But I'm going to keep my property for myself . . . I'm happy if my son has a good time. . . . He's young . . . He should have a good time . . . But I'm not going to pay, no I'm not!"

"That's what everybody says. Mastro-don Gesualdo thinks he's smart. But this time he's certainly found somebody smarter than he. It would be quite something if he were the one to support Don Ninì's mistress.... He might even think he were indulging in youthful escapades himself!..."

The Baroness was laughing so hard that she held onto the furniture not to fall.

"Ah! ah!... That's really a good one!... This time you really said it, Don Roberto!..."

Ciolla was following her pretending he was laughing too, stealthily looking at her, and irritated because she was taking it so cheerfully. But Rosaria, as she came in to pick up the canvas, found her mistress so pale that she almost called for help.

"Jackass! What are you doing? Why d'you stand there stiff as a board? Rather can you see Don Roberto to the door?..."

So Ciolla finally made up his mind to leave, unburdening himself by grumbling at the servant:

"Your mistress is really in a good mood! I'm glad, I'm glad! Laughter keeps you healthy and makes you live long. Great! Great!"

When she went back upstairs, Rosaria saw her mistress in a frightening state—rummaging in the drawers and in the closets, with hands that could not find anything, with eyes that did not see, with foam at her mouth, dressing herself as fast as she could to go to her cousin Motta's for the baptismal ceremony.

"Yes, I'll go... I'll find out what it's all about!... It's better to know the truth."

The people who saw her go by in the streets, out of breath and her bonnet slanted, did not know what to think. In the little square of Sant'Agata there was great curiosity as the guests arrived for the baptism in the Trao house, and Don Luca the sacristan was coming and going, with candlesticks and other sacred implements under his arm. Every moment Speranza stuck her head onto the landing, shaking her skirt, planting her fists on her hips, and shouting against that baby girl who robbed her of her brother's inheritance:

"This baptism will be sensational! The house is full.... The entire aristocracy... We'll be the only ones...not there! No, we won't go...not to make our aristocratic relatives blush.... We don't have anything to do with this, we don't!... Nobody has invited us to the baptism of our niece.... You can tell that she's not our flesh and blood...."

Also the old man Motta had refused, that morning, when

Gesualdo had gone to plead with him to put the holy water or his grandchild. Seated at the table, having a bite, he said no, while he raised the wine bottle that he had had at his mouth. Then, wiping his lips with the back of his hand, he planted a dirty look on his son.

"You go to your daughter's baptism yourself. It's your business. I wasn't born to be together with the big shots.... You come looking for me only when you need me...to shut people up.... No, no ...when there's a profit to be made you don't come looking for me, no indeed!... The contract for the road...the city lands..."

Mastro Nunzio wanted to recite the litany of his grievances, now that he had his chance. But Gesualdo, who already had his house full of people, and who knew that he could never make him change his mind once he had said no, walked out with a heavy heart and with shrunken shoulders. He wasn't feeling cheerful either, the poor man, although he had to put forth a smiling face for all the congratulations and the bows. But finally he unburdened himself with Nanni l'Orbo who at the bottom of the stairs shamelessly kept pestering him by asking for the special candies of the occasion:

"Yes... Go and see!... Go and see that not even the roof beams can hold any longer—now that a baby girl was born in this house."

Barabba and Baroness Mendola's hunter had helped by sweeping, dusting, putting back on its feet the dilapidated altar, which for so many years had been locked in the closet of the great hall that served as chapel. The hall itself was still draped in mourning, as it had remained after Don Diego's death, with the portraits draped and the benches all around covered with black cloth for the relatives who had come to the funeral—as was the custom in the old families. Don Ferdinando, freshly shaven, wearing one of his cousin Zacco's black suits, which rode up his back, went around poking his nose into everything, his face long, his arms hanging out of the short sleeves of the jacket, anxious and suspicious, asking everybody:

"What is it? What are you doing?"

"Here is your brother-in-law," Aunt Sganci told him as she walked into the hall with Don Gesualdo Motta. "You must embrace each other and get rid of all bad feelings, now that there is that little girl between you."

"Greetings, greetings," grumbled Don Ferdinando, and turned his back on them.

But the other relatives who had more sense were friendly to Don Gesualdo: the Mendolas, the Zacco cousins, all of them. As a matter of fact, times had changed; the whole town had been upside down for twenty-four hours, and no one knew what might happen from one day to the next. By now, like it or not, Mastro-don Gesualdo had become one of the relatives, and they had to reckon with him. Thus they all wanted to see the baby girl — a veritable flower, a spring rose. Aunt Rubiera embraced Bianca, just like a mother who has found her long lost child, wiping her eyes with her handkerchief that was wet as a sponge.

"Yes! Yes, I have feelings, too!... I was so happy I couldn't believe it, after having raised you like my own daughter!... I'm a jackass...I've remained a peasant...just like my mother, rest her soul...doing everything straight from my heart...."

Bianca, all decked out under the big bed canopy, so pale that she seemed made of wax, dazed by all that crowd, didn't know what to answer; she looked at the people with wild eyes, tried to sketch a smile, and stammered. Her husband, on the other hand, played his role well in the middle of all those friends and relatives and of those congratulations — his face open and jovial, his shoulders broad and friendly, his ears stretched out to pick up what was being said around him and behind his back. Aunt Cirmena, all excited, answered those who were wishing the parents a big healthy boy, next time, for girls are like crabgrass, and they sweep everything good out of the house to go and get married.

"Eh...you've got to take children the way God sends them, boys or girls.... If one could go to the market to pick and choose them...Don Gesualdo would have plenty of money to buy himself a boy."

"Don't talk to me about it!" Aunt Rubiera finally cut in. "You don't know how much boys cost!... All the pains and troubles!... How well I know!"

And she kept unburdening herself into Bianca's ear, full of excitement, stealthily casting sidelong glances at Don Gesualdo, to see what he would say. Don Gesualdo didn't say anything. Bianca, however, her eyes low, turned all kinds of colors.

"I can't recognize him any more, no, I can't!...not even I who brought him into the world!... D'you remember what a jewel of a son he was?...docile, loving, obedient... Now he'd turn against his own mother, for that bitch of a stranger...and an actress, d'you know her? They say she's got false teeth and false hair.... She must have cast some kind of a spell on him! An actress and a stranger, understand?... He can't see straight.... He's spending a fortune. ... There are bad people...criminals who even help him.... But I'm not going to pay, no I'm not!... You can be sure of that!"

"Aunt Rubiera!" stammered Bianca, all her blood gone to her face.

"What can we do? He's my cross to bear! Had I known all this..."

Don Gesualdo was busy chatting with Cousin Zacco, both speaking right from their hearts—really great friends! The Baroness then blurted out the question boiling inside her:

"Is it true that your husband lends him money...under-handedly?... Have you seen him come here, to talk to him?... Tell me: d'you know anything about it?"

"Of course, of course," answered Don Gesualdo at that point. "You've got to take children the way they come."

To confirm this Baron Zacco pointed at his own girls, all lined up like so many organ pipes, modest and prosperous.

"Why, yes! I have five daughters and am equally fond of all of them!"

"Of course!" answered Marquis Limòli! "That's why you don't want them to get married."

Donna Lavinia, the oldest of them, threw a dirty look behind her.

"Ah, you're here?" said the Baron. "You're always around, like the devil in the litany, you are!"

The Marquis, whose job it was to be the godfather, was wearing his Cross of Malta. Don Luca came in to say that the canon-priest was ready, and the ladies went into the hall, with a great rustling of silk, behind Donna Marianna who was carrying the baby. Through the open doorway you could see a swarming of little flames. Don Ferdinando out of curiosity stuck his head in at the end of the corridor. Bianca was quietly moved to tears by tenderness. Her husband, who had remained on his knees, with his nose against the wall, as Aunt Macrì had told him to, got up to go and calm her.

"Quiet... Don't let them see you!... Before these people we must put on a smiling face!..."

All of a sudden, in the square below there exploded a loud crackling of firecrackers. Don Ferdinando ran away frightened. The others who were attending the baptism rushed to the balcony, candles in hand. Even the canon-priest, with his surplice and his stole on. It was Santo, Don Gesualdo's brother, who was celebrating his little niece's baptism in that way—in shirtsleeves, on all fours on the pavement, the lighted fuse in his hand.

Don Gesualdo opened the window to pour out a bunch of abuse on him.

"Jackass!... You must always think up something!... Jackass!"

His friends calmed him:

"Poor man...leave him alone. It's his way to show his happiness..."

Aunt Sganci, in triumph, put his daughter into his arms:

"Here is Isabella Trao!"

"Motta and Trao! Isabella Motta and Trao!" corrected the Marquis.

Baron Zacco added that she was a graft. The two families becoming one. But Don Gesualdo's face remained somewhat gloomy as he held the baby in his arms. Meanwhile, Don Lucca was serving ice drinks and cookies with Barabba's and the hunter's help. Aunt Cirmena who had taken along her little nephew La Gurna on purpose, filled his pockets and his handkerchief. But all the Zacco girls said no, because the eldest, reserved, had not taken anything, and devoured the tray with their eyes. Don Luca encouraged them to take something, saying:

"It's quite fresh. I went personally to order it at Santa Maria and at the Collegio. No expense spared."

"What the hell!" said Baron Zacco who was looking for an opportunity to show himself friendly. "What the hell! I would like to see that one too!..."

The others chimed in together—indeed! The Trao house was coming back to life. God's will. That little girl herself who had wanted to be born in her maternal home. The canon-priest Lupi went so far as to congratulate Marquis Limòli, who had found a way of not letting the Trao name become extinct with the death of Don Ferdinando.

"Of course, of course," grumbled Don Gesualdo. "It was already agreed... I said 'yes' at the time... When I've given my word..."

And he went to put his daughter, whom all the aunts were stealing from one another, in the arms of his wife. Baroness Mendola wanted to know what they were saying. Baron Zacco, out of consideration, asked for some of the special candles to bring to Don Ferdinando, whom everybody had forgotten.

"Of course, of course. He's the master of the house."

"See?" remarked Aunt Rubiera. "There already is in this world the one who'll take away from you both your daughter and your property."

There was a burst of laughter. Donna Agrippina twisted her mouth and lowered those great big eyes of hers, which said many things, to the floor — as if she had heard something dirty. Don Gesualdo was laughing too, and wore a smiling face for everybody. Finally he even risked a crack:

"And when she gets married, she'll leave her Trao name too! ...but not her dowry; she won't leave that!..."

Baroness Rubiera, who thought this was the right moment, and who did not want to miss the opportunity, pulled him close to the bed, face to face with her — while you could hear Baron Mendola and Don Ferdinando quarreling aloud at the end of the corridor, and everybody ran to see.

"Listen, Don Gesualdo; I don't mince words. I wanted to talk to you about that reckless one — my son. You help me, Bianca."

"Me, Aunt Rubiera?..."

"Excuse me, I can talk only straight from the heart... just like my mother made me.... Now that you too are a father, Don Gesualdo, you'll understand how I feel inside... what a thorn... what a torment!..."

She was looking now at her niece and now at her niece's husband with her sharp eyes, and with the simple and genial smile her parents had taught her to put on for thorny deals. Don Gesualdo was listening calmly. Bianca, embarrassed by those words, looked like a wax statue, with her little girl on her lap.

"You must know the talk that's going around, about Nini and that actress. All right. I wouldn't worry about that. She's not the first and she's not going to be the last. His father, rest his soul, was that way too. So far I've kept him from making a mess. But now he's fallen into bad company, criminals... Listen, Bianca; if I were you, I wouldn't have asked that canon-priest there to baptize my daughter!..."

Bianca, dismayed, moved her lifeless lips without being able to find a word. Don Gesualdo, however, put on a smile when the Baroness blurted out that remark. As she heard people coming back, she finally asked openly:

"Tell me the truth. He has approached you to borrow money, hasn't he?... And did you give it to him?"

Don Gesualdo was now laughing loudly. Then, as he saw the Baroness become as red as a tomato, he answered:

"Excuse me...excuse me... In case... Why don't you ask him?... That's really great!... I'm not your son's father confessor..."

Baron Mendola broke into the room telling everybody, in the middle of outbursts of laughter, the scene he had just had with that bear of a Don Ferdinando, who had refused to come to make peace with his brother-in-law. Baroness Rubiera, without saying more, was wiping her lips with her handkerchief still sticky with sweet stuff, while the relatives were saying good-bye. As they left, each one had a word of praise about the way things had been done. Donna Marianna whispered to Baroness Rubiera that it was good that she had come too, not to attract attention, to keep the backbiters quiet. ... The other replied with a dirty look that Donna Agrippina caught immediately:

"It's really been of help! They're snakes! I won't tell you more! We've put a viper in our bosom!... You'll see in time..."

Don Gesualdo, who had remained alone with his wife, swallowed in one gulp a big glass of water, without saying anything. Bianca, her face haggard, as if she were about to faint, followed his movements with frightened-looking eyes, pressing the baby to her breast.

"Here, would you like a drink of water?" he said. "You must be thirsty too."

She nodded. But the glass was shaking so badly in her hands that she spilled all the water on herself.

"It doesn't matter, it doesn't matter," continued her husband. "There's nobody to see us now."

And he began to wipe the sheet dry with his handkerchief. Then he picked up the baby who was crying, and dandled her in his arms to make her stop, as he walked about the room.

"Did you see what kind of people? How loving, those relatives. But they're not going to take your husband in, they're not!"

Outside, above the square, all the neighbors were at the windows and in the doorways, to see the guests leave. At the Margarones' window, far in the background, above the roofs, there were also more people who stuck their heads out every minute. Baroness Rubiera began to greet them from the distance with her fan and with her handkerchief, while she was talking with Marquis Limòli, so heatedly that they seemed to be coming to blows.

"They're snakes, that's what they are! Nothing but criminals! They're going to eat up that degenerate son of mine in one bite!... But first he'll have to deal with me! Listen, come along with me to the Margarones' for a minute...I haven't seen them for a long time. ... After all that isn't a reason to break with old friends...a childish prank.... You're a well-bred man...and sometimes...the right word at the right time..."

Donna Giovannina came to the door—with a long face. You could see in the background the drawing-room door wide open; and the furniture covers off. An atmosphere of formality, in short.

"What is it?" asked the Marquis going inside. "What's going on?"

"I don't know anything!" exclaimed Donna Giovannina, who seemed about to burst into tears. "There must be somebody out there; but I don't know anything about it."

"Poor girl! poor girl!" The Marquis was lingering in the entry-room, stroking her. He had taken her cheek between two fingers, while he was winking mischievously, and looking around to whisper into her ear:

"What can we do? Too bad! First come first served. Is Donna Fifi with your mother to receive the guests, eh?...Don Bastiano, eh? the Captain at Arms?..."

In fact, Don Bastiano was there in the drawing-room, dressed in civilian clothes—freshly shaven, his brand-new suit shining on him, seated on the sofa next to Mother Margarone, like a fiancé, now and then letting a languid and sentimental glance slide toward the girl, stroking his big new moustache that refused to bend. Donna Fifi, seeing Baroness Rubiera come in, became cocky, haughty, cooing underhandedly at the stranger to spite her.

"Oh, oh," said the Marquis, greeting Don Bastiano, who was feeling rather foolish. "You're still around? Good! Good!"

And while the ladies were chatting all together, he began to talk with the Captain, asking him why the Company at Arms had left without him, if he intended to stay there for some time, if he liked the town and was planning to leave the uniform. Don Bastiano kept to generalities, praising the landscape, the climate, the people, underlining his words with expressive glances toward Donna Fifi, who pretended to be looking out over the balcony with her eyes full of poetry, and bent her head blushing at every one of those compliments, as if they were meant for her. Suddenly the Marquis asked why Don Filippo was not there, and they answered that he had gone out to take little Nicola for a walk.

"Ah! Good! Good!"

Baroness Rubiera bit her lips waiting for Cousin Limoli to lead the conversation toward the subject they had agreed upon. Meanwhile, however, she stealthily observed the languid looks of Donna Fifi, who seemed to be melting under Don Bastiano Stangafame's fiery glances, and could not sit still on the chair, her flat breasts panting like a pair of bellows, and her restless little feet saying so many things as they came out of the hem of her dress every minute. The conversation languished. They talked about the baptism and about the people who had attended it. But meanwhile everybody was thinking about his own business, chatting about trivial things, searching for words, with an absent smile on their lips. Only the Marquis seemed to be deeply interested in what the Captain had to say, as if he had not come there for any other reason. Then, with the corner of his eye seeing the red face of Donna Giovanninia, who was peering in through the half-closed door, he called her in a loud voice:

"Come in, come in, pretty girl. We want to see that pretty face. There's only us here, *en famille*...."

The mother and the eldest sister darted two lightninglike dirty looks at the girl, who was standing in the doorway, hiding her servant's hands under her apron, ashamed of having been caught that way, in her housedress. Marquis Limòli, without noticing anything, asked Donna Bellonia in a whisper:

"When are we going to find a husband for that beautiful girl? The eldest comes first, it's obvious. But then remember that I'm here to act as the intermediary... *gratis et amore*... free of charge, of course.... We're old friends!..."

Donna Bellonia kept giving him dirty looks, although the Marquis pretended not to pay attention. Then she told him in whispers:

"What are you saying?... What kind of ideas are you putting into her head?... She's still too young... she's hardly out of her short dress...."

"I see! I see!" answered the Marquis, looking at Donna Giovannina's white stockings through the corner of his eye.

Donna Fifì had taken the Captain to look at her flowers on the balcony. She picked a beautiful carnation, smelled it at length closing her eyes, and then offered it to him.

"I see, I see," repeated the old man.

At that point Baroness Rubiera decided to leave, chewing a lean smile, the yellow flowers on her hat quivering. While the ladies exchanged kisses and embraces, the Marquis turned to the Captain:

"Congratulations!... Congratulations indeed...Don Bastiano."

"Why?... On what?..."

Surprised and embarrassed the Captain was looking for an appropriate answer. But the Marquis had already turned his back, and was saying good-bye to the ladies with a kind word for each; in a fatherly manner he stroked Donna Giovannina, who was still sulking.

"What's the matter? What's the matter? What's the meaning of this? Girls must be cheerful. Did you hear your mother? She said that there is plenty of time for you to grow up. Chin up, then! Cheer up!"

Baroness Rubiera felt herself exploding under her mantilla. After she had turned around to wave her hand from the street toward all the Margarones lined up on the small balcony, she began to grumble:

"Did you see?"

"What the hell! It wasn't so hard! Even concerning Giovannina, you must put your heart to rest. . . ."

"Of course, of course! I'm very happy to put my heart to rest. . . . A flirt! . . . Did you see the little game of the carnation? We would have been in for something, my son and I. . . . But he almost deserved it! Degenerate! His own mother's enemy . . ."

Soon after they ran into Canali, who was going to the Margarones', and from the distance he had seen all the hand kissing that had taken place between the street and the balcony. Canali set a particular expression on his face and stopped the Baroness to greet her, stretching out the conversation, and planting his searching wide-open eyes on her face:

"So you went to see Donna Bellonia, eh? It was a good thing. Such an old friendship as yours! . . . Too bad Don Nini . . ."

The Baroness wanted to find out as much as possible too, with a nonchalant air, fanning herself and beating about the bush.

"After all . . . pranks . . . youthful pranks . . ."

"No, no, forgive me!" retorted Canali. "I'd like to see how you yourself would feel! . . . A father must keep his eyes open to find out to whom he's giving his daughter. . . . I'm not speaking of your son . . . A good young man . . . a heart of gold . . . The problem is that he let himself be taken in . . . surrounded by false friends. . . . There are plenty of villains around. . . . They fleeced him out of a few signatures. . . ."

The Baroness left him right then and there.

"Did you hear? Did you see?" she kept grumbling to Cousin Limoli.

Then she left him too—who could no longer keep up with her.

"Good-bye, good-bye."

And, pale, out of breath, she ran to Notary Neri's, to see, to hear.... The Notary didn't know anything...anything sure, at least.

"As you know, Don Gesualdo is a sharp fox.... In any case, these things are done underhandedly.... They probably had the contract drawn up by a Notary from another town.... Notary Sghembri of Militello, the rumor has it.... But come now... There's no reason for you to get into that state for a thing like that ...I don't like the way you look."

Rosaria, who was cleaning the chickencoop when her mistress came back home, suddenly heard a terrifying howl from the courtyard, as if upstairs they were slaughtering a large animal—a howl that made her lose her slippers as she ran headlong. The Baroness was still there, where she had begun to undress, leaning against the chest of drawers, doubled over as if she had abdominal colic, moaning and lamenting, as foam was running out of her mouth and her eyes were popping out of their sockets:

"Murderer! Degenerate!... No! I won't let anybody devour my property!... I'd rather leave it to the poor...to the convents and the monasteries...I want to write my will!... I want to make donations!... Call the Notary...right away!..."

Don Nini was having an argument with his Aglae in that dilapidated inn room, which for him had become hell the very moment he had saddled himself with the debt and with Mastro-don Gesualdo. Her bed in disarray, her clothes dirty, her hair disheveled, even her very caresses and the dishes prepared by her friend Pallante had turned to poison for him, since they had become so expensive. As he saw Alessi who was coming to call him, talking about Notary and donations, he grew suddenly pale. In vain the leading lady clung around his neck, scantily dressed, without paying attention to Pallante, who was running in from the kitchen, nor to Alessi, who opened his eyes wide and rubbed his hands.

"Nini! Nini, my darling!... Don't leave me now, in this state!..."

"Goddammit! Let me go...all of you!... D'you think she's joking!... That woman is capable of anything!"

Don Nini, again taken up entirely by his love of property, did not let himself be moved, not even by the fainting scene. He left poor Aglae right then and there, stretched out on the floor as in the last act of a tragedy, with Pallante pulling her dress down over her stockings — to run home without even his hat. At home there was a terrible scene between mother and son. At first he tried to deny everything; then he became furious, complaining that he was kept like a slave, worse than a child, without two tari to spend; and the Baroness threatening that she would go to the Notary's herself, personally, to dispose of her property, just as she was now, in her underskirt, at that very moment, if they didn't want to send for him. Don Nini then went downstairs to bolt the front door, and put the key in his pocket, threatening to break every bone in the houseboy's body, if he so much as breathed a word.

"Ah, this is what I get in return!" grumbled Alessi. "Next time I'll go to the Notary's for sure."

Finally, whether she liked it or not, they managed to put the Baroness to bed. She struggled and screamed that they wanted her to die of a heart seizure, to be free to squander her property.

"Mastro-don Gesualdo!...yes!... It's he who'll devour my property!"

Her son was trying to calm her any way he could:

"Can't you see that you're not well? D'you want to get really sick, to drive me to hell?"

Then for the whole night he never closed his eyes, getting up every moment to run and listen behind the door if his mother was still screaming, terrorized as he was by the idea that his neighbors might hear and come to the house with the police and the Notary, in his heart cursing the leading lady and whoever had introduced her to him, troubled by a host of nightmares, if he dozed off for a moment: Mastro-don Gesualdo, the debt, people closing in on him and filling his house — a tremendous crowd.

Early in the morning Rosaria came to knock at his door:

"Don Nini! Baron, sir! Come and see ... The Baroness has lost her speech!...I'm afraid, if you only saw ..."

The Baroness was lying stretched out in her bed, like an ox felled by the butcher, with all her blood in her face and with her tongue hanging out. Her anger, all the pains and troubles, all those ill humors that must have piled up on her stomach, were gurgling inside her, coming out of her mouth and of her nostrils, dripping on her pillow. And she seemed to want to help herself, even in that condition, trying to grope with her swollen and heavy hands, trying to call for help, with the inarticulate sounds that were being kneaded in the slimy foam.

"Mother! Oh mother!"

Don Nini, frightened, still swollen with sleep, went screaming from room to room hitting his head with his fists running to the balcony in despair, while the neighbors knocked and stormed at the front door that was bolted. After a while, doctor, barber, relatives, curious people — the house was filled. Exactly like the dream of the night before. Don Nini told everybody the same thing, wiping his eyes and blowing his swollen nose as if he were blowing a trumpet. As soon as he saw Notary Neri come in too, he would not move from his mother's bedside any more, and he would ask the doctor every moment:

"What d'you think, Doctor? Will she recover her speech?"

"In time, in time," finally the Doctor answered, annoyed. "What the hell! D'you think it was like sneezing?"

You couldn't recognize Don Nini any more, from one day to the next — his beard unshaven, his hair disheveled, sitting continuously at his mother's bedside, or trying his best with the house chores. Not one fava bean left the pantry without passing through his hands. — So true it is that trouble teaches people sense. — His mother herself would have told him, if she could speak. You could tell from how she looked at his hands, with blood in her eyes, each time he came to get the keys from the doorpost. And he himself, now that everything passed through his hands, finally understood the pains he had caused the poor woman; he felt sorry about it, he tried to earn forgiveness with patience, with loving care, being always with her, watching over her and over the people who came to see her, growing pale each time she tried to loosen the knots of her tongue in front of strangers. He was overcome with great tenderness at the thought that his poor paralyzed mother could neither move nor speak for the purpose of taking property away from him, as she had threatened.

"No, no, she won't do it! Those are things people say in moments of anger . . . I'd like to see her! . . . I'm her flesh and blood after all . . . She would be the first to die of a stroke, if she were to leave her property to any and everybody. . . ."

PART THREE

I

Even before her fifth birthday, little Isabella was put in the Collegio di Maria. Don Gesualdo, now that he had property under the sun and was on the same level as the best people in town, wanted his daughter to be on the same level as well: to learn good manners, reading and writing, embroidery, Church Latin too, and everything else, just like a Baron's daughter; so much more so that, thank God, she wouldn't be without a dowry, for Bianca didn't promise to give him any more heirs. After the baby's birth, Bianca had never recovered her health; as a matter of fact, she was declining from day to day, gnawed inside by the same worm that had eaten up all the Traos—and it was certain that she wouldn't have any more children. A true punishment of God. A bad bargain; although the good man was careful not to complain, not even with the canon-priest Lupi, who had first proposed it to him. When you have made a blunder, you'd better keep quiet and not talk about it, not to let your enemies have the upper hand. —Nothing, nothing had that marriage brought him; neither dowry, nor male child, nor the new relatives' help, nor even what Diodata used to give him: a moment of relaxation, an hour of pleasure, like a glass of wine for a poor man who has toiled all day! Not even that! —A wife who went sour in your hands, who froze your caresses with that face and those eyes of hers, with her being frightened, as if you were making her fall into mortal sin, each time, and as if the priest hadn't put his sign of the cross over it, then, when she had said 'yes' . . . It wasn't Bianca's fault. It was the blood of her race that refused. You can't graft peaches on an olive tree. She, the poor woman, lowered her face, even went so far as to offer it to him, all red as it was, to obey the commandment of God, as if she were being paid to do it. . . .

But he wasn't taken in, no. True he was a peasant, but he had a peasant's sharp nose too! And he had his pride. The pride of a man who, with his own hands and his own work, had managed to earn those fine linen sheets in which they slept turning their backs on each other, and those delicacies he ate with uneasiness under the eyes of that Trao wife of his.

But at least in his own house he wanted to call the tune himself. And if God had punished him precisely in that matter of the children he wanted to bring into the word according to His law, by giving him a baby girl instead of the legitimate male heir he expected, at least Isabella should have everything that he hadn't had, she should be a lady both in name and in fact. Bianca, as if she guessed she didn't have long to live, didn't want to be separated from her little daughter. But he was the boss, Don Gesualdo. He was good, loving, in his own way; he didn't let her go without anything: doctors, drugs, just as if she had brought him a fat dowry. —Bianca didn't find words good enough to thank God, when she compared the house into which He had brought her with the one in which she had been born. There her own brother was missing bread during the day and blankets during the night.... He would have died of hardships, hadn't his relatives helped him in good style, without letting him know. Only from her, Don Ferdinando wouldn't accept anything at all, and yet Don Gesualdo wouldn't have let him go without anything—that man, whose heart was as vast as the sea! Her own relatives told her:

"You can't find words good enough to thank God and your husband. Let him do as he likes; he's the boss, and he wants the best for your daughter."

Then she conjectured that the Lord was punishing her, that He did not want that poor innocent girl in her husband's house, and at night she soaked her pillow with tears. She prayed to God to give her strength and consoled herself as well as she could, thinking that she was suffering in expiation for her sins. Don Gesualdo, who had so many other things on his mind, so many other weighty business concerns on his shoulders, and who was used to seeing her like that, with that face, did not even notice. Sometimes, when he saw her get paler, more haggard than usual, he would say to give her courage:

"You'll see that when you have sent your little girl to the boarding school, you'll feel happier too. It's like pulling a tooth. You can't look after your child, with your poor health. And when she grows up she must know all the things known by so many other girls who aren't as rich as she is. Children must get used to discipline when they're young, each one according to his own condition.... Don't I know it myself...I didn't have anybody to help me. That baby was born with a silver spoon in her mouth."

Nevertheless, at the last minute there were tears and moans, when they accompanied little Isabella to the parlor of the convent. Bianca had gone to confession and to communion. She heard mass on her knees, feeling herself fail, feeling her child being again torn from her womb—that little girl who clung to her neck and didn't want to leave her.

Don Gesualdo spared no expense to keep little Isabella happy in the boarding school: sweets, books with pictures, holy cards, nuts with the wax Infant Jesus inside, a Bongiovanni manger* that took up a whole table; his daughter had what the richest people's daughters had; and the best things to eat, the first fruit in town, and cherries and apricots brought in on purpose from far away. The other little girls opened their eyes wide and stifled big sighs. The youngest of the Zacco girls, and the other Mendolas, who had to be satisfied with the onions and the black olives given by the convent for the afternoon snack, got even by talking about the riches they had at home and on their farms. Those who had neither house nor farms, brought up their aristocratic background, the Police Captain who was mother's brother, the aunt the Baroness, whose hunter wore feathers, father's cousins who owned five estates next to each other in the Caltagirone district. Every holiday, every New Year's Day, as little Isabella received still more costly presents—a silver crucifix, a rosary with gold *Gloria*-beads, a mass book bound in tortoise shell for her to learn how to read—there arose new little wars, little snubs, alliances made and unmade according to whether a cookie or a holy card was given or refused. You could see little eyes shining with haughtiness or with jealousy, burning little faces, whimpers that they would later unburden in the parlor into their mothers' ears. Among all those girls, and in all those families, there arose the same hell that Mastro-don Gesualdo had caused among the grownups and in the town. You wouldn't know any more who could spend money and who couldn't . . . a race among all the relatives as to who would squander the most money on nonsensical trifles, and a general confusion between those who had always been in the front rank and those who would stay behind. Those who couldn't keep up, or

*Giacomo Bongiovanni (Caltagirone, 1772-1859), a sculptor, who was famous for his statuettes humorously capturing scenes from the daily aspects of Sicilian life. His work can be seen in Caltagirone, and at the National Museum of Palermo.

became annoyed with spending all their money to please Mastro-don Gesualdo, blurted out against him such sarcastic allusions and such ironic remarks that later fermented in the little heads of the young students. The nuns also took part in this internal war, depending on their relationships, their likes, the party that wanted to support or to overthrow the Mother Superior. Even the porter sister, even the lay sisters protested vehemently, for they felt humiliated at having to serve without extra pay also the daughter of Mastro-don Gesualdo, of a man who had come up from nothing, like themselves, and who had just become rich. The outside enmities, the dissensions, the fights based on interest and on vanity, went through the cloister, occupied the leisure hours, vented themselves even inside there in the form of gossip, of reprisals, of ugly words.

"D'you know your father's name? Mastro-don Gesualdo?" —"D'you know what happens in your house? That they had to sell a pair of oxen to plant the seed?" —"Your aunt Speranza spins hemp for anybody who pays her, and her children go barefoot." —"The bailiff went to your house to attach your furniture."

One Sunday little Alimena even hid on the belfy stairs to see if it was true that Isabella's father wore the peasant's white cap.

He found his daughter still red in the face, her breast swollen with sobs, turning her head in fear of seeing the nasty eyes of the other little girls glitter behind every grating, staring at his hands to see if they were really dirty with mortar, drawing instinctively back when he stung her with his skin as he kissed her. Just like her mother.

"A peach-shoot cannot be grafted on an olive tree."

So many pinpricks; the same bad destiny that had always poisoned everything for him each day; the same implacable war he was always forced to fight against everything and everybody; and it wounded him even there, through his daughter's love. He kept silent, he did not complain, because he was no fool and did not want his enemies to laugh at him; but at the same time his father's words, the same grudges, the same jealousies came back to his mind. Then he thought that everyone in this world looks after his own interest, and goes his own way. That's what he had done with his father, and that's what his daughter was doing. That's the way it must be. He set his heart at rest, but there always remained a thorn in that heart. Whatever he had done and was doing for his daughter was also precisely what moved her farther away from him: the money he had spent to educate her like a rich girl, the companions among whom he had wanted her to grow up, the largeness and the luxury that sowed pride into the little girl's mind, the very name he had given her by marrying a Trao—he had really reaped a great profit! The little girl kept saying:

"My mother is a Trao. My name is Isabella Trao."

The war burst out still more fiercely among the girls when Nini Rubiera got married:

"If it's true that you're relatives, why didn't your uncle send you any wedding candies? It must be that they don't want you as relatives."

Little Isabella, who could already answer like a grownup, retorted:

"My father will buy me wedding candies himself. We had a falling out with the Rubieras because they owe us a lot of money."

The wax woman's daughter, who was on her side, added several other stories: —the young Baron was broke. The Margarone girl wouldn't have any more to do with him. He was marrying Donna Giuseppina Alòsi, who was older than he, for love of money, because he couldn't find anything better. This was talk that went on in her mother's store, in every café, in every drugstore, and from door to door.

In town people talked only about Don Nini Rubiera's wedding.

"A marriage of convenience!" said Mrs. Capitana who always spoke with frills on her lips.

As she got older, Mrs. Capitana had also picked up the vices of the town; she busied herself with other people's business, now that she did not have any of her own to hide. When she met Cavaliere Peperito, she turned to him with such a mischievous face that made her look twenty years younger—with a smile that intended to guess a lot of things, shaking her head, and graciously offering herself to listen to his confidences and to his jealous outpourings, threatening the Cavaliere with her fan—as if to say what a terrible rake he had been, and that if he now let someone steal his mistress from him, it meant that there must have been some really good reasons . . . sooner or later . . .

"No!" retorted Peperito, beside himself. "Neither before nor later! This you can go and tell Donna Giuseppina! If I can't be the boss, I don't want to be exploited either, understand?... To play the stud...understand? As for this, Donna Giuseppina can set her heart to rest."

Now he spread all of Donna Giuseppina's filth in the square — that if she for a miracle sent you a basket of grapes for a present, she wanted the basket back; and secretly she sold the stockings she herself knitted, such stockings that were a finger thick, servant style. She had even let him see them on her legs to tease him...just to get out of him what she wanted.... But no, he wasn't having any of that!...

To make a long story short, he told all kinds of tales. There were even cudgel blows at the Caffè dei Nobili. Ciolla stayed on his heels to pick up gossip and carry it around. Then one day it was a real feast for him, when Signora Aglae arrived in town together with Signor Pallante, to make a scandal for Baron Rubiera, and get her dues, if the seducer didn't want to see her appear before the altar. She came especially from Modica, enraged, covered with wax, painted, loaded with rooster feathers and pieces of glass, dragging behind her a really lovely little girl as the innocent proof of Don Nini's dirty trick. So people were saying that Don Nini was a philanderer and if he married Donna Giuseppina Alòsi, who was old enough to be his mother, there must have been some big money interests behind it. Some people explained the matter in one way and some people in another. But the young Baron quickly got rid of all those who rushed to congratulate him in order to pull the real truth out of his mouth. Mrs. Sganci, who had negotiated the deal, didn't say anything when her lady friends went to visit her for the purpose of being informed. Maybe Don Gesualdo knew more than the others, but he shrugged his shoulders and managed to get away with answers such as:

"What can you do? Everybody's after his own interest. It must be that Baron Rubiera found that marrying the Alòsi woman was to his advantage."

The truth was that Don Nini had to marry the Alòsi woman in order to save that little bit of a house of which Don Gesualdo wanted to dispossess him. True, now he had become sensible, totally devoted to business; but his mother, buried alive as she was in her armchair,

didn't leave a cent at his command; she wanted him to give account
of everything; she wanted everything to pass under her eyes; without
being able to speak, without being able to move, she had her people
obey her better than before. And she was clinging to her property
like an oyster, and insisted in going on living not to pay Nini's debt.
Meanwhile, the debt was getting bigger from year to year; so much
so that Don Nini spent whole nights thinking about it, often without
being able to close his eyes; and when the money was due, between
the capital and the interest, it amounted to quite a sum. The canon-
priest Lupi, who went to ask for an extension of payment on behalf
of the young Baron, found Don Gesualdo worse than a stone wall:

"What kind of game is this, my dear Canon Lupi? I have seen
neither interest nor capital for more than nine years. Now I need my
money and I want to be paid."

Out of need, Don Nini even humiliated himself to the point of
going to plead with his cousin Bianca, after so many years. He
started from far off: — They hadn't seen each other for such a long
time! He didn't have the heart to show himself before her, that was
sure! He wasn't trying to clear himself. He had been really bad. Now
he had opened his eyes — too late, when he could do nothing about
it, when the load of his errors was heavy on his shoulders. But he
absolutely couldn't pay right at that moment.

"I'm an honest man. I've property after all. Your husband will
be paid to the last cent. But right now I really can't! You know what
your aunt is like! How stubborn she is! We really had to suffer because of her stubbornness! But, after all, she cannot live forever, the
poor woman, in her condition. . . ."

As she first saw him, Bianca remained breathless and speechless, turning now white and now red. She didn't know what to say,
she stammered, she broke into a cold sweat, a convulsion in her
hands that she tried to hide by mechanically smoothing the two
corners of her apron. Suddenly she coughed up blood.

"What is it? What is it? Something wrong with your gums? Did
you bite your tongue?"

"No," she answered. "It happens once in a while. Don Diego
had it too, remember? It's nothing serious."

"Good, good. Then do this for me; talk to your husband about
it. Right now I really can't . . . But I'm an honest man, am I not? . . .

My mother, even if she lives a hundred years, has nobody to leave all her property to."

Bianca was trying to excuse herself. —Her husband was the boss. He had a mind of his own for everything. He didn't want anybody to stick his nose into his business.—

"But then what are you his wife for?" retorted her cousin. "Great thinking indeed! Somebody who wasn't worthy to look you in the face!... He must thank God and my mother's stubbornness if he's been so lucky!... So will you do everything possible to convince him to grant me this extension?"

"And you, what did you tell him?" asked Don Gesualdo, finding his wife still upset, after that visit.

"Nothing...I don't know...I got sick..."

"Good. You did well. Don't worry, I'll take care of business. Snakes in your bosom, that's what relatives are.... Did you see? They look for you only when they need you, but otherwise they don't care whether you're dead or alive. Leave him to me. I'll send your cousin the answer by the bailiff...."

That's how that wedding had taken place, after Baron Rubiera had turned heaven and earth upside down to find the money to pay Don Gesualdo; and finally Donna Giuseppina Alòsi, who had some good land under the sun, had granted her mortgage signature. Don Gesualdo, after getting his claim to those lands, no longer talked about needing money.

"In time..." he confided to his wife. "Leave them alone. They pay neither interest nor capital, and in time those lands will be good enough for Isabella's dowry. What d'you think? Isn't it funny? Uncle Rubiera taking care of your daughter's dowry?..."

Sometimes he would come out with these kinds of funny remarks, when he was alone with his wife, and when he was happy with his day, before going to bed, standing in shirtsleeves, as he was putting his nightcap on. Face to face with her, he really showed himself as he was—good-natured, with his broad laugh showing his big white teeth, even passing his tongue over his lips, as if he were already tasting the good food, like the man that he was, craving property.

When Isabella had grown older, she was sent from the Collegio di Maria to the first boarding school in Palermo. This was another blow for the poor mother, who feared she wouldn't see her any more. To comfort her in the state she was in, her husband said:

"See, we're killing ourselves to do our best for her—each one doing his best—and some day she won't even remember us. That's the way the world goes. In fact, you must get it into your head that you can't have your daughter with you forever. When she gets married she'll go away from this town. Here there isn't anybody who can marry her, with the dowry I'll give her. If I've done so much for her, I at least want to know whom I'm giving my flesh and blood to. At this very moment, as I'm talking to you, the man is already born, who'll enjoy the fruits of my labors, without even saying thank you. . . ."

His heart was heavy too, the poor man, and if he sometimes let himself go, face to face with his wife, for the sake of talk, he did not neglect what was his duty. He went to see his girl in Palermo, whenever he could, whenever his business obligations would let him, even once a year. Isabella had grown into a beautiful girl, still a little frail, somewhat pale in the face, but naturally graceful in all her elegant movements with the delicate complexion and the aquiline Trao profile—in short, a flower from a different plant; rich people's first-class stuff, such that her own father, when he went to see her, felt somewhat uneasy before the girl, who had acquired the same demeanor as her school companions—all of them coming from the first families, all of them bringing to the boarding school the baronial haughtiness of every corner of Sicily. In the parlor they called him Signor Trao. When he wanted to know why, Isabella grew red in the face. Again the same story as in the Collegio di Maria. And his daughter had to suffer the same humiliation because of her background. Fortunately, the Leyra girl, whose affection Isabella had won with her little presents, had begun to defend her with full vigor. She knew the Trao name, one of the first families down south, where her brother the Duke owned large estates. The little duchess had a great name and a haughty manner of speech, although she was in the boarding school without paying; and so her companions accepted the name Trao. And Mastro-don Gesualdo had to accept it too, and had to let himself be called that way, for his daughter's sake, whenever he went to see her.

"You'll see how beautiful your daughter's grown to be!" he would then say to his wife, who was always ill.

Donna Bianca finally saw her again when she got out of the boarding school in 1837, and in Palermo the first cholera rumors were already beginning to spread, and Don Gesualdo had rushed to get her. It was like a blow in the chest for the poor mother when, after such a long time, she heard the sedan chair stop before the front door.

"My girl! my girl!" her arms stretched out, her legs shaky, hurrying down the stairs. Isabella was running up, her arms also open:

"Mother! Mother!"

Then each clinging to the other's neck, the mother tossing her child right and left just like when Isabella was a little girl.

Then the relatives came to see her. Bianca had recovered enough strength to take her daughter around in triumph—to the Sganci house, to the Limòli house, everywhere she had been as a child, before going to the boarding school—now that she was a big girl, with her straw hat on her beautiful blond hair—a veritable flower. They all put their heads out to see her pass. Aunt Sganci, now deaf and blind, touched her face to recognize her:

"A Trao girl! No doubt!"

Her uncle, the Marquis, praised her eyes, blue eyes like stars.

"Two eyes that could see sin," said the Marquis, who always had a crack ready.

When they took her to visit her uncle, Don Ferdinando, Isabella, who had often talked to her schoolmates about her mother's home, in her outbreaks of naive ambition, felt surprised and depressed, sad and disappointed.

Anybody could come in through the dilapidated front door. The courtyard was small, obstructed with stones and rubble. By a small path among the nettles you could get to the toothless stairway, staggering, stifled by the weeds. At the top, the collapsing door was hardly held closed by a rusty latch; and as soon as you entered you were hit by a wave of heavy, humid air, by a stench of mold and of cellar, rising from the floor blazoned with the coat-of-arms, littered with pieces of broken pots, and raining down from the unplastered ceiling, coming from the corridor as black as a cellar, from the dark halls, of which you could catch a glimpse lined up in a long row, bare and abandoned—through the strips of light leaking out of the ramshackle windows. Down at the end there was her uncle's little room, filthy, sooty, its ceiling ready to collapse, and the shade of Don Ferdinando who kept coming and going in silence, just like a ghost.

"Who is it?...Grazia...come in..."

Don Ferdinando appeared on the threshold, in shirtsleeves, yellow and fleshless, looking in astonishment at his sister and at his niece through his eyeglasses. On the unmade bed still lay Don Diego's greatcoat, which he was patching. He quickly rolled it up, together with a bundle of other rags, and threw it into the chest of drawers.

"Ah!... It's you, Bianca?... What can I do for you?..."

Then, as he realized that he was holding the needle in his hand, he stuck it in his pocket, ashamed, still repeating that somewhat mechanical movement.

"This is your niece..." stammered his sister with a trembling voice. "Isabella...do you remember?... She's been away at a boarding school in Palermo..."

He stared at the girl with those wild blue eyes of his, which ran in all directions, and murmured:

"Ah!...Isabella?... My niece?..."

He was anxiously looking around the room, and now and then, as he saw something forgotten on the table or on the lamé chair, some filthy thread, a cotton handkerchief he had laid in the sun to dry, he quickly ran over to hide it. Then he sat on the edge of his little bed, staring at the door. While Bianca was talking with a heavy heart, he kept looking around with suspicious eyes, thinking of something else. Suddenly he went to lock his desk drawer.

"Ah!... My niece...really?"

He stared at the girl with the same hesitation, and then he lowered his eyes toward the floor.

"She looks just like you...exactly...when you were here..."

He seemed to be looking for words, his wandering eyes avoiding those of his sister and of his niece, a slight trembling in his hands, his face lifeless and stunned. For a moment, as Bianca talked into his ear, pleading, as if she were about to break into tears, he straightened up his bent back so that he looked extremely tall—a shadow in his light-colored eyes, a residue of Trao blood reddening his pallid face.

"No...no...I don't want anything...I don't need anything

... Go away now, please go ... See ... I'm so busy ..."

Something that would wring your heart. A state of ruin and of hardship that humiliated her ambitious memories, her romantic fantasies born of the imaginary talks confided to her boarding-school friends — the illusions filling the moody head of the girl, who had come back to her hometown with the intention of playing the leading role in it. The petty luxury of Aunt Sganci, her very house cold and melancholy, the Trao's collapsing palace, which she had often mentioned down there with childish pride — everything now looked smaller, became black, poor, sad. There, across the square, was the Margarone balcony — which she had often mentioned as vast, flooded with sun, full of flowers and of cheerful girls who astonished her as a child with the display of their gaudy clothes. How narrow and squalid it was instead, with that leprous wall weighing on it. And how old had Donna Giovannina become, as she laughed sitting among the dusty flower pots, knitting, dressed in black, enormous! At the bottom of the alley was crouched Grandfather Motta's little house. When her father took her there, they found Aunt Speranza spinning, white-haired, with rough wrinkles in her face. There were loose bricks that made you stumble, a tough boy in shirtsleeves, who raised his head from a packsaddle he was mending, without greeting you. *Mastro* Nunzio was in bed with rheumatism, under a filthy blanket, lamenting:

"Ah, you've come to see me? Did you think I was dead? No, no, I'm not dead. Is this your girl? Did you bring her here to show her to me? ... She's a young lady, no doubt about it! You gave her a beautiful name too! But your mother's name was Rosaria! D'you know? Excuse me, my dear granddaughter, if I receive you in this hovel. ... I was born here, what d'you want me to do? ... I hope to die here.... I didn't want to trade it for the palace where your father wanted to lock me up.... I'm used to getting out on the street as soon as I get up.... No, no, it's better to think about it in time. Everybody the way he was born."

Speranza grunted out some other words they could not hear. When they left, the rough boy accompanied them to the door with his eyes.

Meanwhile, there were strong rumors about a cholera epidemic. In Catania there had been an uprising. Don Bastiano Stangafame arrived from Lentini together with Donna Fifi, who looked already ill, green, fleshless, telling tales that must have turned her hair white in twenty-four hours. In Siracusa, a girl as beautiful as the Virgin Mary, who danced in the theater on the back of trained horses, and went spreading the cholera with that pretext, had been lynched. The people, suspicious, just waited as they made their provisions to run off at the first sign of alarm, and scrutinized every new face that passed.

At that time two peddlers of ribbons and silk handkerchiefs happened to come to town. They went from house to house selling their things, and looked across the doors and into the courtyards. The Margarone women who spent a lot of money to deck themselves out, as if they were still spring chickens, bought a lot of those things; as a matter of fact, since they had no change on hand, those good men said that they would pass by again for it the next day.

Instead, it was doomsday. Ciolla had gone to the judge to report that they had poisoned his hens; as proof he was carrying them, still warm, in his hands. Don Nicolino came back home all out of breath, and ordered his sister to bolt the doors and the windows and not to open to anybody. Doctor Tavuso even had the door to the water cistern locked. The rich people, remembering what kind of dubious character Ciolla was, the one who sixteen years ago had been brought to the Castello handcuffed, armed themselves to the teeth and began to scout the town, in case he should get it into his head to go fishing again in troubled waters. The order was to shoot him without mercy at the first alarm. The two peddlers were not seen any more. In the late afternoon the loaded carts running away from town began to file by. After the *Angelus,* no living soul went into the streets. A litter arrived rather late carrying Don Corrado La Gurna, dressed in black, his handkerchief at his eyes. The dogs barked all night.

The panic knew no bounds when people saw Baroness Rubiera, paralyzed, fleeing away seated in an armchair, because she could not fit in the sedan chair, since she was so enormous, and four men struggling to carry her, with her head hanging to one side, her big face livid, her purple tongue half out of her slobbery lips, with only her eyes alive and uneasy, and her almost dead hands traveled by a constant quiver. And behind her, the Baron, looking twenty years older, bent, gray, loaded with children, his wife pregnant again, and with the other children of the first marriage too. Wherever they passed, they filled the street—a dismal sight. The poor people who could not leave town, looked on, frightened. In the churches they had exposed the Blessed Sacrament. Old grudges were then silenced, and factors were seen returning to the owners what they had been stealing. Don Gesualdo opened his arms and his storehouses to the poor and to his relatives—all his country houses, at Canziria and at Salonia. And he spoke of gathering the whole family together at Mangalavite, where he owned vast buildings.

"Now I'm running to my father to try to get him to come with us. In the meantime, you go to your brother," he said to Bianca. "Make him understand that in times like these we must bury the hatchet.—Even if I had betrayed him . . . We've got the cholera on top of us . . . Blood is thicker than water, after all! We can't leave that poor old man alone in the midst of the cholera. . . . People would then clearly have reason to speak against us, eh? . . ."

"You have a good heart!" stammered his wife with a feeling of tenderness. "You have a good heart!"

But Don Ferdinando wouldn't be persuaded. He was perched at the top of a ladder, a little pot around his neck, very busy gluing strips of paper over all the cracks in the shutters.

"I can't leave the house," he answered. "I've so much to do! . . . See how many holes? . . . If the cholera comes . . . I must stop them all . . ."

In vain his sister kept pleading and imploring.

"Don't leave me with this regret, Don Ferdinando! . . . How am I going to close my eyes at night, knowing that you're alone in this house? . . ."

"Ah! ah! . . ." he answered with an obtuse smile. "At night they're not going to blow the cholera at me! . . . I'm going to stop all the cracks . . . look! . . ."

And he kept retorting:

"I can't leave the house alone . . . I must guard the family papers . . ."

The sacristan's wife, who saw Donna Bianca leave the front door in distress, ran after her, in tears:

"We won't see each other any more! . . . Everybody's leaving. . . . There won't be anybody to ring mass and matins for!"

Mastro Nunzio had also refused to go with his son.

"I eat with my fingers, son! You'd be ashamed of your own

father, at the table...I'm uncouth...I don't belong together with the rich!... No, no! We'd better think about it first! Better to die of cholera than of anger!... Then, you know? I'm used to being the boss in my own house...I'm a peasant...I'm not used to letting my wife walk all over me, no!"

Speranza pointed at Burgio, who was in bed with malaria.

"We don't desert our own people in danger!... My husband can't move, and we don't intend to move!... That's the way we are! ... You know what it takes to support a whole family, when the husband is confined to bed!..."

"But haven't I always told you that you'll be the boss?... Whatever you want!..." exclaimed Gesualdo finally.

"No!... I haven't asked you for charity!... We won't accept anything from you, unless we're in need!... Thank God!... But since you're doing it to help us, we'll go to Canziria.... Don't worry! Now people won't say that you have abandoned your father in the midst of the cholera!... You send us the provisions...we can't eat grass like animals!... By the way... If you also have a few of your daughter's old dresses, one of those that she absolutely wouldn't wear any more... For she's a rich girl — but they will always be good for poor people like us!..."

The Margarones left immediately for Pietraperzia; all of them still in mourning for Don Filippo, who had died of the heartaches brought on him by his son-in-law Don Bastiano Stangafame each time he cudgeled Fifì, if her father didn't send money. They darkened up a whole street. Baron Mendola, who was courting Aunt Sganci, took her to Passaneto, where she caught the malaria fever, the poor old woman. Baron Zacco and Notary Neri went to Donferrante. The town was quite dreary. An hour before dark you wouldn't see anybody else along Via di San Sebastiano but Marquis Limòli, going on his usual after-dinner walk. As a matter of fact, they even let him know that he aroused suspicion with those walks of his, and that they meant to do him in at the first case of cholera.

"Eh?" said he. "Do me in? You'd better think about it first, you who'll have to cover the cost. I'm doing what I've always done, or I'll die anyway."

And to his niece who pleaded with him to go to Mangalavite with her:

"Are you afraid I'll not be here when you come back?... No,

no, don't be afraid; the cholera doesn't know what to do with me."

As Bianca and her daughter were about to climb into the litter, Aunt Cirmena arrived, desperate.

"Did you see? They are all going! Our relatives have turned their backs on me!... I'm saddled with the poor orphan, Corrado La Gurna, too.... A real tragedy in his house!... Both his father and his mother struck down by cholera...the same night!... Nobody has the heart I have, nobody!... A poor woman without help, who has nowhere to go!... If you give me the key to the two rooms you have down there at Mangalavite, next to your cottage!... The millhouse rooms... You're the only relative I can turn to, Don Gesualdo!..."

"Yes, of course!" he answered. "But don't tell anybody else..."

"As a matter of fact I will tell them!... I want to throw it into everybody's face, if I live long enough!..."

II

What they called the cottage, at Mangalavite, was a great big building nestled at the bottom of the small valley. From her window, Isabella could see the broad alpine road bordered with olive trees, the dense green thicket that marked the cave where the water flowed, the cliffs over which the path wound, and farther up the slope spotted with sumac trees, Budarturo, barren and rocky in the glazed sky. The only cheerful brushstroke was a hedge of brier roses always in bloom, forgotten and neglected, at the entrance to the road.

Down the precipices, every cave and the little huts hidden in the cactus thickets were crowded with poor people who had run away from the town in fear of the cholera. All around you could hear the roosters crow and the children scream; you could see rags spread out in the sun, and thin columns of smoke rising here and there, through the trees. Toward the *Angelus* the herds came back through the olive groves around the building—whole droves of colts and oxen gathering in the immense courtyards. Then all night long there was a restless stamping of feet, a sudden awakening of moo-ings and of bleatings, a shaking of cowbells, a stench of stable and manure, so that Isabella could not close her eyes. Every once in a while a wild gunshot ran through the darkness in the distance; wild shouts of alarm reached even down there. The day after, the peasants would say that they had happened to see shadows lurking stealthily over the precipices. Aunt Cirmena swore that she had seen solitary and luminous rockets toward Donferrante. And immediately they sent people to inquire if there had been any cases of cholera. Baron Zacco, on the contrary, who had come from that area, maintained that the fires were seen toward Mangalavite.

Don Gesualdo, apart from the fear of the rockets seen at night and from the suspicion aroused by every new face that passed along the paths climbing up the cliffs, lived there like a king, among his herds, his fields, his peasants, his activities, always on the go from morning to night, always shouting and always showing his boss-face everywhere. Then in the evening he rested, seated among his own people, on one of the steps going up to the road, before the gate, in shirtsleeves, enjoying the cool and the freedom of the countryside, listening to the interminable complaints and the rambling talk of his sharecroppers. And to his wife, who was feeling still worse because of the country air, he used to say to comfort her:

"At least here you're not afraid of catching the cholera. As long as there's no cholera, the rest is nothing."

There he was safe from the cholera, just like a king in his own kingdom, watched over night and day. He had provided every peasant with a good shotgun, one of those flint guns that had been hidden underground since 1812 or 1821,* and he kept such mastiffs that could devour a man. He was helping everybody; and everybody would have had himself killed to guard his hide, in that situation. Wheat, fava beans, a big barrel of wine that was just beginning to spoil. Whoever was in need ran to him to borrow whatever he needed. He kept his hands open, like Providence itself. He had given

---

*In 1812 there was, in Naples and in Sicily, a parliamentary revolution, aided by the British under the Minister Bentinck, resulting in a bicameral legislature. After Napoleon's final defeat, and the subsequent departure of the British from Sicily, Ferdinand IV of the Bourbons took power and established the Kingdom of the Two Sicilies. He abolished the constitution and crowned himself king in 1816. As to the 1821 revolution, there is no historical record.

shelter to half the town, in the haylofts, in the stables, in the guard-huts, in the caves up there, at Budarturo. One day even Nanni l'Orbo had come with his whole troop, winking his eyes and pulling him aside to tell him what was on his mind.

"Don Gesualdo...here we have your own things too. Look at Nunzio and Gesualdo, how much they look like you! They eat four tumoli of bread a month, good health to them! You can't shut your door in their faces.... You've been so generous with everybody? Be generous this time too, for this is God's will."

"What the hell of an idea did you get into your head!... Now my wife and my daughter are here!... At least go into the mill-house, and don't show up around here...."

But all that help and that generosity turned to poison, because of the obstinacy of his relatives, who had not wanted to put themselves under his wings. He often unburdened himself with Bianca, in the evening, as he shut doors and windows and felt safe:

"We're saving so many people from the cholera.... We've so many people under our wings, and only our own flesh and blood is scattered here and there.... They're doing it on purpose...to plague us...to let us have a thorn inside!...I'm not talking about your brother, poor man...that one doesn't understand.... But my father... He shouldn't have left this thorn inside me, not he!..."

He did not know about the other trouble his daughter was about to give him, the poor man! Isabella, who had come home from school with so many nice things in her head, who had thought that at Mangalavite she would find as many nice things as at the Palermo Favorita—marble seats, statues, flowers everywhere, big trees, boulevards kept like so many ballrooms—had experienced another disappointment. She had found alpine paths, stones that made her little shoes wobble, dust-covered vineyards, burned-up stubbles that blinded her, rocky peaks scattered with sumac trees that looked rusty at that height, and where the sunset quickly saddened the evening. And then the days were always alike, in that solitude; a continuous suspicion, a distrust of everything, of the water you'd drink, the people passing by, the dogs barking, the letters being delivered—a pile of damp straw permanently before the gate smoking everything coming from outside—the rare letters delivered on the end of a reed across the smoke—and as the only distraction, the chattering of Aunt Cirmena, who came every night, lantern in hand, with her knitting basket on her arm. Her nephew accompanied her rarely; he'd rather stay home, like a brooding bear, thinking about his problems or his dead parents—who knows... To excuse him, Aunt Cirmena talked about the great talent that boy had—the whole day locked up in his room, his head in his hand, filling sheets of paper bigger than packsaddles with poems that would make even the stones weep. With this kind of talk, Don Gesualdo fell asleep. Bianca didn't talk much either, always short of breath, always between being in bed and going to bed. The only one to pay attention to her aunt was she, Isabella, while she stifled her yawns after those empty days. To her school friends, who were also scattered here and there, she didn't know what to write. Every week Marina di Leyra sent her little pages sealed with her coat-of-arms and crammed full with the confessions of her adventures. She teased her, she questioned her, she asked for her personal secrets in return. It seemed to Isabella as if at every letter Marina happened to be there before her, with her big haughty eyes and her beautiful big lips, to whisper into her ear things that made her face burn, that made her heart beat, as if she had her hidden secret too, to confide to her friend. They had given each other a little diary, and had promised to write there their most intimate thoughts—everything, everything, without hiding anything! Isabella's beautiful blue eyes, those eyes that, Uncle Limòli said, without wanting to, even without looking, seemed to be searching for those thoughts. Within that little head of hers, which was still wearing braids hanging down her back, there was already a swarming, like a buzzing of bees bringing in all the voices and all the scents of the countryside, from beyond the rocky heights, from beyond Budarturo, from far, far away. It was as if the open air, the rustling of the leaves, the hot sun, were setting her blood on fire, were penetrating into her bluish veins, were blossoming in her face, were swelling with sighs her breasts now beginning to grow under the bib of her apron.

"The country is surely good for you, d'you see?" said her father. "It surely makes you pretty!..."

But she was not happy. She felt restless, bored, so much so that her hands lay idle on her embroidery, that she sought certain special places to read her few books—those little volumes that she kept hid-

den under her lingerie in the boarding school. In the shade of the
walnut trees, next to the spring, at the bottom of the road going up
to the cottage, there was at least a great peace, a great silence — you
could hear the dripping of the water in the cave, the leaves rustling
like a sea, the sudden squeaking of a hawk appearing like a dot in
the immense blue. So many small things that slowly attracted her
and made her look for hours at a line of ants following one another;
at a little lizard timidly sticking out its head from a stone crevice; at
a brier rose dangling above the low wall; at the light and the shadows alternating and mingling on the ground. She was overcome by a
sort of drowsiness, by the serenity coming to her from everything
and taking possession of her and gluing her there — her book on her
knees, her eyes wide open and staring ahead, her mind running far
off. There descended on her a melancholy as sweet as a light caress,
which at times squeezed her heart, a vague desire for unknown
things. From day to day a new feeling rose inside her from the poetry
she read, from the sunsets that made her sigh, like a vague trepida-
tion, a subtle intoxication, a mysterious, repressed and deep-seated
excitement that she felt she had to hide from everybody. During the
night she often got quietly out of her bed, so quietly that her mother
wouldn't hear, without lighting the candle; and she would lean at
the window, dreaming, looking at the sky that swarmed with stars.
Her soul vaguely wandered after the noises of the countryside — the
lament of the horned owl, the distant whining of dogs, the confused
forms traveling in the night — all those things causing a delightful
fear. She almost felt as if the moon were raining down on her face,
on her hands, a great tenderness, a great languor, a great desire to
weep. She confusedly thought she was seeing well-known images,
dear memories, fantasies with luminous intermittency like the light
of certain stars, traveling across the great white glow, beyond Budarturo, far in the distance, her friends, Marina di Leyra, another
unknown face Marina showed in her letters, a face that wavered and
changed form, now blond, now dark, at times with the dried-up
rings around his eyes and the melancholy fold of Cousin Corrado La
Gurna's lips. She was invaded by the sense of things, the sadness of
the spring water dripping drop by drop through the maidenhair
leaves, the fright of the solitude lost far away in the countryside, the
desolation of the gorges where the moonlight could never reach, the

jubilation of the rocks rimmed with silver, up there at Budarturo, distinctly outlined in the great glow, like enchanted castles. Up there, up there, in the silver light, she felt she was rising with those thoughts as if she had wings, while there came back to her lips tender words, harmonious voices, poetry lines that moved you to tears, like those blossoming in Cousin La Gurna's heart. Then she thought about that young man people rarely saw, who stayed in his little room abandoning himself to his imagination, dreaming just the way she was dreaming. Down there, behind that little hill, the same moon must be gleaming on the panes of his window, the same tenderness must be pervading him. What was he doing? What was he thinking? Now and then a chill went through her, as the trees rustled and brought her so many distant voices.

"White moon, beautiful moon!... What are you doing, you moon? Where are you going? What kind of thoughts are you thinking?"

She looked at her thin delicate hands, also white as the moon, with great tenderness, with a vague sense of gratitude and almost of pride.

Then she used to come back down from those heights, tired, her mind inert, shaken by her father's snoring, which filled the house. Her mother, next to him, did not even dare to let her breathing be heard; as she would not dare to show all her tenderness to her daughter in front of her husband, shy as she was, with those sad eyes of hers and that pale smile that said so much with the most humble words:

"Daughter! My daughter!..."

Only the hugging of her thin arms, and the expression of her eyes anxiously running to the door would say the rest — as if she had to hide the caressing of her own child, her trembling hands seeking the girl's face, her troubled eyes closely watching her.

"What's the matter? You're pale!... Don't you feel well?"

Aunt Cirmena, seeing the girl so frail, so pale in the face, with those black rings under her eyes, tried to distract her by teaching her new jobs — how to weave small frames with straw, how to make wool oranges and wool canaries. She told her stories and in the knitting basket, she secretly brought her the poems her nephew Corrado wrote.

"These are brand new, written yesterday. I took 'em from his desk, now that he's gone for a walk. He's living in a world of his own, that child. So shy! He needs help, with all that talent; too bad!"

She also suggested remedies for her delicate health—iron syrup, nailheads in a bottle of water. She busied herself helping in the kitchen, her skirt tucked up around her waist, making a good bone soup for her niece Bianca, preparing some special dish for Isabella, who didn't eat anything.

"Let me see to it. I know what she needs. You Trao people are all like chicks under the moon."

That Aunt Cirmena was like the sea. A woman that, if you were good to her, you certainly got a lot back. She often forced Corrado to come along with her at night, to cheer up the company.

"You who can do so many things with your books, with your words, will entertain them. Good God! If you stay hidden out of sight with your books, how are you going to let people know your worth?"

Then when he wasn't there, she spoke even more clearly:

"At his age!... He's not a child any more... He must help himself... He can't always live off his relatives!..."

And he was as proud as Lucifer too, taking umbrage and kicking if somebody tried to help him, to make him look good, if his aunt did everything she could to open people's eyes to the worth of her nephew, Corrado, and stole his papers, and went to show them off herself in the middle of the group of the Motta cousins, deciphering, getting as excited as a broker who's praising the value of his goods, while Don Gesualdo was slowly falling asleep, nodding yes, yawning, and Bianca looked at Isabella who kept her big eyes wide open in the shadow, spellbound with the expression of her delicate face changing from one moment to the next, as if waves of blood lighted it up intermittently. Donna Sarina, all intent on her reading, did not notice anything; she only worried about fixing her eyeglasses every once in a while; she bent toward the lamp, or grumbled about her nephew for writing so small.

"What a talent, eh! As a manager...what can I tell you...to oversee the work in the fields...to manage a large farm, that boy would be worth his weight in gold. My heart tells me that if you, Don Gesualdo, were to put him in charge of some of your businesses, it would really be a golden deal!... And...now that he's not listening...and for a low salary too! The young man's eyes are still shut, so to speak...still without pretenses...and he would be happy with little! Then you'd also do a good deed, you certainly would!"

Don Gesualdo said neither yes nor no, cautious, like a man accustomed to moving his tongue in his mouth seven times before letting out anything foolish. He thought about it, he considered the consequences, he watched his daughter, even when he snored, with one eye open. He wouldn't have wanted that his girl, so young, so inexperienced, still with no notion of the difference between being rich and being poor, should become excited about all that nonsense. He hadn't had much schooling, he didn't know anything, but he understood that those nice things were traps to catch fools. The same kind of tools used by literate people either to tie your hands or to quibble when driving a bargain. He had wanted his daughter to learn everything taught at school, because she was rich, and sooner or later she would make an advantageous marriage. But just because she was rich, there would be many people making plans about her. In other words he didn't like Aunt Cirmena's talk and the behavior of her nephew, who was helping her out with the distant air of one who must be begged to come to the table, of one who wants to sell his goods dear. And the long glances of his little cousin—her obstinate silences, her chin nailed down to her breast, that passion of hers for hiding in lonely places with her books, to play the literary role too—a girl who should have rather been laughing and having a good time....

So far it was only child's play; nonsense to laugh about, or to smack both of them in the head—the girl leaning at the window to watch the flies fly, and the boy who seemed to be studying the weather from the distance, and whose straw hat could be seen above the low wall or above the hedge, hanging around the cottage, hiding among the trees.

Don Gesualdo had good eyes. He couldn't guess all the nonsense fermenting inside those two crazy heads—the kisses blown into the air, and the sun and the clouds taking part in the duet, a mile away—but he could read in the fresh footprints, in the brier rose he found without petals on the pathway, in the naïve air of Isabella, who came downstairs to look for her scissors or for her thimble when

her cousin just happened to be in the room, in his cunning as he pretended not to look at her, like somebody at a fair who again and
again passes before the heifer he wants to buy, without even glancing at her. He could also read in Nanni l'Orbo's thieving face, in his
suspicious behavior, in the silly air he put on, when he got up in the
middle of the sumac trees, hiding his eyes with his hand to look
down at the road, or when he crawled among the cactuses on all
fours, or when he came to bring him those pieces of paper he had
found near the fountain, or those crumbs of plaster chipped off the
bench, pretending not to know anything:

"Don Gesualdo, have you been up there, by any chance, sir?...
Sometimes...just to stretch your legs... The grass is all trampled
down, as if a donkey had been lying there. It wasn't thieves, no, eh!
... Rather, I'm afraid of those spreading the cholera."

"No...in the daytime!... What the hell!... Jackass that you
are!... Don't be afraid, we keep our eyes open."

And he really did, cautiously, to avoid scandals, waiting for the
cholera to be over and to sweep the house, making a clean break
with Aunt Cirmena and all her relatives, without giving the backbiters a chance, telling her off, as she had also begun to play the
know-it-all, to talk hoity-toity, by cutting short all that rambling
nonsense that made even your heels yawn. One day, in front of
everybody, he spat out his ideas:

"Ah...the ballads? Stuff that doesn't fill anybody's belly, my
dear friends."

Aunt Cirmena took offense:

"You figure everything by weight and by volume, Don
Gesualdo! You don't know what it means...I'd like to see you!..."

Then he, with his mocking face, gathered a pile of books and
newspapers from the table and threw them into her lap, laughing
loudly and pushing her by the shoulders as if he wanted to push her
out of the house, like the broker closing the deal, shouting so loudly
between laughs that he seemed enraged:

"All right...take 'em if you like 'em.... You can live off
them!..."

They all looked at one another in the eyes. Isabella got up without saying a word, and walked out of the room.

"Ah!..." grumbled Don Gesualdo. "Ah!..."

But seeing that it wasn't the right moment, he swallowed his anger and turned the incident into a joke:

"She too...she likes ballads. As a pastime...with the guitar ...now that we're vacationing in the countryside...why not? But there's somebody who has worked hard for her, in the sun and in the wind, understand?... And if she has the Traos' hard head, the Mottas are no less tough, when it comes to that...."

"Good," cut in Aunt Cirmena, "that's another story."

"Ah, you think it's another story?"

"There!" broke in Aunt Cirmena, suddenly turning on her nephew. "Your uncle's speaking for your own good. You'll never find another relative who's so fond of you, as he is, listen to me!"

"Of course, of course...you're a sensible woman, Donna Sarina, and you understand fast."

Aunt Cirmena then started to prove that a talented young man could get any place he wanted to—secretary, factor, manager of a large estate. He would have plenty of recommendations.

"Of course, of course," Don Gesualdo kept repeating.

But he didn't commit himself any further. He busied himself with putting the chairs back where they belonged and with closing the windows, as if to say: "Now go away!" But since the young man was turning his back without answering, with the haughtiness of all those penniless relatives, Aunt Cirmena couldn't contain herself any longer, as she furiously picked up her knitting needles and her glasses, putting her basket on her arm without saying good-bye to anybody:

"Now I'd like to know if that's the way to behave! If that's the way to thank relatives for their concern! I'm washing my hands of it ...like Pilate... Everyone to his own house..."

"That's the right thing to say, Aunt Cirmena. Everyone to his own house. If you wait a minute I'll accompany you.... Eh? eh? What's the matter?"

For some time, as he was talking, he had been stretching his ears toward the barking of the dogs, toward the hell of a racket geese and turkeys were making in the courtyard, toward somebody's mad running. Then he heard an unfamiliar voice in the midst of his peoples's chattering. His field watchman stuck his head through the gate, wild-eyed, and motioning to him.

"I'm coming, I'm coming, wait a moment."

He got back a while later, like another person, upset, his straw hat pushed backward, wiping his sweat. Donna Sarina wanted to know by all means what had happened, pretending she was afraid.

"Nothing . . . The stubble up there must have caught on fire . . . I'll accompany you . . . It's nothing serious."

In the courtyard there was an uproar. *Mastro* Nardo, under the shed, was saddling Don Gesualdo's bay mule as fast as he could. By the garden gate, Nanni l'Orbo and many others were listening open-mouthed to a traveling peasant, who was telling incredible stories — all excited, gesticulating, showing his clothes reduced to shreds.

"Nothing, nothing," repeated Don Gesualdo. "I'll accompany you home. There's no hurry."

But you could see that he was upset; he stammered, and big drops ran down his forehead. Aunt Cirmena insisted on being afraid, planting herself right there, searching here and there with her curious eyes, staring him in the face to find out what was going on:

"A case of cholera, eh? They've brought it as far as here? A crook? They caught him in the act?"

Finally, Don Gesualdo put his hands on her shoulders looking straight into the whites of her eyes:

"Donna Sarina, what kind of game is this? Let me look after my own business! Dammit! Goddammit!"

And he quickly showed her the way home, on the other side of the little bridge. When he got back, he turned on all those people who seemed to be in a state of mutiny — Lia who had stopped kneading, her daughter who had also run over, her hands still dirty with flour.

"What's the matter? What's the matter? . . . You, *mastro* Nardo, go ahead with the mule. We'll catch up with you on the way. There, on that side, along the path. There's no need to let all the neighbors know if I go or if I stay. And you look after your own business. And keep your mouths shut, hey! . . . Without blowing the trumpet and going around, here and there, telling what's happening to me! . . ."

Then he went upstairs feeling his legs broken. As soon as she saw his face, Bianca got frightened. But he didn't say anything to her. He was afraid that the mice would play while the cat was away.

As his wife was helping him to put his boots on, he kept making recommendations:

"Look after the house. Look after your girl. I'll be back very soon. The time to get to Salonia for my father, who's not well. Keep your eyes open as long as I'm away, understand?"

Bianca, on her knees as she was, lifted her stunned face.

"Wake up! What the hell has happened to you? You're just like your brother Don Ferdinando! Your daughter doesn't have a head on her shoulders, did you notice? We surely did the right thing to put so many whims into her head! Who knows what she's dreaming about? And the others too...Donna Sarina and all the others! Snakes in our bosom!... So, no visitors, until I come back... And keep your eyes open and on your daughter. You know how girls are when they get something into their heads!... You were young too ... But I'm not going to be led by the nose like your brothers, understand!... No, no! Quiet! I don't have anything against you. ... You did it for me, then. You've been a good wife, docile and obedient, totally dedicated to the home.... I'm not sorry about it. I'm only trying to give you some advice now. To get married, girls don't worry about anything.... At least you didn't make a blunder. ... You're not sorry either, are you? But now it's another story. Now we must watch out not to be robbed—like in the woods..."

Bianca, who was standing by the door, her face pale, opened her eyes wide, and in their depth there was a vague fright, a sad bewilderment, the painful suspension of a clouded mind, such as showed in Don Ferdinando's eyes.

"Ah! You finally understand! You've noticed too! And you didn't tell me anything?... All like that, you women...helping each other out!... Conspiring against those who work themselves to death for your own good!"

"No, I swear!... I don't know anything!... It's not my fault. ... What d'you want from me?... D'you see the state I'm in?..."

"You didn't know about it? What are you doing then? Is that the way you keep an eye on your daughter?... Is this what a mother does?... Everything on my shoulders! I've broad shoulders, I do. I've a belly full of troubles... And I'm in excellent health, I am!... I've got a tough hide!"

And he left with his back bent, under the scorching sun, thinking about all his troubles. The messenger who had come to call him to Salonia was waiting for him at the top of the path, together with *mastro* Nardo who was limping as he pulled the mule. As he saw him from a distance, he began to scream:

"Hurry up, sir. If we get there too late, God save us, it's going to be my fault."

As they went along, he told stories that would make your hair stand on end. At Marineo they had murdered a traveler who kept hanging around the watering trough, during the hot hours of the day. He was ragged, barefoot, white with dust, his face burning, his eyes sullen, trying to do his thing in spite of the Christians who were guarding from a distance, in suspicion. At Callari they had found a body behind a fence, swollen as a wineskin; they had found it from the stench. At night, everywhere, you could see fireworks, rockets raining down, just like on Saint Lawrence night,* God save us! A pregnant woman who had let an unknown man help her, as she was carrying a load of wood to Trimmilito, had suddenly died that very same night, without even being able to say "Christ help me"—her belly full of prickly pears.

"Your father wanted the cholera himself, yes sir. They all told him 'Don't open before the sun is up!' But you know how stubborn he is! The cholera was brought to Salonia by a traveler who went around with a knapsack on his back. In times like these, you can just imagine! Somebody saw him sit down, dead tired, on the low wall near the farm houses. Then all night there were noises on the roofs and behind the doors.... And the grease spots we found here and there after daylight!... Like snail slobber.... Yes, sir!... That jackass of a pharmacist keeps on preaching about sweeping the houses, turning on the pigs and the hens, to keep off the cholera! How could the Lord's animals be the ones to bring the poison, those animals that have no malice in them? Understand, sir?... Enough to make you kill all of them—doctors, priests, and pharmacists— because for every Christian they send into the other world they get two tari from the king! And didn't Archpriest Bugno have the cour- age to preach from the altar! —'My children, I know that you're

---

*In southern Europe, Saint Lawrence night, August 10, is the high point of the shooting-star season, with the sky continuously streaked by meteorites.

angry at me because of the cholera. But I'm innocent. I swear to you on this consecrated Host!' I don't know whether he was innocent or not. All I know is that he's caught cholera too, because in his house he kept those bottles they send from Naples to make Christians die. The fact is that people are dying like flies—Donna Marianna Sganci, Peperito..."

III

When they all got to Salonia, they found the other tenants loading their mules and donkeys to run away. In vain Bomma, who had come over from his vineyard close by, shouted himself hoarse:

"Jackasses! It's a malignant fever!... He's running a very high fever! You don't die of cholera running a fever!"

"I don't care if it's a malignant fever!" grumbled Giacalone finally. "Doctors are paid to say things like that!..."

Mastro Nunzio was really ill. Death had pinched his nose and had left finger marks under his eyes—a shadow of soot that tinged his thinned nostrils, sank his eyes and his toothless mouth into black holes, and veiled his earth-colored face that was dirty with gray hairs. As he heard his son Gesualdo, who was standing by his bed, he hardly managed to open those eyes of his, and said in a cavernous voice:

"Ah! You've come to the feast, finally?"

Santo, like an old owl, was sitting on the doorstep, without saying anything, and with tears in his eyes. Burgio and his wife were hastily putting some wheat in a sack, so as not to starve to death wherever they would be going as soon as the old man would close his eyes. In the courtyard there were also the mules loaded with stuff. Don Gesualdo grabbed Bomma by the jacket, as he was also about to go.

"What can we do, Don Arcangelo? Just tell us! Anything we can do, for my father...everything I have!... Don't spare any expense..."

"Eh! you won't have to spend much.... There's nothing to do ...I've gotten here too late!... Quinine doesn't help any more!...

A malignant fever of the worst kind, my dear man! But he's not dying of cholera, and there's no reason to scare the whole neighborhood as they're doing!"

The old man was listening, with uneasy and suspicious eyes in the bottom of his black sockets. He was watching Gesualdo, who was busy around the pharmacist, Speranza who was screaming and sobbing as she helped her husband with the preparations for leaving, Santo who wasn't moving, stunned, his grandchildren here and there around the house and in the courtyard, and Bomma who was turning his back, shaking his head, making impatient gestures. Finally, Speranza went to her brother to hand him the keys, as she kept grumbling:

"Here! I'm glad you came . . . So you won't say that we, my husband and I, intend to fleece you out of all your things, as soon as our father closes his eyes. . . ."

"I'm not dead yet, I'm not!" lamented the old man from his corner.

Then the other son, Santo, got up like a fury, his face dirty with tears, shouting and turning on everybody:

"And the viaticum, aren't you going to give him the viaticum, you bunch of swine? . . . Are you going to let him die worse than a dog? . . ."

"I'm not dead yet!" again whimpered the dying man. "Let me die in peace first! . . ."

"No, it isn't for the property, no!" answered his son-in-law Burgio going close to the bed and bending over the sick man as if he were talking to a child. "It's for your own sake that we want you to confess and receive communion before you close your eyes."

"Ah! . . . ah! . . . You can't wait! . . . Leave me in peace . . . leave me! . . ."

The evening came and the night passed that way. In the shadow *mastro* Nunzio lay silent and motionless, like a piece of wood—except that every time they forced him to swallow his medicine, he moaned, he spat, he complained that it was as bitter as poison, that he was dead, that they couldn't wait to get him out of sight. Finally, not to be bothered by them, he turned his nose to the wall, and didn't move any more.

It might have been midnight, although nobody would risk

opening the window to look at the stars. Every now and then Speranza tiptoed close to the sick man, touched him, called him softly; but he kept silent. Then she went back to talk in whispers with her husband, who was calmly waiting, huddled on the doorstep, napping. Gesualdo was seated on the other side, with his chin between his hands. From the far end of the big room came Santo's snoring. The grandchildren had already left with the stuff, together with the other tenants — and an abandoned cat miaowed around the farmhouse like a soul in Purgatory, so that all of them lifted their heads, startled, and made the sign of the cross — as they saw those eyes gleaming in the dark, between the beams of the roofs and the holes in the wall; and on that filthy wall you could still see the shadow of the old man's cap, a gigantic shadow, which did not give any sign of life. Then they heard an owl screech three times.

Finally, after dawn, when daylight had been showing for some time through the cracks in the shutters making the lamp on the big barrel look pale, Burgio decided to open the door. It was a gloomy day, with low clouds and a great silence over the lifeless, rocky plain. Here and there, small blackish houses and the far end of the town on a hill in the background, seemed to be slowly rising from the mist — deserted and silent. Not a bird, not a buzzing, not a breath of wind. Only a rustle ran away in fright in the stubbles, as Burgio leaned out, yawning and stretching his arms.

"*Massaro* Fortunato!... Come here, come!" called his wife just then, her voice changed.

Gesualdo, bending over his father's little bed, called him and shook him. And his sister, disheveled, her clothes in disorder, looking still more yellow in that faint light, was getting ready to scream. After a while Burgio finally risked his opinion:

"My friends, he looks to me as if he's been dead a hundred years."

It was then that tragedy exploded. Speranza began to howl and to scratch her face. Santo, who had been jolted awake, was punching himself in the head, rubbing his eyes, crying like a child. But the one more upset than anybody else was Don Gesualdo — although he didn't say anything, as he looked at the dead man who was looking at him out of the corner of his clouded eyes. Then he kissed his hand and covered his face with the sheet. Speranza, inconsolable, threatened to run to town to throw herself into the cistern, or to starve herself to death:

"What am I doing in the world now? I've lost my support, the pillar of the house!"

That crying and moaning lasted the entire day. In vain her husband tried to console her by saying that Don Gesualdo would not abandon them. They were all his children now, orphans in need. Santo, with his face dirty, looked now at this one and now at that one, as they opened their mouths.

"No!" insisted Speranza. "Now he's dead, my father's dead! There is nobody to care for us!"

Gesualdo, who had let her go on for some time, shaking his head, and his eyes swollen, finally said:

"You're right!... I've never done anything for you people!... You're right to complain about everything I gave you!..."

"No," cut in Burgio. "No! Those are only words that come out when one's upset, dear brother-in-law."

Meanwhile, they had to see to it that the dead man was buried, without being able to find a dog to help, even if you were to pay his weight in gold. A carpenter, there at Camemi, nailed four boards together in the shape of a coffin, and *mastro* Nardo dug a grave behind the house. Then Santo and Don Gesualdo had to do the rest with their own hands. Burgio was watching from a distance, fearful of infection, and his wife moaned that she didn't have the courage to touch the dead man. It hurt her in the heart, it did! Afterward, when she had wiped her eyes dry, made the bed, and tidied the house, while *mastro* Nardo was getting the mules ready, and while they were sitting in a group together waiting, she started to talk seriously:

"And now, what's our understanding?"

At that beginning, they all looked one another in the face. *Massaro* Fortunato was twisting the tassle of his cap, and Santo opened his eyes wide. But Don Gesualdo, who had not caught the hint, lifted his face as he was looking for words.

"What's our understanding? Why? About what?"

"About discussing our business, eh! To divide the inheritance that good soul has left, may he be in Paradise! We are three children ... Everyone his share ... according to your conscience.... You're the oldest, you make the division ... and everyone takes his share.

... But of course, if you have his will some place ... I don't deny it
... Then show it to us, and we'll see."

As he heard those words, Don Gesualdo, who was Don Gesualdo, remained open-mouthed. Stunned, he stammered in search for words:

"The inheritance! ... The will! ... The share of what? ..."

At that point Speranza became furious — What? This is what they were talking about. Weren't they all children of the same father? And who had been the head of the family? So far the one to have his fingers in every pie had been he, Don Gesualdo, selling, buying ... Now, everyone should have his share. All that good property, those beautiful lands, Canziria, Salonia itself where they were standing now, had by any chance rained down from the sky? — Burgio, who was calmer, tried to put in some good words; said that it wasn't the right moment, with the dead man still warm. He covered his wife's mouth, and pushed back his brother-in-law Santo, who had opened his ears and shouted:

"No, no, let her talk!"

Finally he wanted them to embrace right there in the very room where they had been left poor orphans. Don Gesualdo was an honest man, with a big heart. He wouldn't have played a dirty trick on them.

"Don't run away! Listen here! Isn't it true? Aren't you an honest man?"

"No! no! Let me hear what they want. It's better to speak clearly!"

But his sister was no longer paying attention to him, as she sat on a rock, outside the door, grumbling to herself. *Massaro* Fortunato tried some other tunes too — the punishment of God on their backs, the time that was getting late. Meanwhile, *mastro* Nardo pulled the mule out of the stable. They remained outside a little longer, sulking at each other. Then Don Gesualdo offered to take all of them to Mangalavite. His brother-in-law Burgio was locking the door and loading on the packsaddle the few clothes he had gathered into a little bundle. Speranza didn't answer her brother's invitation right away, spreading our her shawl to get ready to leave, looking here and there with surly eyes. Finally, she blurted out what she had on her chest:

"To Mangalavite? ... No, thanks! ... What should I come

there for...if you say it's your property?... It would also be too much trouble for your wife and your daughter...two ladies who are used to their comforts.... We poor people can manage anywhere. ... We'll go to Canziria. Rather, we'll go to the plaster kiln my father left, rest his soul.... That's it!... At least there we'll be at home. You won't tell us that you bought the plaster kiln yourself, with your own money!... No, no, I'll be quiet, *massaro* Fortunato! We'll talk about it some other time, if we live long enough. If you live the whole year, you'll see all the feasts. Good-bye, Don Gesualdo. It will be as God wills. Lucky that old man, who's now peaceful underground!..."

She was still grumbling when she was on her way, shaken by the ambling pace of the mule, her back bent, the wind swelling up her black shawl. Don Gesualdo climbed up too, and rode in the opposite direction, his heart heavy with the ungratefulness he kept reaping, turning his head now and then, to look at the closed and deserted farmhouse next to the still fresh grave, and at his own relatives riding away in a line, one after the other, already like black dots in the barren countryside that was now growing dark. After a while, *mastro* Nardo who had been thinking about it, delivered the eulogy for the dead man:

"Poor man! He certainly worked a lot...to bring up his children...to leave them rich.... Now he's underground! D'you remember, sir, when the bridge collapsed at Fiumegrande and he wanted to drown himself?... That's how the world is! Today it's your turn, tomorrow it's mine."

The boss gave him a grim look, and cut him short:

"Quiet, jackass!... You too!..."

It must have been about two hours after dark when they got to the Don Cosimo Fountain, on a beautiful starry night, the whole sky swarming around Budarturo, above the expanse of plains and mountains being dimly outlined. The mule, feeling close to the stable, began to bray. Then the dogs barked; down below some lights appeared in the thicker shadow of the trees surrounding the cottage, and voices were heard, with stamping of feet, as of people running. Along the path climbing up from the valley there was the rustle of dry leaves, and stones bouncing downhill, as if somebody were cautiously going up the slope. Then silence. Suddenly, out of the dark on the edge of the thicket, came a voice:

"Hey, Don Gesualdo?"

"Hey, Nanni, what's the matter?"

Nanni didn't answer, but began to walk beside the mule. After a moment, he mumbled under his breath, almost reluctantly:

"The matter is that I'm here to guard your back!"

Don Gesualdo didn't ask any more questions. They were going down the path, one behind the other. After a while, Nanni l'Orbo only added:

"It was some feast, wasn't it?"

And since the boss kept silent, he concluded:

"I could tell from your face, sir. The world's full of trouble! They come one after the other!"

When they finally got to the fountain, he said:

"Let's get off here, eh? *Mastro* Nardo will go on the road with the mules, and we'll walk this way, to get there faster."

Don Gesualdo understood immediately and didn't need any more words. They were walking silently, along the wall, as if they could see in the dark. After a while Nanni l'Orbo pointed at some stones scattered on the ground, some sort of breach among the thorns crowning the wall, and said in a whisper:

"D'you see, sir?"

Don Gesualdo nodded his head and jumped beyond the enclosure. With his flintlock Nanni l'Orbo lit a sulphur match, and they walked following the footprints, step by step, all the way to the cottage. Under Donna Isabella's window, l'Orbo pointed to the grass, which was all trampled down as if donkeys had been really lying there.

"And the dogs . . . as if they'd been drugged!" remarked Nanni with his air of mystery. "If it weren't for me, who has sharp ears . . . I said to Diodata: 'When the boss is gone, we must keep our ears stretched out, to guard his back . . .' So I sent Nunzio on to the little bridge, while Gesualdo and I came in from the millhouse . . . Yes sir, where Donna Sarina is staying with her nephew . . . 'If the dogs are quiet,' I was saying to myself . . .'"

"All right. Keep quiet now. They could hear you from up there."

The next day, dressed in black and his beard unshaven, he received the visits of condolence. Donna Sarina had just finished her eulogy of both the dead man and the live one, wiping her eyes, and rolling up her sleeves to run to the kitchen to help in that confusion, when Don Gesualdo stopped her unceremoniously in the corridor.

"D'you want to know, Donna Sarina?... You'd really be of great help to me if you left this house. Clear speech makes good friends. I need those two rooms...for reasons of my own. So far I haven't said anything. You must have certainly admired my restraint, eh?"

Aunt Cirmena turned green. She smoothened her dress, smiling, and without losing her head.

"All right, all right. I understand. Since you need those two little rooms.... If you've reasons of your own... Even now, right away...cholera or no cholera!... People won't talk about it, if you kick me out in the middle of the cholera!... You're the boss. Everyone knows what's going on in his own home. Only, if I may, I'll say good-bye to my niece first. Who knows what they'd think if I left without a word.... The backbiters, you know!..."

Bianca couldn't figure it out:

"What? You must go? In the thick of the cholera? Why? What happened?"

Aunt Cirmena put forth some odd pretext: circumstances; everyone has reasons of his own; Corrado received an extremely urgent letter.

"He's sorry too, poor boy. It hit him so suddenly! He had become so fond of this area.... Just a short time ago he was saying: 'My dear Aunt, today I'll take my last walk to the spring'..."

Don Gesualdo lost his temper and cut that stupid talk short:

"Excuse me, Donna Sarina. My wife doesn't understand anything any more. They all get that way in her family.... It should have happened to me!..."

Isabella, instead, had become as pale as a dead body. But she didn't move, she didn't say anything—a real Trao, her face immobile and impenetrable. She even returned her aunt's hugs and affectionate greetings, trying to smile, a thin wrinkle between her eyebrows. Then, when she was alone, all at once, in a gesture of despair, she tore the ruff that was choking her, with a wave of blood to her face, with a sudden dazzle before her eyes, with a cutting pain, a sharp spasm that shook her, groping, beside herself.

She wanted to see him, one last time, at all costs, when they'd all be resting, in the afternoon, and in the cottage no living soul would be stirring. The Virgin Mary would help her:

"The Virgin Mary!... The Virgin Mary!..."

She couldn't say anything else—her mind in painful confusion, her head in flames, the sun beating down on her head, her eyes burning, a blaze consuming her heart, going up to her head, blinding her, making her delirious:

"I must see him! At all costs!... Tomorrow I'll see him no more!... No more!... No more!..."

She didn't feel the thorns; didn't feel the stones of the out-of-the-way path she had taken to get to him secretly. Panting, pressing her breasts with her hands, startled at every step, looking over her path with her anxious eyes. A bird flew off frightened with a piercing shrill. The level fields were deserted, shaded in dark. There was a low wall covered with sad ivy, a small abandoned water basin in which some aquatic plants were rotting, and on the other side of the wall some squares of dusty vegetables, cut across by abandoned roads that ended up drowning into the thick boxwood bristling with yellow, dead branches. Everywhere the feeling of abandonment, of desolation—in the woodpile rotting in a corner, in the decaying leaves heaped up under the walnut trees, in the water of the spring that seemed to be moaning, as it dripped from the clusters of the maidenhair tapestrying the cave like so many tears. Only among the weeds of the path on which he was to come, some humble thistle flowers gleamed in the sun, green berries bent swaying softly, and said: 'Come! Come! Come!' She cautiously crossed the road that sloped down to the cottage, her heart jumping in her throat, beating in her temples, taking her breath away. Among the dry leaves near the wall where he had sat so many times, there were burned pieces of paper, damp, still moving about as if they were living things—burned matches, torn ivy leaves, shoots broken up into small pieces by his feverish hands, during the long hours of his waiting, in the automatic activity of his fantasizing. You could hear the hammering of an ax in the distance; then a melancholy song that lost itself up there, on the trail. What a long agony! The sun was slowly abandoning the path; it was dying palely on the barren cliff, with the ravines looking even sadder, while she was still waiting, always waiting.

"Don Gesualdo, sir... Come here, if you please...I've something to tell you."

Nanni l'Orbo, calling him from the yard, pretended not to be able to set foot any farther, with a mysterious air, until his boss went there to find out what the hell he wanted, and started out by giving him a good scolding:

"I've told you so many times not to show up around here! What the hell!... You just do it on purpose..."

"No, sir. That's why I called you out here. We must talk face to face, about what I must tell you.... Here in the garden. We're expected."

In fact, there were Diodata's Nunzio and Gesualdo, in their best clothes, their hands in their pockets, and small kerchiefs around their necks. Nanni pointed this out to the boss.

"Blood is blood. D'you deny it? Both of them...they've decided to put on mourning clothes for your father, rest his soul... out of respect, without a hidden purpose.... You're the only one, sir, who can help them, without having to pay out any money.... Why, they would like to have that piece of land by the spring, as sharecroppers. They're both good, hardworking boys. They're like you, Don Gesualdo... If you help 'em out, you can at least think that you're not helping strangers!..."

Don Gesualdo was hesitating, on the one hand suspicious for being caught by surprise, and on the other giving in, in spite of his inclinations, to the inner voice that kept insisting inside him on the arguments Nanni had put forth to persuade him. —What were they asking for, after all?...for a chance to work.... He who had so much in his power!... A question of conscience!... Besides, it would be a good deal too....

At a certain point Nanni l'Orbo suggested that they send for Diodata, so that she could express her opinion. Then, to get rid of that problem and to ease his conscience, just as Nanni l'Orbo was saying, as he stared at the two big boys, who followed them step by step, with their hands in their pockets, without opening their mouths, Don Gesualdo blurted out:

"All right...all right, if it's only the piece of land below the spring...if you're not like the porcupine that puts out all its thorns afterward..."

"Yes sir! What does that mean?" Nanni quickly jumped up, taking advantage of the opportunity. "Only that! Half a salma of land in all. We can go and see. It's right here. We'll stake it out right under your eyes—since you're here—so you won't think that we're robbing you.... That's it!... We even have witnesses, you see.... The young lady up there, under the big walnut tree...."

Don Gesualdo looked in the direction Nanni l'Orbo was saying and quickly went pale. Suddenly he changed his color and his manner, and brusquely dismissed everybody:

"All right, we'll talk about it.... There's time. You don't catch people unaware like this, goddammit! I answered yes; now go away!"

At that outburst the two young men slunk away with long faces, while Nanni went into the thicket to enjoy the scene from the distance. Don Gesualdo, all upset, was hurrying up the road, with the agility of a twenty-year-old. Isabella saw him suddenly appear with a face that almost made her faint out of fright. He didn't say anything. He took her by the hand, like a child, and walked her home. She let herself be walked, like a dead woman, her heart dead, unable to see, stumbling over the stones. Only once in a while she thrust her hand into her hair, as if there she felt a great bewilderment, a great pain.

As she saw them come like that, Bianca began to shake like a leaf. Her husband handed her daughter over to her, with a terrible look, shaking his head. But he didn't say anything. He began to walk about the room, now and then wiping the bitterness from his mouth with his handkerchief. Then he suddenly opened the door and left.

He roamed around like a furious ox, slamming doors, turning on whomever he happened to come across. Everywhere you could hear his voice that shook the house:

"Nardo, where have you been all this time? I told you to bring me those shears at the vineyard. The colts aren't in yet? Brasi, that jackass, will cause some of them to get hurt! I'll let him have it as soon as he gets back! —Tell me, Santoro! Did you finish cutting the sumac trees up there?... What the hell have you been doing all day, then?... As soon as the boss is away for a moment!... Murderers! Paid enemies!... —Martino! Light the lamp, Martino, to milk the ewes! In the dark like that, you'll spill all the milk on the ground, jackass!... They haven't lighted the lamp up there yet! What are they doing? Are they saying the rosary?... —Concetta! Concetta! We're still in the dark! What the hell are you doing? What a household, as soon as I turn my back!... What will happen, if I close my eyes?..."

After some time he went to knock at the women's door again, and since they didn't open right away he burst it open with a kick. Bianca then turned toward him ferociously, like a mother hen defending her chicks, with such a face as nobody had ever seen on her—the wild face of the Traos, with her eyes gleaming like a madwoman's above her pallor and her frightening thinness, covering with her own body the body of her daughter who was lying on the bed, her face buried in the pillow, shaking with nervous shudders.

"Ah! You want to kill her then? Haven't you done enough? Haven't you done enough? D'you want to kill her?"

She wasn't the same woman, so much so that Don Gesualdo himself was disconcerted. Now he tried to be as friendly as he could, overcome by an immense dejection, by the bitterness of so much ungratefulness rising in his throat, his bones broken, his heart black as pitch.

"You're right!... I'm the tyrant! I've a tough heart and a tough hide, I do! I'm the working ox.... If I work myself to death it's for you, understand? A piece of bread and a piece of cheese are enough for me.... Well, this means that I've worked to throw everything to the wolves...my own flesh and blood and my property!... You're right!..."

Bianca tried to stammer a couple of words. Then he turned toward her like a fury, his hands in the air, his mouth wide open. But he didn't say anything. He looked at his daughter who was leaning against the side of the bed shaking all over, her face swollen and her hair loose. Then he let his arms fall down and began to walk back and forth in the room, patting his hands, blowing and puffing, with his eyes to the floor, as if he were looking for words, for the ways to make those hard heads understand reason.

"Come, come, Isabella!... It's only nonsense, understand?... It's nonsense to fret...I don't want to fret either...I've so many other troubles! My heart is heavy!... I'd like you to see how many troubles I have on my mind!... You'd burst out laughing, I swear to

God!... You'd see that all the rest is really nonsense!... You're still young... There are certain things you don't understand.... The world, believe me, is a gang of thieves.... Everybody saying: 'Get out of there, and give me what you have'... Everybody looks after his own interest.... Look! look!... Let me tell you... If you didn't have anything, nobody would bother you.... It's a business deal, understand?... A way to secure one's bread and butter for the rest of his life. If somebody's poor, whether a man or a woman—no offense meant—he tries to help himself as best he can.... He looks around; he sees what will suit him...and then he puts all his resources to work to get to it, everybody in his own way.... Somebody, let's say, will try his aristocratic family name, and somebody else what he can do best...the beautiful words and the tender glances.... But if whoever is on the receiving side has any sense, he must watch out for his own interest.... D'you see how stupid it is to cry and to despair?..."

His words died on his lips in front of the pale face and the wild eyes with which his daughter was looking at him. Even his wife couldn't say anything but:

"Leave her alone!... Don't you see the state she's in?"

"Like an idiot she is!" shouted Mastro-don Gesualdo, finally losing his temper. "Like one who doesn't know and doesn't want to know! But I'm not going to be an idiot myself, that's for sure!...I know what it means!..."

And he walked out in a fury.

IV

After the fear of the cholera had passed, and he had gone back to town, Don Gesualdo was served with a summons by his sister, with the authorization of her husband Burgio, demanding their share of the paternal inheritance, of everything he owned—highway robbery—alleging that all the property had been acquired with the profits of the company headed by *mastro* Nunzio; and that now he, Gesualdo, wanted to appropriate everything—he who had supported them all up to that very day! He who had had to lower his head before all of his father's bad speculations! He who had been like Providence for his brother-in-law Burgio during the bad years! He who kept paying his brother Santo's debts at Pecu-Pecu's tavern! —Santo was suing him too, for his share, since he had been a partner of that company, the lazy bum! —Now they spat in his face through the bailiff; they called him a thief; they wanted to put seals on everything, to sequester his property. They dragged him from one lawsuit to the other, before lawyers and prosecutors —a lot of expense, so much bitterness in his mouth, so much waste of time, so many of his other businesses suffering, and his enemies getting fat on it. In the cafès and in the drugstores people didn't talk about anything else —all turning on him because he was rich, and taking his relatives' side because they had nothing! Notary Neri had even become his enemies' defending lawyer, *gratis et amore,* free of charge, because of old and new quarrels that had come up between them. Speranza waited for him on the courthouse steps to spit all kinds of insults at him, in vain pushing her big and heavy children against him, and she pushing even Santo against him, though Santo didn't really have the face of one who would turn against Don Gesualdo, and was doing his best to avoid him.

"You've got no guts, all of you! Just like my husband!... I'm the only one who should wear the pants around here! I'm not myself if I don't send him to jail, that thief! I'll sell the very shirt off my back. I want what's mine, my own father's blood..."

It was still worse the first time the judge ruled against her, and she lost the case:

"See, my friends?... You can buy anything with money these days!... But I'll go all the way to Palermo, I'll go to the King, to see if there is justice in this world!..."

Baron Zacco, having gotten it into his head to make a certain deal with Don Gesualdo, intervened to act as a peacemaker. One Sunday he got all the Mottas together in his house, including Speranza's husband, who was a jackass and couldn't say anything for himself. Santo, who was forced to meet his brother Don Gesualdo face to face, began with excusing himself:

"What can I say?... It's not my fault. They took me to the lawyer.... What was I to do?... Why did we ask for the lawyer's advice?... I'll do what the lawyer tells me..."

Don Gesualdo was conciliatory. Not that he had to be, no! —He knew the law. But out of good-heartedness. He had always helped his relatives as much as he could, and he wanted to keep on helping them. But there was a squabble about proofs and counterproofs with no end to it. Speranza, who saw her share of the inheritance vanish as they began to talk about good-heartedness, turned on her husband and on her children, who didn't know how to defend themselves. Even Santo kept quiet, like a boy who had been caught red-handed. Fortunately, she was there to speak her piece:

"What d'you want to give us, charity? A few salmas of wheat, when it suits you, every once in a while? A few salmas of wine, the kind you can't sell?"

"What d'you want me to give you, Alia or Donninga? D'you want me to strip myself so that you can gorge yourselves, you who haven't done anything? I have a family. I cannot touch my property . . ."

"Your property? . . . listen to that! Does that mean that our father, rest his soul, hasn't left anything? And the plaster business you had together as partners? And when you took the contract of the bridge together? There is nothing left that belongs to him, rest his soul? All the profits were yours only? To buy those beautiful estates? Those you want for yourself because you have a family? . . . But there is a God above, I tell you! . . . What you want to take out of these poor innocents' mouths . . . there is already somebody eating it behind your back! Go and see for yourself, at night, under your own windows, what a coming and going! . . ."

It ended in an uproar. The Baron had to scream and make a hell of a racket so that they wouldn't come to blows right then and there, instead of making peace. Speranza went off still raving, on the one side, and Don Gesualdo on the other, his mouth bitter, tortured also by that other bug his sister had put in his ear. Now, in the midst of so many troubles and headaches, he even had to watch over his daughter and that criminal of a Corrado La Gurna whom Aunt Cirmena, out of spite, had put right there in his way, keeping him in town at her own expense. He had to be on the lookout for everybody that came and went—on the house servants, on the sheets of paper that were missing, on his daughter, who looked like somebody who was planning a big one—pale and thin as she was. . . . She was melting her soul away, the wretched girl! And he had to be gnawed inside and swallow bitterness, not to make things worse. Finally, one night he caught her at the window, in terrible weather.

"Ah!... So it's still going on!... What are you doing here at this time?... To get some fresh air for the summer? I'm going to teach you how to count the stars! You haven't seen me lose my temper yet! I'm going to teach a certain young gentleman how to walk under windows at night! A good cudgel thrashing, if I meet him! So far you've seen my sweet side; but now I'll show you my bitter side as well! I'm going to make you plow straight, just as I plow myself!"

From that day on there was a hell of a racket, morning and night. Don Gesualdo handled Isabella nicely, roughly, trying to drive that idiocy out of her head; but she had it always there, in the ever-present wrinkle between her eyebrows, in her pale face, in her tight lips that didn't say a word, in her gray and obstinate Trao eyes which said instead: "Yes, yes, even if I have to die for it!" She didn't dare rebel openly. She didn't complain. She was losing her youth and her health. She didn't eat any more; but she didn't bend her head—stubborn as she was, a real Trao, with a Motta head on top of it.

The poor man was reduced to the point of having to examine his own conscience. From her parents, that girl had picked up only the shortcomings. But the love of property, no! The sense to understand who was on her side and who was not, the sense to watch out for her own interest, no! She wasn't even as docile and obedient as her mother! She had even spoiled Bianca for him! Bianca too, seeing her daughter turning to skin and bones, had become like a she-cat when you want to take her kittens away, just like it, with her hair standing on end, her back bent with illness and her eyes shiny with fever. She would unsheath her claws and her tongue against him:

"D'you want my child to die of consumption? Don't you see the state she's in? Don't you see that she's wasting away from day to day?"

She would have helped her, secretly, even to go to the dogs, even to break her neck. She would have betrayed her husband for her child. She said to him:

"I'm going back to my brother's. I'm going with my daughter! What d'you think of that?"

Her eyes like coals. He had never seen her like that. One day, behind the doctor who was coming to see the girl, he saw a face he didn't like: an old woman of the neighborhood who was bringing the medicine from the pharmacist, very much the same way as Don Luca the sacristan and his wife Grazia brought his love messages into the Trao house. He had gotten to the point of inspecting the doctor's prescriptions and the paper the pills Bomma sent were wrapped in. In one month he changed maids five times. He might look like a lout, but he was not a fool like the Trao brothers. He kept everything under lock and key; he didn't let a cent by, which might help in the betrayal. He was a chained dog himself, the poor man. Finally, to get out of that hell, he decided to put Isabella in a convent, right there in the Collegio di Maria, just like when she was a child—jailed! His wife could cry and be desperate to her heart's content! He was the boss!

"Listen," said Bianca with clasped hands, "I don't have long to suffer. But leave me my daughter until I close my eyes."

"No!" answered her husband, "that ungrateful one doesn't even feel any compassion for you! We've all worked ourselves to death to bring up an ungrateful daughter!... She lost her love for her family ...when she was away from home!"

They worked out the betrayal right there at the Collegio: more people whom he had been helping out—Gerbido's sister, who was the doorkeeper, Giacalone who brought Aunt Cirmena's presents and passed the notes to the other side of the wheel,* Bomma who held open conversation in his pharmacy to suit Don Corrado La Gurna, who started with his telegraph messages as soon as the girl climbed up the bell tower for that purpose. They did it for a few cents, or as a favor, or out of spite. They were all conspiring against him, to steal his daughter and his property away from him, as if he had stolen it away from others. Finally one fine day, when the nuns had gone to the choir, during the Forty Hours, the girl had her accomplices open the door, and she flew away.

It was the second of February, the day of the Virgin Mary. A great number of faithful had come that year for the feast, because it

---

*A cylinderlike device rotating on its axis in a wall, with an opening designed to transmit any item from the parlor to the inner cloister. It is also used for written or verbal communication.

hadn't rained since October. Don Gesualdo had gone to church too, to pray to God to remove that cross from his back. But that morning the Lord must have turned his eyes elsewhere. As soon as he got back home from holy Mass, that fateful day, he found the house upside down — his wife with her hands in her hair, the servants running here and there. Finally they told him what had happened. It was as if he had had a stroke. They had to send for the barber as fast as they could to bleed him. Lia got a slap in the face, almost enough to smash her teeth. Bianca, more dead than alive, was coming down the stairs as if tumbling, almost running away too from fright. He, purple with rage, foaming at the mouth, couldn't see with his eyes. He couldn't see the state the poor woman was in. He wanted to run to the judge, to the mayor, turn the whole town upside down; have the Company at Arms come from Caltagirone; have both of them arrested, his daughter and her accomplice; have him hanged in the public square, that crook; have him quartered by the executioner; have him leave his bones in a dungeon!

"That murderer! That crook! I want him to die in a dungeon! ... Both of them! ..."

In the midst of this fury Aunt Cirmena appeared, her missal in hand, with a placid smile, dressed in silk.

"Calm down, Don Gesualdo. Your daughter is in a safe place. Pure as the Immaculate Virgin Mary! Calm down! Don't make a scandal, which is worse. D'you see your wife, who seems to be giving up the ghost, poor woman! She's a mother! We'll never know what's in her heart at this moment! I just came to fix up the mess. I'm not like many other people; I've feelings, unlike others. I can't hold a grudge! You know how much I've done for my relatives. You threw me into the street ... during the cholera ... with an orphan to support. ... But never mind! Here I am to settle the matter. I've a good heart; too bad! My loss! But there's nothing I can do about it! Now we must think how to mend things. We've got to marry those two youngsters, now that the damage is done. There is no other way. In fact, as to the young man, you can't complain ... from a good family."

This time Don Gesualdo lost all restraint, no less, his mouth open, as if he were ready to devour her:

"With that bum? ... Give him my daughter? ... I'd rather let her die of consumption like her mother!... In the country! In a convent! You're proposing quite a deal!... It's just like you!... It takes some gall!... You make me laugh with all this great aristocracy of yours...I know what it's worth!... All of you!..."

There was an uproar. Donna Sarina, red as a rooster, unsheathed her cutting tongue too:

"What you say shows the way you are! At least you could hold your tongue, out of respect for your wife, you peasant! Mastro-don Gesualdo! You're the disgrace of the whole family!..."

"Ah! Ah! the disgrace. Go on, you're surely right to talk about disgrace, you!... Procuress! You've been helping out too! You're an accomplice of that thief!... What a nice profession at your age! I'll have you arrested together with him, Donna Sarina my foot! Donna ...d'you know what they should call you?..."

Uncle Limòli arrived in spite of his infirmities, for the honor of the family, to try to make peace too, whether they liked it or not.

"Don't make a scandal! Don't scream so much, which is worse! Dirty linen must be washed at home. Rather, let's see how to get out of this mess. The mess is there, my friend, and we must make the best of it...like it or not. Bianca! Bianca, don't do that; you'll ruin your health.... It doesn't help anything..."

Don Gesualdo left immediately for Caltagirone at breakneck speed. He wanted a warrant of arrest, he wanted the Company at Arms. His Uncle the Marquis, on the other hand, gave the best help possible with caution and expediency. First of all, he immediately went to pick up his niece, and accompanied her to the Santa Teresa convent, recommending her to a relative of his. The house people were silenced, partly with threats and partly with bribes. A little while later the order to arrest Corrado La Gurna came like lightning from Caltagirone. Donna Sarina Cirmena, out of fear, held her tongue too.

Meanwhile, the Marquis was secretly working to find Isabella a husband. She was an only child; Don Gesualdo, whether he liked it or not, had to give her a big dowry; and with his numerous relations the Marquis was certain to find her a really good match. He wrote to his friends; he spoke to the people who could help him in such matters—the canon-priest Lupi, Notary Neri. The latter finally unearthed the right person: a first-class nobleman, whose properties were being administered by the Notary, with his finances in disorder, entangled in lawsuits and debts, but of a great family, who would give a great name to Mastro-don Gesualdo's descendants. When, however, they got to discussing the dowry with Don Gesualdo, it was an entirely different story. He didn't want to be eaten alive. Not one cent! He had earned his money with the sweat of his brow, during his whole life. He didn't like to be bled for somebody who had to come from Palermo to drink his blood.

"Where d'you want him to come from then, from the moon? My dear Don Gesualdo, these are words on the wind. D'you know how things are? I'm going to make a comparison, the kind you yourself make, just so that you understand reason: hail's falling on your vineyard . . . some sort of disaster that happens to fall on your herds. . . . You must send the heifer with broken horns to the fair, and forget about the price. You've got to lower your head, whether you like it or not. After all, you've no other children. . . . At least you know you're making her a great lady! . . ."

At the same time the Marquis went to visit his niece. He was trying to be as friendly as he could, with the good sense one needs to approach certain themes:

"You're right! You're right to cry. Unburden yourself with me, who understands these things. . . . A burning pain, something that feels like dying! Your father doesn't understand anything about it, poor man. He's always been taken up by his business deals, by his peasants . . . a little uncouth too, if you like. . . . But he has worked for you, to make you rich. With your mother's name and with your father's money, you could play a leading part even in a big city, whenever you want. . . . Not here in this hole. . . . Here, even I feel stifled. I was young, I did enjoy my best years. . . . That's why I'm telling you . . . I understand what you must have inside your little heart. When we're young, we think that nothing else exists in the world. . . . Your father is wrong . . . But if he insists on not giving you anything, that young man doesn't have anything either, poor fellow. . . . And then . . . if you have to sweep the house . . . if he can't make ends meet . . . It will be a serious business, understand? There will be quarrels, and regrets, and long faces. Long faces make both you and him ugly, my dear niece. And why? to what avail? If your father has said no, it's going to be no; you won't marry him! You'll die here, in this sort of dungeon; you'll waste the best years of your life. Corrado will stay in exile, at the mercy of the police, as long as your father likes; he has long arms now.... You are not even going to do any good to those you love, if you insist. Your cousin needs to keep free of worries, to work in peace, to make an honest living.... Instead you could marry a great nobleman, and if it's true that that young fellow loves you so much, he should be the first one to be happy for you. That's love... A great nobleman, understand! For the moment, don't talk about it to your girl friends...here in the convent, they'd die of envy, you know.... But I know that they're planning to have you marry a great nobleman. You'd be either a Princess or a Duchess! Quite different from being Donna So and So! Carriages, horses, a box at the theater every night, as many jewels and dresses as you like.... With that beautiful face of yours I know how many heads you'll turn in a big city! When you walk into a ball-room, wearing a low-cut dress, covered with diamonds, everybody asking: 'Who's that beautiful lady?...' And there comes the answer: 'Duchess So and So, or Princess So and So...' Come, come to see your mother who's still sick, poor woman! That blow has finished her off! You know that she is in poor health!... Your father too is waiting for you with open arms. He's a good man after all! He has a heart of gold, one who's worked himself to death to make you rich! ... Now go back home.... Then we'll see..."

Finally, when Uncle the Marquis took the lost sheep back to her parents, it was such a scene as to make the stones weep. Isabella fell to her knees by the bed of her mother, whom she found so changed, sobbing and asking forgiveness; while her mother, poor woman, went from one fainting spell to another, so great was her joy. Then Don Gesualdo arrived, and they were all silent. Finally he started to talk, a little upset too, his eyes swollen — for blood is not water after all, and he didn't have a heart of stone.

"That was quite a trick you played on me! I really didn't deserve it! We've taken the bread out of our mouths, your mother and I, to make you rich!... See the state she's in, poor woman!... If she shuts her eyes, she looks just like a dead body!... But you're our flesh and blood, our child, and we've forgiven you. Now let's not talk about it any more."

But Isabella kept talking about it with her Uncle the Marquis, with Aunt Mendola, with Aunt Macrì, with all her relatives; from all of them she sought help, even from her father confessor—like a madwoman, disconsolate, washing the stones of the confessional with her tears. They all answered:

"What can we do, if your father is against it? He's the boss. He has to lay down the money for the dowry. He's doing it for your own good; he's doing what's best for you. Girls get married according to their parents' wishes!"

The father confessor even pulled out the will of God. And Aunt Cirmena, when she had seen that not even the elopement had been enough to get the money for the dowry out of Don Gesualdo's hands, had shrugged her shoulders:

"What can you do, my dear niece? I did all I could, but without money there is no High Mass. Corrado doesn't own anything; and you don't own anything either, if your father insists on saying no. . . . It would be a great marriage indeed! See how it turned out? That poor young man has even lost his freedom, because of your father's whims! At least leave him in peace, because now all the letters he writes his relatives every day complain about troubles and ask for money; in other words, it's a serious business! . . ."

Marquis Limòli sang another tune:

"My dear child, when somebody isn't rich, he can't afford the luxury of falling in love the way he likes. You are both young and haven't opened your eyes yet. You see only one thing! You should see also what's going to come later—the pot to be placed on the fire, the shirts to be patched up . . . It will be great fun indeed! You were born well, on your mother's side; I know that. But look at your mother, what she had to do, and your uncle Don Ferdinando, and me too! . . . We were all born from Adam's rib, my dear child! . . Corrado came from Adam's rib too. But it is your father who has the money! If he doesn't want to give any to you, you'll both have to go and sweep the streets, and in a month you'll be pulling at each other's hair. On the other hand, you can have a great marriage, and wallow in luxury like a great lady in a great city! . . . Afterward, when you have a cook in your kitchen, the carriage waiting, and your own good income guaranteed by the dowry contract, you'll be able to afford the luxury of thinking about the other things. . . ."

Toward Eastertime the Duke of Leyra came to town with the

pretense of putting his affairs in order in the area, for they needed to be: He was a good-looking man, slender, elegant, a little bald, extraordinarily polite. He took his hat off even in answer to the peasants' salute. He had the same smile and the same courteous manners for all the annoying people by whom he was quickly besieged from the very first day. In town he was the topic of all conversation—what he had said; what he had come for; how long he'd stay; how old he was. The ladies declared that he didn't look older than forty. On the day of the procession of Christ risen, the Caffè dei Nobili was crammed full of ladies. The Zacco women wearing such little hats that made your eyes hurt; Mrs. Capitana fleshless in her perennial mourning that made her look younger and caused her to be still called the pretty little widow—for ten years, ever since her husband had died. The Margarone women all decked out, green, red, yellow, with fluttering feathers and ribbons and great big curls that had grown black with the years, fat enough to burst, their faces the color of bricks. They were all chattering, very busy trying to be noticed by the out-of-town gentlemen. The Duke had gotten his uncle the bailiff to follow him, so that he would look younger, said the backbiters, a fat and ruddy little old man who was to leave him his property, and who meanwhile was courting the ladies—the way men don't know how nowadays, observed Mrs. Capitana.

At the best point, as the statue of the Evangelist came down by sudden jumps from the church of Jesus to that of Mary, and the people screamed "Long live the Risen God," Don Gesualdo's new carriage happened to pass by. He in his tailcoat with gold buttons and the solitaire diamond in the front of his shirt, his wife all dressed up too, poor woman, with her new dress falling all over her—as she was dried up, reduced to a skeleton—and her daughter wearing a new dress that had especially come from Palermo. The crowd opened up to let them pass, without any need to push their way through. Some curious people looked on open-mouthed. The Duke himself asked who they were:

"Ah! A Trao! You can tell, although she looks somewhat ill, poor lady."

Marquis Limòli thanked him, by nodding, and introduced him to his niece. The Duke and the Leyra bailiff made a group of their own, on the sidewalk of the Caffè dei Nobili, with Don Gesualdo's family and Marquis Limòli. All around there was a circle of people who didn't have anything else to do.

Baron Zacco began to talk with the coachman to find out what was going on. Baron Mendola pretended he was stroking the horses. Canali winked here and there:

"Look, gentlemen, what kind of wheel the world is!"

Nobody cared about the procession any more. People were whispering all over the Caffè. From a distance, Don Nini Rubiera, carrying the banner at the end of the pole that leaned against his shoulder, was biting his lips out of spite, thinking about how things had gone for him—with Donna Giuseppina Alòsi as his wife, a swarm of children, the lawsuit for the house Mastro-don Gesualdo wanted to grab with the pretext of the debt, after such a long time. ... His wife, seeing him so wild-eyed and staring at his cousin, planted her sharp elbow into his ribs.

"When are you going to stop it? . . . It's a scandal! . . . Your own children are watching you! Shame on you!"

"Are you out of your mind?" he answered. "What the hell! I've got something quite different on my mind now! Don't you see her hair's already white? That she's a mummy? . . . Are you out of your mind?"

He had gotten older too—flabby, bald, with a big belly, red in the face, his cheeks and his nose embroidered with blood threads that threatened him with the same disease as his mother's. Now he and Bianca looked at each other like two strangers, indifferent to each other, each one with his own troubles and his own interests on his mind. Even the backbiters, after such a long time, had forgotten the talk about the two cousins. But they envied Mastro-don Gesualdo, who had gotten all the way up there, and Donna Bianca who had made such a big marriage. Her daughter would have gotten nobody knew where! Donna Agrippina Macrì and the Zacco cousins darted fiery glances at Isabella's elegant little hat, and at the Duke of Leyra's bows—as he was wearing his gloves and his big satin necktie, which was holding up his handsome aristocratic head, while he was playing with his slim gold-headed cane. Mrs. Capitana remarked to Don Mommino Neri, who had become a reckless rake, after the story of the leading lady:

"It's obvious! All you have to do is to look at him for a moment to know whom you're dealing with. He will probably say nonsensical things. . . . But it's the way he says them! . . . Every word as if he offered it to you on a silver platter. . . ."

Later the noble Duke went to pay his respects to the Motta household. Don Gesualdo was in his drawing room. They had been working all day dusting and airing—the maids, *mastro* Nardo, and he himself. The noble Duke, talked easily and freely about nearly everything—about agriculture with the master of the house, about fashions with the ladies, about old families with Marquis Limòli. He had the whole register of the noble families of Sicily at his fingertips. He even went so far as to confide that his own family came originally from this town. He wanted to pay his respects to Don Ferdinando Trao, and visit the palace, which must be most interesting. With the girl he casually talked about the operas that were then popular; he told a few stories concerning high society; he also told a few anecdotes about the time when the Royal Court, Queen Carolina, and the British were in Palermo—a world of chitchat, like a magic lantern through which you could see pass great ladies, luxuries, and parties. When he left, he kissed Donna Bianca's hand. On the stairs, from the chickencoop, from the woodshed, all the house servants came out to see him pass. Later, in the evening, they could talk only about him, in the kitchen, even the housemaids and *mastro* Nardo, who opened his eyes wide.

The bailiff of Leyra and Marquis Limòli, on the other hand, had started a different kind of conversation—casually, without insistence, and keeping to generalities. The day after, the Duke intervened too—but he confessed that first of all he was in love with the girl, a real flower of the fields, a hidden violet; and he declared with a smile that as for the rest . . . as for business, he meant . . . he had never cared for it directly, unfortunately for him! . . . It wasn't one of his strong points, and he had asked Notary Neri to look after it himself. . . .

A real usurer that Notary, shrewd, greedy, insatiable. Don Gesualdo would have preferred a thousand times to deal face to face with his son-in-law, like two honest men.

"No, no, my dear father-in-law. It's not my cup of tea. I don't know about these things. Whatever you decide will be all right with me. As far as I am concerned, the treasure I'm asking you for is your daughter.

But the negotiations were being stretched out. Mastro-don Gesualdo tried to defend his property, to see clearly in the deal, to ascertain that whatever his noble son-in-law put on the other pan of the scale was all fine gold. True, the Duke owned a lot of land, half a county; but it was said to be in a great mess—lawsuits and mortgages. Notary Neri could not be trusted. The other broker, Marquis Limòli, hadn't even been able to look after his own interest. The canon-priest Lupi wanted to get into play—protesting an old friendship. But Don Gesualdo answered:

"Thanks! Thank you very much, my dear Canon Lupi! But once was enough! I don't want to impose..."

They were all aiming at his property. There was quite a bit of bargaining, with problems coming up at every step, old papers in which one would get lost. Meanwhile, his daughter, on the other hand, was still thinking about the other young man. She implored her father and her mother not to sacrifice her. She kept crying to her relatives begging them to help her.

"I can't! I can't!"

At her father confessor's feet she opened her heart, everything! The mortal sin she was in!... That good servant of God didn't understand a thing. He only kept advising her not to fall into sin again, and he put her heart at peace with absolution. The poor girl went so far as to run to her uncle Trao's house, to throw herself into his arms.

"Uncle Ferdinando, keep me here! You save me! I don't have anybody else in the world! I'm your flesh and blood. Don't send me away."

Don Ferdinando was ill with asthma. He couldn't speak; he didn't understand anything anyway. He made vague motions with his fleshless hand; he called Grazia to help him, like a child, bewildered by every new face he would see.

"Yes, keep me here in place of Grazia. I'll help you with my own hands. Don't send me away. They want to force me into marriage!... In mortal sin!..."

In the old man's clouded eyes, in his pale, wrinkled face there was then the gleam of a recollection. All the gray hairs of his bristly beard seemed to startle.

"Your mother was forced into marriage too. Diego didn't want her to . . . Go, now . . . or your father will come and take you away from here! . . . Go, go away . . ."

Her uncle the Marquis, who was a man of the world, and who knew more than anybody else about the gossip he had picked up here and there, spoke to Don Gesualdo right to his face:

"But, can you understand? You must marry your daughter right away. Give her to whomever you like; but there is no time to waste. Do you understand!"

"Eh? . . . What? . . ." stammered the poor father, going white in the face.

"Of course! . . . You've found a good man who'll take her . . . in good faith . . . But you cannot expect too much of him, after all! . . ."

So that Don Gesualdo, pressed on all sides, pulled by the hair, let them bleed him of his property, and put his name in big letters on the marriage contract: Gesualdo Motta—under his son-in-law's signature which took up two lines: Alvaro Filippo Maria Ferdinando Gargantas di Leyra.

There arrived from Palermo magnificent presents—jewels and dresses which slowly dried the bride's tears, a display of luxuries which made her dizzy and even brought a pale smile to her mother's lips, and which the Uncle the Marquis bragged about everywhere. Only Don Gesualdo grumbled in secret. They expected great things for that wedding. Mrs. Capitana sent a courier to the best dress-maker in Catania. The Zacco women stayed in the house for eight days, sewing. But nobody was invited to the wedding; the bride and the groom in traveling dress, their parents, the witnesses, four candles, and no one else, in the miserable little church of Sant'Agata, where Bianca had also been married. So many memories for the poor mother, who was praying on her knees before that very altar, her elbows on the chair and her face in her hands! Outside there was the sedan chair waiting to carry the couple away. The relatives and the entire town were disappointed and angry. Comments of blame and disapproval were endless—about that wedding that had been carried out as if in secret. Some people went to visit the Margarones and the Alòsis to see if the bride was red or pale in the face. In vain

Mrs. Capitana tried not to be won over and kept saying and saying that it was now fashionable to get married that way. Donna Agrippina answered that that way it didn't even seem like a sacrament to her; poor Isabella!... Aunt Cirmena was chewing other thoughts between her teeth:

"Just like her mother!... You'll see that she's going to be lucky because she's her mother's daughter!..."

Ciolla, seeing the sedan chair across the square, began to shout:

"The bride and the groom! There's the sedan chair with the bride and the groom leaving."

Then he made the rounds from door to door, at the Caffè and in Bomma's pharmacy:

"A letter for Don Corrado La Gurna has gone off too... That's for sure! A letter addressed abroad. The mailman showed it to me in secret. I don't know what was in it; but it didn't look like Donna Cirmena's handwriting. I would have paid something to see what was in it...."

There were many good things in the letter — just to help swallow the pill, she and her cousin, who was despairing and suffering far away.

"Good-bye! Good-bye! If you still remember me, if you still think about me, wherever you are, here are the last words of the Isabella you loved so much!... I've resisted, I've struggled as long as I could, I've suffered...I've cried so much! I've cried so much!... Good-bye! I'll leave, I'll go far from these places that still speak to me of you!... I'll go far... In the festivities, in the middle of all the pomp of the capital, wherever I shall be...nobody will see the pallor under my duchess' crown.... Nobody will know what I'm carrying in my heart...always, always! Remember, remember!..."

PART FOUR

I

Six months had barely passed when new troubles fell on Don Gesualdo. Isabella was threatening to kill herself; his son-in-law had begun traveling abroad and was intimating that he wanted to sue for legal separation, on grounds of incompatibility. There were also other rumors that privately reached the poor father, who ran at breakneck speed to the Carini Villa, where the Duchess was in seclusion, for reasons of health. He came back looking ten years older, and turned on his wife who didn't understand anything, cursing in his heart Aunt Cirmena and all his relatives, who brought him nothing but bitter pills, and was forced to run after the Notary to fix up the mess and pacify his noble son-in-law by dint of money. It was a big blow for the poor man. He didn't tell his wife the real reason, to spare her useless grief; he kept everything to himself; but he couldn't put his mind to rest; he felt as if everybody was pointing a scornful finger at him; he felt his blood come to his face, when he thought about it, all by himself, or even if he met that beastly woman, Cirmena. He was a peasant; he wasn't used to such disgraces! Meanwhile, his daughter, the Duchess, cost him a fortune. First of all the Canziria and Alia and Donninga estates, which he had given her as dowry, and which made his heart bleed, every time he saw them — leased out to any and everybody; split into bits and scraps after all he had suffered to put them together; badly kept; badly farmed; far from their owner's eyes, as if they belonged to nobody. Now and then other bad news reached his ears, worrying him constantly, like so many horseflies, like stinging wasps. In town they said that the noble Duke was sowing debts there with both hands, debts as thick as hail — the same kind of crabgrass ravaging his own lands was spreading over his wife's properties, worse than locusts. That poor Canziria which had cost Don Gesualdo so much work, so many pains; where for the first time he had felt a swarming in his blood as he set foot on his own land as its owner! Donninga for which he had brought on himself the hatred of the whole town! The good lands of Alia, which he had cherished with his eyes for ten years, night and day — the good lands in the sun, without a rock, and so loose that your hands would sink into them and would feel them fat and warm, like living flesh . . . everything, everything was lost into that gangrene! How could Isabella have held a pen in her hand and signed for so many debts? Cursed be the day he had let her learn how to write! He thought he was seeing the shadow of mortgages spread out over the lands that had cost him so much sweat, like a frost in March, worse than a spring fog killing the young wheat. Two or three times, to get out of a predicament, he was forced to let them bleed him. All his savings were going from that open vein—all his work, his sleep at night, everything. And yet Isabella was unhappy. He had seen her that way in the sumptuous Carini Villa! He guessed what was going on when she wrote such letters that gave him a fever, and poisoned him with the subtle scent of those crested little sheets —him whose hide had become too tough even for malaria. The noble Duke, on the other hand, conducted such business through Notary Neri—because 'it wasn't one of his strong points.' And finally, when Mastro-don Gesualdo refused to go any further, fuming and rearing, his son-in-law sent him this message:

"Obviously, my father-in-law, poor man, doesn't know what it takes to support his daughter the way the rank of her new family name requires."

"The rank?... I shine my boots with the rank! I eat dry bread and onions to support the luster of the duchy! Tell my noble son-in-law! In a few years he has devoured a fortune!"

There was a hell of a racket. Donna Bianca, who was in bad shape and spat blood every morning, had a relapse that in two weeks brought her to the brink of death. By now everybody in town knew that she had consumption; all that way those Traos! A family dying out from exhaustion, said the Doctor. Only her husband, who was always on the go, busy with all kinds of deals, with so many worries and so many troubles on his mind, flattered himself with the idea that he would cure her as soon as he could take her to Mangalavite with him, in that balmy air that would bring a dead man back to life. She smiled sadly and didn't say anything.

She had become like a skeleton, docile and resigned to her destiny, without expecting or desiring anything any more. She only wished she could see her daughter again. Her husband had even promised her. But since they were not on good terms with their son-in-law, she hadn't talked about it for some time. Isabella kept promising to come—from one Fall to the other—but she never made up her mind, as if she had sworn never again to set foot in that accursed town, as if she had completely uprooted it from her heart. As her strength was failing, Bianca felt that hope fading away too, like her life which was slipping out of her fingers, and spent her energies thinking about future projects, in a delirium, her face ablaze with the last flames of life, her eyes veiled with tears that seemed to be coming from tenderness and instead came from dejection:

"I'll do this! I'll do that!"

She was like one of those caged birds that try out the songs for the spring they'll never see. The bed was eating up her flesh; the fever consumed her with slow fire. Now, when she was seized by cough, she began to pant, worn-out, her mouth open, her eyes anxious at the bottom of her sockets that looked so deep—groping with her poor fleshless arms as if she wanted to hang on to life as fast as she could.

"All right!" sighed Don Gesualdo seeing his wife in that state. "I'll do this one too!... I'll pay again so that the noble Duke may let you see your daughter!... After all, I was made to carry the burden...."

The Doctor came and went; he tried all kinds of remedies, and all the nonsense he read about in his big books; there was an incredible bill at the pharmacist's.

"At least if it helped!" grumbled Don Gesualdo. "I don't mind spending money for my wife; but I want to spend it so that it helps and I can see it in her face...not to try out new medicines, just like at the hospital!... Now that they've gotten it into their heads that I'm rich, everybody wants to help himself any way he can...."

But the first time he risked some veiled complaint with the Doctor—Saleni, another one of those who were worse than Tavuso, rest in peace—the man planted his scary eyes into his face, and answered gruffly:

"Then why do you call me?"

He had even to plead and implore to continue to do what he liked—even if it didn't help at all. On the eve of the feast of the Immaculate Conception it really looked as if poor Bianca was going to depart from this world. Her husband, who had gone to wait on the stairs, told the Doctor as soon as he saw him:

"I don't like it, Doctor! Tonight I don't like her looks!"

"Eh! Did you just find out? I haven't liked her looks for quite some time. I thought you had understood."

"Isn't there anything you can do, sir? Do everything you can. Don't spare any expense.... Money is meant to help in emergencies like this!..."

"Ah, you tell me now? Now you understand reason? Congratulations!"

Saleni began the comedy all over again: her pulse, her tongue, a little chat at the foot of the bed, with his hat on and his cane between his legs. Then he wrote the usual prescription, the usual garbage that didn't help anything, and then he went off leaving both husband and wife to their troubles. The house had become like a cavern. Everybody kept his distance. Even the maids were afraid of infection. Baron Zacco was the only relative who remembered them in their misfortune — for he and Don Gesualdo had become partners in the contract for the high road and were friends again. He came every day with all his family — the Baroness, fleshless and obedient, their daughters who filled the room, so overaged, heavy, and prosperous, that they could withstand cannon shots. — He wasn't afraid of infection! Nonsense!... And then, when it's your own relatives! ... That evening in the square he had heard people say that Bianca had worsened, and had come earlier than usual. — To help Don Gesualdo forget his troubles for a moment, he pulled him toward the balcony and began to talk about their business deals.

"Listen to a really funny one! Cousin Rubiera is going to bid for the other two sections of the road!... Yes sir! That jackass!... Eh? Eh? What d'you think? He who couldn't even return to you the leading-lady money?... Because of you there is hell between him and his wife, who doesn't want to pay with her own money!... Children, yes, those she brought him for a dowry!... But the money...she wants to keep that for herself! He's fated, that poor Don Nini!... And d'you know who else will come to the auction? Eh? Would you like to know?... Canali; can you imagine!... Canali becoming a contractor in partnership with Baron Rubiera!... Now they've all become hungry for profit!... Eh?... Wasn't I right to say...aren't you laughing?"

But his friend wasn't listening, anxious as he was, his ears stretched out toward the room. Then he got up to go and see if

Bianca needed anything. She needed nothing, as she lay there staring ahead with her childlike eyes—every now and then bringing to
her mouth a handkerchief which then she hid again under her pillow with her fleshless hand. The Zacco cousins sat around the bed
with their hands on their bellies. To break the silence the mother
stammered timidly:

"She looks a little calmer...since we came..."

At those words the daughters looked all at once, and nodded
their approval.

The Baron approached the bed too, showing great interest in
the sick woman.

"Yes, yes, there's no comparison!...her eyes are more alive;
even her face is more vivid.... It's only natural!...hearing people
talk near her!... We must entertain her, talk to her a little.... Fortunately you're in good hands. The Doctor knows his job. And then,
when one has means!... When one has everything!... I know many
others...wellborn too...of good families...who have no bread
during the day and no blankets during the night!... Old and sick,
with neither doctor nor pharmacist..."

He leaned toward Don Gesualdo's ear and blurted out the rest.
Bianca heard, or guessed, with her shiny eyes staring people in the
face, drew from under her pillow her fleshless and pale hand that
looked like a child's and motioned to her husband to get closer. Don
Gesualdo bent over her and nodded yes. The Baron, realizing that
there was no longer any need for being mysterious, spoke up:

"He's not going to come! Don Ferdinando is like a little boy. He
doesn't understand anything, the poor man!... We must pity him.
Let's say it as it is, right here, among us relatives.... What would
he have gone without?... With such a big-hearted brother-in-law
as this one!..."

Again the sick woman waved that hand of hers which spoke by
itself.

"Eh? What is she saying? What does she want?" asked the
Baron.

Donna Lavinia, the eldest of the girls, had gotten up solicitously, to help her with anything she might need. Instead her sister,
Donna Marietta, pulled her father by the coattails. Bianca had
locked herself into a silence that sharpened her worn-out face like a

knife, so that the Baron, who noticed it, changed the subject.

"Sometimes the Lord lengthens our lives just to make us face more troubles...I'm talking about Baroness Rubiera, the poor woman! Eh?...to keep living just to see the property you've put together go to pieces under your very eyes!...without being able to say a word or to move a finger... Eh?... Eh? Her son is a jackass. Her daughter-in-law begrudges her the bites she eats!... I swear to God! She can't wait to see her go!... But not the Baroness, no! She doesn't want to go! She wants to live just to see how her son is going to manage to get rid of that debt to Don Gesualdo... Eh? I just talked to your husband about the great plans Don Nini's got in his head...."

Don Gesualdo kept silent, deep in thought. Then, since the Baron was waiting for Cousin Bianca's answer, with that little smile of his on his lips, he grumbled:

"No, this isn't a laughing matter.... Behind it all there must be the canon-priest Lupi too."

Baron Zacco was dumbfounded:

"That crook? That schemer?... How d'you know?... Who told you?..."

"Nobody. It's just my idea. But you'll see that I'm right. Besides I don't care at all. I have something else on my mind now!"

But the Baron wouldn't keep quiet:

"What? You don't care? Thank you very much! D'you know what they are also saying? That they want to take the City lands from us!... They say that this time they've found the ways and means...and that neither you nor I will be able to stop them, understand?..."

Don Gesualdo shrugged his shoulders. It really seemed as if he didn't care about anything now. Slowly the Baron calmed down, in the midst of the chorus of his own people, who were whispering against the canon-priest.

"A schemer!... A crook!... Nothing can be done in town without his poking his nose into it!"

Donna Marietta, more cautious, pulled her father by his coat-tail again.

"Excuse me! Excuse me!" he added. "It's just talk...to entertain our patient.... We don't know what to talk about.... D'you know what the intriguers like Ciolla are saying?... That in a week there will be a revolution . . . to frighten the honest men. . . . D'you remember in eighteen twenty-one, eh? Don Gesualdo?"

"Ah? . . . What can I say? . . . Now my revolution is at home! . . ."

"I understand, I understand . . . but after all it doesn't look as if . . ."

The Baroness, who spoke when it was necessary, turned to Don Gesualdo with that ominous face of hers, to ask if they had written to the Duchess about her mother being in that state. . . . Bianca had the sharp ear of the gravely ill.

"No! No! There's no hurry!" cut in Baron Zacco.

Meanwhile, Donna Lavinia had gotten up to get a class of water. As the doorbell rang, she also wanted to run and see who it was.

"A two-handed sword!" exclaimed the Baron in a whisper, as if he was saying it in confidence, and smiling complacently. "A real jewel of a girl to have in the house . . . Judicious! . . . And for her cousin Bianca she would throw herself in the fire! . . ."

The mother was also smiling discreetly. Just then the housemaid appeared announcing Baron Rubiera and his wife.

"Him? What gall! . . ." sprang up the Baron looking for his hat, which was on his head. "You'll see he's coming to talk about what I just told you! Is there another way out? . . . Not to see his face, that jackass!"

Like him, his family was in a rush to take leave, looking for the shawls, overturning the chairs, bumping into one another, as if Don Nini were about to break into the room with a drawn sword. The poor patient, overwhelmed by all that commotion, couldn't help saying in a whisper:

"For God's sake . . . I can take no more . . . ."

"No . . . you must go through with it my dear cousin! . . . They're relatives too! . . . You'll see they're coming because of that, to take advantage of the opportunity . . . Pretending they're paying you a visit . . . We'd rather leave . . . It's only fair . . . First come first served . . ."

But the Rubieras hadn't appeared yet. Don Gesualdo went to the entrance room, where he learned from the housemaid that they were waiting in the living room because they had heard that the Zaccos were there.

"All the better," remarked the Baron. "Obviously, Don Ninì wants to talk to you face to face!... If that's the case, we won't move. We'll stay to keep our cousin company, while you're taking care of your business.... Then we'll hear what that idiot has come to talk to you about!"

The housemaid had brought a little lamp in the living room, and in the semidarkness Don Ninì looked really enormous, wrapped up in his overcoat, his wool scarf up to his ears, and on the back of his head his thick hair that hadn't been clipped since May. Donna Giuseppina, on the other hand, had become hunched, her face flabby and wrinkled inside her round hood, her hair a dirty gray, badly combed, smoothened down in a hurry with her hands and held in place with the silk kerchief that she wore tied under her chin, her hands corroded and black, a good housewife's hands, which she moved about to defend her husband's interests — agitating herself inside the little overcoat all stained with mud splashes, which covered her all up, as she showed, in her looks, the carelessness and the neglect of the rich woman who has no need to appear as such — of a wife who has stopped bearing children and who doesn't even have to be liked by her husband. And on her toothless mouth she kept the smile of a poor person, the humble smile of one who comes to ask for a favor, while Don Ninì was groping for words, turning his filthy hat in his hands, with that scarf of his all the way to his nose making him look threatening. His wife encouraged him with a glance and then began:

"We heard that our cousin was ill...Ninì and I ran over right away.... We're relatives after all...the same blood.., Quarrels, interests...it happens, in all families.... But we must push everything aside in certain situations.... Ninì too...the poor man couldn't find peace... He kept saying... 'After all, I'd like to know why...' "

Don Ninì approved with gestures and with his entire body, which he had let sink into the sofa, making it creak; and quickly he started speaking about the subject he had come for — with his wife absolutely insisting that their cousin sit between them, between two fires.

"There's that business of the new contract, dear Don Gesualdo. Why should we fight against each other? For somebody else's benefit?... For we're relatives, after all!..."

"Of course!" cut in his wife. "That's what we came for.... How's our cousin?"

"As God wills!... As if I had the punishment of God on my shoulders!... I can't put my mind to business now...."

"No, no, I don't expect you to...I was just saying... You should put yourself in the hands of a reliable person... If your interest is protected, of course...."

Suddenly Don Nini grew dark in the face, leaned back, planting two suspicious eyes into his:

"Tell me, d'you trust Baron Zacco? Eh? D'you trust him?"

Don Gesualdo, in spite of all the bitterness he felt inside, put a smile on his lips, as if to say that he didn't trust anybody.

"Good! If you knew what kind of man he is!... What he used to say about you, before...before he became hand in glove with you! ... The kind of talk he blurted out!..."

Donna Giuseppina—her cheeks swollen—tightened her lips, as if not to blurt it out herself too.

"Well, let's forget it! Words don't grind wheat.... He's a relative too!... Let's get back to the point. Why are we fighting each other? Why are we supporting judges and lawyers? Why all this bad blood between relatives? For that trifle I owe you? Yes, a trifle. For you it's like a pinch of snuff...."

"Excuse me, excuse me, so it is for you..."

Then Donna Giuseppina intervened, talking about her troubles, her large family, her mother-in-law, the Baroness...as long as she lived...

"Excuse me...what has that got to do with it.... The fact is that one needs money, you know.... I gave mine to your husband."

Don Nini began to apologize, before his wife. Sure, he had borrowed the money...in a moment when he had lost his head... When one is young...it would be better to have one's head chopped off, at times.... He intended to pay...in time...to the last cent, without lawsuits, without further expense...as soon as his mother closed her eyes.... But was it right to embitter the Baroness further against him, good God? Push her into some beastly decision?..."

"Ah?" said Don Gesualdo. "Ah?"

And he looked at Donna Giuseppina as if to ask why she wasn't paying herself.

Embarrassed, Don Nini now looked at him and now at his wife.

Finally she intervened, cutting his words short with the handkerchief she had pulled out of her purse.

"It isn't just this . . . The land deal . . . Haven't you mentioned it yet to Cousin Don Gesualdo? . . ."

"Yes . . . the deal of the City lands . . ."

"I know," answered Don Gesualdo. "The lease expires in August. Whoever wants to bid at the auction, then . . ."

"No! no! Neither you nor I will grab them."

"A new law," broke in Donna Giuseppina with a sour smile, "the lands aren't going to be leased out any more! The City is going to rent them out . . . to the poorest . . . a little bit each. . . . Soon everybody in the village will be a landowner! . . . Don't you know?"

Don Gesualdo pricked up his ears, putting his troubles aside for a moment. Then he sketched an indifferent smile.

"I swear to God!" Baron Rubiera added. "I've seen the bill myself, at City Hall! They say that the City will profit, and everybody will have his own piece of land."

Then Don Gesualdo took out his snuffbox, smelling a trap.

"What? what?"

"Don Gesualdo!" the housemaid called from the door. "Just a moment, sir . . ."

"Take your time!" said Donna Giuseppina. "We're not in a hurry. We'll wait."

"Donna Bianca! She wants to talk with you, sir!"

"Eh? What do they want? What are they saying?" The Zaccos jumped on him as soon as Don Gesualdo got into the patient's room. "I'm the one who sent for you," said the Baron with his shrewd smile.

But he didn't answer, bending over his wife, who was trying to help herself with her eyes and with her poor pale and fleshless hand, which was speaking for her, saying:

"No! . . . Don't have anything to do with that one . . . if you want to listen to me, just once . . . Don't have anything to do with my cousin Rubiera, don't! . . . Remember, I'm talking to you at the point of death! . . ."

Her voice wasn't audible, but her eyes were piercing, so shiny and fixed. Baron Zacco, who had also bent over the bed to hear her, exclaimed in triumph:

"Bless her! She's speaking like one who can see beyond! You couldn't make a good deal with that man! A jackass! A weathercock! Whatever your wife is telling you in such a moment as this is gospel truth, Don Gesualdo! Remember! I'd be very careful to abide by her words, I assure you."

"And Donna Giuseppina! A fake! Evil,..." added Baroness Zacco. "She has shortened her mother-in-law's days! She can't wait to see her go!"

"Go, go and listen to what they have to say. We are here. Go, or they'll stay there forever!"

Don Nini was still seated on the sofa, puffing from the heat of his wool scarf, his hat on his head; and Donna Giuseppina had gotten up to look in the dark at the nice things beautifully arranged on the furniture: the coffee service, the paper flowers under the crystal bells, the clock pointing always at the same hour. As she saw Don Gesualdo come back, she quickly said:

"Was it Baron Zacco who sent for you? There is no reason... We're not mysterious..."

"We're not mysterious!" her husband went on. "It's only a question of reaching an agreement.... All of us who are well-disposed ... If he's well-disposed too...that gentleman!..."

"But," observed Don Gesualdo, "if things are the way you say, I don't know what I can do.... What d'you want from me?"

Donna Giuseppina had even changed her expression, pointing her needlelike eyes to this one and to that one, chewing a smile with her black lips. She pushed her husband completely into the background, and took Cousin Motta totally for herself.

"Yes, there's something that can be done!... There is!"

And for a moment she stared at him, just to impress him more. Then, holding her purse tightly with her hands, she moved close to him with a sway of her hips, in confidence.

"We must make sure that the lands go to our own people... underhandedly..." said the Baron.

"No! no!... Let me explain... The City lands must be rented out, eh? in small pieces, so that every peasant will have his share? All right! Let 'em go ahead and do that. As a matter of fact, let's put forth some more applicants, secretly...shopkeepers, people who don't know what to do with land and won't even get the money for the rent out of it. Everybody has the same right, isn't it true? Then with a little sense, advancing small sums to this one and to that one. . . . They'll go bankrupt within the year and we pick up the land in payment of the debt. Understand? We must do everything possible to prevent the peasants from getting a hold of it. They'd never let their piece of land go any more. They'd rather die on it!"

Don Gesualdo got up at once, his nostrils open and his face suddenly reanimated, and began to walk about the room. Then, going back to face the other two, who had also gotten up, in surprise:

"You didn't think up this one!" he exclaimed. "This is a good one! I know where this one comes from."

"Ah! Ah! You understand? You see?" answered the Baron triumphantly. "First of all, we must stop Nanni l'Orbo's mouth. . . With sense . . . with a little money . . . without hurting anybody, of course! . . . The Law . . ."

"You who know him quite well . . . That one is a crook, an agitator . . . capable of setting the whole town against us. You, who know him well, you should shut him up."

Don Gesualdo sat down again, sorry for having let himself be carried away by the first impulse, and scratched his head.

But Baron Zacco, who was standing just outside with his ears stretched out, couldn't contain himself any more:

"Excuse me, excuse me, gentlemen!" he said as he entered the room. "If I disturb you . . . if you must talk in confidence . . . I'll leave . . ." And sat down too, with his hat on his head.

They all fell silent, each one glancing stealthily at the other — Don Nini with his nose inside his scarf, his wife with her lips tight. Finally she said she was really sorry about Bianca's sickness.

"Really! The whole town is in mourning. Nini has been prodding me for quite some time: 'My dear Giuseppina, we must go and see how my cousin is doing . . .' Business is one thing, but relatives are another."

"Tell me then," Don Gesualdo continued, "who had this great idea of taking the City lands secretly for ourselves?"

At that it was no use pretending any more. Donna Giuseppina talked again about all the turmoil that there was in town, of the revolution they were threatening. Baron Zacco began to fidget, motioning toward Don Gesualdo with his head.

"Eh? Eh? What was I telling you just a minute ago?..."

"After all..." Donna Giuseppina concluded, "it's better to speak clearly and join hands, all of us who have something to lose...."

And she talked again about that trick of chopping up the City lands into so many crumbs for the poorest people—a little each, so as to help everyone!... She was laughing in such a way that her belly was dancing up and down, with anger.

"Ah???" exclaimed the Baron, purple in the face, his eyes jumping out of his head. "Ah???" And he didn't say any more.

Don Gesualdo was laughing too.

"Ah? You're laughing, ah?"

"What d'you expect me to do? I don't care in the least, I tell you!"

Donna Giuseppina was stunned:

"What?... You?..."

Then she pulled him aside, near the chest of drawers where the stopped clock sat, and spoke to him in whispers, with her hands to her eyes. Don Gesualdo remained silent, stroking his chin, with that calm little smile of his that drove people mad. From a distance the two barons kept their eyes on him, like two mastiffs. Finally he shook his head.

"No! No! Tell the canon-priest Lupi that I'm not going to put up money any more for that kind of mess. Whoever wants those lands can have 'em...I have my own..."

The others turned on him all together, shouting, stirring one another up. Baron Zacco was the most excited of them all, now that he had understood what was going on:

"A really good idea! Worthy of a long-bearded man! The best way to avert that trick of dividing the City lands among the indigent! ... Understand?... That means that what's mine isn't mine any more, and everyone wants his own share!..."

Don Gesualdo kept firm; he shook his head and repeated:

"No! No! They're not going to trap me!"

All of a sudden Baron Zacco grabbed Don Nini by the scarf and pushed him toward the sofa, as if he wanted to devour him, and whispered into his ear:

"D'you understand? D'you want me to tell you? All this means that he intends to make all of us look like fools!... I know him!..."

At that commotion, the Zacco women had come to the entry-room doorway. There was a moment of embarrassment among the relatives. Baron Zacco and Don Ninì suddenly calmed down, becoming ceremonious again:

"Excuse me! Excuse me! Who knows what Cousin Bianca will think when she hears us scream...and then for no reason!..."

Baron Zacco smiled in a friendly manner, his face still ablaze. Don Ninì again wrapped his scarf around his neck. His wife, also smiling amiably, took leave.

"All the best to Donna Bianca.... We don't want to disturb her.... Let's hope that the Virgin Mary will perform the miracle...."

Don Ninì, his mouth open, also grunted some words that couldn't be heard.

"Just a moment. I'm coming with you," exclaimed Baron Zacco. And, pretending to be looking for his hat and for his bamboo cane, he stepped next to Don Gesualdo in the darkness of the entry-room.

"Listen... You're wrong, I assure you! That's a serious proposal!... You're wrong not to get together with Baron Rubiera!..."

"No, I don't want trouble!... I already have plenty of worries! ... Besides, my wife said no. You heard her yourself!"

Now the Baron was really about to fly into a rage.

"Ah!... Your wife!... You listen to her when it suits you!"

But he immediately changed his tune.

"It's your decision after all!... It's your decision, my friend!... Don Ninì, wait for us. We're coming."

His wife couldn't make up her mind to go. She seemed not to be able to get away from the patient's bedside — tucking in her blanket, smoothing her pillow, putting the glass of water and the medicines within her reach — her face long, sighing, chewing up *Ave Marias*. She also wanted her daughter to stay and sit up during the night, in case. Donna Lavinia agreed with all her heart, as she also busied herself, solicitous, taking possession of the keys, watching over everything, like the mistress of the house.

"No!..." mumbled Bianca with her hoarse voice. "No!... I don't need anybody!... I don't want anybody!..."

She followed them about the room with her anxious, suspicious, and diffident eyes, with a certain note of rancor in her deep voice. She tried to show herself stronger, by barely lifting herself on her trembling elbows, with her pointed shoulders that seemed to pierce through her nightgown. Then, as soon as the Zacco women had left, she fell back exhausted, motioning to her husband to come closer.

"Listen!...listen!... I don't want them any more!... Don't let those women come any more!... They've gotten it into their heads that you should marry one of them...as if I were already dead."

And she kept nodding and nodding yes, that she was right—her sharp chin in the shadow of her hollow neck—while he, bent over her, talked to her as if she were a child, smiling, but with his eyes swollen.

"They bring Lavinia into your house... They can't wait for me to close my eyes..."

He protested no, that he didn't care about Lavinia at all, that he didn't want to get married any more, that he had had plenty of troubles. And poor Bianca listened to him happily, with her shiny eyes penetrating him, to see if he was telling the truth.

"Listen...more...there's something else..."

She kept motioning with her hand, because her voice was falling, that voice which seemed to come from far away, and her eyes became veiled, now and then, with a shadow. She had even made an effort to raise herself, so as to put her arm around his neck, as if he were all that she had left to cling to life—moving her face that had grown still sharper, as if she wanted to hide it inside his chest, as if she wanted to confess something to him. After a while she relaxed her arms, her face rigid and shut, her voice changed:

"Later...I'll tell you later... Now I can't..."

II

Now everything was going from bad to worse for Mastro-don Gesualdo—his house was upside down; the land laborers did whatever they liked, far from their boss's eyes; the housemaids ran off one by one, for fear of being infected with T.B.; even Mena, the last one who had remained out of necessity — when they talked about her washing the patient's clothes which the washerwoman had refused to take to the river for fear of losing her other customers — gave him a piece of her mind:

"Sorry, Don Gesualdo, but my hide's worth as much as yours though you're rich.... Don't you see the state your wife is in?... It's consumption, God save us! I'm scared, and I'm saying good-bye to you."

And this after they had grown fat in his house! Now they were all running away, as if it were caving in, and there wasn't even anybody to light a lamp. It was like that night at Salonia when he had to place his father in the coffin with his own hands. Neither money nor anything else was of any help any more. At that, Don Gesualdo really became discouraged. Not knowing where to turn, he thought about his old friends — those you think about in times of need — and sent for Diodata to give him a hand. But her husband came instead, suspicious, looking around, watching out where he set his feet, spitting here and there:

"As for me ... even my own hide, if you want it, Don Gesualdo! ... But Diodata has a family, you know.... If she has an accident, God save you and me.... If she catches your wife's disease... We're poor people... You're so very rich; but I wouldn't even have enough to pay the doctor and the pharmacist...."

In short the same old song, the usual tune to bleed him some more. Finally, after bargaining for a while, they agreed on the compensation. All he could do was to shut his eyes and to bow his head. Nanni l'Orbo, quite happy with the deal, concluded:

"As for us, you can even have our hides, Don Gesualdo. We're at your service night and day. I'm going to get my wife and bring her here myself."

But now Bianca was sick with another illness. She didn't like to see Diodata about the house. She wouldn't take anything from her hands.

"No!... Not you!... Go away! What did you come here for, you?"

She was getting annoyed at those hungry people who came to

eat at her expense. As if she were growing fond of property, at that point; as if an old rancor were awakening inside her, a jealousy for the husband people wanted to steal from her—those evil people who had come on purpose, to close her eyes and grab all her things. She had become just like a child, suspicious, irritable, capricious. She complained that they "put something" in her soup, that they changed her medicines. Each time the doorbell rang, she made a scene. She said that they sent people away so that she wouldn't see them.

"I heard my brother Don Ferdinando's voice!... A letter from my daughter came, and they didn't want to give it to me!..."

The thought of her daughter was another torment. Isabella wasn't very well either, so far away, and such a journey would have ruined her once and for all, her husband wrote. Besides, they had known for some time that Bianca was in rather poor health, but they could never have imagined the end so close. Meanwhile, the poor mother couldn't set her heart at rest, and turned on Don Gesualdo and on all those who were around her. You'd have needed a saint's patience. In vain her husband kept saying:

"Look!... What the hell are you getting into your head now! ... Are you even getting into your head to be jealous!..."

He had never seen such black rings under her eyes before. With a sound he had never before heard in her hoarse voice, she said to him:

"You've taken my daughter away from me...even now that I'm in this condition!... I leave this to your conscience!..."

Or she threw it into his face that he had put those other people around her... Or she didn't answer at all, her face turned to the wall, implacable.

Nanni l'Orbo had installed himself in Don Gesualdo's house like a king. He ate and drank. He was there every day to fill his belly. Diodata busied herself with what there was to do, and he ran to the square to have a good time, to chat with his friends, to say that this was needed and that the other had to be done, to uphold the cause of the poor in the question of sharing in the City lands— each one his own piece, as God decreed, and according to how many children each one had to support, there should be as many pieces!

He also knew in detail all the schemes of the big shots, who were trying to grab those lands. Once he started an argument with Canali on this subject, and they ended up by coming to blows—now that the time of arrogance and abuses was over and everyone could speak up.

The day after, *mastro* Titta had gone to Canali to give him a shave, when somebody rang the bell and Canali went to answer the door with the lather still on his chin. As he was sharpening the razor, *mastro* Titta stretched his neck out of simple curiosity and saw Canali in the entryroom talking with Gerbido—both of them with such faces as to open up anybody's ears. Canali was saying to Gerbido:

"But d'you trust him?"

And Gerbido answered:

"Oh!!!"

"That's all."

Canali came back to be shaved, as calm as if nothing had been going on, and *mastro* Titta didn't think about it any more. But just that evening, he himself didn't know why . . . he had a presentiment, as he saw Gerbido lying in wait at the Masera corner, his shotgun at his side! . . . The words he had heard before came back to him.

"I wonder whom that pill is meant for, God save us! . . ." he thought to himself.

There was already a lot of uneasiness in the air, and people had hurried home before the Angelus rang. Farther on, as he met Nanni l'Orbo, who lived in the area, his heart told him that Nanni l'Orbo was the one Gerbido was waiting for.

"What are you doing out at this time, Nanni?" said *mastro* Titta to him. "You'd better go home; we can walk together . . ."

"No, *mastro* Titta, I've got to go by the tobacco shop, and then I'm going to see Diodata for a moment; she's helping Don Gesualdo's wife."

"Do it for me, Nanni! Walk home with me! I'll give you some tobacco myself, and you can wait until tomorrow to go and see your wife. These are not times to go roaming the streets at this hour! . . . Listen to me! . . ."

The other turned the whole thing into a joke; he said he wasn't one to be afraid to be robbed of the money he didn't have. . . . His wife was expecting him with a plate of spaghetti . . . and so many other things.... And for a plate of spaghetti, God save us... he lost his hide!

Two minutes later, as soon as *mastro* Titta heard the gunshot, he said to himself:

"Nanni got that one."

That day Don Gesualdo had other troubles. Speranza sent the bailiff just when she knew it would drive him especially mad. They hadn't left him in peace for years and years, and had made his hair become gray with that lawsuit. Speranza herself had gotten to be like a witch; she had used up her fields and her vineyard—pushed on as she was by anyone who had a grudge against her brother. She kept reviling him everywhere. She purposely waited for him on the road to vomit insults on him. She turned her children against him, for her husband didn't want the aggravation—he was good only to walk his belly around the town—and Santo himself, whenever he needed money, turned his coat and took Gesualdo's side, and spat out on her the same insults he had been addressing to his brother; a weathercock that turned according to the wind.

"It's a real dirty trick, as you see, Don Camillo! They kick me in the shins just when I am up to my neck in trouble. I have sown good and reap evil from everybody, you see?"

Don Camillo shrugged his shoulders.

"Excuse me, Don Gesualdo. I take care of my business. But why did you have a falling out with the canon-priest Lupi?... For the contract of the highroad!... A mere trifle... That one is a servant of God and we need to be friends with him.... Now he feeds the fire together with your relatives.... I don't want to speak ill about anyone; but he'll give you trouble, my dear Don Gesualdo!"

And Don Gesualdo kept quiet; bending his back now that everyone spoke his mind against him, and whoever could, kicked him in the shins. As it became known that his wife had taken a turn for the worse, Marquis Limòli came to see his niece, taking also Don Ferdinando along, both arm in arm, holding each other up. —"Death and the Idiot"—remarked all those who met the two of them in the streets at that late hour, with all the turmoil that there was in town; and they made the sign of the cross, seeing Don Ferdinando still in the world of the living, with that greatcoat of his that wouldn't stay together any more. The two old men sat down in front of the bed, their chins on their canes, as Don Gesualdo told the story of the illness, and his brother-in-law turned his back on him without saying anything, with his face toward his sister, who looked now at this one and now at that one—the poor woman, with those eyes of hers that wanted to cherish everybody—when there was shouting in the street, with people who ran screaming, as if the revolution they all expected had indeed broken out. Suddenly somebody was knocking at the front door, and a voice was shouting:

"Diodata, open up! Run, quick! Go see . . . your husband's been shot . . . he's there, in the pharmacy! . . ."

Diodata ran as she was, with her head bare, howling through the streets. In a minute Don Gesualdo's house was upside down. Baron Zacco came too, suspicious, uneasy, chewing words, looking ahead and behind him before opening his mouth.

"Did you see? Now it's done! They killed Diodata's husband!"

At that Don Gesualdo lost his patience.

"What can I do about it? That's all I needed! What the hell d'you want me to do?"

"Ah, what can you do about it? . . . Sorry! I thought you'd thank me . . . for coming right away to let you know . . . for your sake . . . as a friend . . . as a relative . . ."

Meanwhile, more people arrived. Baron Zacco went to see who it was by opening the door of the entryroom slightly. Every moment you'd hear the front door slam—so many jolts for the poor patient. At a certain point Baron Zacco came in and said, all upset:

"In Palermo there's a hell of a racket . . . The revolution . . . They want to start it here too . . . That crook, Nanni l'Orbo, had to get himself killed just now! . . ."

Don Gesualdo kept shrugging his shoulders, like a man who doesn't care any more, and can only think about that poor dying woman. After a while, Baron Zacco's wife and daughters arrived, dressed in house clothes, their shawls down their backs, their faces long, without saying hello to anyone. You could tell that it was the end. The Baroness kept going over to whisper something to her husband. Donna Lavinia took possession of the keys. As Don Gesualdo saw this, his face went white. He didn't even have the heart to ask if the time had come. He only questioned everybody with his shiny eyes—one by one.

But they answered him with half words. Baron Zacco stretched his face forward, and his wife lifted her eyes toward heaven, her hands clasped. The girls, already sleepy, kept silent, sitting in the next room. Toward midnight, as the patient had slowly calmed down, Don Gesualdo wanted to send everybody out to rest.

"No," said the Baron. "We aren't going to leave you alone tonight."

Then Don Gesualdo didn't talk any more—since there wasn't hope any more. He began to walk up and down the room, his head bent and his hands behind his back. Every now and then he bent over his wife's bed. Then he went on walking in the next room, grumbling to himself, shaking his head, shrugging his shoulders. Finally, he turned to Baron Zacco with a voice full of tears:

"I think we should send for her relatives...eh? Don Ferdinando... What d'you say?"

Baron Zacco grimaced.

"Her relatives?... Ah, certainly... As you wish... Tomorrow ...after daylight..."

But the poor man couldn't restrain himself any more, the words burning inside him and on his lips.

"D'you understand?... He didn't even let her see her daughter for the last time! He's a swine, that noble Duke! For three months he has been writing 'We're coming today, We're coming tomorrow'! As if she would last a hundred years, that poor woman! The proverb is right: 'Out of sight out of mind.' He has robbed us of both daughter and dowry, that criminal!"

And for quite some time he kept on giving vent to his rage with Baron Zacco's wife, who was a mother herself, and nodded yes, as she tried to keep her eyes open which were closing by themselves. He didn't feel sleepy, or anything else, and grumbled again:

"What a night! what an endless night! What a long night, Lord God!"

As soon as dawn came, he opened the balcony door, to call the assistant mason Nardo and send him to all the relatives, for Bianca, poor woman, was very sick—if they wanted to see her. In the streets there was an unusual coming and going, and from down there in the square came a great buzzing of voices. On his return, *mastro* Nardo brought the news:

"There's the revolution. There is the flag on the bell tower."

Don Gesualdo sent him to hell. What did he care about the revolution now? He had the revolution right there at home now! But Baron Zacco tried to calm him down.

"Caution, caution! These are times when we need caution, my dear friend."

Shortly after, they heard somebody knocking at the front door again. Don Gesualdo himself ran to open, thinking that it might be the doctor or one of those people for whom he had sent. Instead he found himself face to face with the canon-priest Lupi, dressed in work clothes, wearing a felt hat, and Baron Rubiera, who was standing aside.

"Excuse us, Don Gesualdo... We don't mean to disturb you... But it's a serious business... Listen here..."

He pulled him into the stable so as to whisper to him the reason why they had come. From a distance, Don Nini, still scowling, nodded his approval.

"We must get the demonstration going, understand? We must shout that we want Pius IX and liberty too... Or the peasants will take the upper hand. You must be there too. Let's not set a bad example, good God!"

"Ah? The old *Carboneria* song?" sprang up Don Gesualdo, furious. "Thanks, thank you very much, Canon Lupi! I'm not interested in revolutions any more! We gained a hell of a lot by starting! Now they've gotten to liking it, and they keep starting others, just to take money out of your pocket. Now I know what it all amounts to: 'Get out of there, and give me what you've got!' "

"D'you mean that you are for the Bourbons? Speak out."

"I defend my property, my dear friend! I've worked hard... with my sweat... Well, then... all right... But now I don't have any reason any more to do what's best for those who don't have, who don't own, anything..."

"Then they'll do you in, understand? They'll sack your house and everything!"

The canon-priest added that he was coming on behalf of those who had something to lose and had to help one another in that emergency, for the good of everybody.... Or he wouldn't have set foot in his house... after the trick of the contract for the highroad...

"Excuse me! Since you lend deaf ears... You know that you

have many enemies! Envious people . . . whatever you call 'em. . . .
They don't feel friendly toward you. . . . They say you're worse than
the others, now that you have money. This is the time to spend that
money, if you want to save your hide!"

At that point Don Nini broke in too:

"D'you know that they accuse us of having had Nanni l'Orbo
killed, to shut him up. . . . You first of all! . . . I'm sorry they saw me
come here with my wife, the other night. . . ."

"In fact," remarked the canon-priest, "let's be fair. Who could
be interested in not letting Nanni talk so much? . . . A hell of a
tongue, my dear sirs! The whole town knows the story of Diodata.
Now they'll unleash even her children against you . . . you'll see, Don
Gesualdo!"

"All right," answered Don Gesualdo. "Good-bye. I cannot
leave my wife in that state to listen to your nonsense."

And he turned his back on them.

"Ah," added the canon-priest following him up the stairs. "I'm
sorry, I didn't know anything about it. I didn't know it had already
gotten this far . . ."

Since they were there, they couldn't help going upstairs for a
moment, to see Donna Bianca—he and the Baron. Don Nini
stopped in the doorway, his hat in his hand, without saying a word,
and the canon-priest—who knew about these things—soon after
nodded to Don Gesualdo, as if to say yes, the hour had come.

"I'm going," said Don Nini, putting his hat back on. "I'm sorry,
but I can't stand it."

At the bedside there was already Don Ferdinando Trao, like a
mummy, and Aunt Macri, who was wiping her niece's face with a
fine linen handkerchief. The Zacco women were pale because of lost
sleep, and Donna Lavinia couldn't stand on her feet any more. Marquis Limoli arrived with the father confessor. At that point Donna
Agrippina sent everybody out. Don Gesualdo, behind that closed
door, felt a knot in his throat, as if they were taking his poor wife
away from him before her time.

"Ah! . . ." grumbled the Marquis. "What a comedy, poor
Bianca! We remain to watch this comedy every day, eh, Don Ferdinando! . . . Even death has forgotten that we are still in the world of
the living! . . ."

Don Ferdinando was listening in a daze. Now and then, he

stealthily glanced timidly at his brother-in-law, whose eyes were swollen and whose face was yellow and bristly, and moved as if he were leaving, scared.

"No," said the Marquis. "You can't leave your sister at this point. You're like a child, damn it!"

Just then Baron Mendola came in, out of breath and began to make excuses in a loud voice:

"Sorry... I didn't know... I didn't think..."

Then, seeing such faces and such silence around him, he lowered his voice and went to finish his speech in a corner, in Baron Zacco's ear. The latter was again talking about the night's sleep they had lost: his daughters without being able to close their eyes, Lavinia who couldn't stand on her feet. Don Gesualdo was looking — true — here and there with wild eyes, but you could tell that he wasn't listening. At that very moment the priest came out, dragging his feet, and so moved that his drooping lips were shaking, the poor old man.

"A saint!..." he said to the husband. "A real saint!"

Don Gesualdo nodded his agreement, his heart swollen too. Now Bianca lay on her back, her eyes wide open, her face as if veiled by a shadow. Donna Agrippina was preparing the altar on the chest of drawers, with a damask tablecloth and silver candlesticks. What good was it now, to have silver candlesticks? Don Ferdinando kept touching everything, just like a curious child. Finally, he planted himself in front of the bed, watching his sister who was at that moment settling her accounts with God, and began to cry and sob. They were all crying. Just then Donna Sarina Cirmena stuck her head through the doorway, out of breath, with her mantilla inside out, hesitating, looking around to see how they would have welcomed her, already beginning to rub her eyes with her embroidered handkerchief.

"Excuse me! Allow me! I've feelings too... I heard that my niece... I have a heart, here, not made of stone!... She was like a daughter to me!... Bianca!... Bianca!..."

"No, Aunt Cirmena!" said Donna Agrippina. "The viaticum is about to come. Don't disturb her now with worldly thoughts..."

"You're right," said Donna Sarina. "Excuse me, Don Gesualdo."

After she had taken communion, Bianca seemed a little calmer.

The panting had ceased, and she managed to stammer a few words. But her voice could hardly be heard.

"D'you see?" said Donna Agrippina. "D'you see, now that she is in the grace of God!... Sometimes the Lord performs a miracle."

They put the relic of the Virgin Mary on her breast. Donna Agrippina took off her tunic cincture and put it under her pillow. Aunt Cirmena brought up examples of miraculous healings: all it takes is to have faith in saints and in holy relics; the Lord can do this and more. Then Don Gesualdo himself began to cry like a child.

"He too!" grumbled Donna Sarina, pretending she was talking into Donna Macrì's ear. "He too... He isn't hard-hearted after all. But I don't understand why Isabella hasn't come... duchess or no duchess!... We have only one mother!... Did they really have to be so finnicky to get such great results?...."

"He's a swine!... He's a beast!... A criminal!..." Mastro-don Gesualdo kept grumbling, his face wild, his arms crossed, his eyes ablaze, like a madman's.

"Eh? What?" asked Aunt Cirmena.

"Ssh! Ssh!" cut in Donna Agrippina.

Baron Mendola bent toward Baron Zacco's ear to say something. Baron Zacco shook his big disheveled and swollen head two or three times. The Baroness took advantage of this good moment to have Don Gesualdo take a little refreshment from Lavinia's very hands.

"Yes, a little soup; the poor man hasn't had anything for two days!"

As they went into the next room, which faced the street, they heard in the distance a noise that sounded like that of a stormy sea. Baron Mendola then told what he had seen on the way over.

"Yes sir! They hung the flag on the bell tower. They say that it means that all the import duties between counties and all property taxes must be abolished. They'll soon have a demonstration. The mail courier brought the news that in Palermo they've already had it ... as well as in all the towns along the way. So that it would be a disgrace if we didn't have it too.... After all, what can it cost? The band, a few yards of muslin.... Look! look!..."

From Via del Rosario there appeared a tricolor flag fastened to the top of a reed, and behind it a flood of people shouting and waving their arms and their hats in the air. Now and then you also heard a shotgun go off. The Marquis, who was as deaf as a gopher, asked:

"Eh? What is it?"

The end of the world, that's what it was! Don Gesualdo stood there, holding his cup. At that point there was a strong ringing at the front door, and Baron Zacco ran down to see. After a moment he stuck his head through the doorway to the entryroom, and called loudly:

"Marquis! Marquis Limòli!"

They discussed for some time in whispers, in the next room. It sounded as if the Baron was putting in a good word with a third party that had just arrived, and also that the Marquis was getting excited.

"No! no! It's a dirty trick!"

Just then Baron Zacco came back in alone, his face ablaze.

"Listen, Don Gesualdo! . . . Just a moment . . . just a word . . . ."

The crowd had reached there, under the house. You could see the flag at the height of the balcony, as if it wanted to get in. You could hear the howling: "Hail," "Death to . . ."

"Just a moment," Baron Zacco exclaimed, then putting aside all restraint, "Don Gesualdo, go to the balcony for a moment! Let them see you, or there'll be hell to pay! . . ."

The canon-priest Lupi was there, carrying the portrait of Pope Pius IX; Baron Rubiera, as yellow as a dead man, waving his handkerchief, and many other people, all of them yelling:

"Hail! . . . Down with! . . . Death to! . . ."

Don Gesualdo, slumped on a chair, his cup in his hand, kept shaking his head and shrugging his shoulders, as pale as his shirt, himself looking like a rag. The Marquis wanted to know by all means what those people down there were looking for:

"Eh, what?"

"They want your property!" finally Baron Zacco exclaimed, losing his temper.

The Marquis began to laugh, saying:

"Welcome! They're welcome to it!"

At that moment, Donna Agrippina Macrì rushed by, with her puce-colored frock flapping behind her, and in the dying woman's room there was a great commotion — chairs overturned, screaming women. Don Gesualdo jumped to his feet, staggering, his hair on end; he put his cup on the table, and began to walk back and forth — beside himself, patting his hands one on top of the other, and repeating:

"The party is over!... The party's over!..."

III

A letter from Isabella, who didn't yet know about the tragedy, arrived somewhat later and it would have made the very stones weep. The Duke wrote too — a small sheet of paper with an inch-thick black border, and the crested seal, also black, enough to break your heart — inconsolable for the loss of his mother-in-law. He said that the truth had to be hidden from the Duchess by the doctors' very advice, for it would have come like a bolt of lightning to her, sickly as she was, just on the eve of her starting on her journey to go and see her mother!... He concluded by asking for some memento of her dead mother for her — some trifle, a lock of her hair, her missal, the wedding ring she wore on her finger...

And to the Notary he wrote to ask if the dead woman, rest her soul, had left any nondotal property. — This came to be known through Don Emanuele Fiorio, the postmaster, who dug up the business of everybody in town — for the Notary didn't even answer, and only to some intimate friends of his he said — like the grumbling man he had become with age:

"It looks like the noble Duke is fishing for the moon in a pond, it looks like!"

The poor dead woman had gone to her grave in a hurry, between four candles in the middle of the uproar of the mutinous people — some wanting this and some wanting that, standing in the town square from morning to night, shouting with their hands in their pockets and their mouths open, waiting for the manna to rain down from the bell tower and its flag. Ciolla, who had finally become a big shot, with a black feather in his cap and with a corduroy shirt-jacket that made him seem like a child, at that age, walked up and down the square, looking here and there as if to say to people:

"Hey! Mind your own business now!"

Don Luca, who was carrying the cross before the coffin, winked amicably, to make way in the crowd, and smiled at his acquaintances, as he kept hearing along his way all those praises that people recited behind Mastro-don Gesualdo's back.

"A bandit! a criminal! One who had become rich while so many others had remained poor and in rags, worse than before! One whose storehouses were crammed full of stuff, and still sent the bailiff around to collect money from others."

Those to scream the loudest were the debtors, who had devoured the wheat in the blade before the harvest. They even threw into his face his being the one most doggedly set against the others getting the City lands—each one his own piece. Nobody knew who had started this charge, but it was a fact. Everybody said so— the canon-priest Lupi, armed to the teeth, Baron Rubiera, wearing his fustian hunting jacket, like any poor devil. They were constantly in the middle of the groups, always friendly and jolly, their hearts on their lips: —that Mastro-don Gesualdo was always the same! He had let his wife die without even sending for a doctor from Palermo! A Trao! One who had brought him the respect of the world! What good had it done her, to be so rich?—

The canon-priest let himself say even more, in confidence: he had even been stingy with the masses for the poor woman's soul!

"I know that for sure. I was in the sacristy. He doesn't even have a heart for his own flesh and blood! Don't let me say more; tomorrow morning I have to say Mass!"

After the first bewilderment, both the gentry and the commoners had become all one family. Now the aristocracy were fervently defending liberty; priests and monks with the crucifix on their chests, or with the cockade of Pius IX, and with shotguns on their shoulders. Don Nicolino Margarone had made himself a Captain, with spurs and a braided cap. Donna Agrippina Macrì prepared gauze pads and talked about going to the battlefield as soon as the war began. Mrs. Capitana collected money to buy guns—dressing in three colors, with a red jacket, a white gown, and a darling little Calabrian hat with green feathers. Every day the other ladies carried rocks to the barricades outside the town gates, with their ribbon-trimmed baskets, and with the band playing in front of them. It was like a feast, morning and night, with all those flags, that crowd in the streets, those shouts of "Hail" and "Down with," every moment, the ringing of the bells, the playing of the band, and later the festive illumination. The only windows to remain shut were Don Gesualdo Motta's. He was the only one to stay hidden out of sight like a wolf, an enemy of his own town, now that he had grown fat, he who kept complaining that they came every day to fleece him — the commission for the poor, the forced loan, the collection for the guns!... They put him on top of the lists, they taxed him twice as much as anyone else. He had to defend himself and fight it out. When they came back from his house, worn out after an hour of bargaining, the gentlemen of the Committee told strange tales indeed. They said that he didn't understand anything any more, an idiot, the ghost of Mastro-don Gesualdo, nothing more than a dead body, who still kept on his feet to defend his own interests; but the hand of God will come down, sooner or later!

Meanwhile, the peasants and the starving people who remained in the square from morning to night, their mouths open, waiting for the manna that never came, inflamed one another, talking about the abuses they had suffered, about the winters of hardships, while there were people with storehouses full of stuff, with fields and with vineyards!... It was all right for the gentry who had been born into it.... But they couldn't bear the thought that Don Gesualdo Motta had been born poor and naked, just like them. They all remembered him a poor laborer.

Speranza, his own sister, preached right then and there, in front of the flag hoisted on City Hall, that the moment had finally come to return what had been unjustly taken, to take the law into one's own hands. She incited her children against their uncle — those children who had become big and strong, and capable of fighting for their rights, if they hadn't been two capons, just like their father, who had quickly calmed down when his brother-in-law had sent a little bundle of money when Bianca was ill, saying that he wanted to make peace with everybody, and that he had enough trouble as it was. Giacalone, whose mule Don Gesualdo had seized in payment for the harvest debt; Pirtuso's heir, who was still quarreling with him about certain monies the broker had carried with him to the other world; all those who held grudges against him because of one thing or another, now fed the fire, calling him everything under the sun — talking about all of Mastro-don Gesualdo's dirty tricks, running him down in every tavern and in every group, teasing even the indifferent ones into joining them, because of that story of the City lands they all had to share among themselves, each one waiting for his own piece, any day now — and it hadn't even been mentioned yet, and whoever mentioned it, they had him shot in the back to stop his mouth. . . . They knew where the bullet had come from! *Mastro* Titta had recognized Gerbido, Don Gesualdo's former servant boy, as he ran away hiding his face with his handkerchief. And so there surfaced again the story of Nanni l'Orbo, who had taken on Don Gesualdo's woman with the children — two poor foundlings who had to hoe their father's fields to earn their bread, and even kissed his hands, like Diodata, that jackass, who, if you gave her a kick, said "thank you"!

By keeping on this track they had managed to unleash them against him too — one evening when they had dragged them into that nonsense at the tavern, and the two boys didn't even have enough to buy a drink for their friends. Don Gesualdo saw Nunzio, the bolder of the two, appear before him. — His grandfather's name, yes, *that* he had given him; but not the property! — They almost came to blows, father and son. There was a great shouting, a quarrel that lasted half an hour. Diodata ran over too, her hair disheveled, and dressed in black. Nunzio, dead drunk, wanted his share right then and there, and told them all kinds of insults — him and her. Uncle Santo, who had made up with his brother after the death of his sister-in-law, helping him to overcome his grief, eating and drinking at his expense, grabbed the door bolt to make peace. Poor Don Gesualdo went to bed, more dead than alive.

In the midst of so many troubles, he had really gotten ill. It poisoned his blood to hear the people talk that way. Don Luca, the sacristan, who had planted himself in his house as if it were already time to bring him the Extreme Unction, insisted that Don Gesualdo open his storehouses to the poor, if he wanted to save his body and his soul. He himself had five children to support, five mouths to feed, and with his wife six. *Mastro* Titta — when he came to bleed him — sang the rest of the tune, holding his lancet in the air:

"See? If some people don't have more sense, this time it's going to come to a bad end! People can't stand it any more! I've been cutting hair and letting blood out for forty years, and I am still the way I used to be, am I not?"

Don Gesualdo, sick, yellow, his mouth always bitter, had lost his sleep and his appetite; he had cramps in his stomach, like mad dogs biting inside him. Baron Zacco was the only friend he had left. And people also said that he must have his own interest in being friends with Don Gesualdo — some scheme on his mind. He came to see him morning and evening, he brought him his wife and his daughters, all of them dressed in black, such that they darkened the street. He left his daughter there to look after him:

"Lavinia's very good at making decoctions."

"Lavinia's really a demon for keeping an eye on the house."

"Let Lavinia do it; she knows all about it."

On the other hand, the Baron scowled if Diodata still dared to show up there, at Don Gesualdo's, with a black kerchief on her head, loaded with children, already as white haired and bent as an old woman:

"No, no, my good woman. We don't need you! You'd better look after your own business, for here the feast is over."

Later, in confidence, he even blurted out sermons to his friend:

"What the hell d'you want with that old woman?... It's no good to let her hang around here, now that she's a widow!... After you had her in your house when she was single.... You know how people talk! Then there is that other story about her husband's death... Though he deserved it!... But after all, it's better to shut people's mouths!... Besides, you don't need anybody, now that my girl is here."

He himself was always busy putting everything in order in Cousin Don Gesualdo's house — sticking his nose in all his businesses, running up and down with the keys to the storehouses and the cellar. He also advised him to see to it that his cash would earn interest — if he had any aside, in case things should get worse.

"Lend on mortage, with a notary contract, of course... a little each, to all those who are shouting the loudest because they have nothing to lose, and are threatening to break into your storehouses and to burn your house. They'll shut up for the time being.... Then, if they manage to get the City lands, you immediately mortgage them. Things can't always go this way. The future will be different, and you'll have put your claws there in time."

But he didn't want to hear about money. He said that he didn't have any, that his son-in-law had ruined him, that he'd rather receive them with gunshots — those who would come to burn down his house or to break into his storehouses. He had become a ferocious animal, green with bile — his very illness making him delirious. He threatened:

"Ah! My property? I want to see them! After it has taken me forty years to put it together ... one tarì after another!... Better cut out my liver and all the rest at once, for all my insides are rotten with troubles ... With gunshots! First I want to kill a dozen of them! If one wants to take your property from you, you take his life from him!"

That's why he had armed Santo and *mastro* Nardo, the old assistant mason, with sabers and carbines. He kept the front door bolted, and two ferocious mastiffs in the courtyard. People said that in his house there was an arsenal; that in the evening he received Canali, Marquis Limolì, and other people as well, to plot together, and one morning you'd find the gallows in the square, with all those who had made the revolution hanging there. So his few friends abandoned him not to be looked upon with suspicion. And Baron Zacco was really running a bad risk still going there and bringing him his whole family.

"Too bad that with you it's all a waste of energy!" he told him more than once.

But finally his wife, seeing that with that man there was no coming to the point, exploded the bomb — one day that Don Gesualdo had dozed off on the sofa, as yellow as a dead body, and her daughter was acting as his nurse, standing guard by the window.

"Excuse me, Cousin! I'm a mother, and can't keep quiet, after all.... You, Lavinia, go into the next room for I must talk to Cousin Don Gesualdo.... Now that my girl is gone, open up your heart, my dear Cousin ... and tell me clearly what's on your mind. ... As for me, I'd be so happy about it ... and my husband the Baron, too.... But we must talk about it clearly ..."

The poor man opened his drowsy eyes wide, still all upset because of the colic:

"Eh? What are you saying? What d'you want? I don't understand you."

"Ah! You don't understand me? Then what is my daughter Lavinia here for? A single girl! You're a widower after all, and you ought to have reached the age of discretion, to make up your mind, and to know what you want to do!"

"Nothing. I want to do nothing. I want to be left in peace, if people leave me ..."

"Ah? That's what you want? You'll be left there as much as you wish.... But meanwhile it isn't right ... you understand!... I'm a mother ..."

And this time, determined, she ordered her daughter to pick up her mantilla and leave with her. Lavinia obeyed, furious as well. Both of them, leaving that house for the last time, drew a cross on the threshold to make their decision final.

"A dungeon, that hovel! Poor Cousin Bianca had left her bones there, with consumption!"

That very evening Baron Zacco paid a visit to Baron Rubiera — instead of getting bored with that peasant of a Mastro-don Gesualdo, who spent the evenings complaining, holding his stomach, in the dark, to save light.

"You don't mind my coming, eh! Cousin Rubiera ... Donna Giuseppina ..."

Don Nini had gone out to take part in a secret meeting where big deals were made. While waiting, Baron Zacco decided to pay his respects to the old Baroness, whom he hadn't seen for some time. He found her in her room, nailed to the big armchair facing the double bed, next to which still was the shotgun of her husband, rest his soul, and the crucifix they had placed on his chest at the point of death. She was wrapped up in an old shawl, her motionless hands in her lap. As soon as she saw Cousin Zacco come in, she began to cry with emotion, stupefied — with big and silent tears that little by little swelled in her muddy eyes, and came slowly down her loose cheeks.

"Great, great, congratulations, Cousin Rubiera! Your head is all right! You still recognize people!"

She also wanted to tell him her own troubles, chewing, puffing, and confusing herself, with her swollen tongue and her purple lips frothing with slobber. The Baron bent over her, lending an affectionate ear.

"Eh? What? Yes, yes, I understand! You're right, my poor friend!"

At that moment her daughter-in-law came in, furious.

"We can't understand a damned thing!" remarked Baron Zacco. "It must be Purgatory for you relatives."

The paralyzed woman darted a lightninglike ferocious glance, raising as much as she could, head bent over her shoulder, while Donna Giuseppina scolded her like a child, wiping her chin with a dirty handkerchief.

"What's the matter? What d'you want? you idiot!... You're ruining your health!... She's really a baby, thank God! You can't believe what she says! It takes the patience of a saint to put up with her...."

Now her mother-in-law opened her eyes wide, looking at her, frightened, nestling her head between her shoulders, almost expecting to be beaten:

"You see? For heaven's sake!"

"I told you," concluded the Baron. "You go through Purgatory on earth, so you can go straight to Paradise."

After a while Don Ninì came in to get the cellar keys. As he saw his cousin, he put a silly look on his face.

"Ah...cousin!... What's new? Is your wife well?... Here, in this house, you can see ... troubles by the shovelful! What, mother? The same old whims? Excuse me, Cousin Zacco, I've got to go downstairs for a moment...."

The keys were always there, hanging on the doorpost. The paralyzed woman accompanied them with her eyes, without being able to pronounce a word, trying as much as she could to turn her head at each of her son's steps—with blotches of sick blood suddenly flaming up in her corpselike face. At that point, Baron Zacco began to recite his complaints against Mastro-don Gesualdo.

"Lord God, I regret and I repent! I've lasted too long with that man! I felt it would be bad to abandon him when in need . . . in the middle of all his enemies . . . out of Christian charity, if for nothing else. . . . But let me tell you! It's too much . . . Not even his relatives can stand him, that man! Imagine! Not even that idiot, Don Ferdinando! . . . He doesn't want to go out of the house any more . . . not to be forced to wear the new suit his brother-in-law has given him. . . . As long as he lives, understand? That's a man of character! Finally, I'm tired, understand? I don't want to ruin myself for Mastro-don Gesualdo's sake. I have a wife and children. Must I carry him around my neck like a rock to drown myself?"

"Ah! . . . Hadn't I told you! But look, in all conscience! What was Mastro-don Gesualdo twenty years ago? . . . Now he wants to walk all over us. Look, my friends, at Baron Zacco who shines his boots and becomes enemies with his relatives because of him!"

Baron Zacco bowed his head, in contrition. He confessed that he had been wrong — but with good intentions, to prevent him from doing any more harm, and to try to get out of him that little good that was possible. Once in a life time, you can be wrong. . . .

"You finally understood? You saw which of the two of us was right?"

His wife shut the words inside his mouth with an elbow thrust:

"Let him talk. It's his turn to say what he now wants of us . . . what he came here for. . . ."

"All right!" concluded Baron Zacco with an amiable laugh. "I've come like the prodigal son, that's it! Are you satisfied?"

Donna Giuseppina was satisfied with tight lips. Her husband first looked at her, then at Cousin Zacco, and didn't know what to say.

"All right," answered Baron Zacco again. "I know that tonight those boys want to raise a little racket in the streets. You just happen to hold the cellar keys in your hands — to keep 'em in a good mood. Remember that I'm not afraid to speak my mind, if somebody gets it into his head to come and annoy me under my windows. I've a lot on my chest too, and I don't want to buy enemies on credit, like Mastro-don Gesualdo! . . ."

Husband and wife looked each other in the eyes.

"I'm a family man!" repeated the Baron. "I must defend my

interests . . . Excuse me . . . But if we play the game of tripping each other! . . ."

Donna Giuseppina cut in, scandalized:

"But what are you talking about? . . . Excuse me, if I meddle in your business. But we're relatives after all . . ."

"That's what I mean. We're relatives! And it's better to hang together . . . in times like these! . . ."

Don Nini held out his hand.

"What the hell! . . . What nonsense! . . ."

Then he opened up completely, now and then looking at his wife . . .

"Come to the theater tonight, for the singing of the anthem. Show up together with us. The canon-priest will be there too. He says that it's not sinful for him because it's the Pope's anthem. . . . We'll talk afterward . . . But we'll have to dip into our pockets, my dear friend. We must spend and give away. Look at me!"

And he shook the cellar keys. The old woman, who hadn't lost a single word of all that discussion, although nobody paid any attention to her, started grunting in stubborn, childish anger, deliberately swelling the veins of her neck to become purple in the face. The uproar began again — her daughter-in-law and her son scolding her at the same time, and she trying to shout more loudly, furiously shaking her head. Rosaria ran over too, with her enormous belly, and her filthy hands in her disheveled, grayish hair, threatening the paralyzed woman as well:

"Look at that! She's become as nasty as a red donkey! What is she missing, eh? She eats like a wolf!"

Rosaria couldn't stop harping on that note. Baron Zacco thought that it was the right time to leave — at that point.

"I'll see you tonight then, for the singing!"

IV

In the theater there was a full house because it was free. Lights, singing, applause rising to the stars. Signora Aglae had especially come from Modica, at the town's expense, to declaim the "Hymn of

Pope Pius IX" and other poems for the occasion. As he saw her dressed in Greek style, with all those curves on her—God bless her—Don Nini Rubiera, in the general ado, felt tears come to his eyes, and clapped more loudly than anyone else, grumbling to himself:

"Damn it!... She's still quite a dish!... Lucky my wife isn't here!..."

But those who had remained outside, who pushed without being able to get in, finally left to scream "Hail" and "Death to" on their own; and all the others in the theater, at the uproar, went out into the square too, leaving the leading lady and Signor Pallante to fuss about by themselves, flags in hand. In a moment there gathered a great crowd that kept swelling like a river. You could hear an immense shouting, and howling which in the dark and in the confusion sounded like threats. Don Nicolino Margarone, Baron Zacco, Mommino Neri, all those who meant well, shouted themselves hoarse, calling "The Lights! The Lights!" so that people could see and no trouble would arise.

The crowd kept shouting for some time on this side and on that. Then they poured like a torrent down Via di San Giovanni. In front of Pecu-Pecu's tavern there was a bench covered with pans full of fried stuff that ended up on the ground—eggplant and tomato under their feet. Santo Motta, who stayed there as if it were both his shop and his home, when he saw all that stuff go to waste, began to scream as if possessed.

"Jackasses! animals! Don't you eat food?"

They almost crushed him too, in the fury. Giacalone and the most eager ones proposed to break down the church door and carry the Saint in procession to make a bigger hit. —Yes and no. —There were curses and blows to the jaws, in the dark, right in front of the church. Meanwhile, *mastro* Cosimo had climbed up the bell tower, and was ringing the bells full blast. The shouts and the sound of the bells reached all the way to Alia, to Monte Lauro, like hurricane gusts. Lights were seen running in the upper town—the end of the world! Suddenly, as if a password had made the rounds, the crowd started out tumultuously toward the Fosso—behind those that looked like the leaders: Baron Mendola, Don Nicolino, and even the canon-priest Lupi, who had stuck himself into that chaos with good intentions, screamed in vain:

"Stop! stop!"

Baron Zacco, whose legs weren't as good as they used to be, landed cudgel blows all over the place, to make even the blind listen to reason.

"Hey? What's going on?... Take it easy, my friends!... Let's not play dirty! In these things you know how you start and you don't know..."

Since many had lent their ears to the talk about breaking down doors and taking care of all the saints, the rabble was now crowding before Mastro-don Gesualdo's storehouses. It was rumored that they were full all the way to the roof. —Somebody who was born as poor as Job, and now had become stuck up, and was a sworn enemy of the poor and the liberals! —With rocks, with cudgels...two or three of them had armed themselves with a boulder and hit the big door with blows that sounded like cannon shots. You could hear the little shrill voice of Brasi Camauro, whimpering like a little boy:

"Dear gentlemen! There's no more religion! They don't want to know about christs or saints! They just want to let us starve to death —all of us!"

Suddenly, out of the uproar came such howling as to give you goose pimples. Santo Motta, battered and bleeding, by rolling himself on the ground managed to have them make some space before the storehouse door. Then the gentry, also shouting, pushing, shoving, forced back the most violent ones. The canon-priest Lupi, holding on to the window grating, was trying to make himself heard:

"...Is this the way?...religion!...other people's property!... The Holy Father!...if we start..."

Other shouts answered from the multitude:

"...equal...poor...dragged by our feet!...the fat ox!..."

To incite the crowd, Giacalone pushed forward Diodata's two bastards, who were in the crush, and cackled:

"...Don Gesualdo!... If there's justice!... Abandoned in the street!... Even God himself complains!... Go and settle with him!..."

From Piazza di Santa Maria di Gesù, from the first houses of San Sebastiano, the neighbors, frightened, saw a flood of people go by, a chaos, glittering arms, hands waving in the air, upset faces ablaze, barely visible in the light of the torches. Doors and windows were slammed. In the distance you could hear screams and cries of women, voices calling:

"Most Holy Virgin! Holy Christians!..."

Don Gesualdo was sick in bed, when he heard somebody knock at the little side door on the alley with such force that they seemed to be breaking it down. Then the rumble of the gathering storm. That very evening, a charitable soul had come to warn him:

"Watch out, Don Gesualdo! They have it in for you, because you're for the Bourbons. Lock yourself in the house!"

He, who had so many other troubles, had shrugged his shoulders. But now, seeing that they meant it, he jumped out of bed just as he was, his kerchief on his head and a pack on his stomach, putting on his pants at random, and leaving his ailments aside at the sound of that voice—shouting:

"Don Gesualdo!... Quick!... Run!..."

Such a voice that he wouldn't forget it in a thousand years! Disheveled, in shirt sleeves, his eyes shining—like those of a cat gone wild—his face green with bile, he walked back and forth in the room, looking for guns and knives, determined to sell his hide dear, at least. *Mastro* Nardo and those few servants who had remained faithful to him out of necessity were committing their souls to God. Finally Baron Mendola managed to get the little side door open. Don Gesualdo, in wait at the window with his shotgun, was about to make a slaughter.

"Eh!" shouted Baron Mendola as he came in all out of breath. "You even want to kill me, on top of everything else? Is this my reward?"

Don Gesualdo didn't want to listen to reason. He was shaking all over with rage.

"Ah, is that the way it is? That's what we have come to, that an honest man isn't even safe in his own house? That his property isn't his any more? Here I am! But Samson will fall with all the Philistines! Even the wolf, when they corner him!..."

Baron Zacco, and two or three other well-meaning people who in the meantime had arrived, were working very hard to persuade him, shouting all together:

"What d'you want to do? Against a whole town? Are you out of your mind? They'll burn everything! They'll start the Slaughter of the Innocents right here! You'll have all of us killed!"

He stood there, stubborn, in a fury, his hair on end:

"If that's the way it is!... If they want to put their hands into our pockets by all means!... If they want to pay me back this way! ... I've been good to them...I've fed the whole town... Now I'll feed them gunpowder, the first one I happen to get!..."

Really! He was determined to make a slaughter. Fortunately the canon-priest Lupi broke into the room, and flung himself on him without worrying about the risk, and pushed and banged him here and there, until he managed to wrest the shotgun from his hands.

"What the hell! Firearms are not for play!"

The canon-priest was out of breath—the top of his head, red and bald, steaming like when he was young; and he stammered in a broken voice:

"Damn it!... God, forgive me! You make me talk like a swine, Don Jackass! We're here to save your life, and you don't deserve it! D'you want them to sack and burn the whole town? I don't care about you, you jackass! But there are things that must not be allowed to start even as a joke, understand? Not even against a mortal enemy! If those who have so far been satisfied with shouting...if they also begin to enjoy laying their hands on other people's property, we're done for!"

The canon-priest was completely beside himself. Also the others turned on that stubborn jackass of a Mastro-don Gesualdo, who was risking getting all of them in trouble; they surrounded him; they pushed him toward the wall; they damned his ingratitude; they stunned him. Baron Zacco went so far as to put an arm around his neck, in confidence, and confessed in his ear that he was with him, against the rabble; but for the moment they had to be cautious, let things take their course, bow their heads.

"Say yes...anything they want, now...there is the Notary right there to put your promises down on paper... A little tact, a little money... Better a wallet-ache than a bellyache..."

Don Gesualdo, sitting on a chair, wiping his sweat with his shirt sleeve, didn't say anything any more—wild-eyed. Meanwhile, downstairs at the front door Baron Rubiera, Don Nicolino, and Neri's son were all doing everything possible to calm down the most violent.

"Gentlemen... You're right... We'll do all you want... We all have mouths to feed... Hail! hail!... All brothers!... One hand washes the other... Tomorrow, by daylight. Whoever is in need should come here to see us... Now it's late, and we're all the same color... ruffians and gentlemen... Hey! Hey, I say!..."

Don Nicolino had to grab by the neck a man who was about to slip through the half-closed door, by taking advantage of the confusion of the rush that surrounded a woman who kept screaming and pleading:

"Nunzio! Gesualdo! My children!... What are they making you do?... Nunzio... Ah Holy Virgin!..."

It was Diodata, who had heard that her boys were right there in that chaos—they too shouting "Hail" and "Down with" against Don Gesualdo—and she had run over with her hands in her hair.

"Holy Virgin! What are they making you do!..."

Meanwhile, Baron Zacco and *mastro* Nardo brought down some casks of wine and helped to make peace by pouring a drink for anyone who wanted one, while from above the canon-priest preached:

"Tomorrow! Come back tomorrow, whoever needs anything. ... Now there isn't anybody home... Don Gesualdo is away in the country... but his heart is here, with us... to help you.... Sure... Everyone must have his own loaf of bread and his own piece of land. ... We'll see to it together... Come back tomorrow..."

"The hell with tomorrow!..." grumbled Don Gesualdo from inside the house. "It looks like you, sir, are arranging everything at my expense, Canon Lupi!"

"Can't you keep quiet! D'you want me to look like a liar?... I said that you aren't here, to save your hide...."

Again Don Gesualdo rebelled:

"Why? What have I done? I'm in my own house!..."

"What you've done is that you are as rich as a pig!" finally the canon-priest lost his patience and howled into his ear.

At that point the others attacked him all together, trying to persuade him, rebuking him, telling him that if the rebels found him there they wouldn't leave stone atop stone, they'd take everything, they wouldn't even leave him eyes to weep with. Until they finally convinced him to flee through the side door. Baron Mendola ran to knock at Uncle Limòli's door.

At the commotion the Marquis, as deaf as a gopher, had thrown a cloak over his shoulders and was standing at his balcony glass door in shirt sleeves looking down, holding his warmer, and with his bare feet in his slippers, when he was suddenly faced with that cataclysm. It took quite some time to make him understand what they wanted from him at that hour—Mastro-don Gesualdo more dead than alive, and the others howling into his ears one by one:

"They want to do him in . . . your nephew, Don Gesualdo! . . . We must hide him . . ."

He winked, with his flabby and droopy eyelids, nodding "yes," while he sketched a cunning smile.

"Ah? . . . Do him in? . . . Don Gesualdo? . . . It's only fair! Your time has come, my dear man. . . . You're the sample and the example! . . ."

But finally, as he heard that they wanted his hide, he changed his tune, with his little cracked voice, pretending to be worried:

"What? . . . He too? What do they want then? . . . Where are we going to end up?"

Baron Mendola explained to him that Don Gesualdo was just the pretext to turn against the rich; but they wouldn't come there to look for money. The old man nodded "no" too, looking around with a little sour smile in his toothless mouth.

Those were two dirty old rooms that had grown old with him and where every habit of his had left a mark: the greasy blotch behind the chair on which he napped after dinner, the bricks loose in the short space beween the door and the window; the plasterless wall near the bed where he used to light the lamp. And in that filth the Marquis was as happy as a prince, spitting his miseries into everyl ody's face.

"Excuse me, my dear gentlemen, if I receive you in this mouse-trap. . . . It isn't good enough for you, Don Gesualdo. . . . The really great relatives you've got mixed up with, eh? . . ."

They put some of those broken bricks under the old sofa that was leaning against the wall, to hold it up, and on it they arranged a temporary bed for Don Gesualdo, who could no longer stand on his feet, while the Marquis kept grumbling:

"Look at what's happening to us! I've seen a lot of things! But I didn't expect this one for sure...."

Yet he offered to share with him his bowl of milk, in which he was soaking some pieces of hard bread.

"I'm like a baby again, see? I can't offer you anything else for supper. Meat is not for my teeth any more, nor is it for my purse!... You're used to quite different things, my dear friend.... What can you do? The world turns around for everybody, my dear Don Gesualdo!..."

"Ah!" he answered. "It isn't this, no, Marquis, sir. It's my stomach that's wrong. It's full of poison! There is a rabid dog there."

"All right," said the others. "Thank God. Here nobody will touch you."

It was a terrible blow for Mastro-don Gesualdo. The excitement, the rage, the disease he had inside him.... The night passed as it did. But the morning after, at the Angelus, Baron Mendola came back, huddled up in his cloak, his hat low on his eyes, looking around before rushing through the door.

"Now something else!" he exclaimed entering. "Somebody reported you, Don Gesualdo! They want to dig you out of here too, to force you to keep the promises made by the canon-priest.... Ciolla, in person... I saw him down there standing guard."

The Marquis, who had again become sprightly and cheerful in the middle of all that commotion, as he sharpened his ears and stuck himself among people to catch a word or two, ran to the balcony.

"Sure! There he is in his shirt jacket, like a little boy.... This means that we're all turning the clock back!..."

Don Gesualdo had gotten up puffing, shouting that it was better to stop it, that he would run downstairs to give Ciolla those promises himself! And since they were looking for him, he was right there, ready to receive them!..."

"Of course, of course," repeated the Marquis. "If they're looking for you, it means that they need you. They certainly don't come

looking for me! They want you to shout 'Hail' and 'Death to' together with them? All right, you go. Hail to you who have what it
takes to make them shout!"

"No! I know what they want!" retorted Don Gesualdo, furious.

"Sorry, but it's not just you now," observed Baron Mendola.
"The fact is that you represent all of us, the entire town!..."

The canon-priest Lupi came in, scratching his head, worried
by the turn things were taking. The spree was still going on. Quite a
nice thing for some people! Those crooks wanted them to make good
on those words of peace he had let fall at that dangerous point and
they hung around the square all day long waiting for the manna to
rain down from the sky:

"You really got me in quite a mess, Don Gesualdo!"

With that remark of the canon-priest's, there was another
squabble between the two of them:

"Me, eh?... Me?... It was me who promised all wonders?"

"Just to keep them quiet, in God's name! Words of the moment
and nothing more! I'd have liked to see you up against those hellish
faces!"

The Marquis was enjoying it all:

"Listen to that! Look at that!"

"In any case," concluded Baron Mendola, "this is nothing but
talk, and we must buy time. Meanwhile, you get out of our way, you
causa causarum, you the 'cause of causes'! At the bottom of a cistern, in a hole, where the hell you like; but it isn't right that so many
family men are in danger because of you!"

"In the Trao house!" suggested the canon-priest. "Your
brother-in-law will receive you with open arms. Nobody knows that
he is still alive, and they won't come and look for you there."

The Marquis approved too:

"Great! That's really a great idea! Cat and dog locked up
together..."

Don Gesualdo kept balking.

"Then," exclaimed the canon-priest, "I wash my hands of it,
like Pilate. As a matter of fact, I'll go and call Ciolla with all the
others, if you like!..."

Don Gesualdo had gotten to the point that they could do whatever they liked with him. Two hours after nightfall, through out-of-

the-way alleys, they went to wake up Grazia, who kept the keys to the front door, and in the dark they managed to get outside of Don Ferdinando's room.

"Who is it?" an asthmatic voice was heard bleating inside. "Grazia, who is it?"

"It's us, Don Gesualdo, your brother-in-law . . ."

Nobody answered. Then they heard somebody rummaging in the dark. And suddenly Don Ferdinando bolted himself in, and began to pile up chairs and tables behind the door, screaming continuously, frightened:

"Grazia! Grazia!"

"Damnation!" exclaimed Baron Mendola. "Here it's even worse! That jackass will make the whole town rush over!"

The canon-priest laughed in his sleeve, shaking his head. Meanwhile, Grazia had lighted a candle stump, and looked them in the face, one by one—dismayed, blinking her eyes.

"What d'you want to do, gentlemen?" she finally dared say, timidly.

Don Gesualdo, who could no longer stand on his feet, pale and worn out, broke forth in a desperate tone:

"I want to go back home!... At all costs... I'm determined!..."

"No, sir!" cut in the canon-priest. "Here you're at home too. There is your wife's share. Ah, damn it! You've been quiet all this time.... Now it's enough!... There, in Donna Bianca's room. The bed is still there...."

Baron Mendola had gotten into a good mood as they were getting the room ready. He was searching everywhere. He poked his nose into the dark corridor, behind the little door. He dug up jokes, recalling old stories. —How many events! How many ups and downs!

"Who could ever tell, eh, Don Gesualdo?"

Even the canon-priest Lupi had a little smile.

"While you're here, you can do your meditation upon life and upon death, to while the time away. What a comedy, this dirty world. *Vanitas vanitatum!* Vanity of vanities!"

Don Gesualdo gave him a black look, but didn't answer. He still had enough stomach left to lock his troubles and his calamities inside it, without sharing them with his friends to make them laugh at him. Then he threw himself down on the bed, and remained alone in the dark, with his pains, stifling his laments, swallowing the bitterness that came to his mouth with every memory. There was only one thing that didn't let his mind rest—that he could have died right then and there without his daughter knowing anything about it. Then, in the fever, there passed before his muddy eyes Bianca, Diodata, *mastro* Nunzio, and others—and another himself, who was slaving and toiling in the sun and in the wind—all of them with a surly face, spitting at him:

"Jackass! Jackass! What have you done? It serves you right!"

With the daylight, Grazia came back to help a little—worn out as she was, panting when she moved a chair, stopping every moment to plant herself in front of him with her hands on her enormous belly, to repeat her complaints against Don Ferdinando's relatives, who left that poor man on her hands, begrudging him even bread and wine.

"Yes sir, they've all forgotten about him—there in his corner, like a sick dog!... But my heart doesn't let me.... We've always been neighbors... good servants of the family... a great family.... My heart doesn't let me, no!"

Behind her there came a swarm of children that turned everything upside down. Then Speranza came too, screaming that she wanted to see her brother, as if he were just about to expire.

"Let me in! He's my own flesh and blood after all! Now, in the state he is in, I can only remember that I'm his sister."

She, her husband, and her children. They filled the whole neighborhood with noise. Don Gesualdo left his bed puffing. Not even chains would hold him there.

"I want to go back home! What am I doing here anyway? After all, everybody knows!..."

They had a hard time convincing him to wait until nightfall. And after the Angelus, Burgio and all the other relatives very quietly accompanied him home. Speranza wanted to stay to watch over her brother, who was so sick, and it was a miracle if all his things hadn't been sacked and looted that very night.

"It doesn't matter if we're suing. People's hearts can be seen in times of need. Business is one thing, love is another. We've quarreled, we'll quarrel until Doomsday, but we're children of the same blood!"

She declared that she'd care for him better than for the apple of her eye—for him and for his property. In front of his bed she lined up her husband and her children, who were looking around with greedy eyes, and repeated:

"These are your own flesh and blood! These won't betray you!"

And he, struggling, weary, depressed, didn't even have the strength to rebel.

So, little by little, they all thrust themselves on him—his nephews roving about his house and his farms, lording around, laying their hands on everything; his sister, with the keys on her belt, rummaging, ransacking, sending her husband here and there, to find remedies and to pick medicinal herbs. As *massaro* Fortunato complained that his legs were no longer twenty years old to run around that way, she scolded him:

"What's the matter? Don't you do it for your brother-in-law's sake. 'In necessity, in prison, and infirmity you can tell amity.'"

She didn't fear Ciolla or all the others of that same gang. Once, when Vito Orlando out of bravado came in with a gun in his pocket to settle certain accounts with Don Gesualdo, she chased him down the stairs and threw a pot of dirty water on him. The canon-priest Lupi himself had to put his tail between his legs, without again getting generous with other people's property—now that Ciolla and the other ruffians had left to seek their fortune in the city with flags and trumpets.

To quiet the others, the canon-priest had resorted to the expedient of walking the streets in procession, with the scourge and the crown of thorns; and so the people gave vent to their frustrations through feasts and Forty Hours, while he kept preaching brotherhood and love of neighbor.

"But he doesn't shell out a cent, he doesn't!" shouted Speranza. "That's all right with me. But if he comes back here to cheat us out of our things, I'll receive him the way he deserves... just like Vito Orlando!"

Meanwhile, Don Gesualdo's house was being sacked and looted all the same. Wine, oil, cheese, even bolts of cloth, disappeared in the batting of an eye. Factors and sharecroppers came from Canziria and from Mangalavite to complain about *massaro* Fortunato Burgio's children, who ruled with an iron fist and sacked their uncle's farms, as if it were nobody's property. And he, the poor man, confined to his bed, was grieving in silence; he didn't dare rebel against his sister and his brother-in-law; he was worrying about his own troubles. There was a dog in his belly devouring his liver—the rabid dog of Saint Vito the martyr that made him a martyr too. In vain Speranza, lovingly, looked for herbs and medicines, consulted quacks and people who knew the secrets of cure-alls. Everyone brought a different remedy—decoctions, ointments, even the relic and the blessed image of the Saint, which Don Luca wanted to try out with his own hands. Nothing helped. The patient kept repeating:

"It's nothing serious . . . just colic. I've had worries. Tomorrow I'm going to get up . . . "

But not even he could believe it any more, and never got up. He had become almost like a skeleton, skin and bones; only his belly was swollen like a barrel. In town the rumor spread that he was finished; the hand of God was seizing him and drowning him in his riches. His noble son-in-law wrote from Palermo for the details. He also spoke of business to be settled and of impending deadlines. In the postscript there were two disconsolate lines by Isabella, who hadn't yet recovered from the recent blow. Speranza, who was there when her brother was feeling moved by the letter, spat out her venom:

"There you are! And now you're fretting too—on top of it all! You could just go to the other world . . . alone and abandoned, like one who doesn't own anything! . . . Whom did you find here to help you in time of need, tell me? Your daughter sends you only nice words. But her husband gets to the point!"

Don Gesualdo didn't answer. But secretly, with his face to the wall, he began to cry, quietly. He seemed like a child. You wouldn't recognize him any more. When Diodata heard that he was so sick and decided to pay him a visit and ask his forgiveness for the disrespect shown by her boys the night of the uprising—she was stunned, seeing him so far gone that he smelled of the grave and with those eyes of his which became so shiny at every new face.

"Don Gesualdo, sir . . . I came to see you because they told me that you're in this state. . . . Please forgive them . . . those bums who have done you wrong. . . . Boys without sense . . . They were put up to it without their even knowing what they were doing. . . . Please forgive them for my sake, Don Gesualdo, sir! . . . "

And you could tell that her words were sincere, poor woman, with that face, hiding her tears by swallowing them — those tears that kept coming to her eyes with each word — and trying to take his hand to kiss it. He made a vague gesture, and shook his head, as if to say that he didn't care any more, by now... At that point Speranza appeared and berated that impudent woman who came to tempt her brother at the point of death to get something out of him, to fleece him to the end. A leech! She had gotten fat at his expense! Wasn't it enough? Now the crows were flying, smelling the carcass. The sick man closed his eyes to escape that torture, and stirred in bed as if he were having another attack of colic. So that Diodata left without being able to say good-bye to him — her head bent, huddled up in her mantilla. Speranza came back to her brother, all love and smiles.

"You have us here to help you now.... We won't leave you alone, don't be afraid... Everything you need... Just say the word. What good would that witch be to you now? She'd devour you, body and soul. You couldn't even receive the viaticum with that disgrace in the house."

She helped him better than a servant, and watched over him with love, without sparing expense or work. As she saw that nothing helped, she even called Tavuso's son, fresh out of the Naples medical school — a young man who didn't even have hair on his chin yet, and charged princely fees. But seeing him brandish his pen to write the usual humbug, Don Gesualdo spoke his mind:

"Don Margheritino, I saw you born! D'you write that prescription for me? Who do you think I am, my dear friend?"

"Then," retorted the budding doctor in a rage, "then call the vet! Why did you send for me?"

He picked up his hat and walked off.

But since the patient suffered all the torments of hell, in the delusion that somebody could find the cure, and to shut up the neighbors, who accused them of being misers, Don Gesualdo's relatives had to bow their heads to doctors and medicines. Tavuso's son, Bomma, and all the know-it-alls in town — they all filed before Don Gesualdo's bed. They came, they looked, they felt, they exchanged such barbarous words to give you goosepimples, and each one left his say on a piece of paper — such scrawls that looked like leeches. Don Gesualdo, dismayed, didn't say anything; he tried to catch what those words meant; he looked suspiciously at the writing hands. Only, not to throw his money completely away, before sending the prescription to the pharmacist, he took Don Margheritino aside and called his attention to his closet full of jars and bottles, bought for his wife, rest in peace.

"I spared no expense, Doctor, sir. I have 'em still there, just as they were. If you'd think they could be of use now . . ."

They didn't listen to him — not even when he again stammered, frightened by those serious faces:

"I feel better. Tomorrow I'm going to get up. Send me to the country and I'm going to recover in twenty-four hours."

They answered "yes," just to make him happy, like a child.

"Tomorrow, the day after tomorrow."

But they kept him there, to milk him, to bleed him — doctors, relatives, and pharmacists. They turned him over again and again, they tapped him on his belly with two fingers, they had him drink a thousand filthy mixtures, they smeared him with such stuff that brought blisters on his belly. On the chest of drawers there was again an arsenal of medicines, just like during Bianca's last days, rest in peace. He grumbled, shaking his head.

"We're already at expensive medicines! That means that there is no cure."

Rivers of money, people coming and going, chaos in the house, the table laid with food from morning to night. Burgio wasn't used to it; he ran to show his tongue to the doctors when they came for his brother-in-law; Santo didn't go out any more, not even to the tavern; and the nephews, when they returned from the fields came to blows: quarrels and arguments among them — each trying to loot more than the other, and such an uproar that it reached all the way to the room of the patient, who stretched his ears, eager to know what they were doing with his property; and he too began to scream from his bed:

"Let me go to Mangalavite. All my businesses are going to hell. Here I'm eating my heart out. Let me go, or I'm finished!"

In his stomach there was something like a ball of lead, that weighed on him, and wanted to come out, always hurting him; now and then it contracted, it became red hot, and it hammered, it jumped into his throat, and it made him howl like hell, and made him bite whatever was close enough. Then he was worn out, panting, in his wild eyes the vague terror of another attack. Everything he forced himself to swallow, to hang onto life—the rarest foods, without asking what they cost—turned to poison for him; he had to throw it up as if it were cursed, blacker than ink, bitter, damned by God. And meanwhile the pain and the swelling increased: such a belly that his legs couldn't hold it up any more. One day Bomma, as he tapped on it, said:

"There's something in here."

"What d'you mean, sir?" stammered Don Gesualdo, suddenly sitting up in his bed, in a cold sweat.

Bomma looked at him straight in the face, pulled his chair up to the bed, looked here and there to see if they were alone.

"Don Gesualdo, you are a man . . . you're not a child, eh?"

"Yes, sir," he answered with a firm voice, suddenly calm, with the courage he had always had when needed. "Yes sir, speak out."

"All right, you need a consultation. You don't have a prickly pear thorn in your belly! It's a serious business, understand? This kind of thing is not for a Don Margheritino and for the likes of him . . . let's say so without malice, here in confidence. Call the best out-of-town doctors, Don Vincenzo Capra, Doctor Muscio of Caltagirone, whomever you want . . . You're not short of money . . ."

At those words Don Gesualdo flew into a rage:

"Money! . . . Not one of you can take his eyes off the money I've earned! . . . What good is it to me . . . if I can't even buy health with it? . . . It has only made my mouth bitter . . . always! . . ."

But he wanted to hear the conclusion of Bomma's speech. One never knows . . . He let him finish, in silence, holding his chin, thinking about his problems. Finally, he wanted to know:

"A consultation? What is a consultation going to do for me?"

Bomma lost his temper:

"What is it going to do for you? Damn it! Whatever it can do . . . At least people won't say that you're dying without proper care. I'm speaking in your interest. I don't have anything to gain one way or the other. . . . I'm a pharmacist . . . It isn't my business . . . I don't know about these things. I've helped you out of friendship. . . ."

As the other was shaking his head, suspicious, with his cunning smile on his lifeless lips, the pharmacist put all respect aside:

"You're a dead man, Don Jackass! I'm telling you!"

Then Don Gesualdo gave a slow and firm glance around, blew his nose, and let himself fall down on his back. After a while, looking up at the ceiling, he added with a sigh:

"All right. Let's have this consultation."

That night he didn't sleep a wink. Tormented by a new anxiety, with chills that seized him from time to time, cold sweats, starts that made him suddenly sit up in bed, his hair on end, always looking into the dark and always seeing Bomma's threatening face—feeling himself, stifling his pain, trying to delude himself. In fact, he really thought he felt better. He wanted to take care of himself, since it was a serious business. He wanted to be cured. He repeated the pharmacist's very words: —he had plenty of money; he had worn himself out for it; he hadn't earned it for the good of his noble son-in-law; to let the ungrateful enjoy it, those who let him die far away. Out of sight out of mind! That's the way the world is; everybody brings grist to his own mill. His own mill, his own, was to recover his health, with his money! There were in this world some good doctors, who would cure him, if he paid them well. Then he wiped away that death sweat, and tried to sleep. He wanted the out-of-town doctors who were coming tomorrow to find him looking better; he was counting the hours; he couldn't wait to see them, there, before his bed. The very light of dawn gave him courage. Then, when he heard the bells of the litter carrying Doctor Muscio and Don Vincenzo Capra he felt his heart open all the more. He quickly pulled himself up and sat in bed, just like one who really feels better. He greeted those good people with a broad smile that was meant to reassure them too, as he saw them come in.

Instead, they hardly paid any attention to him. They were all ears for Don Margheritino, who was telling the story of the illness with a great deal of pretentiousness; they approved by nodding their heads, from time to time—only occasionally glancing absently at the patient whose expression was changing at the sight of those serious faces, at those grimaces and at the long babbling of the little doctor who seemed to be reciting the funeral eulogy. After the youngster had finished babbling, they got up one after the other and again began to feel and to question the patient, shaking their heads with a certain sententious winking—such glances among themselves that they would cut your breath off, no less. There was especially one of those out-of-towners, who was standing there frowning and deep in thought, and every moment he went 'Uhm! Uhm!' without opening his mouth. Out of curiosity, the relatives, the servants, even some neighbors, crowded by the doorway, waiting for the sentence, while in a corner the doctors chattered together in whispers. At a sign from the pharmacist, Burgio and his wife also went to hear, on tiptoe.

"Speak out, gentlemen!" exclaimed the patient as pale as a dead man. "I am the sick man, after all! I want to know how far gone I am."

Doctor Muscio sketched a smile that made him look still uglier. And Don Vincenzo Capra, in a dignified manner, began to explain the diagnosis of the illness: *Pylori cancer,* cancer of the pylorus, the *pyrosis* of the Greeks. There weren't as yet any signs of ulceration; even the adhesion of the tumor to the vital organs was not certain; but the degeneration of the tissues was already evident through certain pathological symptoms. Don Gesualdo, after listening attentively, went on:

"That's all very fine. But please tell me if you can cure me, sir. Without consideration of money . . . paying you according to your merit . . . ."

At first Don Vincenzo Capra fell silent and shrugged his shoulders.

"Eh, eh . . . to cure you . . . of course . . . we're here to try to cure you . . ."

Doctor Muscio, more cruel, blurted straight out the only remedy they could try: the extirpation of the tumor — quite a case, the kind of surgery that would do anybody credit. He showed the ways and the means, getting excited over the proposal accompanying his words with gestures, already smelling blood, his eyes burning in his large face that turned all purple — as if he were about to roll up his sleeves and begin; so much so that the patient opened his eyes and his mouth wide, and instinctively pulled away; and the women, frightened, broke into moaning and sobbing.

"Our Lady of Peril!" Speranza started screaming. "They want to kill my brother . . . to quarter him alive like a pig!"

"Keep quiet!" he stammered passing the hem of the sheet over his face that was dripping heavily. The other doctors kept silent and more or less approved Doctor Muscio's proposal out of courtesy. As he saw that nobody uttered a sound, Don Gesualdo began to say again:

"Keep quiet!... It's my hide... I must speak my piece too... Gentlemen, I'm a man... I'm not a child... If you say that this operation is necessary... If you say it's necessary... yes sir... we'll have it.... But let me speak my piece..."

"It's only fair. Speak out."

"Well... Only one thing... First I want to know if you guarantee to save my hide.... We're gentlemen... I put my trust in you ... It isn't a deal to be made with your eyes shut... I want to see clearly in my business...."

"What kind of talk is this!" cut in Doctor Muscio, fidgeting on his chair. "I'm a surgeon, my friend. I do my job, and don't care about making a charlatan's bets! Do you think you're dealing with Zanni the quack, at the fair?"

"Then the deal is off," answered Don Gesualdo. And he turned his back on them. "Go on, Bomma, you really gave me great advice!"

Speranza, most solicitous saw that the time had come to turn to the saints, and began to busy herself to get a hold of relics and of holy cards. Notary Neri thought that both the daughter and the son-in-law should be immediately informed of the danger Don Gesualdo was in. He wouldn't listen any more. He said that he had a pile of saints and of relics, right there in Bianca's closet, together with the other medicines. He didn't want to see anybody. Since he was condemned, he wanted to die in peace, without operations, away from all those troubles on his land. He clung to life as hard as he could, desperate. He had gone through hard times before; he had always helped himself, in bad straits. He had plenty of courage, and he had a tough hide too. He ate and drank; he insisted on feeling better; he got up from bed two or three hours a day; he dragged himself around the rooms, from one piece of furniture to another. Finally he had them bring him to Mangalavite—out of breath, with *mastro* Nardo on one side and Masi on the other, holding him up on the mule—a journey that took three hours and made him say a hundred times:

"Throw me into the ditch; that's better."

But down there, before his property, he indeed realized that it was all over, that all hope was lost for him, when he saw that now he didn't care at all. The vines were already leafing, the wheat was tall, the olive trees in bloom, the sumacs green, and over everything there spread a mist, a sadness, a black veil. The cottage itself, with its windows shut, the balcony where Bianca and their daughter used to sit and work, the deserted road, even his own field workers, who were afraid of bothering him and kept at a distance, there in the courtyard or under the shed, everything wrung his heart, everything said to him: "What are you doing? what d'you want?" —His own property, there, the pigeons circling in flocks above his head, the geese and the turkeys crackling in front of him.... You could hear the voices and the singsong of the peasants at work. On the Licodia road, down below, people passed on foot and on horseback. The world was still going its way, while for him there was no hope any more, gnawed inside by a worm just like a rotten apple that must fall from the tree—without the strength to take a step on his own land, without feeling like swallowing an egg. Then, desperate that he had to die, he began to hit ducks and turkeys with his stick, to break out the buds and the wheat stocks. He'd have liked to destroy in a single blow all the wealth he had put together little by little. He wanted his property to go with him, desperate as he was. *Mastro* Nardo and the helper-boy had to bring him back to town, more dead than alive.

A few days later, the Duke of Leyra arrived, who had been called by express courier. He took possession of his father-in-law and of the house, saying that he wanted to bring him along to Palermo to have him taken care of by the best doctors. The poor man, now only the shadow of himself, let him do as he wished; as a matter of fact, his heart opened up to hope again; he was moved by the attentions of his son-in-law and of his daughter, who was waiting for him with open arms. He felt as if his strength were already coming back to him. He couldn't wait to leave, as if he were to leave his disease there, in that house and in those fields, which had cost him so much sweat, and which instead now weighed heavily on his shoulders. Meanwhile, the son-in-law was busy with his accountant getting his affairs in order. As soon as Don Gesualdo was fit to travel, they put him in a litter and started out for the city. It was a rainy day. The familiar houses, faces of acquaintances who hardly turned, passed by the windows of the litter. Speranza, and all her family, angry because the Duke had come to lord around, didn't show up any more. But *mastro* Nardo had decided to accompany his boss as far as the last houses in town. In Via della Masera there was a great shouting:

"Stop! Stop!"

And Diodata appeared. She wanted to say good-bye to Don Gesualdo for the last time—there, before her doorway. But, when she came near him, she couldn't find the words, and remained there with her hands on the litter window, nodding her head.

"Ah! Diodata . . . Did you come to wish me a good trip? . . ." he said.

She nodded yes, yes, trying to smile, as her eyes filled with tears.

"Poor Diodata! Your're the only one to remember your boss. . . ."

He stuck his head out of the window, perhaps looking for other people, but since it was raining he quickly pulled it back in.

"Be careful! . . . In the rain . . . With your head bare! . . . You've always done bad things like that! You remember, eh, d'you remember?"

"Yes sir," she answered simply, and kept accompanying her words with nods of her head. "Yes sir, have a good trip, sir."

Very slowly she drew back from the litter, almost reluctantly, and moved toward her house, stopping on the threshold, humble and sad.

At that point Don Gesualdo noticed *mastro* Nardo, who had followed him that far, and put his hand in his pocket to give him a few cents.

"Sorry, *mastro* Nardo! . . . I don't have anything . . . It'll have to be another time, if we happen to see each other again, eh? . . . If we happen to see each other again . . ."

And he slumped back, with a heavy heart because of all those things he was leaving behind—the muddy lane he had walked so many times, the bell tower lost in the fog, the prickly pears striped by the rain, filing by on both sides of the litter.

V

When he came into his daughter's house, Don Gesualdo felt as if he had entered another world. It was such a vast palace that you'd get lost in it. Everywhere there were curtains and rugs, and you wouldn't have known where to put your feet—beginning with the marble staircase—and the doorkeeper, a big-shot himself, no less, with such a beard and such a long overcoat, stared at you from top to bottom, frowning, if unfortunately he didn't like your face, and shouted at you from his big cage:

"There's the doormat to wipe your feet!"

An army of spongers, of lackeys and servants, yawning with their mouths shut, walking on tiptoe, serving you without saying a word or taking an extra step, with so much condescension as to make you not want anything any more. Everything regulated by bell ringing, with a high-mass ritual—to have a glass of water, or to go into his daughter's rooms. The Duke himself, at dinner time, dressed up as if he were going to a wedding.

The first days poor Don Gesualdo had mustered his courage to please his daughter, and had dressed up too before coming to the table, shackled and fettered, with a humming in his ears, his hands hesitating, his eyes anxious, his jaws tightened by all that apparatus, and by the servant who counted his every mouthful from behind his back, and whose cotton glove you could see at any moment stretch out treacherously and snatch your food away. He was also uneasy because of his son-in-law's white necktie, because of the sideboards as high and as glittering as altars, and because of the tablecloth—so exquisite that you were always afraid to let something accidentally fall on it. So much so that he was planning to get his daughter face to face and to tell her what was on his mind. Fortunately, the Duke came to his rescue, by saying to Isabella—after coffee, his cigar in his mouth and his head leaning against the back of his big armchair:

"My dear, I think that it would be better if from now on we had your father served meals in his rooms. He certainly has his own hours and his own habits.... Besides, with the special diet required by his present condition..."

"Of course, of course," stammered Don Gesualdo. "I was just

about to tell you myself . . . I would be happier too . . . I don't want to be in your way. . . ."

"No. It's not that. We are always happy to have you, dear Don Gesualdo."

He was really good with his father-in-law. He filled his liquor glass; he encouraged him to smoke a cigar; he finally assured him that he looked better, ever since he had come to Palermo, and that the change of air and a good diet with regular medicines would have totally cured him. Then he also touched upon business matters. He showed himself sensible; he was looking for the ways and means to keep his father-in-law in his house for some time, without fear that the latter's businesses would go to rack and ruin. . . . A general power of attorney . . . some sort of *alter ego,* of other self . . . Don Gesualdo felt his smile die on his lips. No doubt. His son-in-law — in his face, in his words, even in the tone of his voice, even when he was acting like a friend and being on your good side — had something repulsive, something that made your arms fall in distress, precisely when you wanted to throw them around his neck, like with a real son, and say to him:

"This is it! for your good words, now! Never mind the rest! Do whatever you like!"

So that Don Gesualdo rarely came downstairs to see his daughter. He felt uneasy with his noble son-in-law; he was always afraid that he would again start with that *alter ego* tune. He couldn't breathe, there in the middle of all those trinkets. He almost had to ask for the permission of the servant who stood guard in the ante-room, if he wanted to see his daughter, and had to run away if a visitor arrived. They had placed him in a little apartment upstairs — a few rooms which they called the guest quarters, where Isabella came to see him every morning, dressed in her robe, often without even sitting down, loving and thoughtful, it's true, but in such a way that the poor man felt really like a stranger. Sometimes she was so pale that she seemed not to have slept a wink either. She had a certain wrinkle between her eyebrows, a certain look in her eyes, that he — old and experienced as he was about the world — didn't like at all. He would have liked to take her in his arms, hold her tight, and ask her with a whisper in her ear:

"What's the matter? . . . Tell me! . . . You can tell me in confidence; I've had many troubles and cannot betray you! . . . "

But she too pulled her horns in, like a snail. She didn't confide in him, she rarely talked about her mother too, as if the nail were still there . . . revealing the haughty restraint of the Traos, who kept their implacable resentment and diffidence locked up inside.

So he had to push back his good words and even his tears, which swelled inside him, and keep his own troubles to himself. He spent his melancholy days behind the window pane, watching the horses being groomed and the carriages being washed, in the court-yard as vast as a town square. The grooms, in shirtsleeves and with their bare feet in their wooden shoes, sang, shouted, exchanged small talk and jokes with the servants, who wasted their time at the windows, wore aprons that reached up to their necks, or red vests, and listlessly dragged a dusting rag with their rough hands, in the midst of their vulgar remarks — scoffing faces of crooks, well shaven and well groomed, looking as if they were just taking off their masks. And the coachmen — real big shots too — kept looking on, cigars in their mouths and their hands in the pockets of their close-fitting jackets — now and then talking with the doorman who came from his box for a smoke, making signs and crude sounds toward the house-maids who passed behind the balcony windows, or stuck their heads out provokingly — those impudent ones — to blurt out dirty words and laughter worthy of whores, from their Madonna faces. Mean-while, Don Gesualdo was thinking about all the good money that must be going through those hands — all people who ate and drank at his daughter's expense, at the expense of the dowry he had given her, of Alia and Donninga, the beautiful lands he had cherished with his eyes for so long, morning and night, and had measured out with his longing and had won foot by foot, day by day, taking the very bread out of his mouth; the poor bare lands that needed to be plowed and sown; the mills, the houses, the storehouses he had built with so much hardship, with so much sacrifice, one stone on top of the other. Canziria, Mangalavite, the house, everything, everything would go through those hands. Who could defend his property after his death — alas, poor property! Who knew what it had cost? The noble Duke, he, when he walked out of the house, his head high, a cigar in his mouth, and the top of his cane in his coat pocket, and just stopped to take a look at his horses, he was paid homage as if he were the Holy Sacrament, with the windows being quickly shut, everybody running to his place, everybody bareheaded; the doorman with his gallooned hat in his hands, standing before his box, the grooms immobile by the crupper of the animals, the currycomb resting by their thigh, the chief coachman, a big shot, bending double as he went on with the review and took orders; a comedy that lasted five minutes. Later, as soon as the Duke turned his back, the noise and the chaos started all over again—from the windows, from the porch archway leading to the stables, from the kitchen smoking and flaming under the roof, full of scullions dressed in white, as if the palace had been abandoned to a famished horde, which was paid for the purpose of living it up until the sound of the bell announced a visitor—a solemn occurrence, too. On appointed days the Duchess decked herself all up to wait for visitors—just like a soul in Purgatory. Now and then a brand new coach arrived; it passed like a flash of lightning before the doorman, who hardly had time to stick his pipe inside his coat and hang onto the bell; ladies and uniformed grooms slipped away in a hurry under the high vestibule, and after ten minutes they turned up again to run somewhere else at breakneck speed—truly people who seemed to be paid daily wages precisely for this purpose. He, instead, spent his time counting the roof tiles across the yard, figuring out, with all the love and the attention of his old trade, how much those carved windows had cost, and those massive pillars, and those marble steps, and that sumptuous furniture, and those fabrics, and those people, and those horses, eating and swallowing money just the same way as the land swallowed the seeds and drank water—but they didn't give anything back, didn't produce any fruits, for they were more and more famished, devouring more and more, just like the disease eating up his insides. How many things could be done with that money! How many good hoe strokes, how much sweat of peasants could be paid for! Farms and entire towns could be built . . . lands could be sown, as far as the eye could see. . . . And an army of reapers in June, mountains of wheat to be harvested, and rivers of money to be pocketed! . . . And then his heart swelled to see the sparrows squabbling on those tiles, with the sun dying on the eaves without ever coming down as far as his windows. He thought of the dusty roads, of the beautiful green and golden fields, of the chirping along the hedges, of the beautiful mornings that made the furrows steam! . . . But now! . . . Now! . . .

Now he was shut up inside four walls, with the incessant buzzing of the city in his ears, with the clanging of so many bells hammering in his head, slowly consumed by the fever, gnawed by pains that at times made him bite the pillow—so as not to bother the servant who was yawning in the next room. During the first days, the change, the new air, perhaps even some medicine they had hit upon by mistake, had worked the miracle and had made him believe that he could be cured. Then he had a relapse and he was worse than before. Not even the best Palermo doctors had been able to find a cure for that hellish disease! Just like the ignorant doctors of his town, and these cost more money—on top of it. They came one after the other, these big doctors who traveled by carriage and made you pay even for the servants they left in the entrance room. They observed him, they felt him, they asked him questions, as if they were handling a child or a peasant. They showed him to their apprentices just like Zanni the quack at the fair shows the horned rooster or the two-tailed sheep, and gave explanations in mysterious words. They hardly answered, from the top of their lips—if the poor devil was bold enough to ask about the disease nursing inside him, as if he didn't have anything to do with it at all, with his own hide! They too had made him buy a full pharmacy: remedies that you should figure by the drop, like gold, ointments that you had to smear with a brush, and which opened raw sores on you, poisons that caused stronger colics and brought a taste of copper to your mouth, baths and sudorifics that left him exhausted, without the strength to move his head—and seeing the shadow of death everywhere.

"Gentlemen, what kind of game is this?" he wanted to say. "All right then, if it's always the same old tune, I'll go back home. . . ."

At least there they respected him for his money and allowed him to let off steam if he wanted to know how he was spending it for his own health. While here he felt as if he were in the hospital, taken care of out of charity. He had to be in awe even of his son-in-law, who came in accompanying the big shots that had been called upon for a consultation. They spoke in whispers among themselves, turning their backs on him, without paying attention to him who was waiting open-mouthed for a word of life or death. Or they gave him the charity of an answer that meant nothing, of a little smile that actually meant:

"See you in Paradise, good man!"

There were even those who turned their backs on him, as if they felt insulted. He guessed that it must have been something serious — by the doctor's very faces, by their discouraging shrugging of shoulders, by their long stays with his son-in-law, by their grumbling that lasted quite a long time in the entrance room. Finally, he couldn't contain himself any longer. One day, when those gentlemen were playing the same comedy all over again, he caught one of them by the coattails before he could leave.

"Doctor, sir, talk to me! I am the patient after all! I'm not a child. I want to know what it is, since you're betting on my own hide!"

But that doctor began making a scene with the Duke, as if he had been insulted in his house. It took quite some doing to calm him down, so that he wouldn't forget about patient and disease once and for all. Don Gesualdo heard the others tell him in whispers:

"Bear with him... He doesn't know about manners... He's a primitive man... uncivilized...."

So that the poor patient had to swallow everything, and to turn to his daughter, to learn something from her.

"What did the doctors say? Tell me the truth... Is it a serious disease, tell me?..."

And as he saw her eyes swell with tears that she tried to push back, he flew into a rage. He didn't want to die. He felt a desperate energy inside himself — to get up and go away from that damned house.

"I don't mean because of you... you've done everything... I have everything I need.... But I'm not used to this, you see... I feel as if I were suffocating here...."

She wasn't happy in that house either. He knew it in his heart — the poor father. They seemed to be in perfect harmony, husband and wife; they talked courteously between themselves in front of the servants; after dinner the Duke almost always spent half an hour in his wife's sitting room; he went to wish her "Good morning" regularly before breakfast; on All Soul's day, at Christmas, on Saint Rosalia's Day, and on her name's day or on their wedding anniversary, he gave her jewels, which she showed her father for him to admire, as proof of how fond her husband was of her.

"Ah, ah... I understand... it must have cost quite a bit!...

But you're not happy...one can see very well that you're not happy..."

In the depths of her eyes he read another secret—a deathly anxiety, which would not leave her even when she was with him, which made her start when she heard a sudden step, or when the bell announcing the Duke sounded at an unusual time—and from her deathly pallor she darted some rapid glances in which he felt he could see a reproach. There had been times when he had seen her come rushing, pale, shaking like a leaf, stammering excuses. One night, late, while he was in bed with his own troubles, he had heard an unusual commotion downstairs—doors being slammed, the voice of the housemaid screaming, as if calling for help—a voice that made him sit up in bed, frightened. But the day after his daughter wouldn't tell him anything; rather, his questions seemed to annoy her. In that house they even counted their words and their sighs, each one shutting up his own troubles inside himself—the Duke with a cold smile, Isabella with the good manners he had her learn in the boarding school. The curtains and the carpets muted everything. But when he saw them in front of him—husband and wife, so calm that nobody would ever be able to suspect what was lurking underneath—he felt a shiver down his spine.

On the other hand, what could he do? He had plenty of troubles as it was. He was the worst off, with death breathing down his neck. When he would close his eyes forever, all the others would set their minds at rest, as he himself had set his mind at rest after his father's death, and his wife's. Everyone brings grist to his own mill. And he had brought lots of grist, for the others to come to the mill! Speranza, Diodata, all the others...a real river. Even there, in that palace of plenty, it was all his doing; and meanwhile he couldn't find any rest between the fine linen sheets, and on the feather pillows; he was stifled by the curtains and the beautiful silk fabrics that took the sunshine away from him. The money he was spending to keep the show going, the noises in the courtyard, the servant they kept behind his door to count his sighs, even the cook who prepared him insipid broths he couldn't swallow, everything poisoned him; he couldn't even digest the rarest delicacies; they were like so many nails in his flesh.

"They're letting me starve to death, understand!" he complained to his daughter at times, his eyes burning with despair. "It's not to save money.... It's probably good stuff.... But my stomach isn't used to it.... Send me back home. I want to close my eyes where I was born!"

The thought of death didn't leave him any more; he betrayed himself with his wry questions, with his suspicious glances, and even with his anxious preoccupation to hide it in various ways. Now he no longer was in awe of anyone, and he seized whoever happened to be near him to ask:

"I want to know the truth, my dear sirs ... To put my things in order ... my businesses ..."

And if they tried to reassure him, telling him that there was nothing critical ... nothing serious ... for the moment ... he again insisted, his eyes sharp, on unearthing the truth:

"The fact is that I have so many things to do down there, on my lands, sirs ... understand! ... I can't really stay on a vacation, I can't! ... I must take care of everything, or else everything goes to ruin! ..."

Then he explained where that disease had come from:

"It has been all the worries! ... All the bitter pills! ... I have had so many of them! You see, they have left their yeast right here, ... inside me! ..."

He had become suspicious. He was afraid they couldn't wait to get rid of him. To save the expense and lay their hands on his property. He tried to reassure everybody, with an amiable smile:

"Don't spare any expense ... I can pay ... My son-in-law knows ... Whatever is needed ... It won't be money thrown away ... If I live, I'll still earn lots more money ..."

With his eyes shining, he even tried to win over his own daughter. He knew that property, alas, puts hell between father and children. He took her on her word. He stammered, caressing her like when she was a child, meanwhile looking at her on the sly, his heart throbbing in his throat:

"Don't I have everything I need here? I have everything to be cured.... We'll spend whatever is needed, won't we?"

But the disease overcame him and took all illusion away from him. In those moments of discouragement the poor man thought aloud:

"What does it do for me? . . . What good is all this? . . . It wasn't any good for your mother either!"

One day, the Duke's administrator paid him a visit—obliging, all kindness, just like his boss when he was getting ready to strike. He asked about his health; he expressed regret about the illness that lasted so long. He understood very well, he was a businessman just like Don Gesualdo, the kind of disorder . . . how many losses . . . the consequences . . . such a vast estate . . . without anybody who really could look after it . . . Finally, he offered to take it upon himself . . . in the interest of the house he served . . . of the Duchess . . . He had been a faithful servant of the noble Duke's for many years. . . . So he took Don Gesualdo's business to heart as well. He proposed to relieve him of every burden . . . until he would be cured . . . if he agreed . . . giving him power of attorney. . . .

As that man spat out his poison, Don Gesualdo's face became more and more upset. He didn't breathe a word, he listened with his eyes wide open, and meanwhile kept thinking of a way to get out of the mess. Suddenly, he began to howl and to shake, as if he had been again seized by the colic, as if his last hour had come, and he could neither hear nor speak any more. He only stammered, raving:

"Call my daughter! I want my daughter!"

But as soon as she rushed in, frightened, he said no more. He withdrew into himself, thinking about how to get out of those bad straits—grim, suspicious, turning the other way not to let out any glance that might betray him. He just planted a very long one of those glances on that gentleman who was leaving like an idiot. Finally, slowly, he pretended to calm down. He had to use all his cunning to escape from those claws. He began to nod yes and yes, as he was staring at his dismayed daughter's face, with loving eyes, with a paternal smile, and with an amiable manner:

"Yes . . . I want to put everything I have into your hands . . . to relieve myself of the burden. . . . You'll do me a favor in fact . . . in the state I'm in . . . I want to give up everything . . . I have a short time to live anyway. . . . Send me back home to prepare the document for the power of attorney . . . for the donation . . . whatever you want . . . There I know the Notary . . . I know where to lay my hands . . . But first send me back home . . . Then, whatever you want! . . ."

"Ah Daddy, Daddy!" exclaimed Isabella, tears in her eyes.

But he felt he was dying from day to day. He couldn't move any more. He felt he didn't have enough strength to get up from the bed and leave because they took money away from him—the very blood from his veins—to keep him a prisoner there, within reach. He puffed, he raved, he howled with pain and with rage. And then he fell back exhausted, threatening, foam at the mouth, suspicious of everything, eyeing first the servant's hands if he drank a glass of water, looking everybody in the eyes to discover the truth, to read his verdict there—forced as he was to resort to cunning tactics to learn something about what mattered to him.

"Call that man who came the other day.... Bring me the papers to sign.... It's only right, I have thought about it. I'll put somebody in charge of my business, until I'm cured...."

But now they were not in a hurry; they kept on promising him, from day to day. The Duke himself shrugged his shoulders, as if to say that it was not necessary any more. A greater, closer terror of death seized him at that indifference. He insisted, he wanted to dispose of his property, as if to cling to life, to perform an act of energy and of will. He wanted to make his last will, to prove to himself that he was still the boss. Finally, to quiet him, the Duke told him that it wasn't needed because there weren't any other heirs...Isabella was an only child....

"Ah?..." he answered. "It's not needed...she's an only child?"

And he lay back again, grim. He'd have liked to answer that there were others—other heirs born before her, they too his flesh and blood. Guilt feelings arose inside him along with bile. He had bad dreams—ugly faces, pale and irate, appeared to him in the night; voices, jolts that woke him up suddenly, in a pool of sweat, his heart hammering. So many thoughts came to him now, so many memories, so many people filed by before his eyes: Bianca, Diodata, and still others—they wouldn't have let him die without help! He wanted another consultation; the best doctors. There must be doctors for his illness, if you knew how to find them, and pay them well. This is what he had made his money for, he had! At home they'd made him believe that if he had let them open his belly... All right, yes, yes!

On the appointed day, he was waiting for the consultation from early morning, shaven and combed, sitting up in bed, his face the color of the earth, but firm and resolute. Now he wanted to see clearly into his own affairs.

"Speak out freely, gentlemen, sirs. All that has to be done will be done!"

His heart was beating somewhat faster. He felt a swarming spasm of anticipation at the root of his hair. But he was ready for everything; he almost uncovered his belly so that they could help themselves. If a tree has gangrene, it's no big deal. You cut off a branch! Instead, now the doctors didn't even want to operate on him. They had qualms, they had "ifs" and "buts." They looked at one another and chewed half words. One of them was afraid of the responsibility; another one observed that it was no longer called for . . . by now . . . The oldest of them, with such an ominous face that it made you die before your time, I swear to God, had already begun comforting the family, saying that it would have been useless even earlier, with a disease of that kind . . . .

"Ah . . ." answered Don Gesualdo, becoming suddenly hoarse. "Ah . . . I understand . . ."

And he let himself slide slowly down until he was stretched out in bed, out of breath. He didn't add anything, for the moment, he kept quiet to let them finish talking. Only, he wanted to know if the moment had come for him to take care of his affairs. It was not a joking matter now! He had so many serious affairs to settle before . . .

"Quiet! Quiet!" he grumbled as he turned to his daughter, who was crying by his side.

With a corpselike face, with eyes like two nails at the bottom of their livid sockets, he was waiting for the answer they owed him, after all. It was no joking matter!

"No, no . . . There is time. This kind of illness may go on for years and years . . . But . . . of course . . . to be ready . . . to settle your affairs in time . . . wouldn't be a bad idea . . ."

"I understand," repeated Don Gesualdo with his nose under the blanket. "I thank you gentlemen, sirs."

A cloud came down on his face and stayed there. Some kind of rancor, something that made his hands and his voice shake, and leaked out of his half-closed eyes. He motioned to his son-in-law to stay; he called him to his bed, face to face, the two of them alone.

"Well . . . is this notary going to come . . . yes or no? I must make my will. . . . I've some qualms of conscience . . . Yes sir! . . . Am I the boss, yes or no? . . . Ah . . . ah . . . you're listening too? . . ."

Isabella threw herself on her knees at the foot of the bed, with her face against the mattresses, sobbing and in despair. His son-in-law quieted him from his side of the bed.

"Yes, sure, yes, sure, whenever you want, as you want. There is no need to make a scene . . . Look how you have upset your daughter! . . ."

"All right!" he kept grumbling. "All right! I understand!"

And he turned his back, just like his father, rest his soul. As soon as he was alone he began to moo like an ox, his nose to the wall. But then, if people came in, he kept quiet. He nursed inside himself both the disease and the bitterness. He let the days go by. Rather, he saw to it that he had as many of them as possible, to earn those, at least, one after the other, as they came—and that was it! As long as you have breath you have life. As breath became shorter, little by little, he also became used to his own troubles; he became hardened to them. He had big shoulders, and he would last a long time, thanks to his tough hide. Sometimes he even felt a certain satisfaction within himself, under the sheets, as he thought the kind of face the noble Duke and all the others would make, when they saw that he had such a tough hide. He had gotten to the point of becoming fond of his disease, he listened to it, he caressed it, he wanted to feel it right there with him, to keep on going. His relatives had become hardened to it too; they had learned that such a disease could last years and years, and they took it calmly. Unfortunately, that's the way the world goes; after the first excitement, everybody keeps going his own way and minding his own business. He didn't complain either, he didn't say anything, like the cunning peasant that he was, not to waste his breath, not to let out what he didn't mean; only every once in a while he let go of such glances that meant a lot —when he saw his daughter coming before him with that disconsolate face of hers, and then helping out her husband, keeping him a prisoner there, under her eyes, with the pretext of being fond of him, to nurse him there, for fear that he would play a bad trick in his will. He could guess that she herself had some other secret troubles, and sometimes her mind was somewhere else, while her father was at the brink of death. He was gnawed inside, as he got worse; his blood had turned into so much poison; he became more and more obstinate, sullen, implacable, his face to the wall, answering only in grunts, like an animal.

Finally, he made up his mind that his time had come and he prepared himself to die like a good Christian. Isabella had quickly come to keep him company. He pushed himself up with his elbows and sat up in bed.

"Listen," he said to her, "just listen to me . . ."

His face was upset but he spoke calmly. He kept his eyes on his daughter, and nodded his head. She took his hand and burst into sobs.

"Quiet," he continued, "stop it. If we start this way, we won't get anywhere."

He was panting because his breath was short, and also from emotion. He looked around, suspicious, and kept nodding his head in silence, still panting. She too turned her tearful eyes toward the door. Don Gesualdo raised his fleshless hand, and cut a cross in the air, to mean that it was all over and that he forgave everybody, before going.

"Listen . . . I have something to tell you . . . now that we are alone . . ."

She threw herself on him, desperate, crying, sobbing "no, no," her wandering hands stroking him. He stroked her too, on her hair, slowly, without saying a word. After a while he continued:

"I'm telling you . . . yes. I'm not a child . . . Let's not waste time without reason."

Then he felt overcome with tenderness.

"You're sorry, eh? . . . You're sorry too? . . ."

His voice sounded more tender also and his sad eyes had grown softer, while something trembled on his lips.

"I have loved you . . . I certainly have . . . As much as I could . . . the way I could . . . When one does what he can . . ."

At that point he drew her slowly to him, almost hesitatingly, looking her straight in the eyes to see if she wanted it too, and hugged her very close, laying his bristled cheek on her fine hair.

"I don't hurt you, do I? . . . Like when you were a little girl? . . ."

Also other things came to his lips—waves of bitterness and of emotion, the hateful suspicions some crooks had tried to put into his head—because of business deals.

He passed his hand over his forehead, to push them back, and changed the subject.

"Let's talk about our business. Let's not waste our time with nonsense, now . . ."

She didn't want to, she went raving up and down the room, she threw her hands into her hair, she said that it was breaking her heart, that it was like a bad omen, as if her father were about to close his eyes forever.

"But no! Let's talk about it!" he insisted. "There are serious problems. I cannot waste time now."

His face was growing darker, the old rancor shone in his eyes.

"Then it means that you don't care at all . . . just like your husband . . ."

Then as he saw her resigned to listen, sitting beside the bed with her head bent, he began to give vent to all the heartaches she and her husband had given him with all those debts. . . . He recommended his property to her, to protect it, to defend it:

"You should rather have your hand cut off, see? . . . when your husband again asks you to sign papers! . . . He doesn't know what it means!"

He explained what they had cost him, those farms—Alia, Canziria—he reviewed them all one by one, lovingly; he recalled how they had come to him, one after the other, little by little—the wheat fields, the pastures, the vineyards; he described them in detail, almost clod by clod, with their good qualities and their bad ones. His voice trembled, his hands trembled, his blood still aflame in his face, tears rising in his eyes:

"Mangalavite, you know . . . you know it too . . . you were there with your mother. . . . Forty salme of land, all full of trees! . . . You remember . . . the beautiful oranges? . . . Your mother too, poor thing, would refresh herself there, in her last days! . . . Three hundred thousand a year . . . they yielded! About three hundred onze! And Salonia . . . golden wheat fields . . . a land that worked miracles . . . blessed be your grandfather who left his bones there! . . ."

Finally, he began to cry like a child out of tenderness.

"Enough," he then said. "I must tell you something else . . . listen . . . "

He looked her straight in the eyes full of tears to see what effect his request would make on her. He motioned her to come still closer, and to bend over him who was lying on his back, and had trouble finding the words.

"Listen! . . . I have some qualms of conscience . . . I would like to make a bequest to some people toward whom I have obligations. . . . Very little . . . It won't be much for you who are rich. . . . Think of it as a token that your father asks of you . . . at the point of death . . . if I have done something for you too . . . "

"Ah, Daddy, Daddy! . . . What are you saying?" sobbed Isabella.

"You'll do it, eh? You'll do it? . . . Even if your husband shouldn't want you to . . . "

He took her head between his hands, and lifted her face to read in her eyes whether she would obey him, to make her understand that it really mattered to him, and that he had that secret in his heart. And while he was looking at her like that, he thought that he too saw that other secret, that other hidden torment, in the depths of his daughter's eyes. And he wanted to tell her other things, he wanted to ask her other questions, at that point — opening his heart to her as if to a father confessor, and reading into hers. But she kept her head bent as if she had guessed, the Trao's obstinate wrinkle between her brow, drawing backward, shutting herself up inside herself, haughty — with her own troubles and her own secret. And he then felt himself become a Motta again, just as she was a Trao — suspicious, hostile, made from another mold. He relaxed his arms, and said no more.

"Now send for a priest," he concluded in a different tone of voice. "I want to settle my accounts with God."

He lasted for a few more days this way, wavering between better and worse. In fact, he seemed to begin improving somewhat when suddenly, one night, he grew worse rapidly. The servant who had been put to sleep in the next room heard him stirring and raving before dawn. But since he had become accustomed to these antics, he turned over, pretending not to hear. Finally, annoyed by that tune which didn't seem to come to an end, sleepily, he went to see what was going on.

"My daughter!" grumbled Don Gesualdo in a voice that no longer sounded like his own. "Call my daughter!"

"Ah, yes sir. I'm going to call her right now," the servant answered, and went back to bed.

But he didn't let him sleep, that pest! Now he hissed and squeaked, and now he snored worse than a double bass. As soon as the servant closed his eyes, he heard a strange noise that jolted him out of his sleep — hoarse yelps, like from one who puffed and panted, some kind of rattling that bothered you and gave you goose pimples. So much so, that finally he had to get up again, furious, swearing and chewing dirty words.

"What's up? Have you got an itch now? Are you going to cut out this tantrum? What do you want?"

Don Gesualdo didn't answer; he kept puffing as he lay on his back. The servant removed the lampshade, to look him in the face. Then he rubbed his eyes well and suddenly he didn't feel like going back to sleep.

"Ohee! Ohee! What am I going to do now?" he stammered, scratching his head.

He stood there for a moment looking at him that way, holding the lamp, wondering whether it was better to wait a while or to go downstairs right away to wake up the Lady and turn the whole house upside down. In the meantime, Don Gesualdo was growing calmer, his breath shorter, and trembling all over, only now and then grimacing with his mouth, and his eyes still staring and wide open. All of a sudden he stiffened and quieted down completely. The window was beginning to whiten. The first bells were ringing. You could hear the stamping of the horses in the courtyard, and the rattling of the currycombs on the cobblestones. The servant went to dress, and then he came back to straighten out the room. He drew the bed curtains, opened the windows wide, and stuck his head out for a breath of fresh air — smoking. The groom who was walking a sick horse, lifted his head toward the window.

"Morning, eh, Don Leopoldo?"

"And night too!" answered the servant yawning. "It's quite a present I had to get stuck with!"

The other shook his head, as if to ask what was new, and Don Leopoldo signaled that the old man was gone, thank God.

"Ah...so...quietly?..." remarked the doorman who was dragging his broom and his slippers through the entrance hall.

Meanwhile, other servants who had come by decided to go inside and take a look. Soon the dead man's room was filled with people in shirtsleeves and smoking their pipes. The wardrobe maid, seeing all those men from the window across the courtyard, came too — to stick her head in from the next room.

"What an honor, Donna Carmelina! Come in, come in; we're not going to bite you.... And he isn't either...he won't lay his hands on you any more — you can be sure of that..."

"Shut up, damn you!... No, I'm afraid, poor man!... He has stopped suffering."

"And so have I," added Don Leopoldo.

So he told the group how that Christian had plagued him — one who turned night into day...and you never knew how to take him ...and he was never satisfied.

"Never mind serving those who were really born better than we ... Enough, we shouldn't talk about the dead."

"You can tell how.he was born,..." the chief coachman remarked gravely. "Look at his hands!"

"Sure, these are the hands of someone who cooked his own mush!... See what it means to be born lucky.... And so he dies between batiste sheets, like a prince!..."

"Then," said the doorman, "should I go and close the front door?"

"Eh, of course! It's a family matter. Now we have to advise the Duchess' maid."